I0824150

MEDIEVAL BADGES

THE MIDDLE AGES SERIES

Ruth Mazo Karras, *Series Editor*

Edward Peters, *Founding Editor*

A complete list of books in the series
is available from the publisher.

MEDIEVAL BADGES

THEIR WEARERS AND THEIR WORLDS

Ann Marie Rasmussen

PENN

University of Pennsylvania Press
Philadelphia

Published by
University of Pennsylvania Press
Philadelphia, Pennsylvania 19104-4112
www.upenn.edu/pennpress

Printed in the United States of America on acid-free paper
10 9 8 7 6 5 4 3 2 1

A catalogue record for this book is available from the Library of Congress.
ISBN 978-0-8122-5320-7

Contents

Acknowledgments

This book has accompanied me for the past ten years. The seeds for it were planted earlier than that, however. In 2003 I collaborated with a modernist colleague, Dick Langston, to propose a special session for the 2004 Modern Language Association (MLA) convention in New York City. Not only was the special session accepted by the program committee, the title of my paper on sexual badges, "Wandering Genitalia in Medieval German Literature," made it into the *New York Times* article (published on December 27, 2004) that gleaned from the conference program enough apparently salacious or fatuous titles to skewer the research being presented at the conference. In any case, it made me think that when it comes to research topics, one might as well embrace the old saw that there is no such thing as bad publicity, and the MLA talk became the basis for my giving invited lectures on medieval sexual badges.

At the time, I had planned that these talks would become part of a book about obscene texts in medieval German literature. As I reworked the talks into (now published) articles, I slowly realized that my study of medieval badges was raising a host of vexing issues about visual representation in the late medieval world. This insight marked a turning point, though I did not grasp that at the time. I had embarked on a new scholarly path and entered into unfamiliar terrain. I consigned the project on obscenity to the (digital) desk drawer and began writing the book you are reading now.

At some point after the euphoria of new scholarly curiosity has passed, it dawns on a person that the research journey upon which she has embarked will be long and difficult. Turning back, that is to say, abandoning the project, feels like a viable option. I expressed thoughts like these many years ago to Romedio Schmitz-Esser, who was then a postdoctoral researcher at Duke University, and he replied, "Ann Marie, you must write this book." Romedio's simple words and the gravity of his tone admonished me to bear up and reassured me that the project mattered.

In 2016 I started a research project on medieval badges with a small team of experts that was made possible by an Insight Grant from the Social Science and Humanities Research Council (SSHRC) of Canada. The intellectual companionship of the scholars and graduate students who belong to this team, Hanneke van Asperen, Steven Bednarski, Flora Cassen, Lloyd de Beer, Sara Fontes, Torsten Hiltmann, Amy Jeffs, Hartmut Kühne, and Caley McCarthy, has been a source of constant inspiration.

I am immensely grateful for the intellectual generosity of colleagues from many fields who share my enthusiasm for medieval badges, beginning with the members of the SSHRC Insight Grant badges team. They have corrected my mistakes; expanded my thinking; gently coaxed me out of the weeds; taken me on badge-related excursions to museums and churches; answered my pleas for publishable material with photographs, maps, off-prints, and scans; and repeatedly refrained from saying, "I told you so" when the scales fell from my eyes and I discovered what it actually means to assemble 120 images for publication, even without the complications wrought by pandemic lockdowns. I thank Willy Piron who responded to innumerable image requests and queries with sainted patience and kindness. I thank Christiane Andersson, Jörg Ansorge, Hanneke van Asperen, André Dubisch (European Hansamuseum, Lübeck), Dirk Jakob, Françoise Labaune-Jean, and Kay-Peter Suchow for sharing images for publication. I am grateful to museum colleagues Isabelle Fronty (Musée de Cluny), Volker Hilberg (Schleswig-Holsteinisches Landesmuseum), Lyle Humphrey (North Carolina Museum of Art), Anders Jansson (Kulturen, Lund), Bart de Sitter (Art in Flanders), Karin Schnell (Bayerisches Nationalmuseum), and Jan de Wilde (Yper Museum), and to Robbi Siegel of Art Resource. I owe a huge debt of gratitude to the Family Van Beuningen Collection and to Hendrik-Jan van Beuningen. It was an honor to meet him in 2013. I especially thank Ferdinand and Christine Vaandrager for their hospitality and for granting permission to publish images of badges from the Family Van Beuningen Collection.

This book has been through so many versions that I have lost track. For reading the entire manuscript in one of its guises and providing valuable feedback and encouragement, I thank Michael Andersen, Steven Bednarski, Lloyd de Beer, and Jennifer Lee. Alis A. Rasmussen, aka Kate Elliott, helped me make my fictional sketches better. I thank Jerry Singerman and the other skilled editors at the University of Pennsylvania Press for their support and advice. Over the years I have had the good fortune to work with outstanding research assistants. I thank Sara Fontes (who also built an awesome badges project website), Erik Grell, Caley McCarthy, and Max Symulski. Special thanks go to Hannah Gardiner, who in spite of nightmares caused by close study of *The Chicago Manual of Style* became an eagle-eyed editor and cheered me on through the final phases of revising, editing, and assembling this book.

Over the past ten years my research on medieval badges has been supported by grants from the following organizations: the Social Science and Humanities Research Council of Canada, the German Academic Exchange, the Arts and Science Faculty Research Council at Duke University. and the Josiah Charles Trent Memorial Foundation. Thank you. I am grateful to Princeton University for generous research funding that paid for most of the high-resolution images in this book. At the University of Waterloo, I thank Tom Barber, Ruth Knechtel, and Angela Roorda for teaching me how research funding works at a Canadian university. Tom's unique combination of political shrewdness with seemingly eternal optimism continues to inspire me to just keep applying.

I thank the colleagues in North America and in Europe who invited me to give talks about medieval badges. I have enjoyed these opportunities for intellectual exchange. Preparing made me think hard about what I wanted to argue about medieval badges, and from our discussions I always learned something significant that flowed back into this book. Thank you to Ingrid Bennewitz, Michael Ott, Ludger Lieb, Tobias Bulang, Bruno Quast, Monika Unzeitig, Rosemarie McGerr, Jehangir Malegam, Sarah Blick, Diane Wolfthal, Alison Beringer, Christian Schneider, Joe Sullivan, Hester Baer, Jim Schultz, David Pan, Gail Hart, Russell Berman, Bethany Wiggan, Catriona McLeod, Racha Kirakosian, Jane Toswell, Olga Trokhimenko, Chris Nighman, and Annemarike Willemsen, and to dear friends Clare Lees, Julian Weiss, and Gina Psaki.

At Duke University I shared drafts of Chapters 1 and 2 with first-year students in writing seminars; their feedback was invaluable. Thank you.

I thank my colleagues in the Department of Germanic and Slavic Studies at the University of Waterloo for their collegiality and friendship: Emma Betz, Michael Boehringer, Alice Kuzniar, Grit Liebscher, Paul Malone, Barbara Schmenk, James Skidmore, and Andrea Speltz. Special thanks go to Janet Vaughan, for untangling so many bureaucratic and financial threads. I also wish to thank Jola Kormornicka for organizing the regular side-by-side writing sessions where I worked on this book and Sam Schirm for driving on that last-minute, evening dash to Toronto Pearson airport to get my Canadian work visa straightened out.

In the 2019–2020 academic year I was honored to hold a position as Stanley Kelley Jr. Visiting Professor for Distinguished Teaching in the German Department at Princeton University. It was an intellectual feast. I thank Janine Calegero, Devin Fore, Florian Fuchs, Mike Jennings, Tom Levin, Barbara Nagel, Sally Poor, Lynn Ratsep, Fiona Romaine, Ed Sikorski, and

Nikolas Wegmann; graduate students Sebastian Klinger, Peter Malhkouf, and William Stewart, as well as Paul Babinski and Sean Toland who have now completed their PhDs, and undergraduates Molly Banes, Janice Cheon, Thomas Jankovic, and Jason Qu. I also thank Suzanne Conklin Akbari, Janet Kay, Beatrice Kitzinger, AnneMarie Luijendijk, Daniela Mairhofer, Helmut Reimitz, Melissa Buckner Reynolds, and Maggie Schleissner.

Friendship is sustenance. Beth Eastlick, Mary Kay Delaney, Racha Kirakosian, Astrid Lembke, Heidi Madden, Jean O'Barr, Sally Poor, and Sonja Rasmussen, kept me company and looked after me the first time I was in lockdown, which was after knee replacement surgery in 2018, and thank you to Anne Moscrip who drove me home. Since 2017, fellow members of the Medieval Global Storyworlds book club, Bettina Bildhauer and E. Jane Burns, have made studying non-European medieval literature a total delight, and our transcontinental and transatlantic reading group has provided heaps of practice for conducting meetings over Zoom. Thank you to Mitch Reyes for his Scholarly Writing Retreat, where I worked on this book. These workshops taught me how much I love side-by-side writing. I thank my Portland, Oregon, friends and side-by-side writing buddies Isabelle de Marte and Katja Altpeter-Jones, as well as Judith Bennett and Cynthia Herrup. Thanks always to Barbara Altmann and Jane Hacking for treasured companionship on our nearly annual writing retreat getaways.

Thanks always to Christophe Fricker, Tim Senior, Christine Oeien, Amanda Lee, Isabelle Lee, Mary Kay Delaney, Fritz Mayer, David Delaney Mayer, Michael Delaney Mayer, Kellie McGown, Paul Delaney Mayer, Kate St. Romain, Catherine Green, Paul Green, Vee Green, Markus Stock, Ruth von Bernuth, Kathryn Starkey, Beth Eastlick, Tom Ferraro, Olga Trokhimenko, and Helen Solterer. I do not know how I would have gotten through the many sloughs of despond into which writing takes one if I had not been able to rely on Kristen Neuschel's understanding, friendship, and excellent advice.

I remember here two dear friends whose writing and thinking profoundly influenced me and this project, and whom I miss every day, Sarah Westphal and Jonathan M. Hess. I also remember my beloved father, Gerald Rasmussen, who I think would have loved this book.

For helping me in ways large and small to complete this work, I thank my brother, Karsten Hans Rasmussen; my sister-in-law, Christine Lewandowski; my sisters, Sonja Rasmussen and Alis A. Rasmussen; and my niece, Rhiannon Rose Silverstein. I thank my cousins Helle Mølgaard and Nina Krüger for the wonderful times we have spent exploring Denmark. I also thank my ninety-two-year-old mother, Sigrid Marie Rasmussen, who will be delighted to see this book in print.

This book is dedicated to my son, Arnbjorn Stokholm, who has patiently listened to and cogently summarized so many of its arguments about medieval badges that he probably could have written it himself.

I

What Are Medieval Badges?

The road from Mont-Saint-Michel
northwest toward Caen,
July 1421, midmorning

The old man rests in the shade by the side of the road. All the other pilgrims have gone ahead. The boy did earnestly offer to stay behind. He is a good boy, this nephew of his; he has been raised well. He worried that an old man alone would be set upon by that unsavory pack of armed toughs who were snoring under the elderberry bushes at the edge of the village as they passed by early this morning. Probably the same ruffians whose drunken street brawl awakened half the village last night. "I am safe. The archangel Saint Michael will protect his own," he said to his nephew and the others, pointing to the bright, new badge sewn on his cloak.

His jest that the sainted archangel might even speed his catching up with them by carrying him back to their side like a mouse in the clutches of a hawk did bring a scowl to the face of that wretched, garrulous friar. In truth, the old man knows that the peace of resting in the shade of the linden tree, listening to the melodious song of the lark,

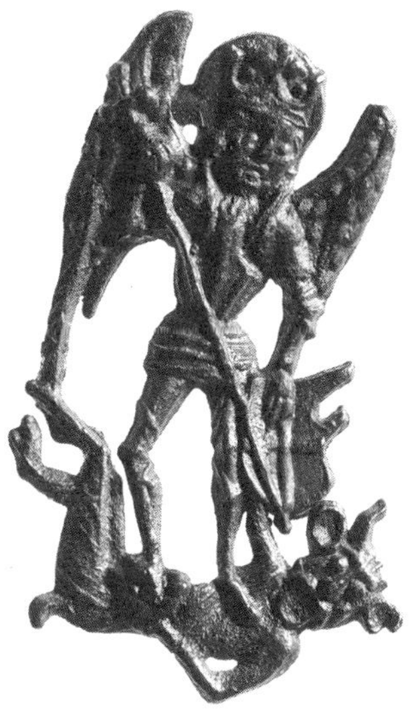

Figure 1.1. Pewter badge, winged archangel Saint Michael wearing armor and stabbing flailing demon, attachment unknown, Mont-Saint-Michel, France, 1000–1599, find site unknown, 25 mm (height). London, British Museum, inv. 1913,0619.37 (Kunera 11267). Photograph and permission from © The Trustees of the British Museum.

resting his aching bones and aged heart may come at a high price. Those fractious youths are doubtless on the road now, too. They are dangerous and unpredictable, as he well knows, having been such a one himself many years ago when he bore arms in the service of the English lord. Am I afraid? he asks himself. Perhaps. But one weighs risk differently at his age. Violent death, though painful, is swift, and in this case not certain, while another hour of listening to that clacking friar's endless sermonizing will drive the peace of Saint Michael out of his heart and awaken the old bloodlust in him again. A bargain then. Is it one that Saint Michael would understand? He muses that the archangel did not seem to have much patience with clerics himself. The lark trills and sings. He closes his eyes, and the voice of his beloved, long dead, arises unbidden in his mind, singing that beautiful, strange old song he so loved, "Can vei la lauzeta mover . . ."

A sharp jab in the side startles him awake; his inadvertent shudder is accompanied by peals of raucous laughter and shouts. A face—young, scarred, hungry—leans down into his own.

"Old man," it says in heavily accented but serviceable French, "hand over your money purse and perhaps we won't eat you this time!"

Another knife poke in his ribs. More gusts of laughter punctuate the joke, and words fly, though not in French.

"Just slit his throat, you need the practice!"

"That's our ditherer, all sweet words and no action!"

"Quick, be quick, before that Michael swoops in and carries him away!"

Raising his head slowly, he gazes into the eyes of the four young predators gathered around him and sees that they will kill him.

Why is he not frightened? he wonders. Has he faced death, meted out death so many times in his life that it no longer holds any mystery for him? What recognition is this? Unbidden, a memory from so long ago, its freshness miraculous, springs into his mind: he is a little boy, holding his older sister's hand, peering down the wooded track for Papa. And then Papa is there! Again he hears Papa's voice:

"So, children, fresh meat for dinner tonight. Children! Mama has slit the old pig's throat!"

His childhood language—little used, half extinguished. These young roughnecks speak the Flemish tongue of his childhood village, and they bend their vowels as his father did. There is a chance. He speaks carefully, slowly, watching and judging the young men, trusting the language to seek its own path.

"Well met, countrymen. Having a little fun with the old folk, are you? I will gladly share my bread with you, but I fear you will find that Saint Michael has left this old pig too lean for your liking."

Surprise, even shock, crosses their faces. They hesitate. It is one thing to murder strangers. That is the sort of thing that binds such companions, much like going to the whorehouse together. But to kill an old man whose accent summons up the complexities of home, who might well be kin to one of them, such a killing and the knowledge of such a killing could sever friendship, turning boon companions into enemies bound to pursue vengeance.

Still, perhaps it is not so. One more test then. The small, red-haired one, whose filthy, torn hose and rundown shoes contrast sharply with his new, colorful jacket and well-made short sword, speaks up.

"Why are you on the road, Old Father?"

"I come from visiting Saint Michael, as you can see."

The old man points to the shiny, new Saint Michael badge sewn onto his cloak.

"And I walk, for so far no wings have sprouted from my back."

This last remark provokes, unexpectedly, new shouts of laughter from the young men. The red-haired one flashes open his jacket, revealing a badge pinned to his linen tunic above his heart: a crowned, engorged, bewinged penis that runs forward on little legs and shod feet.

"We can still fly, Old Father. Do you know our destination?"

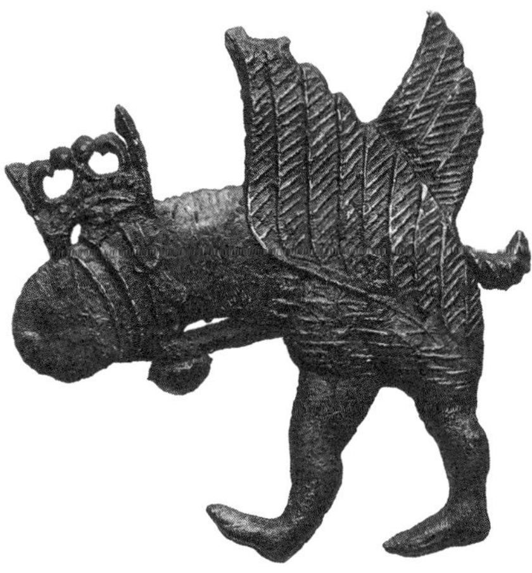

Figure 1.2. Pewter badge, crowned, belled, walking penis with wings and tail, pin, origin unknown, 1375–1424, found in Nieuwlande, Netherlands, 29 × 28 mm. Langbroek, Netherlands, Family Van Beuningen Collection, inv. 1856 (Kunera 00634). Photograph courtesy of Family Van Beuningen Collection.

The old man smiles. Like the long vowels and harsh consonants, it summons something familiar from long ago.

"Ah, the house of little daughters in Ypres. You're racing home tail first then?"

They howl with laughter. He has passed the test. Now he dares to put his hand in his pocket, bringing forth the bread. The ruffian slices, each one eats, the bread is gone. No matter. He will live to eat another day.

In the foregoing fictional sketch, the Saint Michael pin worn by the pilgrim who was once a soldier and the walking, crowned phallus pin worn by the red-haired hooligan are based on real, surviving medieval objects made of cheap metal and displaying vivid images and symbols that were widely familiar in the Middle Ages. In English, these objects are called badges, a word of unknown origin that is first attested in the fifteenth century. In most medieval European languages, however, these objects were called signs: *sigillum* or *signum* in Latin, meaning little signs or seals; *enseignes* in French; *zeichen* in German or *teken* in Low German and in Dutch. Calling these objects signs signaled clearly the presence of another layer of meaning, and thus, their communicative function. Badges were meant to be seen and to be understood.[1]

Mass-produced by pouring lead-tin alloys in molds carved of stone, badges were cheap to make and to purchase, and they were widely used throughout the High and late Middle Ages. Badges are usually small objects, around four-by-four centimeters, and sometimes as tiny as two-by-one centimeters. They are two-sided objects, although in nearly all cases the back of the badge, not intended for display, features only scored lines (see, for example, figures 3.12, 4.2, and 6.2).[2] In the High Middle Ages, larger badges were made that were not solid, plaque-like objects, but rather featured a lattice-grid of lead-tin alloy clearly intended to be pinned or mounted against a background showing through. This feature is seen in the fourteenth-century badge from the city of Ypres, which is nearly ten-by-eight centimeters in size in its current, fragmentary state (figure 1.3). By the late Middle Ages, very thin, ultra-lightweight, flat, single-sided plaques with an image in light relief were being mass-produced in a new mode of manufacture: die stamping or embossing (plate 4).

Many badges were associated with secular life. They featured images using all manner of secular symbolism, from familiar symbols associated with courtly love and friendship, such as garlands, clasped hands, and crowned hearts, and with civic organizations or elite households, such as the personal devices of swan, stag, or rose, to symbols and images that are enigmatic or obscene, such as penis and vulva creatures. The majority of surviving badges, however, were closely associated with religion and were most often linked to specific charismatic or holy sites that had become pilgrimage centers. Pilgrims would acquire a site-specific badge at the holy site they had visited; in the opening sketch, the pilgrim who was once a soldier has been to Mont-Saint-Michel on the northern coast of France, where for centuries Saint Michael's shrine attracted pilgrims to the offshore abbey and church that had grown up around this charismatic site.[3]

Badges were made to be worn and seen and were most commonly sewn or pinned on clothing. There were some badges, including small, decorated, three-dimensional lead ampullae (also known as phials) that were made to be worn around the neck. These ampullae were often associated with shrine sites where a liquid was acquired as part of the pilgrimage, for instance, Canterbury or Walsingham. More can be learned about the way medieval religious badges

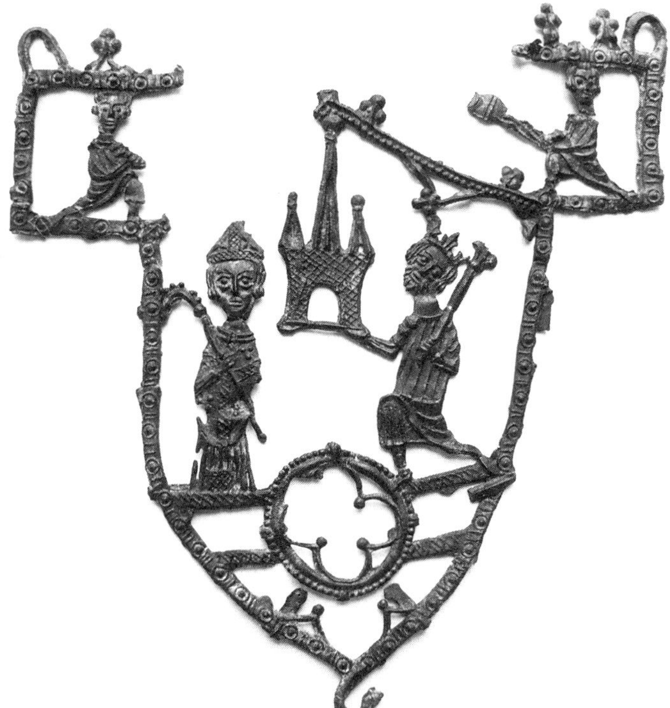

Figure 1.3. Damaged openwork pewter badge, kneeling king and standing bishop in elaborated shield-like framework, eyelets, origin unknown, 1325–1374, found in Ypres, Belgium, 98 × 89 mm. Yper Museum, inv. SM 005187 (Kunera 06816). Photographer: Els Deroo. Photograph courtesy of Yper Museum.

were worn from surviving medieval works of art. Late medieval artists sometimes depicted medieval religious badges in their works. Plate 1 and figure 1.4 are details from an altarpiece, *The Seven Acts of Mercy*, which was created in 1504 for the Cathedral of Saint Laurence in Alkmaar in the Netherlands by an artist known as the Master of Alkmaar. The badges in these images are worn by people who crowd together on a city street, where burghers are shown performing acts of religious charity directed toward the poor.

On plate 1 a small crowd of poor wanderers gathers in front of a city home, where they are being welcomed for the night by a well-dressed couple. The wanderers include Christ, the bearded and hatless figure standing at the back of the group, and three pilgrims, recognizable as such by the badges they wear on their hats and cloaks. The way in which badges communicate through the use of familiar iconography is visible in plate 1. Some of its painted badges can be easily identified even five hundred years later because they are connected to famous pilgrimage sites in western Europe. On the far left, the brown hat has a mirror badge in the center that probably represents the city of Aachen, Germany. It is centered between two small badges, one of which is the scallop shell that commemorated a pilgrimage to the shrine of the apostle Saint James the Greater at Santiago de Compostela in Spain. To the right, the hat of the man wearing red (from left to right) has something that may or may not be another Santiago de Compostela badge; a badge with three communion wafers in a monstrance, associated most likely with the Precious Blood (also known as Holy Blood) or Eucharistic pilgrim site at Alkmaar itself; and papal crossed keys from the Holy City of Rome. The pilgrim in a blue cape likewise has a scallop badge from Santiago de Compostela on his hat and crossed swords on both his hat and cape, perhaps from Mont-Saint-Michel.

Figure 1.4 from the same altarpiece features a woman with a badge-like object on her hat. Carrying a child in a kind of cloth wrap that is anchored with a shoulder strap, she stands at the back in the crowd of eight people representing the neediest of the poor: children, babies, widows, the aged, the infirm, the disabled.[4] Again, Christ is shown standing in solidarity with them and watching the act of mercy being carried out by the well-dressed burgher couple, who are giving the travelers drink. The placement of the small item on the woman's hat suggests it is a badge of some kind. Unlike the badges in the previous panel, however, it is not possible to identify this one. Whether the lack of detail was deliberate on the part of the artist or is due to the artwork's present condition (the painting was damaged during the Reformation and has been restored) cannot be discerned. The badge's shape does resemble

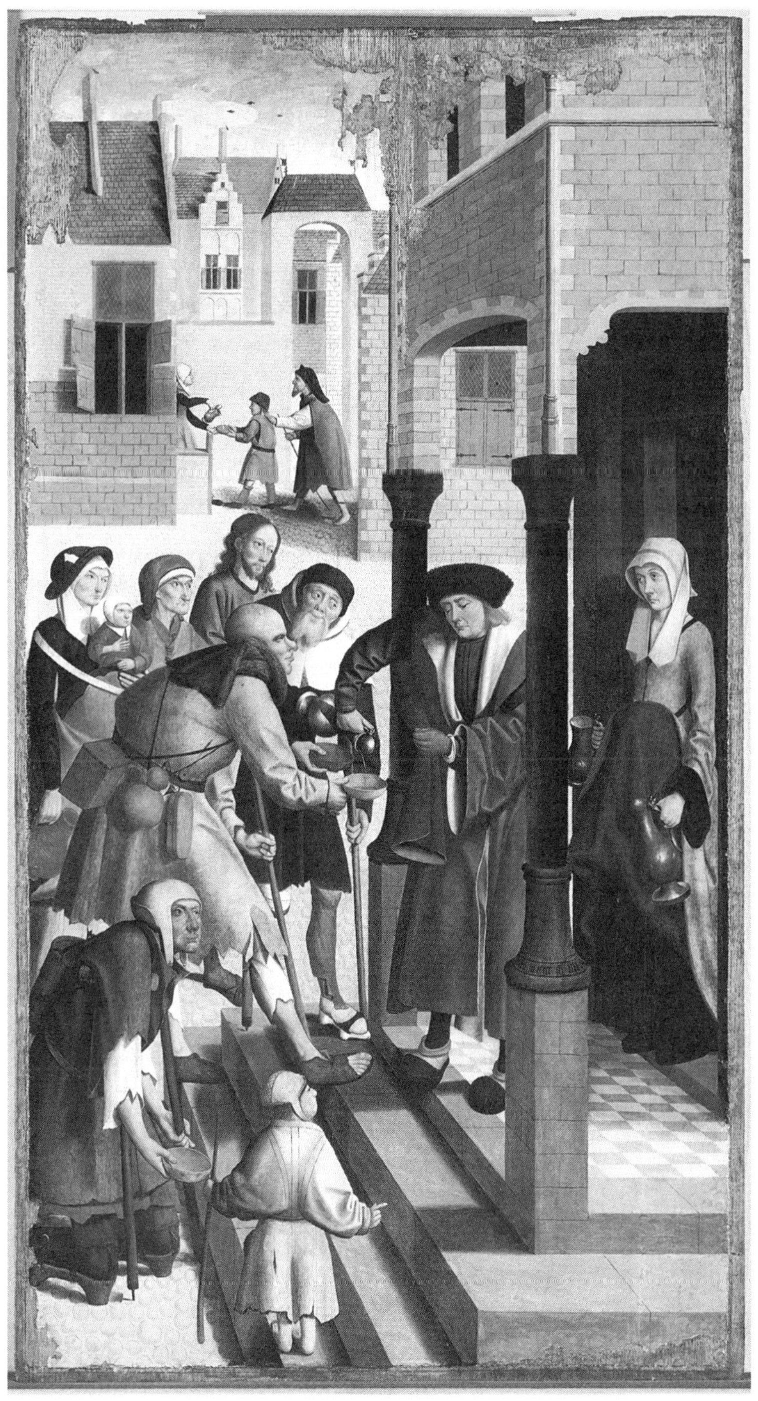

Figure 1.4. The Master of Alkmaar, *The Seven Works of Mercy*, oil painting on panel, 1504, detail from panel two of six, 103.5 × 56.8 cm. Amsterdam, Rijksmuseum, inv. SK-A-2815-2. Photograph courtesy of Rijksmuseum, Amsterdam.

that of the middle badge worn by the man in red in the previous panel, and this shape fits that of known badges from Alkmaar itself. A local reference would make sense, because it contributed to the idealized reality being created by the altarpiece, in which pilgrims flock to Alkmaar to partake in its holy site and the good citizens of Alkmaar hurry to their doorsteps to perform good works by caring for the pilgrims. The shape and placement of the woman's badge might also indicate a pilgrim badge manufactured not out of metal but out of paper, parchment, or small pieces of leather known as scrip. This book focuses on badges made of pewter (often known as lead-tin or tin alloy) because so many of them survive, but as will be discussed in more detail in Chapter 2, the range of materials in which badges were produced was great.[5] Those made of extremely perishable materials, such as paper or parchment, are known primarily from written or pictorial sources. Such a pilgrim badge was probably even cheaper than the already inexpensive lead-tin alloy badges shown on plate 1. The detail of depicting a paper or parchment badge or scrip would be consistent with the other poor folk gathered here; a young woman carrying a child can afford only the very cheapest devotional object.

The oldest medieval badges date from the last decades of the twelfth century. Their number and use increased steadily throughout the High Middle Ages, reaching a high point in the fifteenth century and largely disappearing in the first decades of the sixteenth century following the Reformation. At least twenty thousand medieval badges survive to this day.[6] In the fifteenth century, the time of their greatest popularity, hundreds of thousands would have been in use at any given moment in time. Historian Carina Brumme estimates that the total number of badges once manufactured in the last two centuries of the Middle Ages (that is to say, from ca. 1300 to 1500) to be somewhere between ten million and twenty million.[7] This number is staggeringly large, and it implies that each badge shown in a figure in this book is but a surviving example from the many duplicates produced using a single mold, as is explained in more detail in Chapter 3. The surviving badges demonstrate that they were made and used in many contexts. There are religious badges, heraldic badges, political badges, civic badges, satirical badges, comical badges, sexual badges, obscene badges. The sheer number of surviving badges and the diverse and wide-ranging contexts both religious and secular that they evoke suggest that badges were ubiquitous, woven tightly into the fabric of ordinary, late medieval life.[8] Their ordinariness is part of what makes them so intriguing now. Who made badges and out of what materials? Who bought, gifted, and wore badges, and why? Most intriguing of all, what might they have meant, and what can they tell about thought, belief, and practice in the late medieval world? This book seeks answers to those questions.[9]

Crucially, medieval badges display vivid, easily recognizable images. They are in effect very small sculptures displaying images from religious and secular iconographies that were familiar and intelligible all across medieval Europe. Because of their distinctive iconographies, nearly always linked to a specific place or to a specific corporate group, it is often possible to determine *where* a badge was made and acquired. Its image conveys this information. Sometimes it is possible to determine where a badge was found, especially for badges found in modern archaeological digs. Yet the *when* of a badges' manufacture and use is much harder to decipher. The surviving badges themselves provide very few clues. The kinds of contextual information typically supplied by archaeological sites that allow scholars to date objects (strata of finds, coins, dendrochronology of surviving timbers, and so on) are often entirely lacking for badges, especially those that became part of museum collections early on. Stylistic criteria or the use of a datable symbol, such as a nobleman's newly adopted heraldic device or a holy site's acquisition of a new relic, can sometimes allow the general assignment of a badge to a short span of decades in a specific century. While badge designs did change over time, these changes often happened relatively slowly, in part because the design elements for any specific badge were closely tied to a stable visual program that sought to unmistakably identify the badge's giver or place of origin.

Documents and texts about pilgrimage from the decades before the year 1200 provide a first glimpse of the manufacture and use of badges, where they appear as a part of religious devotion and pilgrimage.[10] A late twelfth-century pilgrims' guide to Compostela, where the shrine of Saint James the Greater flourished from the eleventh century on, describes stalls and shops in an enclosed area in front of the cathedral known as a parvis selling to pilgrims, alongside wine flasks, sandals, scrip, belts, and medicinal herbs and spices, "small scallop shells which are the insignia of the Blessed James" (crusille piscium, id est intersigna Beati Jacobi), such as the ones depicted in plate 1.[11] In the French biography *Vie de Saint Thomas Becket* (*Life of St. Thomas of Becket*), from around 1174, Guernes de Pont-Sainte-Maxence notes similar practices: "Pilgrims to Jerusalem bring back palm crosses, those to Rocamadour lead figures of the Virgin, and Compostela shells cast in lead."[12] These twelfth-century mentions of Saint James badges, whether made of ordinary scallop shells or of shells fashioned out of lead-tin alloy, suggest that badges were already an ordinary part of pilgrimage.

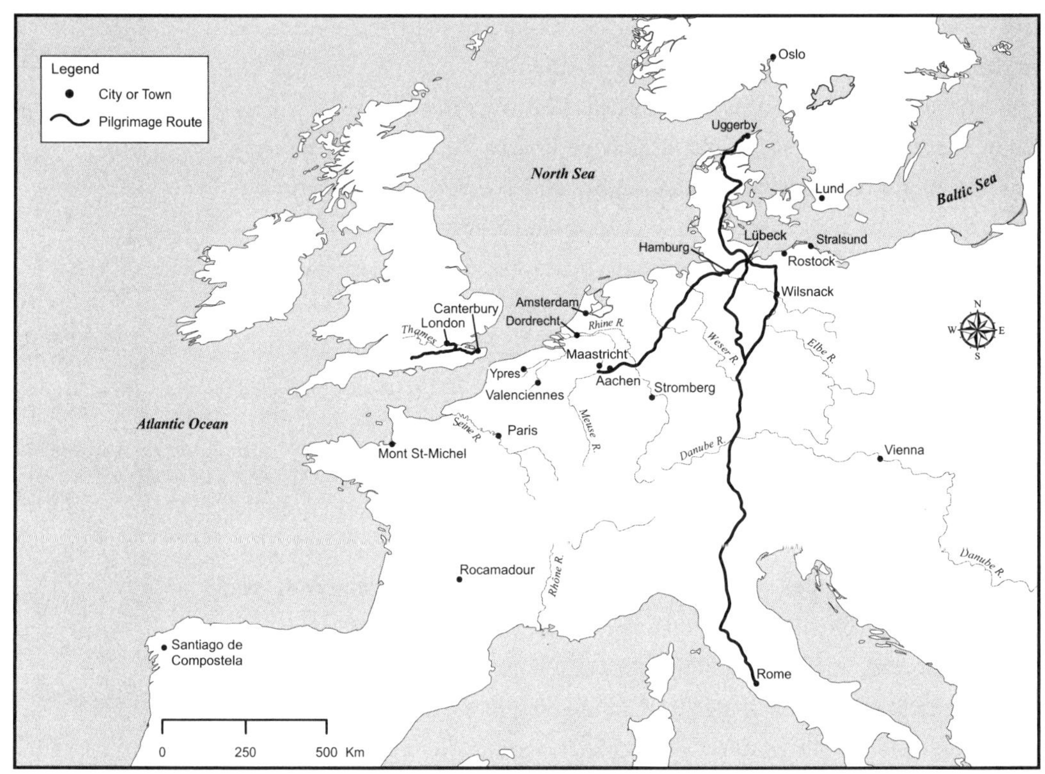

Key towns and cities mentioned in this book and some land-based medieval pilgrim routes. Map: Gordie Thompson.

By the mid-thirteenth century, badges were being used for both secular and religious purposes across Europe, and their manufacture and use increased throughout the Middle Ages. Yet there is a clear geographic pattern to the survival of the badges.[13] The vast majority, whether religious or secular in purpose, have been found in northwestern Europe, including a band stretching east around the Baltic as far as Gdańsk (Danzig): in the cities of what are now the Netherlands, Belgium, northern France, and England, in German-speaking regions north of the Alps, in Denmark, Norway, and Sweden, and in trading centers and cities along the Baltic Sea. Most badges were also made in these regions, but many originated in the great pilgrimage sites in southern Europe, such as Rocamadour in France, Compostela in Spain, and Rome, where badges were made and sold to pilgrims and travelers who carried them back north. Badges are only rarely found south of the Alps, however, including badges made in southern regions.

This pattern of find distribution raises a number of intriguing questions. Identity markers of various kinds (clothing, hair, heraldic symbolism, and so on) were found everywhere in late medieval Europe, from the Mediterranean to the Baltic. Badges were manufactured both north and south of the Alps as well. Yet surviving badges overwhelmingly come from these northerly regions of Europe. Does this state of affairs reflect an as-yet-unexamined characteristic of regional European culture?[14] After all, the area in which badges are found contains the great northern cloth and trading cities of the mercantile age. These cities played a large role in the rise of capitalism and were key players in the spread of the Reformation. Perhaps badges were part of a vibrant and unique cultural form of identity formation and communal belonging that must have played a significant role in the rise of modern Europe and that is still only partially understood. If so, then badges might represent part of a pattern of large-scale regional, cultural difference between northern and southern Europe whose historical contours are still only incompletely understood.

Or are there other plausible explanations? The distribution of badge finds might reflect not medieval practices but modern phenomena, arising from, perhaps, survival conditions or from scholarly and curatorial practice. Perhaps badges survived better in the mud of northern waters. Perhaps archaeologists in the north have been more alert to and interested in badges. Badges have been collected privately and in museums since the 1840s in England, France, and the Low Countries (Belgium and the Netherlands), where publishing on them also began. The long trend away from antiquarianism and toward modern scientific and scholarly, or disciplinarily based, approaches to medieval badges has had its ups and downs, and these approaches vary from country to country in northern Europe.[15] Since the 1980s, however, more museum curators and private collectors in northern Europe have been curating and publishing catalogues and articles about their collections. Perhaps scholarship on badges found in southern France and Italy has not had the benefit of similar endeavors and has been more sporadic.[16] Before advancing a hypothesis about regional cultural differences concerning badges and community formation, these more mundane and modern potential causes for the uneven distribution of surviving medieval badges must be ruled out. These issues await further study and so lie outside of the realm of this book.

The passage of time has rendered badges as we see them today, tarnished and blurred, when new badges would have been bright and colorful. The lead-tin, or pewter, alloys out of which badges were made would have been shiny, looking something like aluminum foil, and would have had crisp, clear lines delineating the images.[17] Many badges would have sported embellishments of various kinds, most commonly paint or bright backings of other materials (for example, metal foil or painted paper). Though small, badges would have been eye-catching, and they would have communicated meaning quickly and easily.

Displayed on capes and hats as people went about their business, badges were mobile, because they moved through space with their wearers. This mobility meant virtually everyone in northwestern Europe in the Middle Ages would have encountered badges in some way, and virtually everyone could have afforded one because as mass-produced objects made of easily obtained and widely available materials, they were cheap. What distinguishes badges from other ordinary, ubiquitous, visible objects is that each displayed an image whose meaning was widely known and understood.[18] Badges were more than personal adornments. They employed once common, widely understood symbols to create and communicate meaning. A few of these symbolically laden, meaning-making images are still with us today, such as an image of the heart as a symbol of tender love. Others, such as a knight kneeling before a lady, are still intelligible to a modern viewer as a symbol of love, although the full implications of the image are no longer well known. Many other symbols and images, however, are now obscure. The devices and images associated with medieval heraldry and secular politics are no longer widely known, while many religious images fell out of use after the Reformation, as is the case for the otherwise easily recognizable badges from Wilsnack (figure 1.5), now a sleepy small town in the province of Brandenburg, Germany, but which before the Reformation was home to one of the most popular Holy Blood pilgrimage sites north of the Alps.

Badges make and communicate meaning through their use of these once widely used and commonly understood images and symbols. Reading this

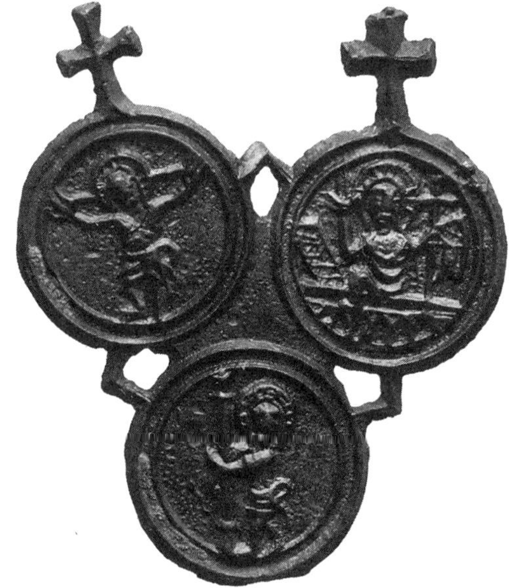

Figure 1.5. Pewter badge, the Precious or Holy Blood wafers of Wilsnack, eyelets, Wilsnack, Germany, 1475–1522, found in Nieuwlande, Netherlands, 36 × 31 mm. Langbroek, Netherlands, Family Van Beuningen Collection, inv. 1709 (Kunera 00130). Photograph courtesy of Family Van Beuningen Collection.

once ubiquitous symbolic language is done by deciphering the references being made, usually not a difficult task because so much comparable medieval material survives and because the languages of symbolism and imagery in which the badges participate were not meant to be esoteric or secretive but rather to communicate easily and well. Even obscene badges, for which the hypothesis must be entertained that the graphic, yet abstruse nature of the imagery is intentionally enigmatic, do not overthrow the thesis that badges were intended to communicate meaning easily and well.[19] The manner in which obscene badges combine a variety of symbols and elements for the viewer to decode, rather like a riddle, suggests that these badges deliberately toyed with the cultural expectation that badges would be easy to read.

The passage of time has made it more difficult to understand what scholars call the pragmatics of badge use and their symbolic systems of meaning-making. Badges were worn: they were made to be worn, they are shown being worn, and the fact that they are found hundreds of kilometers from the sites to which they refer shows us that they were carried and worn far from their sites of origin. Badges were selected, worn, and used by people to communicate something about themselves to others. Badges established a relationship between the wearer and that which was being referenced by the image itself, which might be referring, for example, to a pilgrimage site designated by a saint, or to a lordly household, or to a voluntary, civic association. Why would the badge wearer choose a specific badge, and was wearing a badge always a voluntary choice? Perhaps badges allowed their wearers to make statements to the world about the wearer's beliefs, experiences, and status. A badge from Mont-Saint-Michel or from Compostela suggested that its wearer had been on pilgrimage; a badge, or device, sporting a Lancastrian rose denotes that the bearer supported or belonged to that noble English household; a penis badge might have been acquired during carnival (no evidence survives regarding the actual use of such sexual badges but for a variety of reasons that are discussed in Chapter 8, this scenario is at least plausible). The badge's function to relay a message about its bearer tells us that there was a social dimension of meaning-making at work. A badge communicated meaning, not only to the person wearing the badge but above all to everyone who viewed the badge as it is worn. Did the viewer validate, share, or reject the proffered meaning? The creation and negotiation of shared, symbolic meaning was constantly in play. The meaning produced by badges was profoundly dynamic and social, and understanding the pragmatic, communicative aspect takes the scholar and the reader into the very fabric of late medieval social life, which was complicated and contradictory.

Let us return for a moment to the badges shown in the altarpiece *The Seven Works of Mercy* (plate 1 and figure 1.4). The badges that the Master of Alkmaar chose to show on these panels represent Alkmaar's charismatic pilgrimage site, the Eucharist miracle at the Cathedral of Saint Laurence, alongside some of the best known and most widely visited pilgrim sites in Europe—Rome, Compostela, and Aachen. The depiction of badges on the altarpiece is part of a theological argument about the efficacy and benefits of performing corporal acts of mercy. Crucially, on the panels no cleric mediates these pious acts being carried out by the good burghers; there are no priests, monks, or nuns. Rather, Christ himself is present, a symbolic depiction that removes from the image institutional mediation in the form of the church officials, so that in the painting Christ and Christ alone directly sanctifies these ordinary, civic acts of mercy. (The missing element of institutional mediation would have been powerfully present, of course, in the staging of the altarpiece in its church setting and liturgical use.) The depicted badges participate in the painting's theological argument that works of mercy inherently merit forgiveness of sins, a view strongly rejected by the Lutheran Reformation. The badges clarify for the medieval viewer that the persons wearing them are pilgrims and therefore fitting and needy recipients of the burghers' civic acts of religious charity. The depicted badges also close the distance between the faraway and powerful holy sites where they originated and Alkmaar itself, bringing the aura of divinity of those distant shrines directly into Alkmaar's city streets and further sanctifying the secular street space where these acts of mercy are taking place.

Secular-themed badges communicated in similar ways. They were often related through shared iconography to the dense and profuse world of medieval heraldry, whose symbolism pervaded the world of elites both secular and religious across Europe. Heraldic symbols were designed following a tightly scripted language consisting of colors, shapes, and symbols to indicate to the initiated (i.e., those who could read the signs), for example, the bearer's paternal and maternal lineage or his corporate belonging. Heraldry included the use of what are known as devices, meaning a flexible symbol or image, individually designed to connote a specific person, household, or elite association and sometimes created to mark special events, such as a grand wedding or an important peace treaty. Devices were identity markers, claims that signaled belonging and that communicated important messages about the wearer. Many surviving badges were devices. An example of a personal device can be found in the portrait of *Henry V of Mecklenburg, The Peaceful* (1479–1552), who in this artwork from around the year 1510 appears to have adopted a late medieval weapon axe as a personal device (plate 2).[20]

The portrait features three images of the device, which is probably a *voulge*, a type of polearm, an axe-like weapon head mounted on a long pole. (Being designed to attack opponents wearing plate armor may account for the voulge's unsettling resemblance to an old-fashioned can opener.) Life-sized depictions of a voulge decorate the robe Henry V is wearing, perhaps appliqued onto or woven as part of the fabric. The one on the right is fully visible; the one on the left, partly glimpsed. A third, miniature voulge, in the form of a shiny metal badge, hangs as a pendant from a chain around Henry's neck, positioning the miniature sharp, deadly, cleaving weapon at Henry's throat.

Sacred or Profane?

As the reader will have discerned in the preceding paragraphs, this book treats all badges as a single object category that shared modes of manufacture, purpose, and function in order to explore the argument that medieval badges, whether secular or religious (or both), operated as a kind of pan-European, symbolic mode of communication. At the same time, in its argument the book often distinguishes between badges whose function was primarily religious and those whose function was primarily secular, or profane.

Using these two broad categories provides a measure of clarity when grappling with such a vast amount of material. The online database Kunera, which provides annotated images of over fifteen thousand individual badges and is an invaluable resource for studying badges, is organized according to the categories, religious and secular, allowing a systematic disposition of a vast amount of material. Most scholarship on medieval badges treats either religious badges—pilgrimage badges mainly—or secular badges, such as devices, without considering any overarching shared characteristics. A differentiated approach often makes sense. Religious badges were overwhelmingly associated with saints, divine personages, holy sites, and charismatic religious centers. They participated in the medieval Christian faith world, an extensive, shared, and changing network of stories, legends, theology, philosophy, belief, and practice, sometimes overlapping, sometimes contradictory. This web of story, doctrine, and practice was managed, usually locally, by the many, varied, and sometimes competing institutions of late medieval

Catholicism. Many of the profane badges, on the other hand, were bound up with aspects of quotidian life, for example, with city governance, with chivalry and knighthood, with lordship and political power, with civic associations and festivities. Compelled identity markers such as Jewish badges, which are discussed in more detail in Chapter 4, could be considered a subset of these political badges.

That being said, new scholarship on the Middle Ages has profoundly unsettled the modern distinction between religious and secular culture on which so much modern historical work about both the near and distant past is based. When studying medieval badges, the problem with relying on a near absolute and categorical distinction between the sacred and profane constructs an opposition that misrepresents the medieval world. Seeing the secular and religious spheres in the medieval world as distinct and in opposition to one another has played a role in creating a modern vision of medieval culture as animated by a power dynamic in which the secular world is dominated (indeed oppressed) by the religious orthodoxy of a powerful, unified Church. Over and against such a vision of past oppression, the modern, secular world can create an emancipatory story about itself, emancipation above all from the oppression of a totalitarian-like Church. This modern vision of the medieval past pervades modern culture. Ask students in North America or Europe at the beginning of class about people who lived in the Middle Ages, and they will usually say that medieval people were God-fearing, pious, and uncritically submissive to religious authority, religious ideology, and oppressive religious dogma, which in turn ruled the secular world. What students say sums up modern misconceptions about the past that flourish in spite of having been overturned by the scholarship of the past forty years. Like the work of social history out of which it grows, the study of medieval badges demonstrates the limitations of framing the medieval past in terms of a putative opposition between a weak, submissive secular realm and an ideologically unified, politically dominant religious realm. Setting aside one view allows another view to emerge of the fundamental historical and cultural uniqueness of the late medieval European world, which was characterized by the mingling of disparate religious and secular cultures through conflict, competition, negotiation, and disputatiousness. In the Middle Ages, the sacred and the profane overlapped and interacted in ways that are invisible or alien to modern people: obscenity in sacred spaces; profane parodies of the sacred; what many modern people would define as superstition integrated into the sacred realm; symbols and images moving back and forth between the religious and the secular worlds.[21] When studying medieval badges, it quickly becomes apparent that the distinction between sacred and profane badges is useful primarily as a heuristic or organizing device. Used as an interpretive model, this categorical distinction obscures more than it reveals.

Whether sacred or profane, badges were all manufactured and designed in similar ways. They shared symbols and participated in extensive, shared networks of stories and beliefs. All badges functioned and created meaning in similar ways. Religious and secular badges (even sexual ones) cohabitated the same world, as the fictional sketches imagining a roadside encounter in France or the lead foundry workshop on Mont-Saint-Michel are meant to suggest. They were disparate pieces of a social whole. All badges, whether sacred or profane, were signs of belonging whose display was also about power. All badges, whether sacred or profane, were media that participated in widely held medieval beliefs about the intimate connections between the natural and the spiritual worlds and about the struggle between various supernatural forces of ascendancy over human beings. All badges, whether religious or profane, were designed as media with these struggles in mind. Exploring the many, fundamental ways in which all badges resembled one another means this book sets aside the modern presumption of a clear, bright line distinguishing magic from religion, because in fundamental ways all badges, including the religious ones, participated in what modern people might call magic. Some badges represented humankind's effort to control the visible and invisible forces within and around them. Other badges represented human beings' efforts to create and project into the world visible, collective identities. All badges were a way of doing something. They took action. In a complex world fraught with perils natural and supernatural that was at the same time a world of opportunity and possibility, badges took a stand.

Why Badges?

Badges have intrigued me for the past ten years, since I, a literary scholar, stumbled more or less by accident over these material objects that are more usually studied by art historians and historians of religion. Around 2005, I was writing an article on three short, anonymous, late medieval, obscene German tales that featured human genitalia (male and female) wandering about a fictional landscape as speaking, mobile protagonists in their own right, each with the pronounced character profile of a beguiling if rather bad-mannered trickster-rogue.[22] An illustration in a scholarly article on these texts showed images of small objects, badges as it turned out, that were exactly the kind of fantastical penises and vulvas wandering about the world on their little legs and feet that were featured in the literary texts.[23] There was no discussion of the images per se, and of their connection (or lack of it) with the texts; they were just there. I was immediately curious. What were these objects? Where were they from? How were they used? What did they mean? Following the footnotes led to a small but significant body of scholarship on what are known as sexual badges: articles, catalogues, modern databases. But the answers that I found through my research did not take me far enough. After giving a number of lectures and presentations on the sexual badges, it dawned on me that one way to understand the sexual badges would be to study them, not in the context of texts with which they shared motifs and iconography but in the context of all badges, whether religious or profane. I realized that all badges were radically similar in key ways regardless of their widely differing images: they were made in the same way and from the same materials; they were of similar sizes and were worn in the same way; and they alluded in similar ways to larger, shared spheres of shared meaning. Surely if they shared so much, their cultural functions must have been similar even though their meanings were manifold.

As I sought to understand this unique, copious, and understudied body of evidence and my exploration widened to include all badges, I have become, in some sense, a North American champion of badges. Badges need champions because time has cost them the very qualities that made them eye-catching and engaging in the past. The surviving badges are downright ill-favored. They are so small that they are hard to look at when displayed in a dimly lit museum vitrine. Chemical changes to the lead-tin alloy have made them not bright and shiny but darkened and tarnished. Their once bright, crisp images are often eroded and blurred, as can be seen in plate 12b. Any paint, paper backing, or other embellishment is gone (with only a handful of exceptions). As they survive today, badges lack nearly all the qualities possessed by those surviving medieval objects that most capture and hold the modern imagination, such as medieval cathedrals, altarpieces, paintings, statues, precious illuminated manuscripts, and tapestries (think of the Unicorn Tapestries, for example) usually brilliantly restored. Badges have little in common with these; they are not big or bold or colorful or even restored. To engage with badges requires patience, understanding, and imagination. Once extended, however, these habits of mind will be rewarded with new insights into medieval culture and into a fascinating chapter into the history of the way human beings use objects to create and share meaning.

Informed Imagination as a Way of Thinking About Badges

One answer to the problem of making badges accessible and interesting to modern people is to imagine badges in use. Each chapter of this book, which is primarily a scholarly study, opens with a fictional sketch of my invention, in which I imagine specific badges in specific, everyday moments of late medieval life. The stories take place in northwestern France and Belgium (encompassing but not limited to Flanders), which is the setting of the sketch at the beginning of this chapter, and in southwestern Sweden. All the fictional scenarios take place in the same roughly one-hundred-year time frame, from about 1375 to 1475. The formative political event in French and Belgian settings is the violence of the Hundred Years' War. The Swedish stories are set during and after the Kalmar Union, the union of Denmark, Sweden, and Norway under one royal crown, which in Sweden dissolved into peasant uprisings and civil war after the death of Queen Margaret I in 1412. Badges were in widespread use during this time, not only in the urban and manufacturing heartland of northwestern Europe, represented here by the cloth-making city of Ypres, but also on its edges along the Baltic and in Scandinavia.

To write these fictional sketches, I relied on the same research, scholarship, and informed analysis that underwrite the chapters in this book. Learning more and more about the past, about everything from bell-making to theological discourses on free will, stirs the imagination in unexpected ways. A dialogue or conversation opens up in the mind, as the detail and frameworks gleaned from reading scholarship vivify the landscape of the past. The fictional scenarios are a product of that dialogue, a process that I call informed imagination. They began to assert themselves as I started to write the scholarly study in earnest. The badge material I was reading, analyzing, and integrating into my own thought insisted on suggesting stories, and those murmurings became impossible to ignore. I decided to experiment by interlacing storytelling and fact-finding in order to make the process, or method, of informed imagination legible to the reader. I hope that the fictional scenarios will draw readers in and provide an animated backdrop, as it were, for the scholarly chapters that make up the bulk of this book. I also hope that the fictional scenarios will encourage readers to similarly deploy informed imagination when they encounter objects and stories from the past. I am not the first scholar to make such an attempt. Others, such as Barbara Hanawalt with her study *Growing Up in Medieval London*, have tried something similar to mixed reviews.[24]

Many scholars read historical novels for pleasure, some scholars write them, and historical novelists mine the work of scholars for their own writing. Yet in our finished products scholars tend to hold far apart these two approaches to the past: fictional reimagining and historical scholarship. It is as though they meet offstage, as though they confer behind the scenes, a secret conclave or exchange of information whose continued and necessary existence can only be traced by the initiated through encoded references in a book's or an article's acknowledgments. The relationship between the two is not precarious; it is robust. But it is also private. It is as though they have not been able to settle on a public means of communication. The form I have adopted in this book takes another step toward putting this conversation in the open.

Using a fictional as well as a scholarly approach to the distant past seeks to capitalize on the strengths of both. Scholars and students alike owe an enormous intellectual debt to the careful, detailed, patient work of decades of scholars, toiling away in libraries, classrooms, and field sites across Europe, North America, and farther afield. Their sustained attention to evidence of all kinds within the context of the ethical frameworks of inquiry demanded by scholarly disciplines is foundational to our work. Yet scholarship is necessarily disparate and fragmentary, held separate in discrete disciplines by the very techniques and testable methods unique to each discipline that give them integrity.

Scholarly ways of studying the past foreground difference. Scholarship challenges the researcher to become aware of and set aside her own assumptions about the past, and about the objects or thought or events she is analyzing. It seeks to inhibit quick and facile judgment or understanding based on what the scholar already knows or believes to be true. Instead, it deliberately slows down the process of comprehension by asking the researcher to painstakingly learn and follow the research methods and evidence of her discipline and to thoughtfully engage with positions, interpretations, or schools of thought contrary to her own. These protocols, if you will, are forms of applied reasoning. Scholarship based in a disciplinary framework employs tools intended to open up a space that allows the mind to reassemble the object of study with attributes and meanings made visible through the scholarly process itself. Reason, emotional distance, and objectivity privilege the discontinuity between the past and the present. Scholarly practices create a bridge between past and present that recognizes separation yet creates connection so that lost meanings and beliefs can be partially recovered, can become partially visible or audible again. The researcher, however, partially and imperfectly attempts to make space in which to voice the uniqueness, the incommensurability of the past.[25]

It is a truism useful to repeat that all knowledge is partial, fragmentary, limited. The surviving evidence, in whatever state of present-day muteness, is residue of a time that was. Once it all existed, not as the kind of harmonious or unified whole that the ordering and systemizing patterns of our research methods and disciplines impose on it, but rather in the kind of fractious immediacy of competing realities, unexamined certainties, and disjunctive beliefs of terror, piety, injustice, doubt, and delight commingled that characterize our experience of the world even now. There is no way back to this fractured state of contradictory wholeness, at least through the lens of scholarship, which as I said above must for its own health and integrity insist on difference, on discontinuity between past and present. Yet fiction and storytelling take a different path to the past. Sharing the scholar's belief that the structures of fissure, rupture, and completeness are indelibly unique for each time and place, the writer animates that place and asks the reader to engage his or her own imagination as well. The writer imagines the past. This act places its trust in continuity, at worst in a belief that people in the past were exactly like ourselves, at best in a belief that the human spirit can grant access to the lived experience of the past across the unbridgeable gap of time and space.

The topic of badges lends itself particularly well to adopting the method of informed imagination to move between fictional scenarios and scholarship because the objects are numerous, compelling, and ordinary, yet direct evidence concerning their use and the beliefs attached to them is limited. Most of what can be surmised about badges is based on indirect evidence. It consists largely of the badges themselves, the sites where they have been found, images from medieval paintings (including illuminations in late medieval books), an extremely limited number of texts, such as surviving documentation from legal disputes that touched on badges. The nature of the surviving evidence sets radical limits on what can be known for sure. Only a few written texts or documents have survived that might afford a glimpse of a medieval person talking about badges or their reasons for making, wearing, gifting, or not wearing a badge. There are no letters from mothers scolding their sons for wearing lewd badges; no young husband's journal detailing the badges he has brought back for his wife from pilgrimage; no reforming mendicant's treatise recounting the social rituals and practices of the devout city guilds and what their badges signify. There are no coming-of-age novels reminiscing about boozy good times had at carnival and the badges that accompanied them. And it goes without saying that there are no interviews or consumer surveys: What is your age, sex, ethnicity, and profession? When did you first see or become aware of badges? At what age did you first acquire a badge?

Was it a religious, political, or lewd badge? Did you acquire it through purchase, gift, or by some other means? Did you wear it? Gift it? Carry it in your belongings? Use it in a different way? When and where did you do so? How many badges did you own or use in the past? How did you dispose of them and why? How many do you own now?

Such questions, impossible to answer, circle around and lead back to the most important questions to which this book seeks answers: Why did medieval people make and use badges? To whom were they speaking when they used them? To themselves, to neighbors, friends, or strangers, or to the supernatural forces beneficent and malignant that in their belief crowded the world? What acts were they performing with badges, and what were those acts saying about the world, about religion, magic, nature, and sexuality, about their own bodies and the bodies of others, about their identities and those of others? Badges have much to teach about medieval views of the world: beliefs about religion and magic; beliefs about the interconnections between the natural and the spiritual world and the ways in which human beings can intervene in them; medieval understandings of personhood at the intersection of individual and collective identity; and so on. Fiction informed by scholarship imagines ordinary medieval people with their badges, and these acts of imagination, however limited, can work together with scholarship to bring the reader a little closer to the lived reality of medieval people.

This book experiments with both scholarly and fictional writing, to see if they can cohabitate between the same covers. At the same time, and in the interest of clarity, the book clearly marks the difference between the genres of fiction writing and scholarly writing by keeping the two separate. A fictional scenario or sketch opens each chapter, and it is followed by academic writing. I have used this format to show that the two genres are doing different kinds of work. The fictional sketches present context and set the stage for analysis by imagining in detail medieval people using badges, both religious and secular. The subsequent analyses follow best practices for academic writing by presenting the reader with claims, arguments, and evidence drawn from the methods, work, and findings of different fields of studies, including art history, visual studies, literary studies, religious studies, history, anthropology, and gender studies.

2

How Do We Know About Medieval Badges?

The city of Ypres, on the Ieperlee Canal,
the first Sunday in August, 1394

The evening breeze brings the scent of marsh and the far-off sounds of the Thundach festivities to the deck of the gently rocking barge. The young man has been given guard duty so that the rest of the crew can join the throngs to cheer the jousts between the teams of Ypres and Lille before lining up for the free beer that the city fathers dispense on tournament day. They have handed him a fat cudgel, worn deep brown with age, as a sign of his new office and as a defensive weapon. How they laughed, roared really, at the sight of him weighing in his slight hands the heavy thing, now lying at his feet. He is so young that they call him mama's boy, and thin as a reed. The litheness gained in a childhood and youth spent tumbling and balancing is no use to these brawny dockers hauling barrels, bales and crates, animals and people, onto and off of the barge. Luckily the barge dog, a cranky old fellow with a bad eye, worse breath, and the worst temper, took to him from the start.

He pats the dog's head. He cannot haul and lift, but he has earned the place he begged from the barge owner whose wife found him hiding between the barrels of wine last spring. He had crept there from the inn where he and Pa had been left behind by the troupe as Pa's fever worsened.

He had no money for the hostel and no coins for the priest for burial, so he had tracked the sums in his head as Pa's delirium increased. He was the only object of value left. The innkeeper's wife, who smiled and gave him milk now and again, knew that, too. He had caught her glancing his way while chatting with the brothel keeper from up the river. Quietly, in the night, death took Pa, and quietly he slipped away and let the darkness swallow him, too.

On the barge, he has kept the promise he made to the barge owners. He has made himself useful. He has eavesdropped on traders haggling at the market and on the merchants whispering among themselves. He has memorized the numbers on their accounting sheets, never hidden from the sight of an untutored street lad like himself. And then he has done sums in his head. He has whispered better numbers to the owner while he is bargaining, and he has kept them from being cheated by flashy city merchants and folksy con men alike. They are making more money, and the six of them—the owner and his wife, their three-year-old daughter, the two dockers, himself, even the dog—all eat better.

Now he leans cross-legged on a barrel, the dog's back resting against his leg while he shapes with a carving tool the little plank of oak. It is for the servant girl he has been meeting for a year. He smiles, remembering that moment in the fall when they met for the fourth time as if by chance in the alley leading from the wharf to the market.

As if by chance? And she was again, as always, carrying the fish market shopping basket. They had walked through the cold drizzle and then sought refuge—at least from the wet, if not from the cold—inside a church to resume a conversation that seemed to have never stopped since they first met in June. There she shyly told him that she had taken on the unwholesome chore of fish market bargaining so that she could keep an eye on the river traffic and spot his barge.

Since then they have been making plans. There is urgent work to be done on the barge; the wife's second confinement approaches, and another docker has been hired. The barge owner has agreed that a hard-working, healthy young woman may join them on board if it causes no trouble. She must lawfully leave her employ, and, as always, no woman who is shared by men—common women as they are called on the farther reaches of the Rhine—is allowed on his barge.

Marriage then. Why not? It is true that during the festivities, all afternoon and night, girls like her will have been roving through the crowds, looking for a quick partner or two from elsewhere for a small fee. She is smart about it, though. She does not drink away the money but sets it aside for their future. She is careful to avoid the drunken brawlers and homeboys who take without paying, and quick to outwit unscrupulous con men who seek to capture girls like her and haul them far off to brothel servitude in other cities. She and the young man hide nothing from each other.

Marriage then. He is good at sums, she is strong and resolute, and they have a promise of shelter and work on the barge.

Around dawn the dockers and the owners will stagger back reeking of wine and beer, and then they will sleep like the dead. No telling when the new wares will finally be loaded. She will be waiting for him in the little glade just beyond the city ramparts, and he will bring her this gift and with it his proposal.

The small piece of oak has a fine shape now, narrow and rising to a point like the beautiful, towering windows in the great church, and with a small rim framing its center.

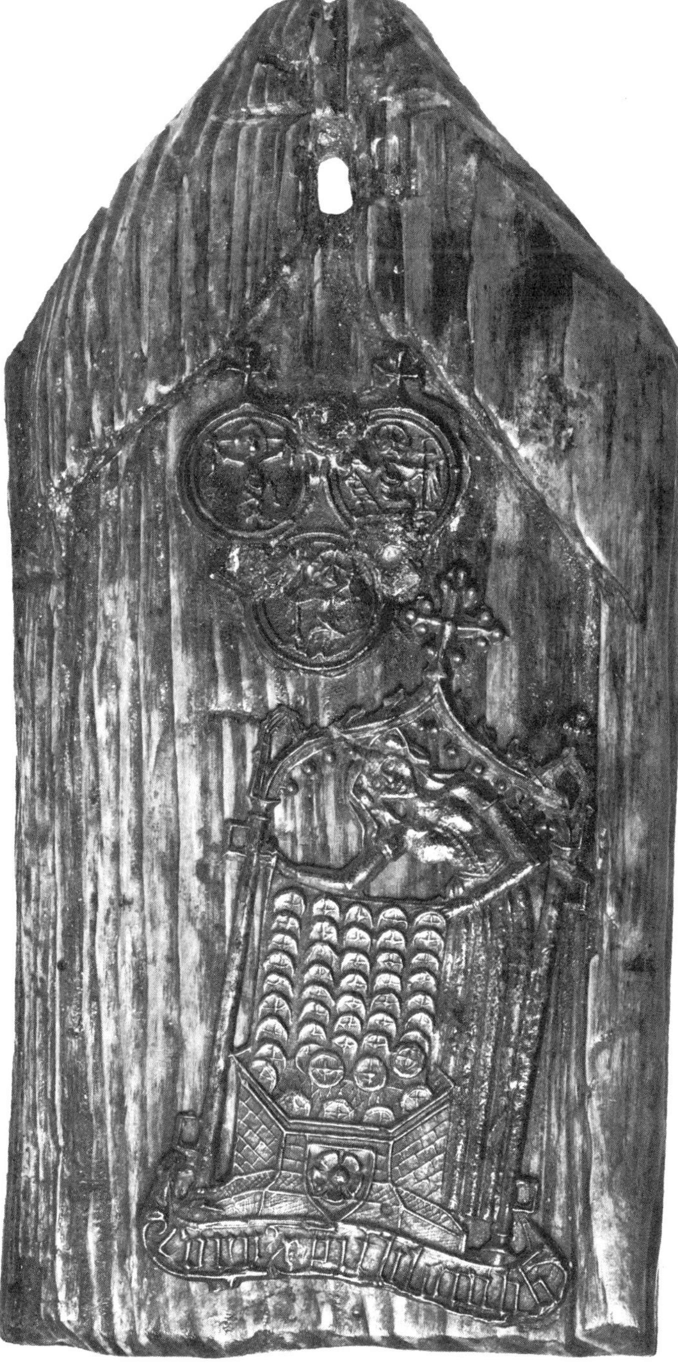

Figure 2.1. Wooden plank, carved in shape of Gothic window with Holy Blood religious badges (top, Wilsnack; bottom, Blomberg) affixed, 1475–1524, found in Amsterdam, 35 × 32 mm. Amsterdam, Bureau Monumenten & Archeologie, inv. MW2-6 (Kunera 04673). Photograph courtesy of Monuments and Archaeology, City of Amsterdam.

He takes from one pocket the two bent nails hidden there, and from another a small badge retrieved from the reedy riverbank where a drunken bargeman tossed it, shouting an oath.

The pendant is shaped like a shield, with a fine embossed, raised edge, and it hangs from a little chain whose eyelet can be fastened to the board by a nail. The shield is bright and shiny, silver-white, and it frames two tiny figures, the Blessed Virgin Mary and the Christ Child, she who protected Ypres's ramparts and saved it from the English besiegers just ten years ago, a great victory and endurance now being celebrated again in the town. They shine, too, like the frame and the little lions (how they resemble the old dog!). It is true that the holy ones are a little off-center, as the bargeman shouted in fury, claiming to have been cheated, to have purchased a remade thing, not a new one. The Christ Child is off to one side, almost peeping out from behind the shield's edge. A tiny shard of broken glass is wedged in the upper corner. But what of it? The Virgin Mary is smiling and so is her Child. They are safe within their little world, for a shield is a kind of rampart, a thing of strength and protection. They bring safety and blessing to those who care for them.

He takes the nails, and with great care he centers the badge and fastens it top and bottom to the little plank. It is a lovely sight. The badge has depth, and the Virgin and her Child hover between their white

Figure 2.2. Pewter badge, enthroned Madonna with Christ Child on her left in shield-shaped pendant topped by facing lions, pendant, origin unknown, 1325–1374, Ypres, Belgium, 44 × 25 mm. Yper Museum, SM 003510 (Kunera 06596). Photographer: Els Deroo. Photograph courtesy of Yper Museum.

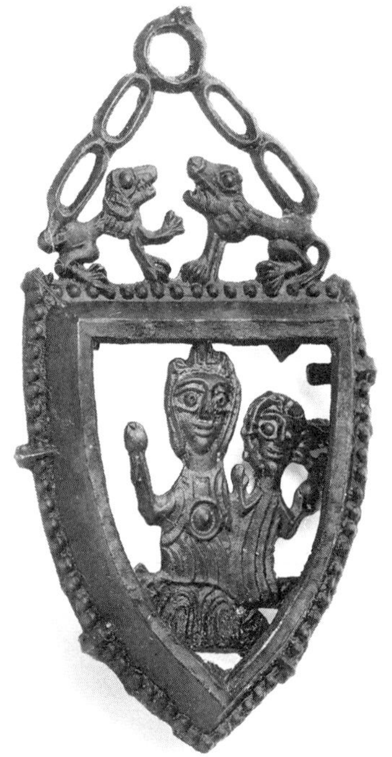

shield and the warm brown tones of the oak. The gift is done. Hung on a wall or set upon a table, it is a little chapel of one's own, where private prayers can be said. He speaks to it now. May the Blessed Virgin Mary and her Child bless his words and strengthen his entreaties and may they convey to his sweetheart the sincerity of his words. For he has told her the truth, that he sails on a barge that moves from this small river to the great ones beyond, that it is a good life, moving goods and people as the season demands and the weather permits, and that she can come with him and marry him and they will make their own way together.

Collecting and Cataloguing Medieval Badges

An important entry point into modern interest in medieval badges is Paris in the 1850s, when the French archaeologist Arthur Forgeais (1822–1878) began retrieving, preserving, and collecting ancient and medieval artifacts that were emerging in Paris as a result of the massive public works program of rebuilding and redesigning central Paris, which was undertaken in the 1850s and 1860s under the directorship of Georges-Eugène Haussmann (1809–1891).[1] Many of these artifacts, including huge numbers of medieval badges, were found in the Seine River, which was being dredged and rechanneled and over which new bridges were being built. Forgeais's collection must have been enormous. Along now-obscure pathways and via various Parisian art dealers over many decades, the river was most likely the ultimate source for hundreds of medieval badges in major museum collections. In Paris, parts of Forgeais's collection went to the Musée de Cluny–Musée national du Moyen Âge and to the Musée Carnavalet. In the first decades of the twentieth century, museums in Berlin and Prague acquired badge collections from French art dealers that had previously been in private hands, parts of which probably also go back to Forgeais. As the collection records of the British Museum in London show, from the 1830s on, badges from France, perhaps connected to Forgeais, were donated to its collections as well.[2]

The majority of surviving badges have been found in or alongside rivers, in archaeological sites, and by collectors using metal detectors, who are known in the United Kingdom as mudlarks because their primary "hunting grounds" are the mudflats of such tidal rivers as the Thames. In London, their finds, as well as badges uncovered during construction and archaeological excavation, are mostly housed in two large badge collections at the Museum of London, one belonging to the museum itself and one part of the Museum of London Archaeology. Similar collections based on local finds are housed in regional museums in England, the Low Countries, northern France, and northern Germany. The preservation of badges in museums has continued in these regions of Europe to the present day, supported there in part by various frameworks that encourage people to come forward with their finds. For example, in Denmark treasure and finds of historical importance are known as *Danefæ* and belong to the state. Finds are assessed and compensation (*godtgørelse*) can be paid by the state to the finder.[3] In England, Wales, and Northern Ireland, the Portable Antiquities Scheme is a voluntary program designed to encourage finders to report small finds of archaeological interest, such as badges. Because badges rarely contain more than ten percent precious metal, they are not considered treasure, which is subject to the United Kingdom Act of Parliament Treasure Act of 1996. This legislation establishes a legal obligation that finders of objects meeting various criteria (more than three hundred years old, more than ten percent precious metal, other provisions for prehistoric material) report their finds for valuation and possible reward.

Antiquarian interest in medieval badges continued into the twentieth century, but there was never much scholarly interest. They thus remained marginal to the scholarly research and teaching that came to shape modern perceptions and beliefs about the Middle Ages. Things began to change in the 1970s with the pioneers of modern badge research who emerged in Germany, the United Kingdom, France, and the Netherlands. Beginning in the late 1980s, major museum and exhibition catalogs began to be published. Scholars who were key to this change include professor and librarian Kurt Köster (1912–1986). A German pioneer in the field of pilgrim badge research on many fronts, Köster recognized the value for badge research of medieval church bells, of which thousands survived, in use, into the twentieth century.[4] Medieval bellmakers cast medieval pilgrim badges into the bells themselves. Köster's systematic database for pilgrim badges, completed after his retirement and now housed at the Germanisches Nationalmuseum in Nuremberg, was the basis for the online German reference tool, the Pilgerzeichendatenbank (database of pilgrim badges).

Another pioneer in the field of badge research was the historian Brian Spencer (1928–2003), who was the keeper in charge of Medieval Collections at the Museum of London Archaeology from 1975 to 1988. He recognized early on the historical value of the pilgrim badges that were turning up regularly in archaeological digs and being found by mudlarks in the tidal flats of rivers such as the Thames. After publishing catalogs of the badge collections in the Kings Lynn Museum in Norfolk (1980) and the Salisbury Museum (1990), his catalog of the badge collection of the Museum of London Archaeology saw a first edition in 1998 and a second edition in 2010.[5] In Scandinavia, the historian Lars Andersson published in 1989 a thorough catalog of religious pilgrim badges held in museums large and small across Sweden, Norway, and Denmark.[6] The French art historian Denis Bruna published a catalog from the first major exhibition of badges in France in 1996; his catalog of the collection in the Musée de Cluny–Musée national du Moyen Âge appeared in 2006.[7] In 2004, Arnaud Tixador published a catalog of the badges that had emerged from extensive archaeological excavations in the cloth-making city of Valenciennes in northern France.[8] In 2013 and 2016, Henryk Paner published two catalogs of medieval badges found in Poland, where there are especially rich finds from the former Hansa city of Gdańsk (in German, Danzig).[9] Finally, the large and diverse assemblage of religious and secular badges, administered by the Medieval Badges Foundation in the Netherlands, was collected actively by Hendrik-Jan van Beuningen (1920–2015) from the 1960s until his death.[10] In 1993, van Beuningen began the process of making the collection accessible and visible by publishing the first volume of the catalog *Heilig en Profaan* (Sacred and Profane), of which there are now four volumes (1993, 2001, 2012, 2018).

The print catalogs and monographs edited or authored by Andersson, van Beuningen, Bruna, Paner, Spencer, and Tixador remain primary reference materials for badges. Yet the ongoing process of classifying, ordering, and making accessible this scattered and essentially visual evidence presents a challenge. Tens of thousands of badges survive, and that number constantly grows because of new finds. Badges were made and found across a wide geographical area. These locations matter for understanding their manufacture, use, and meaning. Because each badge is a miniature, mass-produced, sculptural object that communicates visually, a picture is truly worth a thousand words. Badge research has profited immensely from the foresight of scholars who realized that these challenges could be handled by the new forms of classification, publication, and accessibility made possible by computer technologies and the internet.

The most prominent example of using modern technology to construct a reference work for badges is the database Kunera (Centrum voor Kunsthistorische Documentatie, Radboud Universiteit, Nijmegen, Netherlands). Planning for Kunera began in 1998, and the database was launched shortly thereafter.[11] This immense and invaluable resource organizes images, documentation, and bibliographies regarding individual medieval badges in a searchable, online database. Willy Piron and A. M. Koldeweij keep Kunera updated by continually adding new bibliographic items, photographs, and objects to its database, whether from private collections, museums, or new finds. Kunera features dynamic maps showing badge find sites when known. In December 2012, the Kunera database contained 10,734 images of religious badges (8,006 from known find sites; 2,728 from unknown sites) and 2,805 secular badges (2,490 from known find sites; 315 from unknown sites); in October 2020, that number had grown to a total of 15,407 images, comprising 12,069 images of religious badges (9,079 from known find sites; 2,990 from unknown sites) and 3,338 images of secular ones (2,974 from known find sites; 364 from unknown sites).

The Database of Pilgrim Badges (Pilgerzeichendatenbank) is much smaller, containing about 1,500 images of religious badges found in German-speaking lands and in central and eastern Europe. It is now housed and maintained at the Museum for Decorative Arts (Kunstgewerbemuseum), which is part of the State Museums of Berlin (Staatliche Museen zu Berlin) transforming Köster's pioneering research into an accessible and expandable reference tool.

The work of cataloging medieval badges remains far from complete. Medieval badges continue to be found. They routinely come to light during construction work in the Low Countries, in northern Germany, and around the Baltic, for example, areas where they were widely used; engineering and construction work in and around historical harbors and waterways turns them up. The arrival of cheaply available metal detectors has only increased the volume of discoveries. Badges in regional museums and private collections in northwestern and eastern Europe await classification and cataloging, as do eastern European cast imprints on surviving medieval bells. Study of and interest in medieval badges, from an ever-wider range of approaches, enriches our understanding of these objects and their manifold functions and meanings, while at the same time the actual number of known medieval badges available for study continues to grow.

Approaches to Studying Medieval Badges

Bearing vivid images that were designed and produced at a specific holy site or in a specific city or region, medieval badges are nearly always identifiable in the sense that in most cases a badge's image can be recognized and connected to a specific place. The tight connection between a specific image and a specific place is especially true of religious badges. Most churches and holy sites in medieval European Christendom venerated specific, local saints or wonder-working objects that were deeply connected to local legends and devotional practices, creating a unique site profile within the overarching matrix of Christian doctrine and liturgy. Administrators and officials of the holy sites where religious badges were sold guarded the rights to design and manufacture badges, trying to ensure that badge designs capitalized on unique features of a site.[12] That most religious badges can be identified even today testifies to their success. The local holy site also received some portion of the revenue stream generated by badge sales and controlled those sales, which were limited to the immediate environs of the site. As far as we know, religious badges were sold only at the site for which they were made. A badge's devotional efficacy was inextricably entwined with the shrines at the holy site from which it originated.

There are, of course, exceptions to the rule of easy badge recognizability. Secular badges are often more difficult to connect to a known great household, civic group, or large city, in part because less research has been done on them and in part because the visual images they employ (a rose, for example) are often more generic. Some religious badges cannot be connected to a specific holy site, often because that site was obscure, short-lived, or left little or no trace in the written record, or at any rate none that can be related to the badge imagery. Many local pilgrimage shrines in northern Germany and Scandinavia, for example, ceased when the Reformation took hold, and their lore and legends disappeared from memory.

The normal ease of identifying the specific holy site from which a religious badge originated means that much can be learned from paying attention to the places where religious badges were found. Pilgrims purchased badges at holy sites, and then they transported those badges with them as they traveled, often eventually disposing of them.[13] The sites where badges are found and the numbers of specific badges found at those sites can tell us a lot about where medieval pilgrims went and how popular different religious sites were. Such analysis corroborates written evidence to make visible, for example, the popularity of such holy sites as Wilsnack and Canterbury or the interconnectedness of specific sites into regional pilgrim routes, and it can also create new knowledge about local pilgrim sites and shrines that disappeared from view.[14]

The growth of research interest in medieval badges that began in the 1970s was fueled in part by fundamental, postwar shifts in the field of history in North America and Europe away from political history and toward social history. To use a visual metaphor, the field moved from a close focus on the top of the political and social order (kings and popes) and on abstract thinking (clerical writing and theology) to a wide-range lens that encompassed the study of everyday life and social structures in the Middle Ages. To the fore came such topics as the study of women, children, sexuality, pilgrimage, popular forms of piety, the urban poor, medieval slavery, and medieval peasants, as well as the study of everyday, widely available things, often made of cheap materials, a category of objects to which badges belong.

The past twenty years have also witnessed renewed interest in the study of material culture. This trend encompasses modern and contemporary studies as well, yet it is particularly well suited to studying the distant past. This approach depends to a certain extent on archaeology and art history and on their processes of collection, preservation, and conservation.[15] Contemporary work in the field of material culture goes decidedly beyond the close study of historical artifacts, exploring rather the ways in which practices of collecting and preservation, both institutionally and as practiced by individuals, intersect with the assumptions of changing regimes of representation. Located at the intersection of art history, archaeology, museum studies, and cultural studies, groundbreaking work in the field of material culture often focuses on quotidian objects of all kinds, across cultures and times, and explores the kinds and modes of meaning-making that are assigned to these objects.[16] In medieval studies, this trend has encouraged new research on badges because it has created a larger scholarly conversation around the nature of the surviving things, whether precious or ordinary, that medieval people made and used, asking not just about their functions but also about the beliefs and practices attached to them.[17]

Badges and Archaeology

Because badges are objects made of metal, they can be examined using modern scientific isotope analysis, which was undertaken and documented for many badges cataloged in the *Heilig en Profaan* series. The findings suggest, among other things, that badges were routinely made from recycled metals, which suggests in turn that badges were recycled themselves.

The study of badges is hindered by the frequent lack of archaeological context. Archaeological evidence, when known, is extremely valuable for understanding medieval badges. Knowing and recording exactly where an ancient object is found, and its relationship to other objects and traces in its vicinity, remains the bedrock of modern archaeological analysis. In this regard, badges have suffered. The retrieval, collection, and preservation of badges began in the early nineteenth century, preceding the emergence of the modern science of archaeology and its scientific practices of excavation that systemically capture data. For most surviving badges, this means that rich data about their find sites are lacking. In many cases, little more than the find site's geographical name (for example, the river Thames or the city of Bruges) survives; in many other cases even that is unknown.

Badges are often found in waterways, which does not tell very much about them beyond what an identification of the image on the badge indicates about the distance between the place where the badge originated and where it was found. Badges are often discovered as single finds outside the limited confines of a scientific excavation. When a find site is known, or when medieval badges are found as a part of archaeological excavations in constellation with other surviving artifacts and sometimes within the surviving traces of medieval habitations and then excavated, recorded, and studied according to the methods of modern archaeology, much can be learned about the ways medieval people used badges.

Take as an example the small, carved wooden plank shown in figure 2.1.[18] It is a created ensemble of objects. It includes two readily identifiable badges, the uppermost one from Wilsnack in northern Germany and the lower one from Blomberg (Lippe, North Rhine-Westphalia), both associated with veneration of the Holy Blood. These are affixed to a small wooden board, crudely yet effectively carved in the architectural shape of an arch and furnished with a hole at the top to facilitate mounting it in some fashion on, perhaps, a post, frame, or wall.

The object is one of about three similar wooden objects found in waterways in the Low Countries. This one, discovered in the Amstel River in Amsterdam, could easily have been made somewhere else given Amsterdam's prominence as a harbor trade city in the Middle Ages. The carved board's origin must be described as unknown but there is still much that can be learned from it. The badges affixed to the board are from late medieval holy sites; Wilsnack was a flourishing pilgrimage site by the first decade of the fifteenth century, while the Blomberg holy site was not active until the 1460s. The Blomberg badge provides a rough date for this specific object, which cannot be older than 1460. (I have taken liberties by using the idea of affixing a badge to a homemade, carved board to illustrate a scene that would have occurred nearly one hundred years earlier; the youth cannot be making this particular object, but he is making something like it.) The considerable distances between Amsterdam where the carved board with affixed badges shown in figure 2.1 was found and the holy sites associated with its badges—about 335 kilometers separate Amsterdam and Blomberg and about 600 kilometers separate Amsterdam and Wilsnack—indicate that someone carried these badges from one place to the other.

Most intriguingly, the board was purpose-carved, as is indicated by the wall-mount hole and the careful creation of a framed space imitating an architectural feature associated with high-value stonework and also commonly seen in late medieval, painted altarpieces, where saints are shown enclosed in arched, crowned niches. The board may be a homemade altarpiece or icon intended for intimate or domestic use, built up around the badges, which occupy the spatially honorable position within the arch. Someone carefully crafted this object to give the badges a similar function to that of saints in an altarpiece or niche. The entire ensemble is a fine example of the popular piety for which the late Middle Ages are so well known and provides more evidence that badges, which were personal and portable, played a role in this religious development.[19]

Three modern archaeological excavations have yielded rich knowledge of the production and function of badges: excavations at Mont-Saint-Michel; in the city of Valenciennes in the 1990s; and in the so-called "drowned meadows" excavations in Ypres (Ieper), Belgium, which took place in the 1970s. At Mont-Saint-Michel, a badge-making workshop was abandoned precipitously in the fifteenth century, most likely in response to an English assault on the abbey and village that took place in 1434 during the Hundred Years' War. From this abandoned workshop survive a range of molds, sometimes complex, which demonstrate the range of badges and objects and the techniques of mass production being used in a single workshop (these are discussed in more detail in Chapter 3).[20] In Valenciennes, the found badges are also linked to manufacturing but not their own.[21] Valenciennes was a cloth-producing city in the Middle Ages, and the excavations turned up numerous small, ground-level workshops containing one or two large looms. The badges found in these rooms probably belonged to the people who worked and traded in them, perhaps the weavers.

The case of Ypres is of special interest, both because so many badges survive from the city and because the rich archaeological evidence is still not fully analyzed with regard to badges. To understand the significance of the Ypres finds, a little historical background is in order.

The prosperous, walled cloth manufacturing and trading city of Ypres, on the banks of Ieperlee Canal and thus connected via the Ijzer (Yser) River to the North Sea, was embroiled in the events of the Hundred Years' War (1337–1453), which was fought primarily between England and France.[22] In July 1383, Ypres was besieged by the English army of Henry Despenser, Bishop of Norwich, in league with Ypres's archrival, the city of Ghent. The siege lasted for eight weeks, until Ypres's French ally, the Duke of Burgundy, marshaled a large army intending to attack the besiegers, causing the English to raise the siege and recross the channel by the end of October in defeat. Ypres's victory, traditionally attributed to the protection given to the city's ramparts by the Blessed Virgin Mary, was celebrated annually for generations thereafter in Ypres as *Thundach* (modern Dutch, *Tuindaag*) in the first week of August. Why does this history matter to understand medieval badges? Because it is part of the story of significant archaeological excavations at a site known as the "drowned meadows," which was on the south side of Ypres at the Rijselpoort, which opens onto the road to Lille, France.

Medieval Ypres was a walled city. Over the course of the High Middle Ages, suburbs sprang up around the outside of the city walls, flanking the roads leading to the city gates and spilling out from there, a normal pattern of urban development for late medieval European cities. By the year 1383, however, Ypres's suburbs appear to have been shrinking, a sign of the city's gradual economic decline.[23] When the English siege began, the suburbs were abandoned, and the English occupied the vacant suburbs instead. After the siege was raised, some of the suburbs, including those south of the city, were abandoned for good. Over the course of centuries, habitations crumbled, rotted, and disappeared, and the ground, which became progressively marshier, was used as animal pasturage, conveniently located just outside the city gate. In the nineteenth century, Ypres began to grow again. The train station was located just west of the old city walls; new suburbs with multistory apartment buildings sprang up to the east and north. The drowned meadows south of the city remained unbuilt, perhaps because of the marshy conditions that rendered the area an unfavorable or expensive site for construction.

In World War I, Ypres was on the front line. Shelled and bombarded continually, by the time the war was over, the city had been entirely destroyed by German shelling (today's enchanting medieval city was painstakingly rebuilt in the 1920s and 1930s). Because of its position in a kind of no-man's-land between the city and the front line of the German army, however, the drowned meadows were not shelled and remained nearly untouched. The excavations, which took place in the 1970s, yielded, among other things, a rich store of medieval badges, some three hundred in all, both religious and secular. Because of the meticulous care taken to document the excavation, it might be possible to place the badges found here in rich contexts of habitation and possible use—an exciting prospect indeed.

Badges survive in unexpected contexts as well. In his study of medieval pilgrim badges in Scandinavia, Lars Andersson records thirteen religious badges found during the restoration of medieval churches and altarpieces that had been hidden close to or in an altarpiece or its base or found under the choir floorboards.[24] Badges under floorboards may have been dropped or lost, of course, but the other badges must have been deliberately tucked away into the spots where they were found centuries later. These religious badges from distant holy places found their way into new sites of divine power. Perhaps craftsmen, artisans, parishioners, or priests deposited the badges in these places, as part of rituals or actions whose purposes can never be known to us. The example of religious badges cast into medieval bells supports the notion that religious badges were deliberately placed in hidden places, with medieval craftsmen and artists seeking to provide divine protection by placing a religious badge in their works.

One of the most interesting and unexpected sources of information about medieval badges comes from medieval church bells, which survived in large numbers across northern Europe into the twentieth century. According to historian Cornelia Oefelein, the first church bells that had pilgrim badges cast into their fabric were made in Cologne foundries in the fourteenth century; the practice was most popular in northern and central Germany and Scandinavia.[25] An example of such a bell is shown in figure 2.3. It was cast in the fifteenth century for a Franciscan monastery in the prosperous northern German trading city of Lübeck.[26]

Figure 2.3. Medieval bell, Saint Catherine's Church, Lübeck, Germany. Photograph courtesy of photographer: Dr. Jörg Ansorge, Horst, Germany.

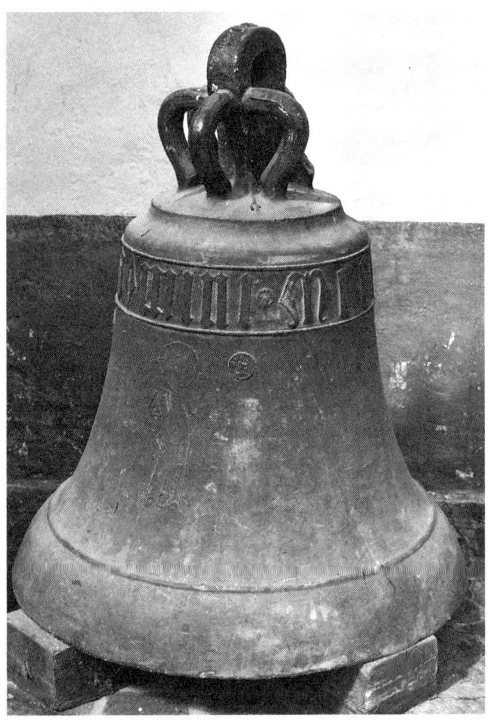

In the Middle Ages, large bells were not usually produced centrally and transported long distances but rather were made on site. This means that the master craftsmen, called bell founders, whose foundries or workshops specialized in this complex, difficult, and expensive manufacture traveled from place to place, following commissions and work.

The evidence of late medieval bells suggests that medieval bellmakers often cast religious badges into the fabric of the bell by carefully pressing a badge into the clay bell mold; when the molten ore was poured in, the badge melted, leaving an indelible, clear impression inside the bell.[27] Another technique was to imprint the clay with the badge and then keep the badge for reuse; it is nearly always impossible to tell which technique was used. In any case, it is often possible to recognize and identify a religious badge from the impression left in a bell. The Wilsnack badge impression on the bell from Saint Catherine's in Lübeck (figure 2.4), for example, is clearly recognizable, as is the impression of a Saint Odile badge (figure 2.5) that was cast into a medieval bell from the village of Schlatkow (Mecklenburg–Western Pomerania), Germany.

Many medieval bells contain more than one cast of a religious badge. One bell from 1473 in the parish church of Uggerby, Denmark, a village on the northern tip of the Jutland peninsula, shows traces of six religious badges cast

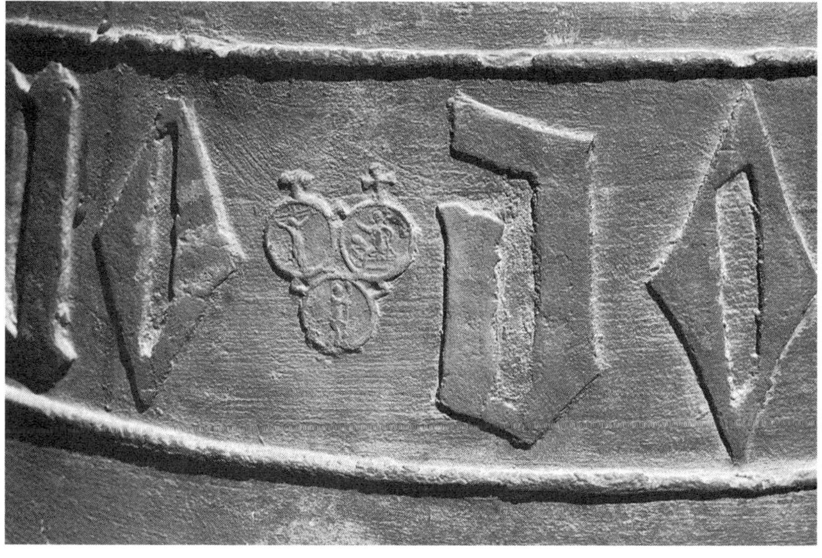

Figure 2.4. Medieval bell, detail showing cast of badge from Wilsnack, Germany, Saint Catherine's Church, Lübeck, Germany. Photograph courtesy of photographer: Dr. Jörg Ansorge, Horst, Germany.

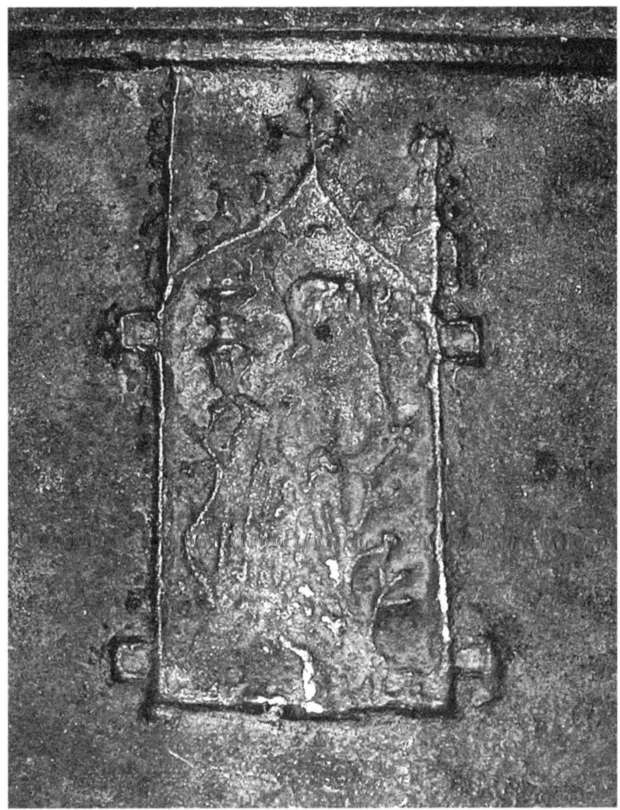

Figure 2.5. Cast of pewter badge on bell, Odile as abbess holding chalice on the left, Schlatkow (Mecklenburg-Vorpommern), Germany, bell cast in 1446. Photograph courtesy of photographer: Dr. Jörg Ansorge, Horst, Germany.

into its fabric. Although the condition of the bell is poor, four of the badges are still identifiable: Saint Theobald, whose holy site was Thann, Alsace, France (Kunera 03912); Saint Helper (*Sankt Hjælper*), an image of crucified Christ wearing a long gown, which comes from Kliplev in southern Denmark (Kunera 03835); Saint Odile, whose holy site was in Odilienberg, Alsace, France (Kunera 03909); and crossed keys with Vera icon from Rome (Kunera 03961).

The outlines of an itinerary are suggested by these four badges in the Uggerby church bell. The holy sites of Odilienberg and Thann, about one thousand two hundred and fifty kilometers south of Uggerby, were part of the same regional pilgrimage route, and the Kliplev holy site is situated directly on the ancient main road running from Hamburg in the south to the tip of Jutland in the north. Someone present or proximate when the bell was made in Uggerby—whether the master craftsman bellmaker and his workshop, local patrons, or well-traveled local pilgrims we will never know—had journeyed on these routes and acquired the badges that left their traces in the Uggerby bell.

Casting religious badges in bells demanded forethought; it could only have been carried out by the founders who made the bell. The surviving evidence suggests that this was a common practice in the late Middle Ages. In the late nineteenth century, diligent and passionate amateur historians in German-speaking lands and in Denmark began making systematic inventories of medieval bells, which meticulously describe each bell inside and out and are often accompanied by sketches. It is well that this evidence was collected then, because thousands of bells manufactured in the late Middle Ages were destroyed or melted down in the twentieth century, both during World War I and World War II. The larger question remains: why did these craftsmen put religious badges in the bells that they made? What does it mean that a bell wears, as it were, badges? Chapter 4 offers some answers to that question.

Art Historical Approaches to Badges

The quick and reliable identification of badge images relies on decades of art historical scholarship, which has made intelligible and accessible the systems of visual communication and the meanings associated with these images and symbols that pervade the medieval world. Art historians have also taught us that this iconography is not a fixed set of symbols with fixed meanings, but rather a complex and flexible system of visual communication with a wide variety of purposes and functions and in which context, material, and audience codetermine meaning.

Art historians have studied other kinds of evidence pertaining to badges as well, namely, badges in medieval manuscripts. Best known are representations of badges that were painted into religious books containing texts intended for private devotion, usually (though not exclusively) prayer books known as Books of Hours.[28] At the end of the fifteenth century, workshops in Bruges, Ghent, and the surrounding areas had specialized in creating richly illustrated prayer books for wealthy lay patrons. The illuminators working in these workshops painted pictures of religious badges in the lavishly decorated pictorial margins and frames of these prayer books, as can be seen in plate 3.

The painted badges are not fantasy badges or imagined ones. The illuminators used real badges as models for the paintings, although they made changes to the size or shape and often did not reproduce legibly any text on a depicted badge. Some of the surviving prayer books display the same set of badges from important local and regional shrines and sites, likely highly appropriate for the customers for whom these books were made. Other manuscripts contain images of different religious badges. These manuscripts may have been produced on commission for specific patrons, who perhaps selected religious badges based on the saints for whom they felt a special affinity.

The painted badges in these richly illuminated manuscripts did not start a trend for putting religious badges in manuscripts, however. Carefully rendered to achieve a trompe l'oeil effect (the optical illusion that actual badges are sewn to the page), the painted badges were imitating a decades-old trend in which medieval lay owners of devotional books had been adorning them by adding devotional objects, most often, though by no means exclusively, by sewing in badges. This trend was facilitated by a new mode of manufacturing, in which the image was stamped or hammered onto a thin piece of metal, often a precious metal such as gold, creating a very thin badge that added almost no depth to a page and that could be easily pierced by a needle. Plate 4 shows an array of gold and silver embossed badges sewn to an uninscribed manuscript page in a mid-fifteenth-century Book of Hours from Bruges.

Several recent works study medieval uses of devotional books. In her study from 2008, art historian Hanneke van Asperen documented the evidence found in about ninety manuscripts in which religious badges were still or, more often, had once been attached to a manuscript page.[29] Most badges in manuscripts were removed at some point in the past, but they left an indelible trace on the book's pages. These traces include sewing or needle holes where a badge, now lost, had been carefully stitched onto a page, and offsets, where a missing badge had left an imprint on adjacent pages.

Sometimes an offset preserves enough detail from the original badge to allow for identification. There can also be smudge-like traces of the original metal. Modern science can help a little further. Sometimes enough microscopic dust from the badge is embedded in the parchment or paper to allow the identification of the metal from which the badge was made. Many were of silver or gold, which helps to account for both their placement in expensive books and their eventual removal. Traces of related devotional objects are also found. Art historian Kathy Rudy argues that the round offsets in Books of Hours may indicate, not pilgrim badges, but rather Eucharist badges, which were the same size and material as pilgrim badges but served the devotional purpose of commemorating the book owner's taking the Eucharist at Communion.[30] Other badge-like objects, for example made of paper or leather, are sometimes found, as well as objects of a similar size to badges and used for similar, devotional purposes: tiny veils sewn in place to cover precious or meaningful images; tiny, hand-colored woodcuts of saints (perhaps the pilgrim woman in figure 1.4 has such on object on her hat); tiny strips of parchment turned into rolls; tiny embroideries; or printed drawings from other sources.[31]

A fifteenth-century Book of Hours from Paris (Paris, Bibliothèque de l'Arsenal, MS 1176 A rés) contains an example of this practice (see plate 5).

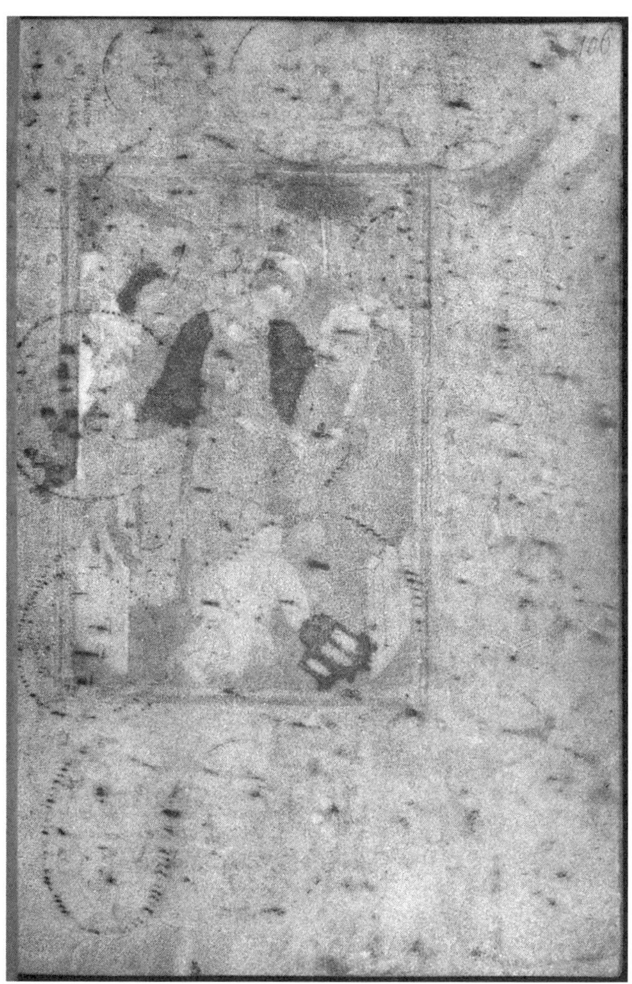

Figure 2.6. Master of Guillebert de Mets, detail of Book of Hours of Elizabeth von Munte and Daniel Rym with offsets and needle prickings from now lost sewn-in badges, parchment, Flanders (Ghent?), 1420–1430, 13.3 × 16.7 cm. Baltimore, Walters Art Museum, inv. Ms W 166, fol. 106r. Photograph courtesy of Walters Art Museum.

Carefully assembled at the front of the manuscript are three devotional objects.[32] At the top left is an embroidered square featuring a floral frame surrounding symbols and objects associated with Christ's crucifixion and death (the *arma Christi*), with these surrounding the holy initials IHS, also known as a Christogram or Christ's monogram. At the top right, there is a tiny piece of parchment on which have been painted in gouache the crossed keys of Saint Peter with a double-armed cross and an image of Christ's face showing a bearded, long-haired man surrounded by a halo. This image, ubiquitous in the late Middle Ages, is the Vera icon (Latin *sudarium*), variously known as the Veronica, the Veil of Veronica, or the Holy Face, a piece of cloth revered in Rome as a precious relic that was believed to show Christ's face.[33] Below these objects is a round, silver, stamped badge featuring Saint Martha standing on a dragon, the stitches fastening it to the page clearly visible. This page is an example of the practice of a Book of Hours or prayer book being used as, in John Harthan's words, "albums for the safe-keeping of pilgrim's badges, ex votos and other objets de piété."[34] The objects carefully placed at the front of this Parisian Book of Hours were not merely souvenirs. Rather, like the manuscript's subsequent illuminations, they could be activated, as it were, by the reader through contemplation and prayer for devotional exercises, and they personalize the manuscript as well.[35]

Van Asperen's work shows that having large numbers of badges or objects in a single manuscript was the exception. Most devotional manuscripts contained only a few badges, carefully selected and placed to reflect the individual religious beliefs and preferences of the book's owner or user. A Book of Hours made around 1450 for Maria van Elderen has traces of only one badge next to a prayer to Saint Anne, the mother of the Blessed Virgin Mary.[36] We will never know for certain when or by whom the badge, now present only as a ghostly trace, was sewn into the manuscript and how the badge was acquired. The person who added this badge to the prayer book need not have gone on a pilgrimage, though she or he may well have done so. However she acquired it, the badge placement, the wear marks on the page, the words of the prayer, and perhaps even the original owner's name strongly suggest that the primary association of this Saint Anne badge was not so much pilgrimage as it was, more capaciously, holiness and personal devotion. The religious badge's function and use far exceed pilgrimage. The medieval book owner who inserted this badge in this book inserted herself or himself into the book's devotional narrative.

Late medieval devotional manuscripts are a rich source of information about the functions and uses to which medieval people put religious badges. Representations of badges are found as well in medieval sculpture and painting, as is attested in some of the illustrations of this book. These art historical sources remind us that medieval religious badges belong in a larger category of devotional objects that has much to tell about the growth of lay piety in the late Middle Ages and about the heterogenous rituals and practices that grew up around it.

The End of Badges

The manufacture, production, and use of badges peaked in the fifteenth century; in the first decades of the sixteenth century, badge use declined precipitously so that from the height of their popularity around 1500, religious badges fell rapidly into disuse in northwestern Europe after the Protestant Reformation. The illuminated devotional manuscripts filled with drawings of all kinds, among them pages littered with religious badges, and the personal devotional manuscripts transformed into personal shrines by badge collections or the addition of a single religious badge or other objects stand at what turned out to be the waning life of religious badges. In a few tumultuous decades the Reformation swept victoriously across the same territories of Europe where religious badges had played a major role, altering the cultural and religious landscape there forever. The rapid disappearance of religious badges in northwestern Europe was a side effect of the Protestants' deep, fervent, and all-encompassing rejection of late medieval Catholicism's devotion to the saints and wonder-working objects. Although Protestant doctrine proceeded from and intensified the personalization of piety and devotion to which the personalized manuscripts bear witness, at the same time it kicked away the prop, the worship of saints, as an intermediary between God and the believer, replacing it with an immediate and intimate connection between the two in which pilgrimages to regional shrines and objects such as religious badges had no place. The late Middle Ages also saw the beginnings of the mass production of what might be termed generic holy images, such as crucifixes that lacked the iconographic and geographic specificity of medieval badges featuring the crucified Christ. Such generic signs could compete with or replace site-specific ones.

Of course the material traces of Catholicism hardly vanished from reformed areas. Far from it. Church buildings and works of art were adapted for Protestant worship. Costly items such as cloth and fabric, which represented a considerable investment of resources and were an integral part of liturgical and ritual performances, were re-purposed for Protestant liturgical use. The largest and most valuable still existing collections of medieval textiles are in Protestant churches in northern Europe.[37] But religious badges appear to have been different. Not only were they casual signs that had little intrinsic value, they appear to have been so tightly tied to an ensemble of pious, Catholic practices linking together pilgrimage, the sale of indulgences, and various liturgical and para-liturgical practices and performances that the fundamental, wide-ranging changes to these structures and practices of belief led also to the abandonment of religious badges.

The changes in religious and cultural practice brought about by the Reformation provide a cogent explanation for the disappearance of religious badges. Secular badges, however, continued in use after the Reformation; the story of the shifts and changes in their meanings and uses in early modern Europe has still not been told.

The mass use of pewter badges as political devices declined in the decades after the Reformation and there was a bifurcation in the continued use of political badges, with elites increasingly using costly device-like items often with esoteric images, while at the same time the use of compelled badges was on the rise.

Elites continued to use badges and devices as personal signs (in the mid-sixteenth century, Robert Dudley, Elizabeth I's favorite, used the bear and ragged staff badge or emblem wherever he could), but these were often—indeed usually—made of costly and precious materials. They were jewelery-like. Hat badges made of precious materials became popular with elites (many portraits of Habsburg family members and close associates in the Low Countries show them), and these hat badges often sport images from classical stories.[38] These classical references are interesting because they suggest a trend away from the kind of wide intelligibility of images that was so typical of medieval badges and toward more deliberate obscurity of reference. Whereas in High and late Middle Ages, political badges and devices were usually designed to be widely recognizable, some early modern hat badges and devices were more individual and their meanings more esoteric. Having or lacking access to the knowledge necessary to interpret the device might then have signaled closeness to or distance from the device wearer.

On the other hand, the use of compelled badges increased in the late fifteenth century and continued into the sixteenth century. Different kinds of compelled badges are discussed in Chapter 4: beggar's badges, sanctuary men badges, heretical crosses, and Jewish badges. Medieval descriptions of these badges stressed that they must be large. In late medieval and early modern England, for example, male and female sanctuary seekers were compelled by statute to wear when outside of their lodgings a badge that was "ten inches length and breadth."[39] This large size sets the compelled badges apart from late medieval pewter badges, which are often so small that they required close, face-to-face proximity in order to be read. Compelled badges, however, were by regulation designed to be recognizable from a distance, so that the wearer could be identified before someone who did not belong to that category or wished to distance themselves from it could keep from getting too close. In this case, physical distancing really was social distancing as well.

Compelled badges imposed a social stigma. What was happening here may be roughly analogous to semantic narrowing in the linguistic sphere, a common linguistic process in which the meaning of a word becomes less general and inclusive. Perhaps by the beginning of the sixteenth century the display of an inexpensive political badge, which was never a neutral act in the first place, was losing its association with political allegiances that were adopted voluntarily. Instead, the meaning of wearing a political badge that one had been given was narrowing, so that it was increasingly viewed not as a claim of self-chosen political or social belonging but rather as a statement of political or social belonging that had been compelled by an authority.

Research into badges using frivolous or obscene imagery might explore changes in carnival practices and in discourses about the use of frivolous, ribald, sexual, and obscene imagery in public locations to understand why badges using this imagery disappeared. Perhaps the imagery itself migrated into other, less benign areas of public discourse (witchcraft, for example) or into less public circles. The use of badges employing widely understood imagery related to friendship declined as well. Perhaps this change reflected an increasing use in the early modern period of visual symbols and systems of signification that were decipherable not by many but only by a select few. It is quite possible, too, that images manufactured through new modes of rapid image technology production replaced pewter badges in many spheres of life.

To assert that the heyday of badges, which began in the late twelfth century and persisted to around 1500, came to an end is not to say that badge-like objects vanished altogether, of course. Ex-voto images remain in widespread use in Catholic areas to this day.[40] Vestiges of political badge use can be found in the discrete lapel pins worn by members of lay religious orders or of political parties. Girl Scout and Boy Scout badges visually signal mastery of specific skills or lore. An alternate frame of reference for understanding the decline in the use of medieval badges might highlight transformation over time, investigating how changes in the social order and social practice affected identity-signaling practices or whether new materials and technologies assumed some of the social and symbolic features previously fulfilled by badges. Investigating the interplay of text and image in cultural systems of meaning-making is as pertinent and urgent today as it was five hundred years ago, and an article by linguist Anatol Stefanowitsch published in 2020 on some linguistic similarities in functionality between badges and emojis suggests that, in some new ways, badges are with us still.[41]

3

How Were Badges Made, Designed, and Used?

Mont-Saint-Michel,
late August 1434

The ancient abbey towers over the village clinging to the steep slopes of the tiny coastal island. In a metalworking shop at the village's north edge, the summer heat is compounded by furnace fires in which lead is melted. A small group of skilled metalworkers ply their trade. They are hard at it, manufacturing small lead and tin alloy objects for the pilgrim trade: bells, rattles, rings, tiny pendant horns, many different badges showing the archangel Saint Michael crushing a demon underfoot and sometimes impaling it for good measure, and even tiny swords to pin to one's hat.

The craftsmen work quickly, producing many objects in a single day. They are stockpiling items now. Saint Michael's feast day on September 29 will bring thousands of visitors. The Mont-Saint-Michel Abbey expects even more pilgrims to arrive for that most holy day, October 16, commemorating the founding of the abbey centuries ago, a time shrouded in mystery, when Saint Michael appeared to Aubert, the bishop of Avranches, a city across the bay, instructing him to build a church on the rocky tidal island.

The village children enjoy acting out the story, especially the part in which Saint Michael finally gets Bishop Aubert's attention by burning a hole in his skull with his finger. Aubert has become a saint, too, his skull, hole and all, preserved at Avranches. On the Mont, Saint Michael is supreme, a saint so powerful that some say he is more powerful than Saint Jacques, whom the English call James, and whose shrine is many days' travel south, at Compostela in Spain.

It is a wonder of sorts that the pilgrims still come. The hostile English army is still encamped in sight, on the mainland. Their on-again, off-again siege has worn on so long that many born in its early days have grown old never knowing any different. Nearly thirty years now! These English men-of-war and their troops have become like bad neighbors, whose vices and weaknesses, as well as strengths, are well known. One

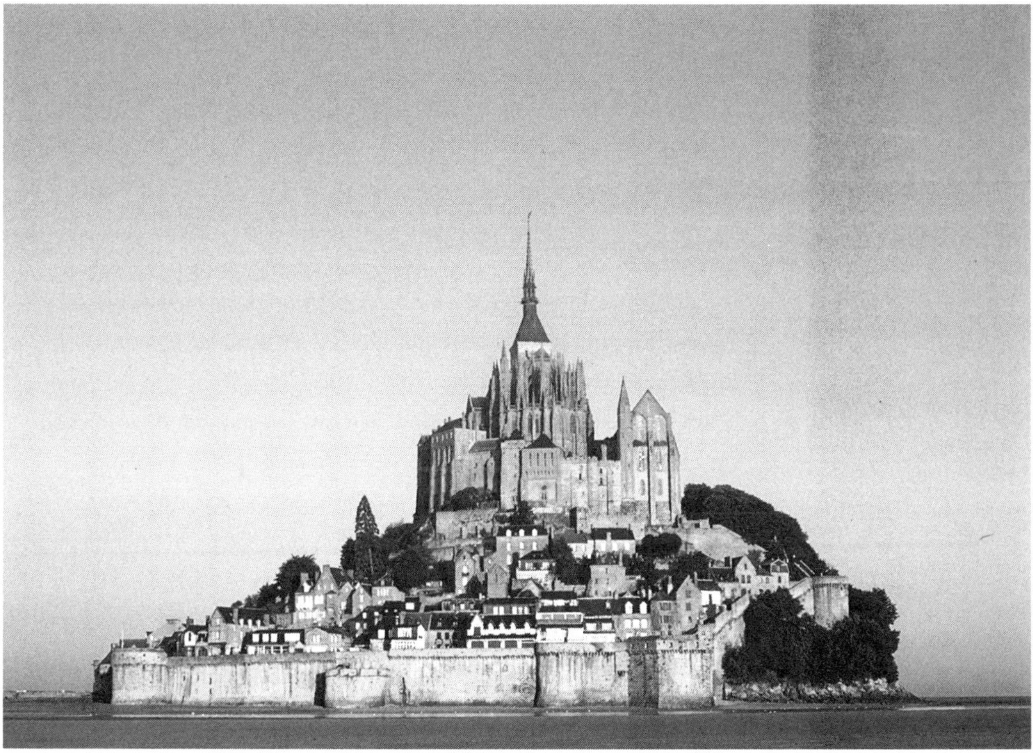

Figure 3.1. Mont-Saint-Michel at high tide, Mont-Saint-Michel, Normandy, France. Photograph and permission from HIP/Art Resource, New York.

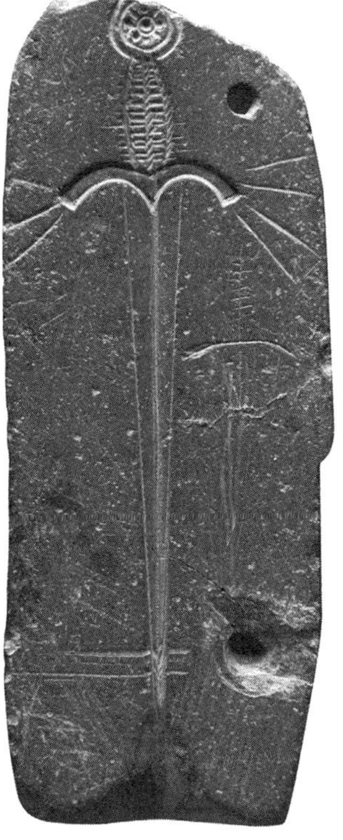

Figure 3.2. Fragment of sandstone shale pilgrim badge mold, an engraved sword and, as graffiti etched beside it, a small sword, Mont-Saint-Michel, France, c. 1434, 95 × 38 × 8 mm, inv. 2004-2-4. Photographer: Hervé Paitier, Inrap. Photograph courtesy of Françoise Labaune-Jean.

can haggle with them, and for payment they will let pilgrims and supplies pass.

But to reach the Mont, pilgrims must also face unknown, unpredictable evil. They must brave difficult roads made even more perilous by marauding bands of armed men who roam the countryside, stalking the weak and preying on the innocent. Lawlessness and disorder lurk everywhere.

Does it really matter, the villagers say, who these men claim to be? French, English, barons, peasants, king's men, outlaws, liberators, or lords: they are thieves, the lot of them, bringing disorder at best and death at worst. The foolish young men run away to join them, and so the old are left to bring in the harvest. The silver penny tossed by a captain to a pleading mother as he leads away the last milk cow will not still the children's hunger. Those who take the seed grain at knife point and set fire to the barn, well, what is there to say to that?

It is a blessing that the pilgrims still arrive. With them comes custom for the village, trade for the metalworkers. Making a living for oneself and one's family is not to be taken for granted in such troubled times. Everyone has experienced their share of the troubles: the evils of siege; the violence and predation of armies large and small; the plight of the displaced and wounded who wash up like tidal flotsam on the abbey's doorstep, so many of them sick, starving, or dying, in desperate need of food and shelter.

Nor have the monks, lords of the village on the Mont, put their trust solely in Saint Michael. The abbey chancel, more than three hundred years old, is dilapidated and in desperate need of repair. Rumor has it that an architect has visited the abbot. Sketches of a soaring edifice with a window grander than that at the shrine of the Blessed Virgin Mary at Chartres were laid out on the abbot's table after dinner was cleared away.

But these brothers are hardheaded, and thanks be to Saint Michael for that! They have poured their treasure into ransoms and payoffs and into improving the fortifications that have kept marauders at bay, unable to conquer the little isle, its abbey, and village. Thanks to the shrewdness, foresight, and resources of the brothers, the isle's inhabitants and the abbey's treasures both spiritual and material have been spared the worst depredations of these interminable wars with the English and their ever-shifting allies. It has been a struggle, but somehow the everyday rhythms of prayer, farming, and commerce have been maintained.

The metalworkers labor precisely, quickly, and carefully. They melt the raw material: scrap; discarded objects; a few, precious ingots from the mines. Stone molds, each made of several parts, are ready on the long, low workbench. Each is hand-carved in shale or schist rock, which is easy to work yet durable and long wearing. Each consists of several parts that have been carefully assembled and tightly joined.

Each mold is being carefully checked by the new worker. He has made sure that the channels funneling the liquid metal to the hollows inside are unobstructed and the delicate grooves for venting air are smooth. The molds may appear small and humble, but the new man, a fine technician in his own right, admires the ingenuity of their designs.

Take, for example, the three-piece mold for making the tiny bells that pilgrims attach to their clothing. The cleverly designed mold allows the eyelets to be cast as an integral part of each tiny bell. Skill and precision fit everything together so that the top mold containing the design joins the bottom mold with the attachment rings, with the tiny bell inside. Such a waste of time, effort, and precious resources when sloppiness produces exquisite bells with misaligned dangles and sewing rings!

Careful handling is required for the exquisite, detailed Saint Michael badge molds, made at great expense by goldsmiths working in the employ of the monks, who retain ownership of the molds and lease them to the shop. Fewer of these badges are made, because they sell for more than five times the cost of their humble cousin, the Saint Michael sword, and they often require further embellishment.

The new man's young son works alongside him, opening the cooled molds and marveling at them. What will emerge? His family is new to the village, and he is not yet familiar with this workshop's molds, although soon enough, he judges, he will be able to recognize them from their backs like the other workmen.

The boy carefully breaks open the first cooled mold and reveals Saint Michael in a brooch-like circle. The small eyelets, left and right, so tricky to manufacture and crucial to the value of the object because they allow the badge to be sewn to clothing, are perfect. It is an exquisite object. The six petal-like curves are outlined with small, pearl-like dots. Inside this frame, the archangel Saint Michael stands erect, wings out-spread, wearing robes and with a brooch or badge pinned to his chest. Saint Michael looks impassively out at the boy, holding his gaze.

The saint's head, wings, and torso, calm and immobile, fill the upper half of the badge. The action is taking place in the bottom half of the badge. A lance gripped high in Saint Michael's right hand draws the eye diagonally down across his body to its lower end that is impaling the maw of the monstrous dragon lying pinned and flailing under Saint Michael's feet. Beside the dragon's head, Saint Michael's left hand holds a shield. Behind him and within the lower half of the badge, two souls are being weighed on a scale.

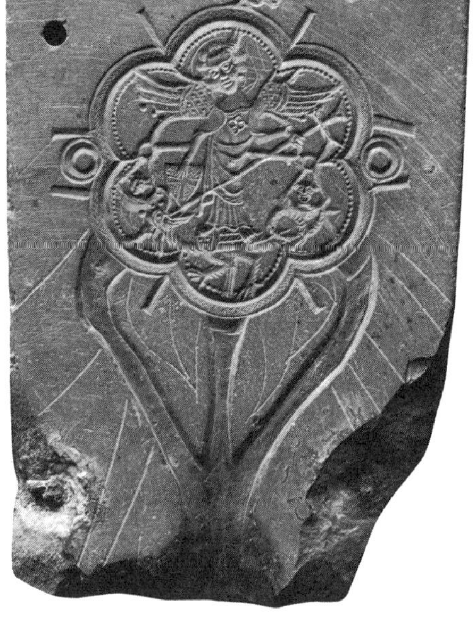

Figure 3.3. Black schist pilgrim badge mold, winged Saint Michael slaying dragon in six-petaled frame, Mont-Saint-Michel, France, c. 1434, 95 × 71 × 15 mm. Photographer: Hervé Paitier, Inrap. Photograph courtesy of Françoise Labaune-Jean.

Figure 3.4. Drawing of individual pieces of black schist pilgrim badge mold showing winged Saint Michael slaying dragon in six-petaled frame. Drawing by Mathilde Dupré and Françoise Labaune-Jean, Inrap. Courtesy of Françoise Labaune-Jean.

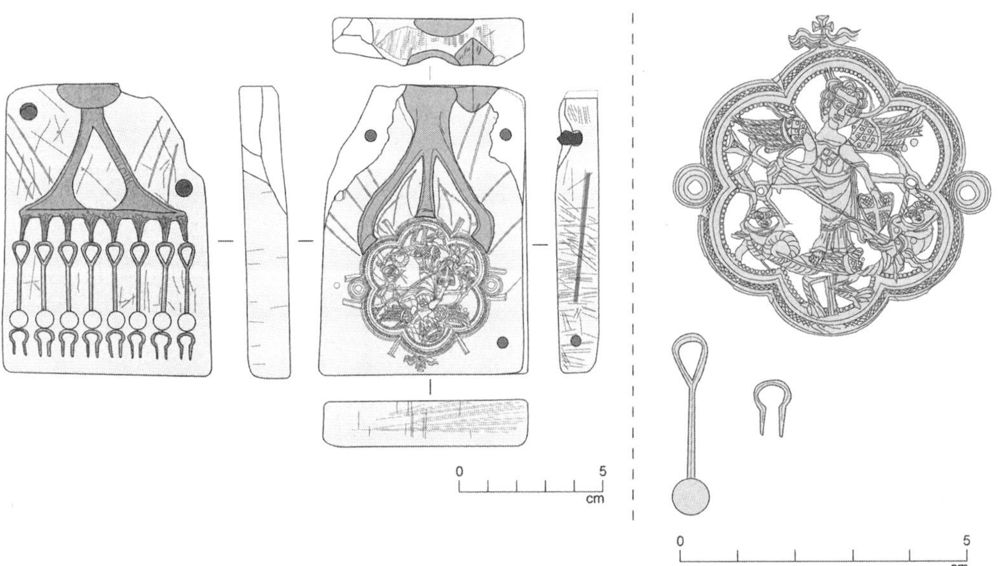

Ingenious, the interlocking pieces of this mold! Designed to make full use of the high-quality stone, it also produces eight little clappers to be mounted inside bells, and eight tiny, needle-fine pincers that must be affixed to the six-petaled Saint Michael badge in order to hold in place a backing of painted paper.

The boy carefully nests all the tiny pieces into a basket padded with wool. When it is full, he will run it down the lane to his mother in the embellishment workshop. He is eager to go, to trade the blistering heat of the smithy for the cool shade of his mother's place. There will be the cool touch of her hand as she strokes his cheek, the finer smells of oils and eggs, the dry delicious crunch of the bread she will have saved for him in her apron pocket, the coos and cries of his baby sister, whom he will hold while his mother's deft hands unpack the badges and the small pieces and distribute them on the workbench by size and complexity, reserving the difficult pieces for the most skilled artisan in the group, herself.

Opening the next mold discloses a little horn, with incised decorations and a simple ring attachment at the top. The boy fingers the pottery horn that dangles on a strip of leather around his neck, a gift from the workshop foreman, whose brother-in-law oversees the pottery works nearby. The horn is already chipped. A lead one would last much longer. Simple, easily bent, but a fine object nonetheless! How it shines in the summer light!

From the final mold, another archangel Saint Michael emerges, a long-legged, proud, young man not much older than himself. No wings! No halo! Instead, Saint Michael is a soldier, an officer doubtless, to judge by the expensive armor he is wearing. He is bareheaded and his hair curls over his ears. He stands tall and strong, his feet planted on the chest of a demon writhing in helpless agony across the bottom of the badge. Saint Michael's hand, lowered beside his knees, holds a shield emblazoned with the fleur-de-lis, the symbol of a great baron. His other hand is raised high, clasping a sword that is preparing to descend on the hideous, horned, winged devil that lies chained on its back beneath the saint's feet. The demon looks out at the viewer, imploring help, while Saint Michael gazes at the viewer, too, commanding attention. See what I do; I do it for you; you can do it too.

The goldsmiths employed by the abbot to design and carve the molds are justly praised. These exquisite objects the molds yield honor the saint. Yet the boy has overheard grumblings in the shop. Some say that the abbot demands too high a fee for the use of the molds. Others

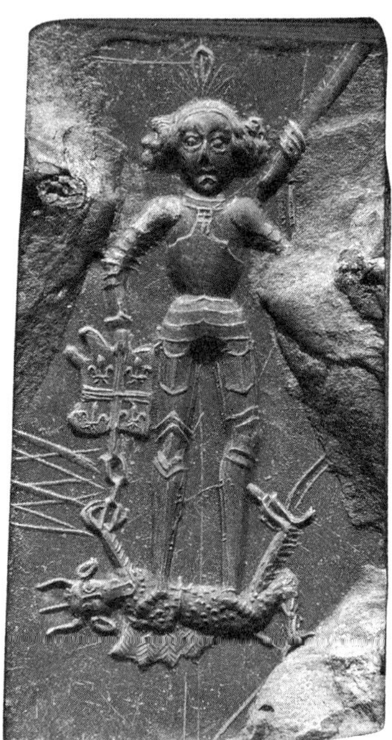

Figure 3.5. Fragment of sandstone shale pilgrim badge mold, archangel Michael wearing fifteenth-century combat armor and holding on the left a shield and aloft on the right a sword, standing on flailing demon, Mont-Saint-Michel, France, c. 1434, 80 × 40–43 × 13–19 mm. Photographer: Hervé Pairier, Inrap. Photograph courtesy of Françoise Labaune-Jean.

report the gossip of traders and merchants, who say that the concession fee demanded by the abbey to lease the property is too high.

The journeymen, two of whom have come from the city of Ypres, whisper as they furtively pass around badges that the boy never has seen properly. When the others catch him or his father glancing their way, they put the things back in their work aprons with a smirk. Yet they show these objects to one another and laugh, and say that in Ypres and in other cities to the north, a master craftsman can be a free agent, not under the thumb of an overlord who compels him to make certain kinds of badges and forbids him to make other kinds. There is money to be made in manufacturing other badges, they say, especially at festivals and carnival time, or for the establishments much frequented by young men such as themselves.

Is there harm in such talk? Is that why Papa is so worried? Or does the sour look on Papa's face concern the English ships and boats gathering and massing for days now on the ocean side of the isle? Papa counts them every evening as they walk. He mutters to Mama that there are ten more every day, and Mama prays.

Thanks to the work of modern archaeology, imagining a day in the life of the medieval craftsmen who produced badges (and perhaps craftswomen as well, as pictured in the previous fictional sketch) can draw on historical facts.[1] Starting in 2002, archaeological excavations, proceeding in advance of the rebuilding of the primary school on Mont-Saint-Michel, discovered five levels of medieval habitation. The second level was a badge-making workshop, a metal smithy where small objects made of lead-tin alloys and associated with the pilgrim trade were produced, among them badges linked to the abbey's thriving pilgrimage worship of the archangel Saint Michael. The workshop must have been precipitously abandoned and then destroyed by fire, for the valuable molds, many nearly intact, were still on site. Later, rubble filled in the ruin, and a third building was erected. The dates of coins and objects found in the badge-making workshop and its sudden destruction accord well with historical record: in the late summer of 1434, the English laid siege to Mont-Saint-Michel from the sea, bombarding it and setting portions of the village on fire, probably including the badge-making workshop. What was doubtless a terrible calamity to the workmen and the abbey is a stroke of good fortune for the modern world. This unique survival left the entire chain of production assembled on site. Nothing remotely like it has been found anywhere else.

Religious objects dominated production in the destroyed workshop, yet some secular objects were made there as well: pendants, rings, buttons. This makes sense because the mode of manufacture for all these cast objects, as well as for all cast badges, religious or secular, pious or obscene, was exactly the same.

It is true that when their workshop was destroyed, the badge smiths at Mont-Saint-Michel, though apparently working to the shop's full capacity, were not producing obscene badges. While one can only speculate on the reasons, a number of possibilities present themselves. Perhaps the abbey monks, who designed, ordered, and owned the molds and were the village overlords, had interdicted the production and sale of such lewd objects. This is the hypothetical version I have chosen for the sketch, in which the journeymen laborers have in their pockets obscene badges such as those found in the city of Ypres farther north.

But other, equally plausible explanations present themselves. Perhaps there were no local customs or practices that made such objects desirable, and so there was no market for them. Perhaps the lack of obscene badges was a matter of the season. Perhaps such objects were only made at specific times of the year, such as carnival season in February and March or for planting festivities in the month of May. This final explanation, though not as dramatic as the first, also seems plausible from a historical point of view. What matters is that secular (though not sexual) and religious objects were being produced side by side in a workshop that primarily served the abbey at Mont-Saint-Michel, a workshop whose main focus of business was the pilgrim trade, and that such commingling was the norm in such workshops across late medieval Europe.

Badges represent one small product of the vast network of medieval metalworking trades.[2] Metalwork required specialized training, access to specifically equipped workspaces or workshops, cooperation with others in the production process, access to valuable or semivaluable raw materials, and access to some kind of sales network. The small metalworking workshops such as the one described above were an ordinary feature of medieval life across northern Europe. Metalworkers, called founders, produced objects in all kinds of precious, semiprecious, and ordinary materials, from gold and silver to iron, pewter, and tin. Badges were made in small foundries, or workshops, by lead- and tinsmiths, specialists at the bottom of the metalworking trade. They worked with alloys of lead and tin, also called pewter (unlike its medieval counterpart, modern pewter contains no lead because of lead's highly toxic qualities). Pewtersmithing itself does not require a complex foundry. Lead and tin melt at a very low temperature; a cauldron, tongs and ladles, adequate fuel, some kind of protective clothing (aprons or gloves), and the necessary molds are all that is required.[3] Figure 3.6 represents through images the way a mold works. The mold (figure 3.6, image 2) is composed in this case of two matrices (figure 3.6, images 1 and 3), which are held firmly together with the molten lead then poured in through the opening on top. After a minute or less, the mold is opened to reveal the badge (image 4) with the "tail" of lead that has hardened in the pouring channel. When this tail is pinched off and presumably tossed back into the cauldron of molten ore, and perhaps some tattered edges are quickly smoothed, the badge (image 5) is finished.[4] The process of casting a badge is very fast because molten pewter hardens so quickly. The process is so simple that anyone could carry it out easily as I did: hold the mold in one hand, use a ladle in the other to pour in a dollop of molten ore, tap lightly to encourage the ore to flow, count to twenty slowly, open the mold, and there is the badge.

Like most artisans, leadsmiths learned their trade through a system of apprenticeship and journeying that brought laborers into the trade at a very young age and that usually required mobility, because the apprentices and journeymen often moved from town to town following the work.

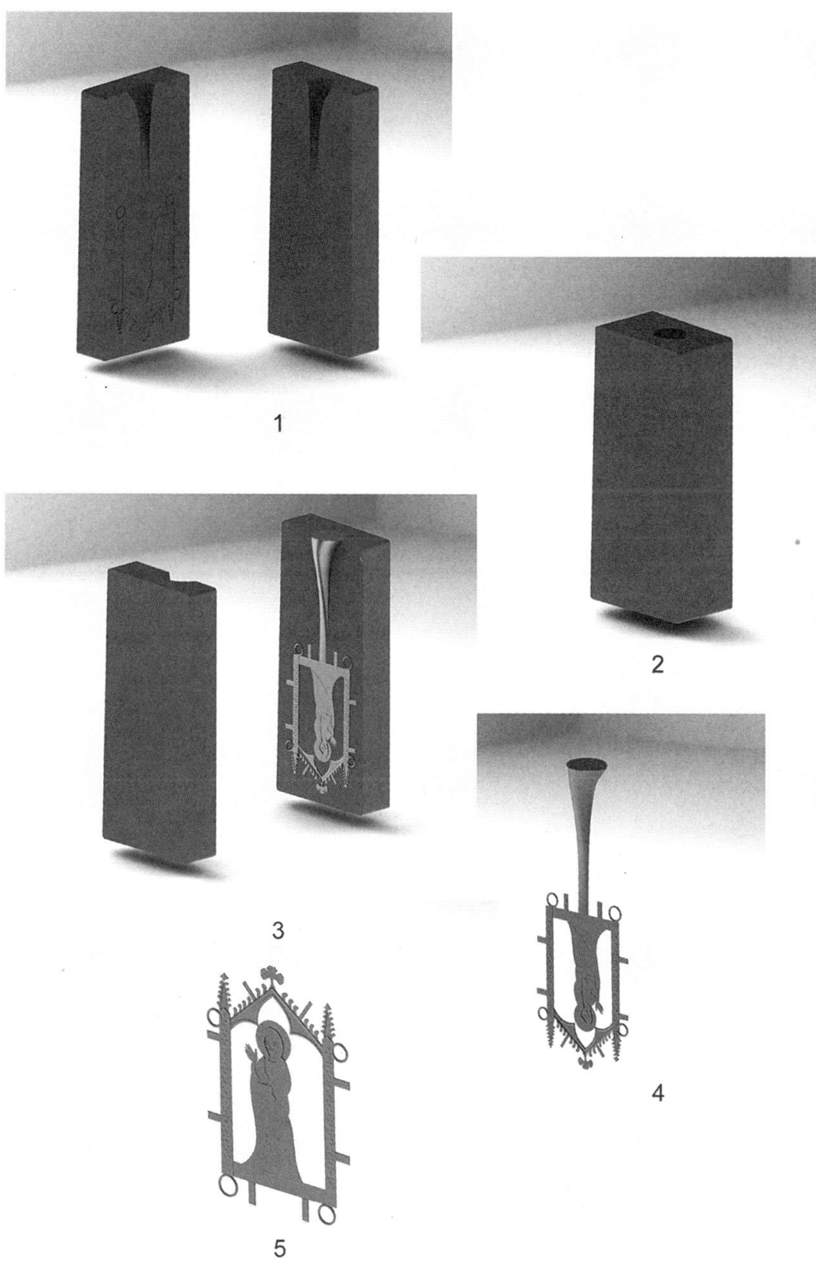

Figure 3.6. Reconstruction of system for use of mold to make a pewter badge. Reconstruction by Philippe Labaune, Independent. Courtesy of Françoise Labaune-Jean.

To make these cheap, mass-produced objects, leadsmiths used alloys, defined as solid metal materials made from two or more chemical elements. They normally used lead and tin. There were numerous advantages to making pewter objects using lead-tin alloys. The alloy created heavier objects. The cheap and plentiful lead counteracted some of the problematic qualities of tin. Above all, using alloys allowed the leadsmiths to recycle materials and to stretch the use of the tin, an expensive, rare metal.

Metallurgic analysis of the surviving badges tells the story of these alloys well. Virtually every badge subjected to analysis is made of lead-tin alloy, yet each one shows a different ratio of its component elements, tin and lead (sometimes there are trace elements of other metals, too).[5] This finding is best explained by the hypothesis that leadsmith workshops did not manufacture their alloys by following a set formula for combining raw ores, but instead routinely melted down recycled materials for use in recasting, most likely relying on experience to recognize the best consistency for casting. That leadsmiths routinely used recycled materials is also supported by surviving administrative records from late medieval cities across Europe, which set standards for the objects produced in leadsmith workshops by requiring that specific amounts of tin be used for specific kinds of products. Such attempts to create quality standards imply, of course, that objects were being sold that had been made out of substandard alloys that contained so little tin that the objects tarnished quickly and were so malleable that they broke easily. Some of these low-quality objects, for example, spoons, survive. In general, it is safe to say that these lead-tin alloys created objects that were cheap, highly malleable, and easily damaged.

During the fourteenth and fifteenth centuries, lead foundries mass-produced these small pewter objects for everyday use and adornment, including thousands and thousands of inexpensive badges.[6] They manufactured many other objects: bells, toys, embossed strips for ornamental purposes, and more prosaically, pipes, lead cames for window-glass fittings, and such household objects as spoons and dishes. These workshops would have produced badges and other small objects for local patrons great and small. They manufactured objects for religious establishments, such as abbeys and cathedrals, which often preserved relics of specific saints and martyrs, promoting them as a focus for intense, mass piety. The metalsmiths worked for great secular lords, producing, for example, tableware, harness fixtures, and heraldic pins. They doubtless worked on commission, designing and producing objects for tradesmen and merchants. Perhaps some of them acted as traders themselves, setting up booths or tables at local markets to sell their wares.

Millions of these small items, and especially badges, must have been made, sold, used, lost, worn out, discarded, and remelted during the three hundred years studied in this book.

The pewter (lead-tin alloy) objects produced in these workshops were ordinary, as shown in the list above. They were manufactured in a variety of ways. By the late fifteenth century, more and more objects were die-cut or stamped or embossed on hammered strips. For centuries, however, the most common mode of badge manufacture involved melting raw materials or more often scrap metal and pouring the molten ore into multipiece molds crafted from stone. Indeed, the secret to the complexity of badge images lies not in the process of casting them but in the molds themselves.

In the workshop at Mont-Saint-Michel, as was pointed out previously, molds were made of local sandstones and schist, which were easy to carve yet durable. The design and manufacture of molds was a separate step in the production of metal objects. While simple molds may well have been produced in the workshop, elaborate designs needed molds consisting of different pieces that fitted together (see figure 3.4, for example). These were valuable objects, and their production was a specialized process. It required goldsmiths, silversmiths, and leadsmiths to create iconographically appropriate designs suitable for this mode of manufacturing—the molten ore enters the mold at one place, so all parts of the design must be connected to allow the ore to flow—and then carve those designs, in reverse in stone, while engineering the individual pieces of a mold so that they were perfectly aligned and could be quickly and tightly assembled and disassembled again and again.

The craftsmanship exhibited in some of the surviving molds is extraordinary, as the plume badge mold in figures 3.7 and 3.8 demonstrates. The piece is tiny, only a few centimeters wide; yet the object's proportions are lovely, and the many fine lines are sharp, straight, and carefully spaced. Note that the space on the stone was maximized for badge production by adding two small round bangles at the lower edge.

Surviving records tell us that some badge molds were made by goldsmiths, artisans at the highest end of the metalworking trades who were trained in drawing and design. At Mont-Saint-Michel, the abbey commissioned and owned such expensive molds and leased them to the workshop, as seen in the sketch in the opening of this chapter. Some of these smiths, whatever the original metal in which they worked, were not only craftsmen and artisans but also designers and artists, exercising their creative talents to produce objects that spoke powerfully to the collective imagination of the Middle Ages.

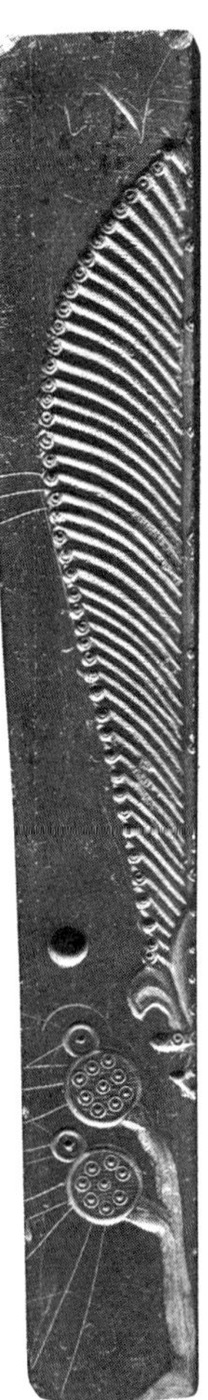

Figure 3.7. Fragment of grey schist pilgrim badge mold showing half of pewter plume and below it two bangles, Mont-Saint-Michel, France, c. 1434. Photographer: Hervé Paitier, Inrap. Photograph courtesy of Françoise Labaune-Jean.

Figure 3.8. Drawing of badge mold pieces from Mont-Saint-Michel and of reconstructed plume badge. Drawing by Stéphane Jean, Inrap. Courtesy of Françoise Labaune-Jean.

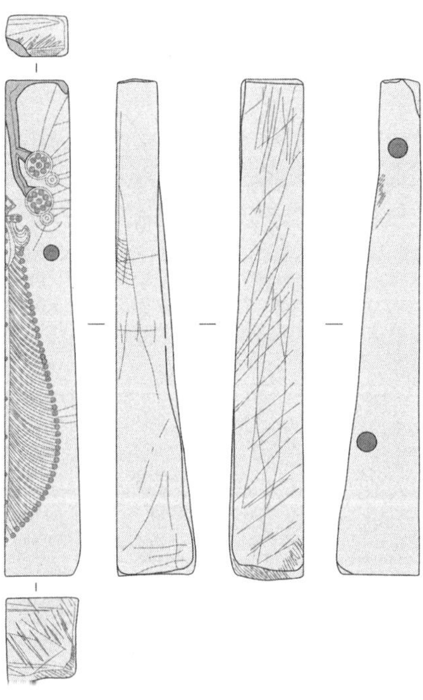

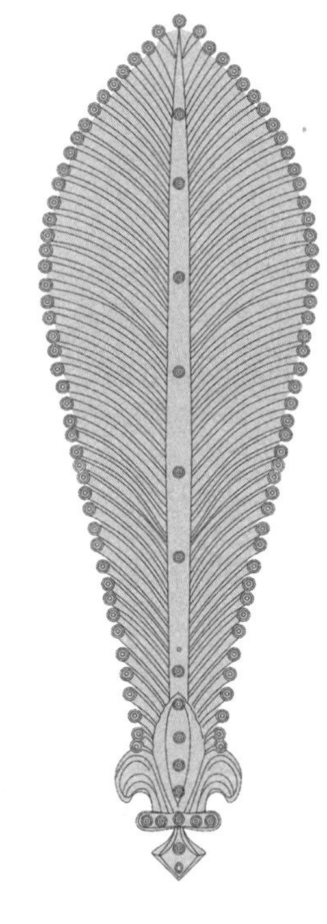

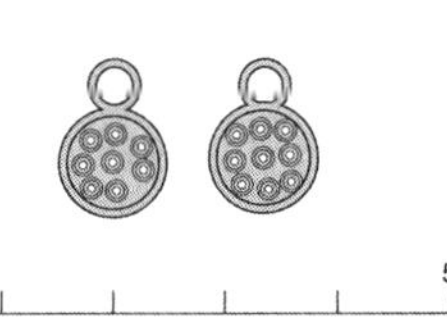

Mass-produced medieval objects are not perfect, exact replicas of one another in the way that modern, mass-produced objects are. Rather, human designing and making left traces on each object. Mass production of cast badges, for example, meant reusing a badge mold repeatedly until it wore out. When a broken mold was repaired and reused, the repair often left a trace on the badges cast from it. When a new mold was carved using the same design, the new badges deviated in minor yet identifiable ways from those produced in earlier molds. The surviving evidence indicates that busy workshops had more than one mold with the same design in production at the same time. However that may be, it is rare for badges made from the same mold to survive.

Most of the surviving badges of the same design and from the same site clearly come from different molds. What clues might these facts offer regarding the number of badges manufactured and circulated in the High and late Middle Ages? In the past, scholars assumed that a single mold could produce a few hundred objects before being worn out and discarded; many scholars now find these numbers far too conservative. Molds were not only valuable objects; they were durable. It is now considered likely that molds were used for many years, that they passed from workshop to workshop, and that, in sum, from a single mold thousands and thousands of badges were produced. Add to this fact the sheer speed and simplicity with which pewter badges are actually cast: given enough fuel, raw material, molds, and semiskilled hands, even a rudimentary workshop would have been able to produce hundreds of badges in a single day, and the 130,000 badges reputed to have been sold at the holy site of Einsiedeln in Switzerland in a single day no longer sound quite so much like "typical" medieval hyperbole or self-aggrandizing exaggeration. Historian Carina Brumme calculates that somewhere between ten million and twenty million badges were manufactured between about 1300 and 1500.[7]

If this is the case, and all the evidence suggests that in fact millions of badges were produced, then the number of surviving medieval badges (perhaps twenty thousand in total) is not large at all. The question then becomes, why do so few badges survive? The answer to this question may lie in the materiality of the badges themselves.

Brumme offers two answers that arise from looking closely at the material from which the badges were made. First, she draws our attention to a unique, chemical property of tin. It does not oxidize or corrode, although to the eye, tin's process of deterioration looks rather like rusting. But when the temperature falls below 13.2 degrees Celsius (55.76 degrees Fahrenheit), tin crumbles to dust. The German term for this process is "tin plague" (*Zinnpest*). Tin is an allotropic element, which means that under certain external conditions, usually related to either pressure or temperature, such elements modify their atomic structure and take on a different appearance. One example of an allotropic element is carbon, which, when subjected to extremely high pressure, becomes a diamond. In the case of tin, the allotropic reaction is triggered by temperature. When the temperature drops, tin changes its atomic structure and turns into gray powder. The colder it is, the faster this change happens. The process is irreversible and stops only when the temperature rises. Mixing tin with copper or zinc accelerates the process; mixing tin with lead or antimony halts or slows it. Being in an aerobic or an anaerobic environment has no effect on it. In sum, cold is the great enemy of tin. Badges with a high tin content, manufactured and used in northern Europe, would not have lasted very long. While badges made with low tin-content alloys would have survived better, in time most badges not conserved in unusual conditions would have crumbled away.

The second answer has already been glimpsed. Metal was a valuable resource in the Middle Ages, and metal objects of all kinds were routinely recycled by being melted down and recast. Badges were no different. They were made of recycled materials, as the chemical analysis of the surviving badges suggests. Probably so few survive because they were routinely recycled themselves. Brumme points out that about 70 percent of the known badges come from just ten specific sites, where the badges were not just in wet earth but actually underwater. How can this be explained? That so many badges would be lost in these places is unlikely. What about a ritual practice that saw medieval people throwing badges into water at these sites, enacting superstitious belief or folk practice? This hypothesis has been thoroughly debunked.[8] Brumme's argument is more prosaic and plausible. She looks closely at the ten sites and at assemblages of objects there. The sites are all along old canals or other waterways used for transportation in the late Middle Ages. The badges are found mixed with other metal objects: nails, coins, hooks, and the like. According to Brumme, these sites represent loads of old metal that had been collected for recycling and were being transported by water that for some reason sank and could not be recovered.

The hypothesis that badges were routinely recycled is supported by the legend of the holy badge that will not melt, which appears in a number of miracle books. Here is a late version, found in the Amersfoort (Netherlands) miracle book of 1474, about the Amersfoort badge of the Blessed Virgin Mary (figure 3.9): "A fellow from Osterhout was supposed to melt lead for casting. But he didn't have enough [material] so he looked for some more and all he could find was a badge of Blessed Virgin Mary of Amersfoort. So he added it to the others and it melted and then he finished filling the mold.

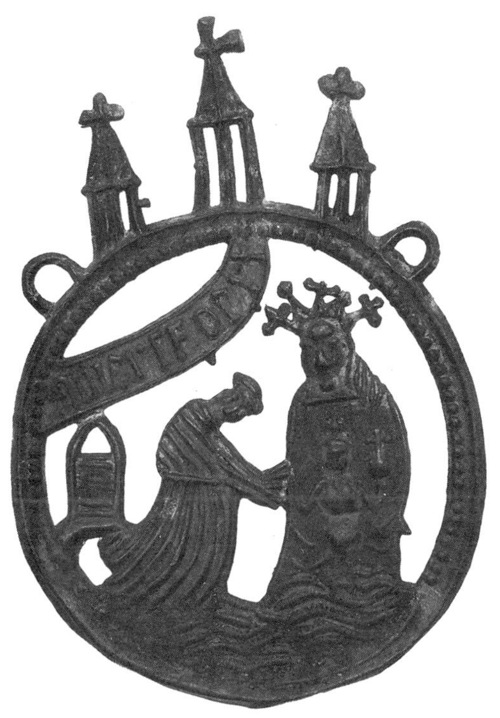

Figure 3.9. Pewter badge, round beaded frame surmounted by three towers and enclosing a banner inscribed with AMERSFORT above a bending woman pulling out of water a statue of the Virgin Mary and Child, two eyelets, Amersfoort, Netherlands, 1450–1499, found in Amsterdam, 65 × 45 mm. Langbroek, Netherlands, Family Van Beuningen Collection, inv. 2984 (Kunera 06506). Photograph courtesy of Family Van Beuningen Collection.

But the excess that flowed out immediately re-formed into the badge of the Blessed Virgin Mary."[9]

My interest in this story is different than the medieval author's, for whom the quotidian circumstances of the badge's miraculous intactness were both necessary and beside the point. For the author, the story's larger context within a miracle book, an ongoing collection of stories demonstrating the divine power of the Amersfoort religious site, determined its meaning. Like all the stories in the book, the story of the badge that would not melt was making the point that the holiness and spiritual forces compacted and consolidated at Amersfoort and its holy site of the Virgin Mary were so strong and so present in every object and person who came in immediate contact with it that they overcame not only demonic hostility but nature itself, here the element of fire.[10] My point with this story is different. Badges both profane and religious were routinely treated like scrap metal; they were melted down and reused.

That the practice of recycling badges goes back all the way to the beginning of badges in the late twelfth century is suggested by the fact that a similar miracle story was recounted over two hundred years earlier, where it featured among the miracles attesting to the holiness of the English medieval martyr and saint Archbishop Thomas Becket. In this case, the object in question was a badge-like object, a pewter ampulla, which is a tiny vessel, sometimes featuring an image, intended to hold a drop or two of holy water and worn suspended around the neck (see plate 6a).

Again, the routine of scrap-metal recycling is the backdrop for the miracle:

> A certain Augustine, a citizen of London, skilled in the arts of the founder, was melting down old ampulla so that he could make new ones from the old, to be devoted to the sacred ministry and the divine cult. He added one of the vessels of the new martyr, which people carry about. When everything was liquifying, one ampulla was seen to be floating in the melted tin. The founder, marvelling, took his tongs and pressed the unmelted tin into the liquid. But it did not entirely yield to the heat, retaining a degree of solidity. Marvelling at what he saw, he reasoned that the furnace was ineffective because it was not hot enough, and built up the kindling under the vessel, but he could not overcome the firmness of the metal. Wherefore, investigating the cause of the phenomenon, he realised that something of the body of the holy martyr had infused the container, which conferred strength upon it and repelled the assaults of combustion.[11]

This anecdote appeals both to the reader's faith and to her skepticism. The founder (i.e., leadsmith) proceeds in a rational way. The badge will not melt. Why do objects not melt? Because they are too cool. The badge is floating on the surface of the molten liquid, so the founder takes tongs and plunges the badge deeper. It still will not melt. Reason takes another stab at the matter. The founder deduces that the entire vat of molten lead is too cool; the fire is not hot enough. He adds more fuel. Again, the badge does not melt. Only now, when physical laws have been twice tested and overturned, does the founder turn to a metaphysical explanation: the divine power of the saint has miraculously infused the physical structure or nature of the ampulla (the container) itself, making it heat resistant. The ampulla's divine mediality has remained untouched.

Fastening and Embellishing Badges

Badges were made with a fastening device because they were intended to be worn in ways that were visible to others. Images of pilgrims in medieval altarpieces and book illuminations (as well as in other forms of art, such as statues and carvings) show religious badges affixed to outerwear, usually pinned or sewn onto hats. In this detail from an altarpiece in Brandenburg, Germany, three figures, a man, a woman, and a child, have religious badges on their hats, including badges from nearby Wilsnack (figure 3.10).

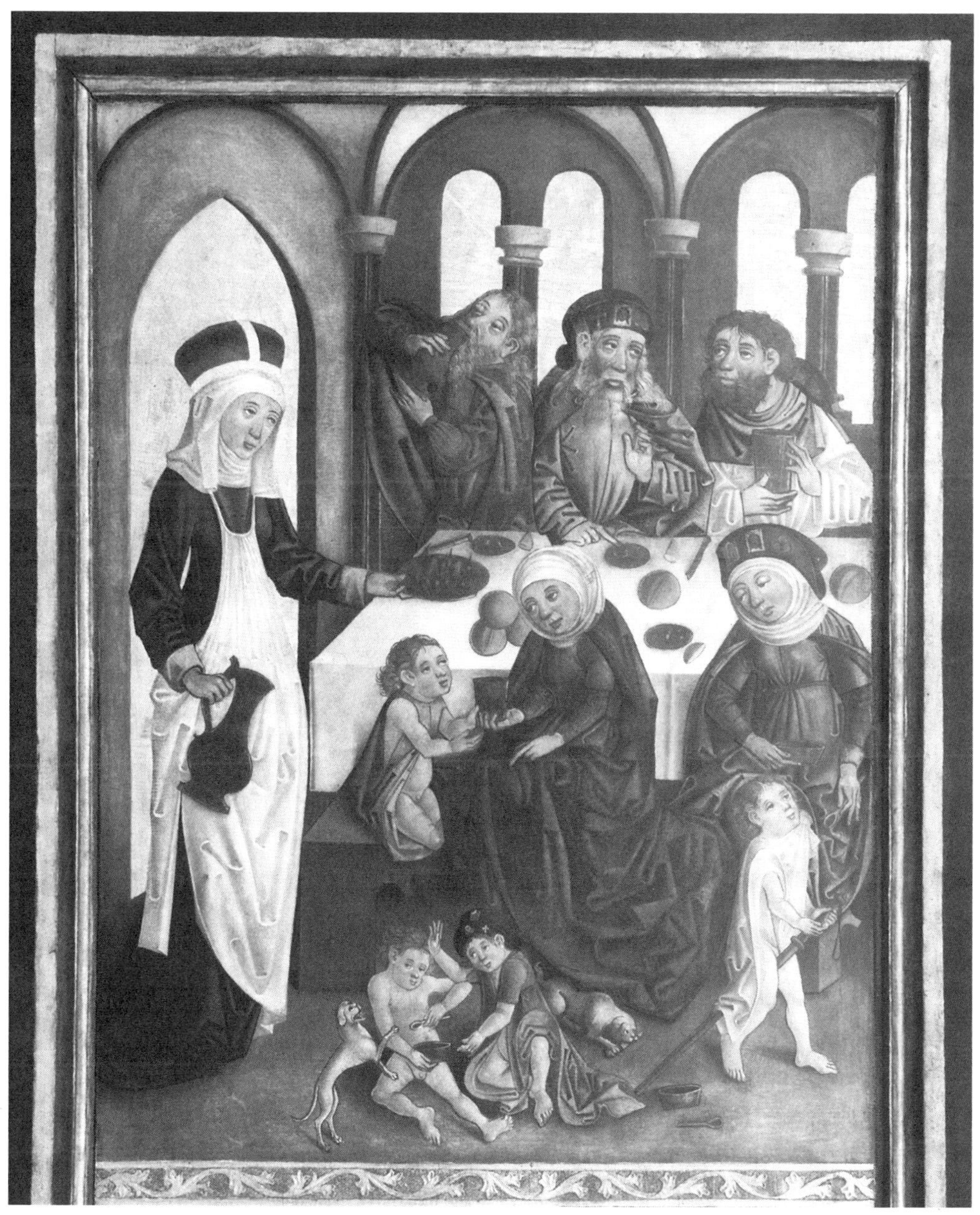

Figure 3.10. Detail from Saint Hedwig Altarpiece, at back and seated at table a man with four religious badges on hat, including one Wilsnack badge, in the middle ground far right a woman with three religious badges on hat, including Wilsnack badge, in foreground on floor a child with three pilgrim badges on hat. Church of Saint Catherine, Brandenburg, Germany, c. 1500. Photograph courtesy of photographer: Dirk Jacob.

Sewing a badge onto a piece of clothing was the typical fastening method for badges manufactured in continental Europe. Such badges were made with tiny eyelets that allowed the badge to be stitched in place. Eyelets can be clearly seen on the right side of the badge in figure 3.11 (those on the left have broken away), which features the thirteenth-century German Saint Elizabeth (1202–1226), known variously as either Elizabeth of Hungary because of her birthplace or Elizabeth of Thuringia by virtue of her marriage, whose charismatic center was Marburg, Germany.[12] The back of this badge, shown in figure 3.12, has been carefully scored in a manner typical of many badges.

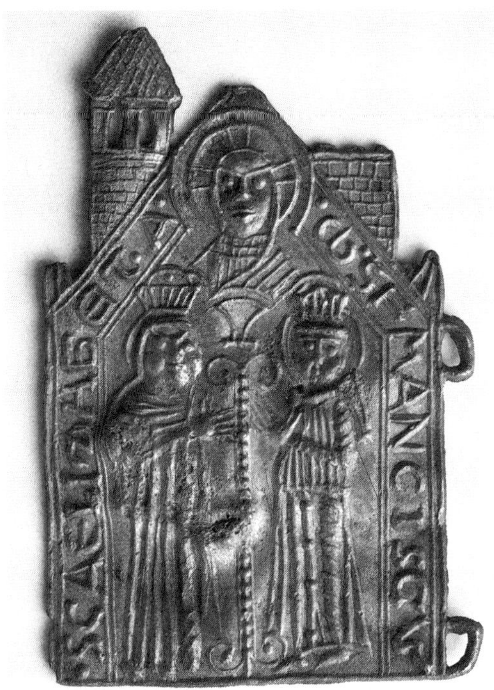

Figure 3.11. Front of pewter badge, Elizabeth of Hungary and Francis of Assisi face one another inside a pointed arch surmounted by turrets and under an image of God the Father with alpha and omega letters on either side and saints' names inscribed left and right, eyelets, Marburg, Germany, 1300–1399, found in Lund, Sweden, 57 × 39 × 5 mm. Lund, Kulturen, inv. KM 5876 (Kunera 03906). Photograph and permission from Kulturen.

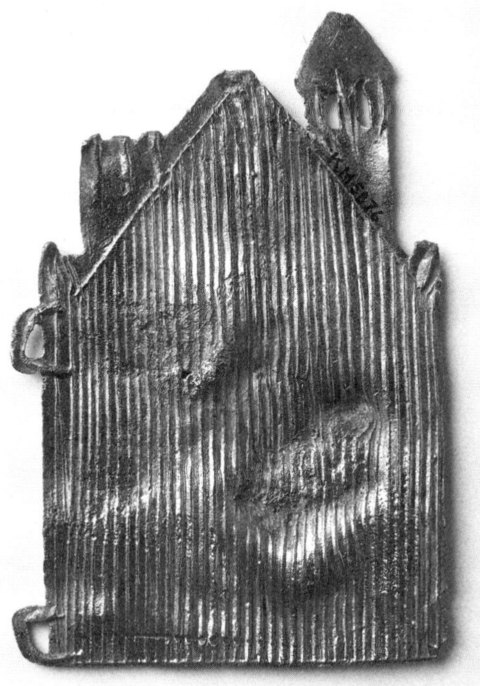

Figure 3.12. Back of pewter badge, Elizabeth of Hungary and Francis of Assisi, eyelets, Marburg, Germany, 1300–1399, found in Lund, Sweden, 57 × 39 × 5 mm. Lund, Kulturen, inv. KM 5876 (Kunera 03906). Photograph and permission from Kulturen.

Eyelets can be discerned on many of the badges shown in this book. There was a second mode of fastening, however. Rather than eyelets, many badges feature a simple stick pin on the back, much like the brooches and pins we wear today. The badge of a mermaid holding a mirror in one hand and a comb in the other features a visible stick pin running horizontally across the back of the badge (plate 6b); stick pins aligned horizontally or vertically can be discerned in other images in this book.[13]

Happily, the distribution of these two modes of fastening is roughly contiguous geographically: badges with pins on the back were manufactured in England, badges with eyelets in France and Germany, with both modes of badge fastening being manufactured in the Low Countries. I write "happily" because this clear geographical distribution means that simply looking at the way any badge was fastened allows a good guess about its place of manufacture. In both cases, however, the fastenings are extremely vulnerable to damage, largely because of the softness and malleability of pewter. The eyelets and pins protrude, and so they break off. The pins must be bent in order to be thrust into the cap or cloak, and they often break. Few badges survive with the pin intact, although the pin mount or the pin latch can often still be seen.

Some badges were manufactured to be affixed or worn by other means, for example, to dangle in some way. Such badges might feature a single eyelet or ring, which if situated at the top of the badge made it a pendant, while if situated at the bottom of the badge indicated that something was supposed to dangle from the badge in turn. For example, the badge in figure 3.13 builds the chain attachment into the design of the badge, incorporating the front attachment as a realistic detail of the dog chain and collar.

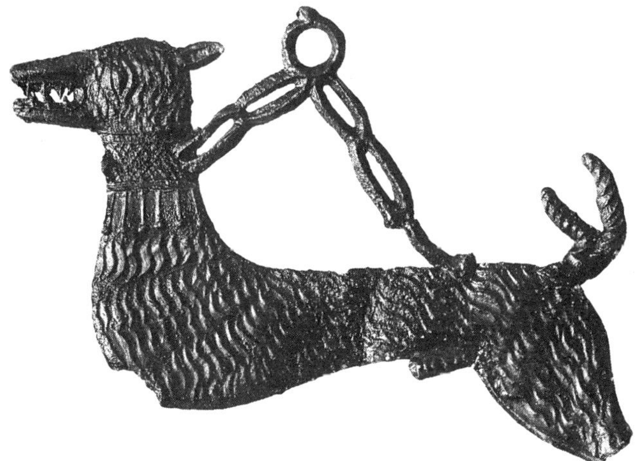

Figure 3.13. Pewter badge with chain remnant, crouching hound, pendant, origin unknown, 1400–1449, found in Nieuwlande, Netherlands, 34 × 42 mm. Langbroek, Netherlands, Family Van Beuningen Collection, inv. 1857 (Kunera 00676). Photograph courtesy of Family Van Beuningen Collection.

The tiny vessels known as ampullae, such as the one shown in plate 6a, nearly always featured a single eyelet at the top so that the ampulla could be worn suspended from a chain or another object; some surviving ampullae show wear marks on one side, where the vessel rubbed against something, perhaps the body or the clothing of the wearer.

Badges were small, often only about three-by-three centimeters, sometimes smaller and sometimes larger, but they were made to be worn and meant to be seen. Yet now, the surviving lead badges and pins are only shadows of their former selves. They are often damaged, with smaller obtruding pieces broken, the pin backs snapped off, a part rubbed away, the entire object eroded, split, or bent from wear. They are dark in color from tarnish, erosion, and age.

What the badges look like now is very different from what they looked like when new. Their fragile condition and dark color belie what would have been their most important, eye-catching feature. When first made and purchased, lead alloy badges were a bright, glossy silvery-white, with a shininess that reminds a modern viewer a bit of aluminum foil. New badges must have been so shiny that they caught and glinted in every bit of light—the unpainted ones, that is. The eye-catching qualities of new, shiny lead were enhanced and embellished in numerous ways. Some were painted or touched up with paint in key places. Wilsnack badges were embellished with red paint, representing Christ's blood. It is easy to imagine the Saint Michael badges enlivened, for example, by dots of paint for the eyes of both demon and saint, underscoring the compelling force of the saint's full-frontal gaze. Other badges were embellished with tiny stones or pieces of glass and mirrors.

Many openwork, or fretwork, badges, such as the ones that would have been produced by the mold in figure 3.3, also survive. These badges are not solid plaques but rather consist of design elements with open space between them. Most badges such as these, when turned over, reveal on the back and along the frame many tiny flaps or tabs, whose purpose was to be pinched down over and hold in place some sort of backing material, perhaps a scrap of cloth, a piece of gold leaf, or a piece of paper or parchment that was colored or painted with an image, any of which would have contrasted strongly with the shiny white of the original alloy. (The drawing in figure 3.4, which reproduces all the pieces of the mold of which figure 3.3 is a part, includes matrices for these tiny clips.) Most surviving openwork badges such as the one shown in figure 1.3 consist now only of a frame or its fragments, making it plausible that a now-lost element, such as a piece of parchment or paper, completed the badge. Perhaps a heart-shaped badge such as figure 7.3 contained a tiny, simple portrait painted or sketched on paper. Most surviving openwork badges

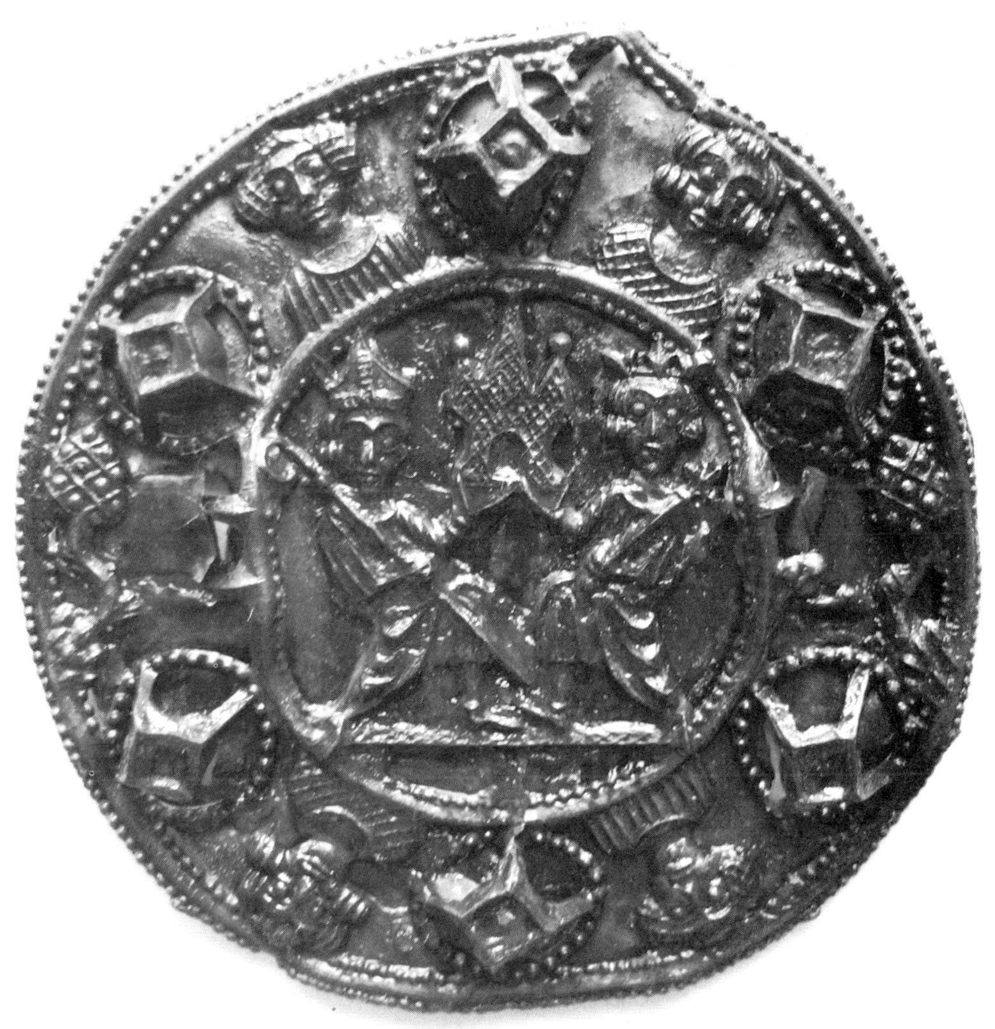

Figure 3.14. Pewter badge, king and bishop hold a tower, origin unknown, 1325–1374, found in Ypres, Belgium, 58 × 56 mm. Yper Museum, inv. SM 005143 (Kunera 06817). Photographer: Els Deroo. Photograph courtesy of Yper Museum.

are by definition incomplete; they included and were designed for a background element.

Only a handful of badges survive with any of these elements intact—paint, mirror, shininess, paper, gold. A graphic designer's reconstruction of such a badge from Ypres, Belgium, graces the cover of this book. It seeks to imagine the vivid, eye-catching qualities that virtually all badges would have had when first made and worn. Figure 3.14 shows the original. A round badge about five centimeters in diameter, the Ypres badge's frame is embellished with small stones alternating with male and female heads (to judge by their hairstyles). At the center of the badge kneel two dignitaries, recognizable by their attributes as representatives of worldly and religious power, the one on the left with his miter and staff being a bishop, the one on the right with crown and scepter being a prince or king, together holding high a small model of a three-towered building. This badge also has pinch tabs or clips on the back. Most unusually, it also preserves a small round disk of some material now also nearly black in color attached to the back. The badge was designed to accommodate this backing, which has been carefully slit so that a fastening pin on the back (no longer present) could remain functional.

A glance at the surviving badge in figure 3.14 shows that time has nearly erased the ensemble of contrasting effects intended by this design, which now presents as tonal, shading differences of the color silver. When new, however, the lead frame and the heads would have been bright, shiny silver in color, and the stones on the rim were green. The background color might have been a bright, shiny gold, in any case a contrasting color, so that the king and bishop in the middle would have shone silver against a contrast, all surrounded by a glinting bright, silver-colored frame adorned with deep green stones. Though made of simple and inexpensive materials, this object is intended to be seen and to be special. Whoever purchased, commissioned, gifted, or wore this object was making a weighty gesture.

The perishable nature of most of these materials and pewter's rapid loss of luster underscore the transitory nature of individual badges. It is hard to imagine any badge lasting a lifetime in the Middle Ages, much less five or six centuries into our times. In general, most individual badges were not only inexpensive but also short-lived. The enormous difference between what a badge looked like when new and what it looks like now can only be bridged in the imagination when one understands the changes that time has wrought on the surviving objects.

Designing Images for Badges

Across the spectrum of surviving badges, there is a huge difference in the quality of workmanship, design, and artistic expression. Some badges are exquisitely well made, some are crudely done, and there is everything in between. Different badges from the same holy site can share the same defining symbols and images yet vary immensely in design and in the mode and quality of execution. Badges of Saint Servatius, whose holy site is in Maastricht, Netherlands, were found in the fourteenth-century habitation layer in recent excavations at Harburg (now a borough of Hamburg), and they demonstrate this variation in quality in badges manufactured around the same time at the same site and for the same saint.[14]

The fragment of a plaque badge in figure 3.15 features a crudely drawn stick figure, apparently made from a quickly carved mold using simple lines and circles. (Similar techniques were used for badge production at other popular pilgrimage sites; see, for example, figures 5.15 and 5.16). The bishop's hat, or miter, consists of a triangle created by three thick lines that meet on the top in a ball; the face appears to be a kind of rectangular protrusion with dots indicating eyes and nose; the hair is represented by three small balls arranged symmetrically on either side of the oblong head; torso and attributes of office (crosier, key) are shown with thick, clear lines. This kind of design is schematic rather than representational. It must have been a familiar mode of artistic representation for medieval audiences, because many surviving Servatius badges are designed in this way. The similarities between the Hamburg-Harburg fragment and the intact example shown in figure 3.16, which was found in Dordrecht, Netherlands, are readily recognizable, even though the insignia are reversed on the Hamburg-Harburg fragment, which is also, if anything, even cruder in its execution than the badge in figure 3.16.

The badge designs produced at Maastricht for Saint Servatius were diverse. Some were complex in design, such as those representing a famous, beautiful reliquary containing the skull of Saint Servatius, one of the most sacred objects in the Maastricht cathedral's treasury (see figure 5.1). The badge design focuses on a sensitively rendered face, with wide-set eyes, carefully trimmed beard, and sunken cheeks, surrounded by attributes localizing the badge: the bishop's miter, the angels on either side holding the bishop's insig-

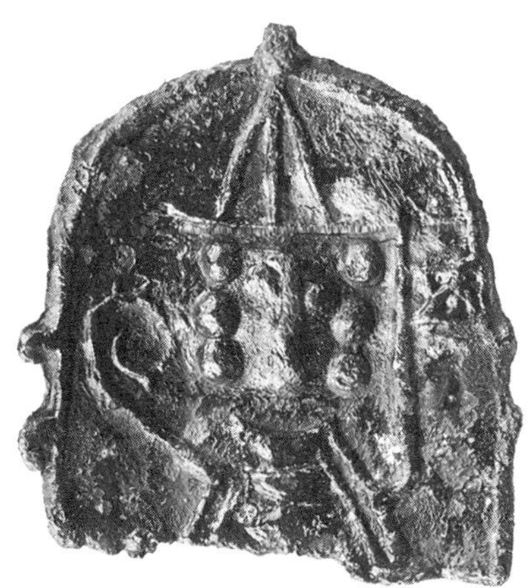

Figure 3.15. Pewter badge fragment, face and upper torso of Saint Servatius, Maastricht, Netherlands, before 1396, found in Hamburg-Harburg, Germany, 25 mm (width). Hamburg-Harburg, Archäologisches Museum Hamburg (AMH). Photographer: Torsten Weise. Photograph courtesy of Archäologisches Museum Hamburg (AMH).

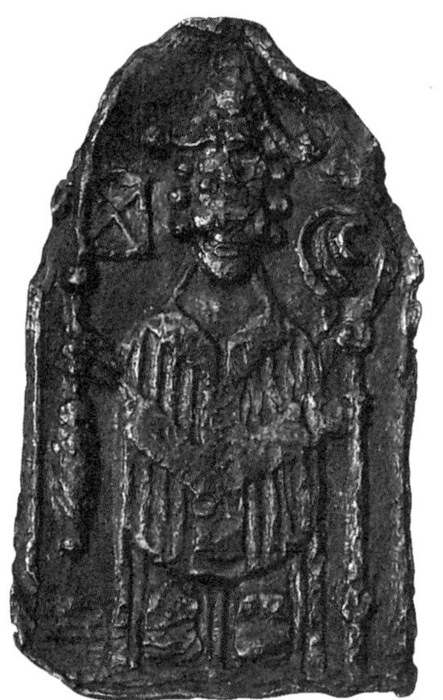

Figure 3.16. Pewter badge, Servatius as bishop holding key, eyelets, Maastricht, Netherlands, 1275–1374, found in Dordrecht, Netherlands, 34 × 22 mm. Langbroek, Netherlands, Family Van Beuningen Collection, inv. 3334 (Kunera 06360). Photograph courtesy of Family Van Beuningen Collection.

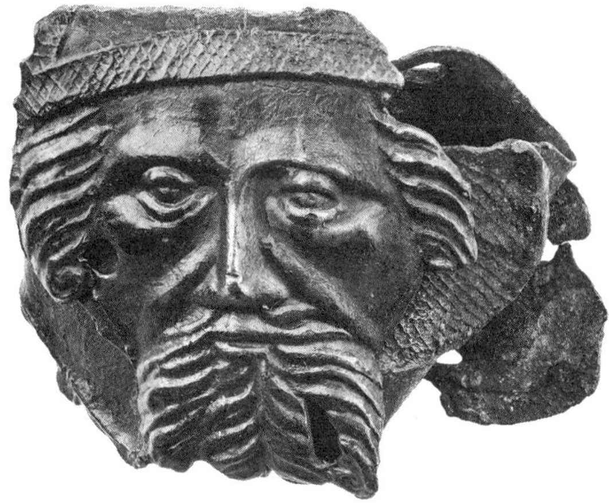

Figure 3.17. Pewter badge folded, face of Saint Servatius, Maastricht, Netherlands, before 1396, found in Hamburg-Harburg, Germany, 33 mm (width). Hamburg-Harburg, Archäologisches Museum Hamburg (AMH). Photographer: Torsten Weise. Photograph courtesy of Archäologisches Museum Hamburg (AMH).

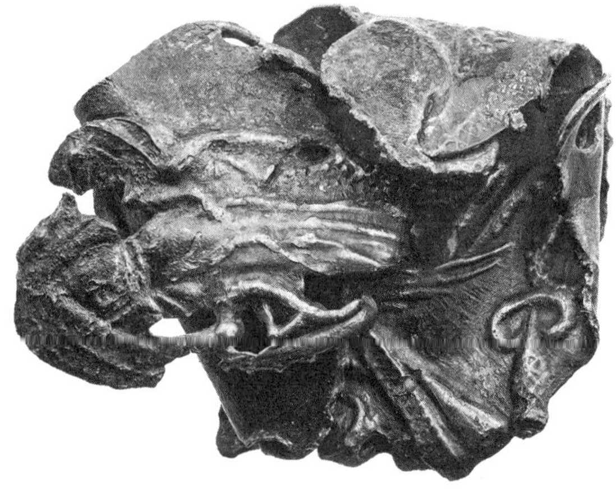

Figure 3.18. Back of folded Saint Servatius pewter badge, with bishop's miter folded on top, Maastricht, Netherlands, before 1396, found in Hamburg-Harburg, Germany, 33 mm (width). Hamburg-Harburg, Archäologisches Museum Hamburg (AMH). Photographer: Torsten Weise. Photograph courtesy of Archäologisches Museum Hamburg (AMH).

nia of office, a key and a crosier (bishop's staff) whose tip is thrust into the jaws of a winged dragon that sprawls across the saint's chest.

A Servatius badge using the same design as figure 5.1 was found in the medieval habitation layer in Hamburg-Harburg, but the highly malleable pewter object has been deliberately folded into a square with the saint's visage alone facing outward, as though to create a close-up view of the face alone that reminds one of a portrait (figure 3.17). A view of the back of the badge in figure 3.18 shows how carefully the various attributes have been tucked into one another.

Why was this badge folded? Folded badges have been found elsewhere, and the practice is old; a crucifix from the pilgrimage site in Stromberg, Germany, folded so that the face of Christ alone is visible at the top of the tiny bundle, was found in a late thirteenth-century habitation layer in Rostock, Germany. The folded badge as it came out of the ground is shown in the middle of figure 3.19; to the right, beside the unfolded back of the cross, are tiny arrows indicating the places where the badge was folded.

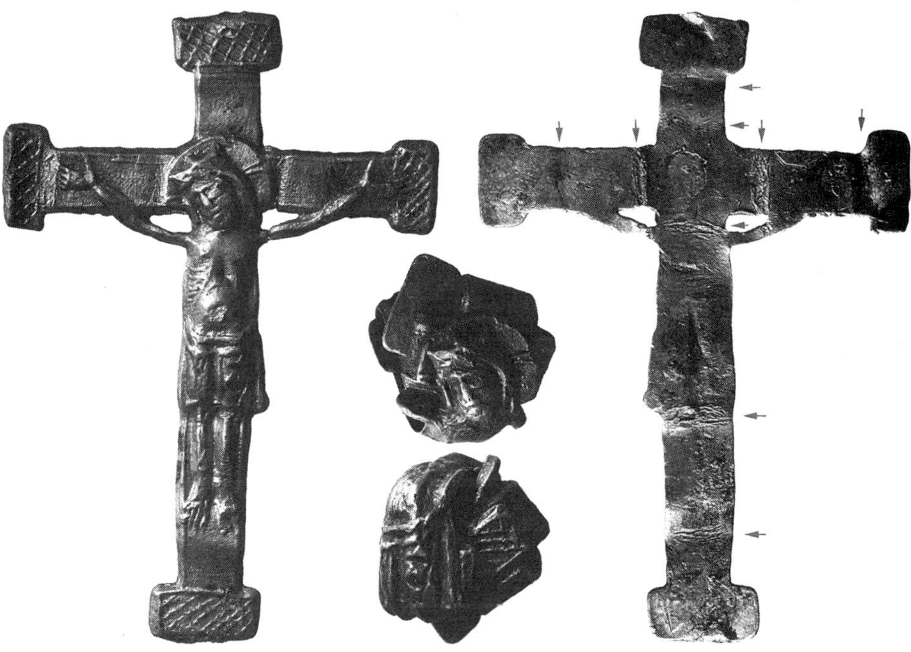

Figure 3.19. Pewter badge, crucified Christ, Stromberg, Germany, before 1269, found in Rostock, Germany. Left, front of badge; center top, folded badge as originally found folded into ball, head of Christ on top; center bottom, back of folded badge; right, back of badge with arrows highlighting fold marks. Photograph courtesy of photographer: Dr. Jörg Ansorge, Horst, Germany.

A few explanations for folded badges spring to mind. Perhaps it needed to fit in something small (a pocket or pouch) for travel; perhaps it needed to fit on a small scale to be weighed for its value as scrap metal; perhaps the saint's face, showing an older man with many cares on his shoulders, mattered more to the badge owner than the symbols of office or the allegory of divinity (angels) vanquishing evil (the dragon) that the attributes enact. It is just as likely, however, that bending the badge participated in its original, spiritual purpose. The practice of folding objects such as coins to create tokens that make and mark a vow to a saint is known from the Middle Ages into the early modern period; perhaps these badges from holy sites had been used in a similar way.[15]

A modern viewer contrasting the schematically rendered Saint Servatius images in figures 3.15 and 3.16 with the representational Saint Servatius images in figures 3.17 and 5.1 may be moved to ask, "What makes these Saint Servatius badges from Maastricht similar badges at all?" They are so different in execution, style, and design that it might seem a stretch to recognize them as coming from the same place, much less group them together in the same category.[16] The point for the medieval badges, however, is that these huge stylistic and aesthetic differences can coexist. What the Saint Servatius badges share is a stable set of images and symbols (bishop's miter, beard, dragon, staff) confidently speaking the same language, as it were, and saying "Servatius" unequivocally. This iconographical language of visual communication is stable; the variations in design and execution are, one might say, registers or dialects within it.

The surviving evidence suggests that the modes of badge production, modes of fastening, and forms of embellishment changed little across the High and late Middle Ages and across Europe. Only in the mid-fifteenth century are stamping and embossing added to the repertoire of manufacturing techniques, allowing the creation of the wafer-thin, nearly weightless badges that were sewn into medieval devotional manuscripts. When turning to an exploration of the images on medieval badges, however, a different story emerges. In the design and symbolism of images on badges can be discerned creativity and inventiveness based in widely shared, complex iconographical systems of symbols and references. The badge images draw on and participate in all aspects of medieval culture practice and symbolism, be they learned or popular, highbrow or lowbrow, clerical or lay, religious or secular. Badge designs range from crudely done ones that look to our eyes like bad knockoffs to exquisite objects, such as the Saint Michael badges, and from objects that speak of devout piety, to political devices of all kinds, to tokens of love, to scurrilous, scandalous, and lewd badges.

Badges were more than mass-circulated objects; they were also intended to broadcast a specific message. This means that badges had to solve the design problem of being both distinct and instantly recognizable at the same time. Religious badges provide the most cogent examples for illustrating this process and so are discussed in detail in the following paragraphs.

Religious badges were associated with the religious veneration of a specific saint or a specific relic—a holy object—at a specific place. They memorialized an ordinary aspect of the late medieval Christian landscape, which across Europe was packed with holy sites, some old, some new, some thriving, some failing, each different and each seeking to distinguish itself from the others. In terms of design, the problem each religious badge sought to solve was twofold; it had to be instantly recognizable while also being completely different from all the other badges. Even in the late Middle Ages, linguistic literacy was largely an elite attribute that was concentrated in specific places (cities and church institutions) and professions (courts, clerics and members of religious orders, merchants). Because badges were a type of mass media, each badge had to (ideally) accomplish its design work without words, using such elements as image and shape alone. This does not mean that letters and inscriptions were missing from badges (far from it!), but medieval religious badges could not, for example, take a generic image and plaster a place name across the top to indicate a site in the way a modern souvenir from, say, the American West might display a generic image of a mountain while featuring a distinguishing place name, for example, Yellowstone or Yosemite, in bright letters. When words appeared on religious badges, they were complementary design features usually supplementing the primary carrier of meaning, which was the image. The purpose of a religious badge was to echo and display the holy site's drive to distinctiveness and uniqueness, while at the same time being instantly recognizable. A successful religious badge was one that was immediately iconic.

The richness and diversity of late medieval religious life is reflected in the stylistic and symbolic diversity of badges and their imagery. The huge range of potential designs is well represented by the Saint Servatius badges from Maastricht, for example, as well as in the badges from other holy sites, such as Rome, Mont-Saint-Michel, and as we shall see, Aachen, Germany. The distinct symbols and imagery associated specifically with each of these holy sites were varied, combined, and recombined to produce fresh, yet legible signs.

Religious badges often feature architectural formats alluding to the changing styles of the High and late medieval church. Aachen badges, for example, often show a stylized building with three towers, capturing a distinctive feature of the Palatine Chapel where the holy relics were held. The fourteenth-century badge in figures 3.11 and 3.12 from the city of Marburg and venerating Saint Elizabeth (1202–1227) shows two church towers framing the face of God, making the upper part of the badge into a fortress-like gable symbolizing spiritual strength. This architectural element transforms the rest of the badge into an enclosed space, an interior space known as an edicula that is inhabited by the two saints gazing out at the viewer, Saint Elizabeth on the left and Saint Francis on the right, their spheres of influence chastely separated into discrete domains by the staff separating them. The badge is architectural in conception, and the architecture does symbolic work. At the same time, the fact that one of the church towers on the badge is higher than the other may represent a realistic detail of the actual church site in Marburg. Work on the great pilgrimage church ground to a halt in the mid-fourteenth century, leaving one tower unbuilt. It is possible that the second tower is missing because of damage to the badge itself, but it is also possible that the badge was deliberately designed to reflect the contemporary state of the building as pilgrims would have seen it.

The Holy Wafers of Wilsnack

Stylistic diversity of badges from a single holy site was the norm, as it were, for religious badge production across Europe. There were exceptions, however, and one of the most striking of these are the badges from the Holy Blood pilgrimage church in Wilsnack (Brandenburg, Germany). These badges do not vary in their design, which corresponded in a visually indelible way to the miracle story they commemorated.

Wilsnack was once home to one of the most popular and controversial pilgrimage sites in late medieval northern Europe, although its importance declined precipitously after the Reformation. Its badges are worn by the pilgrims depicted on the mid-fifteenth-century German altarpiece in the church of Saint Catherine, also in Brandenburg; the badge shown in figure 3.20 was found in the Hamburg-Harburg excavations that also produced the Servatius badges discussed previously. The badges depict three Holy Communion hosts, or wafers, which were revered at the church of Saint Nicholas in Wilsnack. The hosts were believed to have survived a devastating fire in 1383 that burned the church and village to the ground and then to have miraculously bled. Pilgrimage to the site started very soon after this fire and rapidly increased. The miraculously bleeding hosts were associated with Corpus Christi, with devotions associated with Christ's passion, and with the late medieval religious veneration of the Holy Blood, all trends in devotion that flourished in late medieval northern Europe.[17]

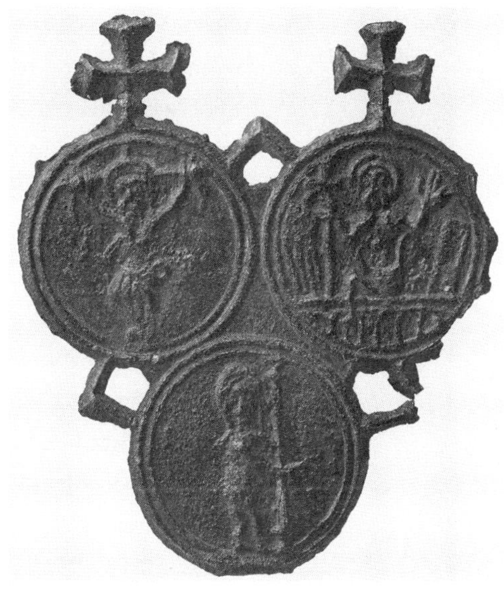

Figure 3.20. Pewter badge, Holy Blood site in Wilsnack, Germany, before 1396, found in Hamburg-Harburg, Germany. Hamburg-Harburg, Archäologisches Museum Hamburg (AMH). Photographer: Torsten Weise. Photograph courtesy of Archäologisches Museum Hamburg (AMH).

The Wilsnack badge always has the same design. It consists of three small circles, arranged in a triangle and touching at the center, each sphere impressed with an image and two topped by tiny crosses (usually missing from the surviving badges because of their extreme fragility). Each circle features a specific image that when read clockwise from the bottom, narrate the Passion of Jesus Christ, the story of His crucifixion and resurrection. The bottom image depicts Christ bound to a whipping post; the left-hand image depicts the next episode in the story, Christ's crucifixion; the right-hand image shows the final episode, Christ's resurrection, and depicts Christ emerging triumphant from a tomb or grave, a banner in His hand. Originally, all or parts of the badge would have been painted red, but the paint has worn off on most surviving badges.

The design of this badge corresponds in a visually indelible way to the holy objects venerated in Wilsnack and to the Christian theology they embody: round wafers made of wheat, often engraved or inscribed with designs, that had been consecrated by a priest for use in the Christian ritual called the Eucharist, which commemorates Christ's Last Supper with his disciples and in which bread and wine are consumed.[18] Roman Catholic theology teaches that the wafers become sacramental bread that have been transformed through the priest's consecration into the body of Christ. This doctrine is called transubstantiation. The Wilsnack badge unites all these elements: the circles represent the wafers; the images tell the story of Christ's passion, in which his blood was shed through his being whipped and nailed to the cross; the consecrated, transubstantiated nature of the holy wafers, which according to the miracle of 1383 proved that they had become the body of Christ because they had bled, was shown through the red paint.

Through their contact with shrines and other holy objects, a medieval religious badge could become what scholars call a eulogia, a blessed present or object. While clergy and theologians would likely have drawn a bright line between eulogiae and relics, it seems likely that some pilgrims did not distinguish between the two so clearly.[19] For them, a religious badge partook in the sanctity of the shrine and became a kind of secondary relic itself. In this way, badges became a kind of media. Badges were thought to be laden or charged with holiness that they both contained and transmitted. Such badges acted upon the world. At the same time, their complex iconography distilled theology in both its most universal and most local features into visual symbols that invited narration. In this way, too, the badges were agents, because they initiated storytelling, which in a religious context might have been a retelling of the New Testament story of Christ's passion and crucifixion, or the legend of a great emperor using his power to spread the power of a saint, or the story of a bishop, martyr, or apostle whose remains were venerated locally.

For modern viewers, a badge such as that from Wilsnack is an image, a reproduction, as it were, of the original miraculous hosts that survived the 1383 fire and miraculously bled. But the surviving medieval evidence suggests that for the medieval pious who thronged to Wilsnack, such a badge, once touched to the shrine itself to activate, as it were, the holiness inherent in the image, became not a replica or an image or a reproduction of the holy wafers but another example of it. The miraculous holy wafer badges were experienced as a part of or as an extension of the Wilsnack miraculous holy wafers. The badge wafers were those wafers; they were Christ's blood. In this way of thinking, their holiness could not be used up or divided and was infinitively reproducible. In fact, the more the wafers' holiness was tapped into and used, the more holiness they generated.

One interesting difference between the Wilsnack badge, on the one hand, and the Mont-Saint-Michel, Maastricht (Saint Servatius), and Aachen badges on the other is that there is only one unique Wilsnack badge design, which never changes, while badges from many other important sites, such as Canterbury, Mont-Saint-Michel, and Aachen, feature diverse designs. In a way, though, the Wilsnack badge design is so perfect that it could not be improved on. The badge wafers may well have been mimetic representations of communion wafers dispensed to the pious at the pilgrimage church in Wilsnack. Communion wafers were of varying sizes and often quite small—in Aden Kumler's words, "small enough to be pinched between index finger and thumb"—and they were often engraved or inscribed.[20] The badge is also an indexical sign in the sense that the now-vanished red paint re-creates the blood from Christ's crucifixion, the key events of which are represented in the tiny images, and it is symbolic in the sense that it sums up key elements of Christian theology. Economic and political factors were, however, also at work in the success of the Wilsnack pilgrimage site. It is likely that in Wilsnack, a very late pilgrimage site located in a small town in the well-organized bishopric of Havelberg (then in Brandenburg, now in Saxony-Anhalt), the manufacture of badges remained tightly under the control of the Premonstratensian Order, who administered the bishopric and served as its bishops. Surviving evidence from Havelberg suggests that the badges may even have been manufactured in or near the cathedral close.

Aachen, on the other hand, was a large medieval city that would have had many craftsmen with the requisite skills to make and sell badges, whether directly licensed by the religious authorities or not. The holy days on which the relics were displayed to the public, which happened only rarely (for certain relics, only once every few years) yet on well-publicized days, drew huge crowds of pilgrims. Many of them would have wished to purchase religious badges, perhaps overwhelming the capacity of licensed badge manufacturers or the ability of the license holders to police the merchandise offered for sale, and so provided business opportunities for itinerant or intermittent badge makers. Finally, the molds from the workshop at Mont-Saint-Michel show a variety of badges being made, presumably catering to different tastes and pocketbooks.

Religious sites associated with charismatic, divine power proliferated in the High and late Middle Ages. Mont-Saint-Michel, Aachen, and Wilsnack were major, transregional holy sites that attracted thousands of pilgrims from near and far; hundreds of badges survive from these sites. There were also small holy sites that had primarily local significance for short periods; some of the obscure badges that are now difficult to localize may come from these sites. There was also everything in between. Holy sites competed with one another for pilgrimage traffic, with its attendant revenues. Their fortunes rose and fell with changes that came with shifts in politics and changes in cultural patterns of belief, as will be discussed in more detail in Chapter 5. The institutions in charge of these holy sites strove to keep their sites going, to stand apart from others, and to claim and maintain a distinct identity within the expansive, theologically heterodox, politically elastic, and regionally diverse framework of late medieval Catholicism. Religious badges played a role in this process. They traveled, visible on the cloaks, capes, and hats of the pilgrims who had purchased them or had been gifted them, carrying the story of a specific holy site to other places, regions, or lands. To use a modern analogy, one part of the badge's job was to create a "brand" for the holy site.

Some badges succeeded in creating enduring brand recognition. Even now, after five centuries have passed, one need only the most fleeting acquaintance with some medieval religious badges to identify the saints and places they represent. From common badges associated with famous places, such as the three-sphered Wilsnack badge and Saint Michael with sword upraised and demon underfoot to rare badges from well-known holy sites such as Saint Ursula in Cologne and obscure badges from now-forgotten medieval pilgrimage sites such as Karup in Denmark, once seen, many religious badge images are instantly recognizable again. Each one strives to be both memorable and instantly recognizable, and many successfully accomplish this. Although these artisans and artists left no theoretical writings, their creations show that they understood how to design images that are unforgettable.

An Inventory of Forms and Meanings

Badge images are memorable and recognizable because they draw from a visual language that was common and shared across the linguistically, politically, and economically diverse territories of northern Europe in the High and late Middle Ages. This symbolic language represents an image-based, meaning-making system of signification that was intended to communicate clearly, widely, and well. Aspects of this symbolic, image-based language are still present in modern culture; more important, however, in even a cursory examination of medieval badges, patterns of meaning-making emerge. Deeper study of medieval badges shows that badge designs combined and recombined various elements of this shared symbolic language. Badge forms, decorations, and images can best be imagined as stable, known resources deployed by producers and consumers inventively in new ways, responding to circumstances (of season, of price point, of locale, of patron or consumer demand, of available materials) whose specifics are lost to us. What we see in the surviving badges is a partial inventory of their forms and images and the ingenious uses to which they are put.

Examples of badges that use, deploy, contextualize, and then differentiate a few tightly linked generic elements are circular badges featuring a forward-gazing human head or bust (a page-boy haircut identifies it as male). Who or what is being represented? Some of these circular badges featuring a male bust anticipate this question, which must be asked once the original context for the purchase, wearing, or gifting of the object has receded in time. Becket badges of this type alter the portrait so that it uses physical traits (miter, cleft chin) associated with Thomas Becket.

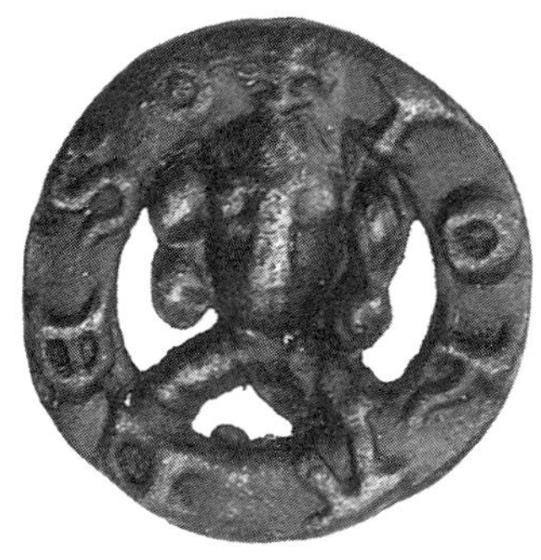

Figure 3.21. Pewter badge, man's head in round frame bearing inscription +IOHANES, pin, origin unknown, 1300–1399, found in The Hague, Netherlands, 13 mm (diameter). Langbroek, Netherlands, Family Van Beuningen Collection, inv. 4312 (Kunera 17150). Photograph courtesy of Family Van Beuningen Collection.

Other such circular badges display some version of what is known as the John's Head, which refers to John the Baptist, the messianic preacher who baptized Christ and who according to the Gospel of Mark was beheaded by King Herod; some of the badges add a horizontal, slightly cupped line underneath the head to indicate visually the platter on which Herod's stepdaughter, Salome, received the head of the imprisoned saint, which she had demanded in return for performing a dance at court. These badges are miniaturized versions of the religious artifact known as the Saint John's platter, or *Johannesschüssel*, the earliest known example of which, carved out of limewood around 1210–1220, is preserved in Naumburg, Germany.[21] In many badge examples, such as the one in figure 3.21, the name "Johannes" is added, making its religious reference unmistakable.

The Johannes badge is one example of a type, originating it would appear in the Low Countries, in which an inscribed circle frames a bust, which to judge by the hairstyle is usually male. These badges are typically very small (seventeen to twenty-two millimeters in diameter), and they are attached by a pin. They also often feature a string of letters, sometimes forming such words as AVE or AMOR, but often not. The scholar Thomas A. Bredehoft has suggested that such strings of apparently random letters are pseudo-inscriptions invoking the power of literacy itself. Some, however, are clearly abbreviations, such as IANBAT (Kunera 00722), which refers to Johannis Battista or Baptista. Others may well be examples of a common medieval word truncation practice in which each letter stands for the first letter of each word of a short, memorable phrase that the knowledgeable reader can easily expand. An example is AMAMAM standing for Ave Maria repeated over and over again.[22] Many of these strings of letters probably represent phrase truncations that I have been unable to decipher, for example, IONTVCONA (Kunera 00721), MVODNAI (Kunera 00273), and AMOEVMS (figure 3.22). It is also possible that some of these truncations refer to mottos or to a special saying known only to a few.[23]

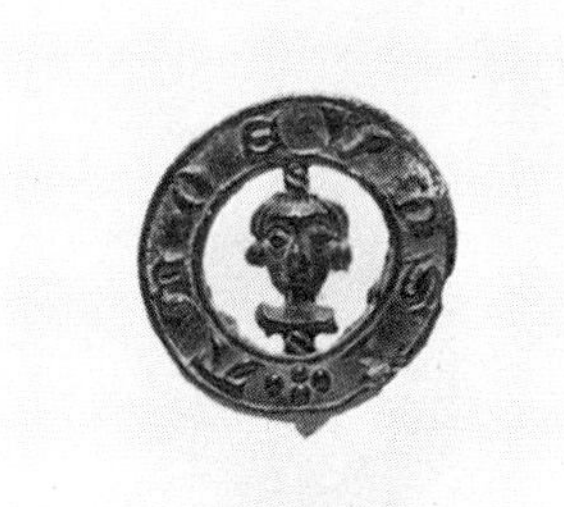

Figure 3.22. Pewter badge, man's or woman's head in round frame with inscription AMOEVMS, pin, origin unknown, 1300–1399, found in Paris, 18 × 18 mm. Paris, Musée de Cluny–Musée national du Moyen Âge, inv. 5766 (Kunera 01660). Photographer: Gérard Blot. Photograph and permission from © RMN-Grand Palais/Art Resource, New York.

Many badges survive that consist of a small human face in a circular or hexagonal frame, sometimes with letters and sometimes not. The frame on the badge in figure 3.23 is inscribed with letters spelling out the word "AMOURS." This simple French word, meaning love, used on a badge found in a Dutch-speaking city, was a clear cultural signal in the Middle Ages. In the universe of badges, the word *amours* (alternately spelled *amors* or *amo[u]r*) is usually associated with secular images and contexts having to do with courtly, or chivalric, love. Its use in this context places the bust in a different context with a different, secular meaning, probably as a love token or symbolic representation of the lover himself.

It is striking, however, that the way in which the folded badges, shown in figures 3.17, 3.18, and 3.19, highlight a human face is similar to the style used in the bust badges. Reliably datable to around the year 1270 because of the excavation layer in which it was found in Rostock, the Stromberg badge may be the oldest object in this grouping. Someone manipulated this badge by folding it and created a tiny, new object focused on Christ's suffering face. The folded Servatius badge highlights the portrait-like qualities of this face of an older man. The bust badges re-create this singular focus on a face, albeit in an unindividuated way.

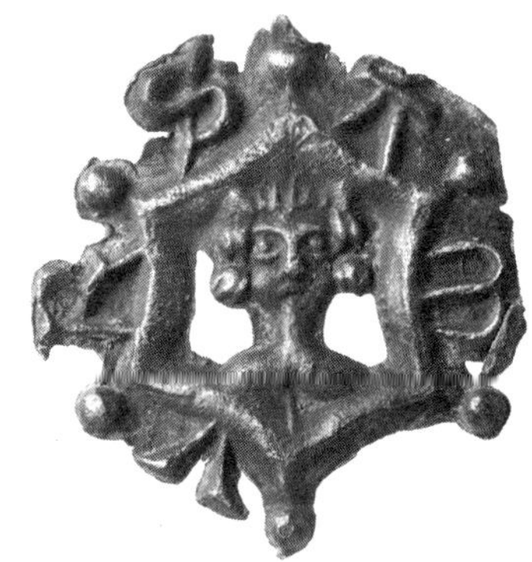

Figure 3.23. Pewter badge, man's head in hexagonal frame, inscription AMO[V]RS, attachment unknown, origin unknown, 1400–1449, found in Amsterdam, 23 × 22 mm. Amsterdam, Amsterdam Museum, inv. NZK5-298-3 (Kunera 17175). Photograph courtesy of Monuments and Archaeology, City of Amsterdam.

The stable design element of the bust, usually but not always recognizably male from its hair or head covering, is varied and combined with inscriptions and shapes suggesting a specific context and meaning. Because these inscriptions are legible even today, such badges can often be placed in specific contexts, sometimes religious (saints), sometimes secular (courtly love). Crossover and creative interchange between the religious and secular realms, in the sense it is used by the scholar Barbara Newman, was a hallmark feature of this symbolic visual language.[24]

This chapter began by exploring the materiality of medieval badges: the processes of mold making and casting by which many of the surviving medieval badges were manufactured and the properties of the metal alloys out of which they were fashioned. Such processes and physical properties represent material forms of constraint—they set limits for what a maker or user can do—but at the same time they represent a set of options and potentials. In the case of badges, these possibilities include the ability to mass-produce objects; to experiment with a variety of design formats, from simple to complex; and to respond quickly and easily to changing events and the needs of different audiences with new visual programs and with objects with varying prices. The chapter also explored the visual design potential of badges as a manifestation of their materiality. The surviving badges show us how the production of religious badges exploited these possibilities to produce new designs in a wide variety of qualities. These designs relied on what I have called widely understood inventories of form and of symbols that could be linked to specific sites and their stories in order to create unique, yet easily legible visual representations. The material qualities of badges also allowed the created image-objects to be manipulated by users. The materiality and the conditions of production of medieval badges allow a glimpse into the late medieval world of visual representation in which images were available and accessible to everyone and everywhere.

4
What Did Badges Do?

A northern German town, 1450s

Standing in the cool pit whose air is so sharply savory of earth that it is more taste than smell, the master bell founder steps back from the enormous structure he has been inspecting, a massive clay bell as tall as a man and still damp. It rests on a wooden base and is pinned through the middle by a spindle, which holds the narrow wooden template that rotates around the outside of the clay bell, shaving, smoothing, shaping it. He turns his eye now on his anxious companions, the workshop foreman and the master of the laborers. Because they are in the pit, protected by the makeshift roof of a temporary structure, the noonday sun bypasses them.

Above the clay bell, on the edge of the pit, the brick oven stands ready. In the woodshed beyond, before everyone's eyes, the master has ordered a great stack of wood taken apart so that he could see into its very core and bottom, testing that every piece waiting there is hardwood, sound and dry. He has reached up to his elbow into the pile of charcoal to extract a hidden piece, testing its weight and density in his blackened fist. He has counted and recounted the vessels of hardened tallow. Now, as the workers silently await the master's final verdict, sounds rush in: the sighing of the late summer wind, water splashing as the workers wash up, axe blows ringing as wood is split, murmuring and laughing among the workers and their wives and children as they gather.

The workshop foreman can stand the tension no longer.

"Sir?" he stammers, "will it do?"

The master frowns, and then striking the foreman and the master of the laborers on their backs, his face breaks into a grin.

"Good work, my men. Good work! I see you have learned from our previous misfortunes. The quality of the clay work is magnificent. Call everyone together! Send someone to fetch that rascal, the priest. When this bell is cast and done, he shall baptize it, but for now, let him come and share our prayers and our blessing of it."

The foreman scrambles up the ladder, looking forward to this work pause now that the inner clay bell is finished and the master has judged it to be good and to surveying the faces of the gathered workers and their families.

To be sure, much remains to be done and many worries still attend; the tallow must be melted and smeared on the clay bell, layer after layer, to the right thickness; the inner rim of the template must be precisely trimmed so that it can keep rotating, shaving, shaping, smoothing the tallow layer until the master pronounces it perfect. Then more clay will be mixed to the proper consistency and carefully layered over the hardened tallow so that it forms a thick inner core between the two layers of clay.

When the tallow is melted and removed, the clay bell will have become a cast, the tallow having left behind that carefully shaped void between the two layers of clay into which the molten ore will be poured to make the bell. The arduous, hot, and dangerous tasks remain: melting and pouring off the tallow, drying and heating the clay mold, melting the metal in the brick oven, and finally, pouring the molten liquid into the space left by the tallow in the clay mold to make the bell.

Only after the cooling and the removal of the clay will they see their bell; only then will they be able to touch it, ring it, and hear whether the master's calculations, for which he is renowned and which are far too subtle for the likes of the foreman to understand, have again produced a great, deep-voiced sounder whose rich tones will echo far and be known to all. Yet the inner wall of the bell is ready and nearly finished.

"Come now! Come here! It's time! We gather to give strength to the bell!"

As the foreman calls, his wife appears, guiding his aged, blind father, whom she seats on a bench by the wall. The skilled craftsmen and the day laborers, the apprentices and the hangers-on, their women and children, crowd around the pit, arranging themselves in a ring. The foreman's bright-eyed little girl enters hand in hand with the priest.

The master steps forward and the group moves back, giving him space to walk between themselves and the bell pit. He pulls a leather pouch from under his shirt and removes from it four small objects. He slowly circles the group, displaying the objects on his outstretched, open palms. As he passes by, folk kneel, or curtsy, or bow their heads, and murmur whatever prayer they know, the Creed perhaps, the Lord's Prayer, a Hail Mary.

Someone has brought the old blind man forward and seated him on the stool. The master stops in front of him so that he can touch the objects. The old man's long years in the craft have already told him what the objects must be: lead badges of saints that will now be pressed into the still damp clay of the bell at four places, north, south, east, west. He smiles and begins to speak: the oldest member of their workshop initiating the old workshop rite.

"Yes, Master, you have chosen well. My fingers tell me that Blessed Odile is here. Blessed Odile, remember me, blind now in age as You were in youth. May the Blessed Odile who gave Her sight for God lend Her voice to this bell. Let Her guard the south. Saint Odile, protect us all."

The master continues his slow walk, speaking to the group before stopping again to address the foreman's little daughter, who is still clutching the priest's hand.

"Workshop companions, we who together have created this clay bell and who together will transform it into a great metal bell, gather around and look in my outstretched hand. Do you see there these great lords and

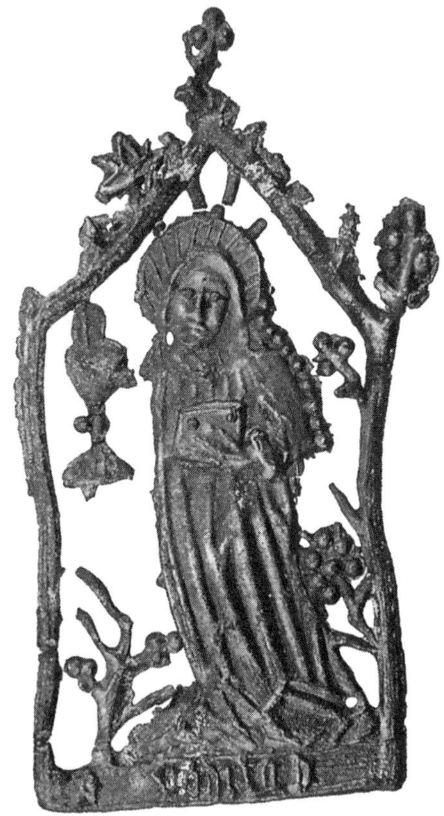

Figure 4.1. Pewter badge, Odile as abbess with book in left hand and chalice in right, inscription S ODIL--, attachment unknown, Hohenburg, Germany, 1450–1499, found in Arnemuiden, Netherlands, 79 × 43 mm. Langbroek, Netherlands, Family Van Beuningen Collection, inv. 4426 (Kunera 16502). Photograph courtesy of Family Van Beuningen Collection.

great ladies? Great in spirit and great in God. They shall inhabit our bell. Some of us have walked to Their great places to bring Them back to us, so that They might lend Their power to our bell's voice. Child, you have a keen mind and spend too much time listening to the stories told by this priest instead of helping your mother. Do you know any of these saints?"

"Oh, yes, master."

"Then speak up, child, and teach your ignorant elders."

"Oh sir, these are great men, master, and they have ever so strange names, master, the priest taught me them, master, and they are Casper, well, that one is easy, and M . . . , M . . . like meat, no, like milk, yes, Melch-ior, and then the last one, it starts round, master, Ball, but it is strong, like bold, and it is Bald-a-zer, and they were kings from ever so far away and they wanted to worship the Baby Jesus just like I do, and we have them in our church, too, sir."

"Well said, my child. Good people, mark this innocent child's piety and take it as example. And which direction shall they inhabit, child?"

"I think east, sir."

"Child?"

"Oh yes, sir, I almost forgot, sir, Blessed Three Kings, protect us all."

The master moves again, stopping in front of a young laborer who has newly joined the workshop.

"You now, young man, whose broken arm has healed so well after that beam nearly crushed you, do you know any of these two remaining?"

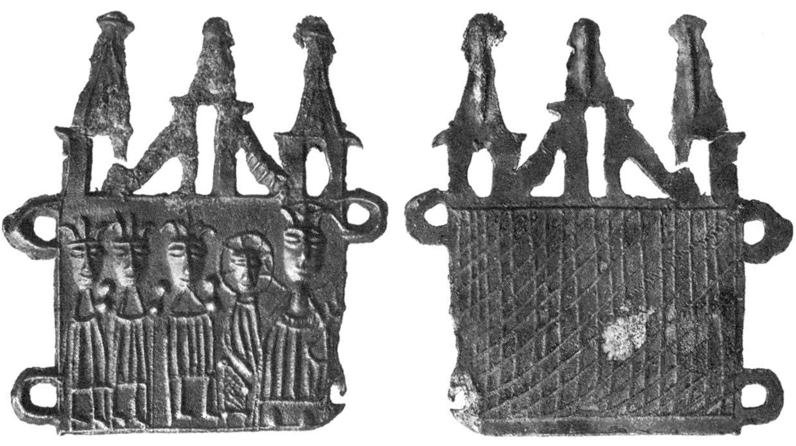

Figure 4.2. Pewter badge, the three kings in front of the Virgin Mary and Christ Child, eyelets, Cologne, Germany, 1300–1350, found in Stralsund, Germany. Photograph courtesy of photographer: Dr. Jörg Ansorge, Horst, Germany.

"That is the Blessed Virgin Mary, master, with Her Son on Her lap."

"Yes."

"And may She lend Her voice to our bell, sir, bless and protect us all. And give Her west, sir."

The master takes a few steps and stops in front of a very young man and woman, each holding a sleeping baby.

"Now, who is the fourth? You, young man, to whom did you give thanks after your wife was safely delivered of twins last winter, who by some miracle survived to suckle and snore in our presence?"

Awkwardly clutching a sleeping infant in his arms, the young laborer leans forward to study the badges in the master's outstretched palm. At last, he straightens up and aims a beseeching look at his wife. The momentary hush that falls over the group coincides most unfortunately with her whispered response to his unspoken entreaty.

"It's Christ on the cross, you ignorant fool! Speak up!"

A common shout of laughter rings out, startling the sleeping infants into shrieking fits so heartfelt that every infant and toddler in the room joins in. Drowned by the noise, blushing to the roots of his shaggy blond hair, and prompted by his wife, the young laborer stumbles

Figure 4.3. Pewter badge, Virgin Mary and Child, Kenz (Mecklenburg-Vorpommern), Germany, found in Rostock, Germany. Photograph courtesy of photographer: Dr. Jörg Ansorge, Horst, Germany.

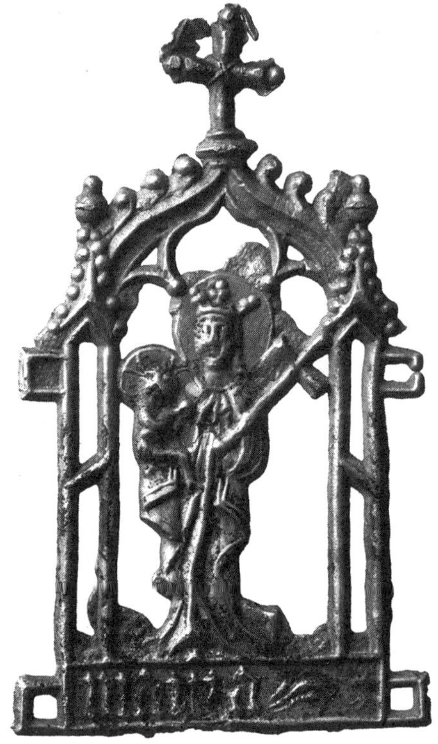

through the ritual blessing. As he does so, the master gives one badge each to the most experienced and dependable craftsmen of the workshop. Down the ladder into the bell pit they go to depress the badges carefully into the clay and make them a part of the fabric of the bell.

"Silence, now!" roars the master. Again, the gathering stills itself, and the master speaks the final prayer.

"Saint Odile, Great Magi, Blessed Virgin Mary, and Christ Yourself, You have come to us from Your holy places, bringing us Your strength and divine protection. We beseech You now to lend Your voices to this bell. May this bell carry the prayers of the devout to the ears of God! When it sings, may Your voices carry across the land! May this bell scatter the blessing and protection of Your holiness across the fields and forests, villages, castles, and cities, wherever it may be heard! May Your voices roar with God's own fury, driving out the demons, the wicked and the depraved. Bell of Odile, of the Great Kings, of the Blessed Virgin Mary, and our Lord Jesus Christ, we beseech You, drive out the demons who bring tempests, evil, and misfortune. May the wicked scream in terror and cower in pain when they hear Your voice. May the evildoers turn from their mischief and ill-doings to flee far, far from

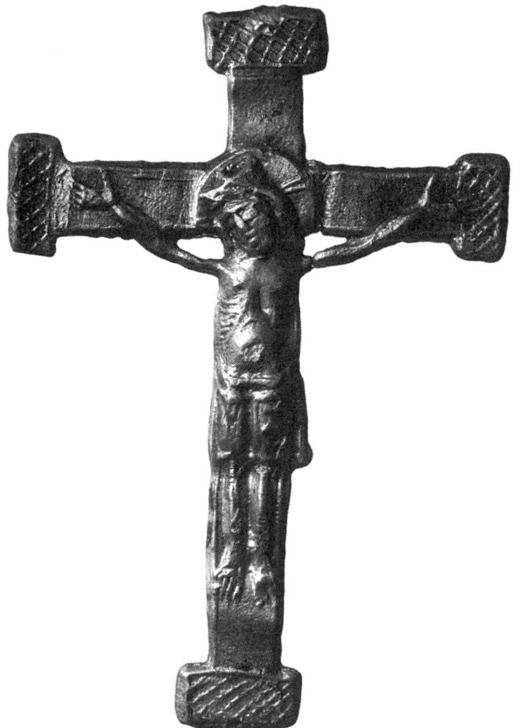

Figure 4.4. Pewter badge, excavated folded into a ball, crucified Christ, Stromberg (Westfalia), Germany, before 1269, found in Rostock, Germany. Photograph courtesy of photographer: Dr. Jörg Ansorge, Horst, Germany.

us when they hear Your voice. We beseech You, protect us from the evil that lurks everywhere, bless us with Your goodness, and carry our prayers to God. Amen."

"Amen."

The master speaks again.

"Well, well, there is still much to be done. But we shall cast a good, strong, capable bell, shall we not? And we shall put the goodness of our hearts and the resoluteness of our faith into this work, shall we not? And now, friends, finish your meals. The wife has brewed her special ale for you today and it waits outside. Find your mugs. There is beer for all."

This chapter is about some of the ways medieval people might have used badges to take action or to make claims about themselves and others. I call the reader's attention again to the fundamental characteristics of badges: manufactured with pins and eyelets for fastening, bright and shiny, often highly embellished, small, and designed to draw the eye. Badges were made to be seen.[1] In our imaginations we can erase the tarnish that dulls and blurs the surviving badges, revive their original brightness and pin them in our imaginations to the hats and cloaks of the rich and the poor, the powerful and the vulnerable, in the late Middle Ages. Yet, badges are small; one must see them close up to fully decipher them. This combination of small size and eye-catching display means that badges steer and fix the viewer's gaze, dictating a mode of interaction between wearer and viewer. In order for the badge to unfold its semiotic (meaning-making) potential, wearer and viewer must interact in close physical proximity. To use a linguistic analogy, because of how they were designed to be worn and seen, badges insist on face-to-face conversation. Their recognizable images, vivid colors, and small size invited wearer and viewer to enter into conversation with the badge and with one another.

The nature of the relationship being established by a badge between wearer and viewer was open to negotiation and interpretation. According to the circumstances, badges might also have functioned at times as personal adornment, amulets, insignia, or devices. Exploring badges in relationship to these categories increases our understanding of the values, expectations, and beliefs that medieval people associated with badges and helps us better imagine the many uses to which badges might have been put. The ubiquity of these categories in the late medieval world signals the complexity of medieval society: its many hierarchies and groupings; its urgent need to make identities visible, easily recognizable, and known; and the role badges played in carrying out many functions.[2]

Arguing that badges could function, depending on context, user, and wearer, in different ways—sometimes like personal adornment, at other times like amulets, and at yet other times as insignia or devices—means that in principle badges did not serve a single purpose or have a single meaning. Rather, multiple uses, purposes, and meanings were possible. A badge of Saint Odile, such as the one in figure 4.1, for example, was intended to be worn. Perhaps it was worn at one time by a traveler who visited Saint Odile's holy site in Hohenbourg in Alsace, France, and returned to the bell maker's workshop with it, signaling the traveler's status as a pilgrim and his or her piety as well. Perhaps the traveler gave it to the bell maker, whose act of melting the badge into the bell suggests, as is imagined in the opening sketch, that for him the bell's sounding force is made divine by its contact with the pilgrim badge from Odile's shrine, which has transmitted the overawing force and power of Odile's divinity into the bell itself.[3]

A second example comes to mind. French King Louis XI (1423–1483) was well known for his piety and was portrayed wearing a simple pilgrim's badge on his hat.[4] His household accounts record the purchase of forty-two religious badges during the king's pilgrimage to the shrine of the Virgin Mary in Embrun, France. It seems likely that these badges were distributed to members of the royal household, which would have included officials, bureaucrats, servants, and others. Were the badges then worn as signs of religious devotion or had the circumstances by which individuals in the royal household acquired them turned them into livery, that is to say, a device or sign that identified its wearer as a member of the king's retinue? Multiple purposes and multiple meanings remain in play.

Personal Adornment

Human beings have always practiced different ways of decorating and adorning themselves. At times medieval badges, especially secular ones, may well have functioned primarily as adornment. Yet adornments can also perform a wide variety of symbolic tasks that communicate meaning within specific cultural frameworks, as much in the present as in the past. Wedding rings, for example, whether plain gold bands or ornate, expensive, or custom-made, are a common marker of marital status. They are both public—everyone in this cultural sphere knows what they mean—and private—in that the actual ornament, its selection and design, can be an intimate part of two people's story of themselves as a couple. Objects used for personal adornment can also bear intimate, personal stories: a gift from a lover, a precious object inherited from a grandfather never known, earrings passed from mother to daughter. Objects worn as adornment whose symbolic references are often only intelligible to the parties concerned can be given to mark friendship, a practice that is explored in more detail in Chapter 7. People still carry lucky charms, thus continuing an ancient practice in which an adornment functions as an amulet, an object that is thought to bring solace or give protection against evil or disease.

Medieval people, whether rich or poor, male or female, young or old, wore objects made of precious materials that signaled social status and identity. In the early Middle Ages (ca. 700 to 1100) elite warriors in northern Europe used heavy silver bracelets or armbands, laconically called "rings" in literary sources such as *Beowulf*. Such armbands were typically gifts from an overlord (this an intimate rather than a distant political relationship) and announced the bearer's status as a member of the overlord's retinue. These same elites carried sumptuously decorated weapons, as those from the Staffordshire hoard find dating to around 700 CE make clear. Hilts and fittings for swords, knives, helmets, belts, and buckles were recovered, all of them enameled and gilded with artwork of stunningly high quality that proclaimed the original bearer's high status.[5] From the late Middle Ages, manuscript illuminations, paintings, and sculpture provide a rich source of information regarding customs of dress and personal adornment. They show elites and the wealthy wearing all manner of exquisitely crafted objects made from costly materials, often displaying heraldic symbols announcing the bearers' place in an elite lineage, or their belonging to an elite household, or their membership in a prestigious association such as the Order of the Golden Fleece (see plate 10 and figure 6.14, which are discussed in more detail in Chapter 6).

Medieval objects made of precious materials are now rarities. Subject to changes in fashion and in political and social structures, they often became obsolete. Because high status items crafted of gold, silver, and gems were also valuable for the intrinsic worth of the material out of which they were fashioned, they were often broken apart and recycled. Early medieval armbands that have been found in hoards have often been systematically hacked into pieces, testimony perhaps to ritualized practices of preparing objects to be deposited as offerings to a divinity or perhaps to the practice of hacking the objects made of precious material (chiefly silver) into pieces by weight to be used as a kind of currency. The precious gold and garnet sword, shield, harness, belt, and armor fittings in the Staffordshire hoard have been broken and cut off their original settings, then folded and bent in order to pack them tightly into a small space, presumably to allow for easier transport. These objects have come down to us because whoever originally hoarded and hid them never returned to fetch and recycle them.

Gold and silver objects were melted down and refashioned. Gems were recycled. Thievery was (and is) a fact of life. Plunder was the paycheck for most medieval soldiers. Fashions change; debts come due; dowries must be paid; castles, dwellings, and city walls have to be repaired and rebuilt. The costly objects in the treasury of a noble or merchant family, a city council, a cathedral, a monastery or convent represented a kind of savings account—one that was always drawn upon.

Then as now, people also used many kinds of nonprecious, inexpensive materials for adornment, including but by no means limited to badges. In the late Middle Ages, young women and young men alike adorned their hair with garlands of flowers and grasses, a custom presumably shared across social classes. Images from late medieval manuscripts show both men and women wearing garlands. Ephemeral, inexpensive objects were often used for adornment: embossed leather, beads, trinkets, feathers (some of these, if from an exotic species, could be expensive, too). The small bells produced in the molds of Mont-Saint-Michel presumably fall into this category; bells sewn onto clothing show up in medieval illuminations in a variety of contexts and there are casual references to them in texts as well. Objects made of flowers, grasses, feathers, paper, or embossed leather were once ubiquitous, but such items usually do not survive the passage of weeks or years, much less centuries. They are the most transitory of such adornments.

Medieval badges overlap with these categories. They were cheap yet durable, and they were intelligible and meaningful in a variety of situations. Like the high-status objects that they sometimes imitated, badges could be adornments, assertions of status, and visible, intelligible signs of a personal bond.

Amulets: Interactions with the Supernatural

As medieval historians have long pointed out, the categories of magic, science, and religion are modern ones, as is the modern intellectual framework that carefully separates these categories from one another.[6] In the medieval world, there were no such clear divisions. Yet it does not follow that medieval people were any less rational or more superstitious than modern people, only that the belief structures and intellectual frameworks in which they lived and died offered different possibilities for explanation and action.

The relationships that badges sought to memorialize, create, or control encompassed the breadth and depth of human social relations, from the secular to the spiritual, from the real to the imagined, from the visible to the invisible. Among the most intriguing of the relationships suggested by the badges are those that sought to communicate with, personalize, direct, and control powerful forces of the spirit world. Both religious and profane badges could function in these ways.

For most medieval people, little in the world, from stone to metal to green growing things, was inanimate.[7] All things, including humans, were composed of elemental forces that were in constant tension and struggle with one another. This view of reality encompassed not only the natural but also the supernatural world. Invisible forces and presences were powerful, mysterious, and omnipresent. Their invisible and unpredictable operations materialized in the world with terrifying force. One theory of evil in this worldview was that it existed in the world in the form of demons and spirits who attacked the lives and bodies of human beings, their social and political collectives, and the natural world they inhabited with terrible, sudden, unpredictable, destructive, and malicious force. As Ruth Mellinkoff so vividly states, "Infinite in number, alive and active everywhere, demons were believed to be watching for chances to cause destruction of sacred objects, to capture the souls of good Christians, create famine, storms, illnesses and deaths, and do all sorts of other harmful and fearsome things."[8] People lived in fear of demons, as modern people do now of bacteria and viruses. As the well-known Russian medieval historian Aron Gurevich noted, "Demons were a sort of medieval virus with which the whole sinful world was infected."[9]

This worldview did not necessarily contradict monotheistic Christianity, which represented for medieval Christians the most powerful force that could harness, curb, order, and restrain this invisible world of natural and supernatural forces. The triune God who had created this swirling world of forces visible and invisible, along with the lords and ladies of his retinue (saints, archangels, martyrs, apostles), vouchsafed for order and virtue. They stood up for goodness, fought against evil, and rewarded their loyal subjects.

The medieval world practiced many different ways to interact with this spirit world. The Church claimed a monopoly on beneficial intercessions of all kinds, from individual prayer through collective forms of liturgy and ritual. Priests had a special role as intermediaries between the laity and the divine. The divine contained a multitude of beings ready, willing, and able to protect and aid the faithful, from those renowned throughout Christendom such as the archangel Saint Michael, to regionally important saints and holy sites, to those whose influence was largely local. Led by Christ and the Blessed Virgin Mary, this army of saints battled the demonic forces ranged against it. In the mass, the priest orchestrated and choreographed a sustained summoning and conjuring of the divine. Drawing on all the senses, the mass created out of the individuals gathered a greater power whose obedience, submissiveness, and neediness strengthened those powerful forces of good. Other kinds of spiritually informed collectives such as confraternities focused on devotional piety, their statutes and actions drawing them together under the self-sought protection of powerful saints whose cults they served and who in turn would aid and protect them.

In the medieval worldview, words had power in many ways.[10] The liturgy, the right words sung in the right way, opened a channel through which the power of the divine could flow. Individuals built relationships with specific saints through prayer. The right words said in the right way could also function as charms and incantations intended to frighten, distract, or confuse the swarms of invisible, hostile forces waiting to pounce, as was imagined in the opening sketch. The right words said in the right way could represent secret knowledge that sought to harness the invisible, hostile, and elemental powers for human profit, for example, in metalworking or in alchemy. In all walks of life and in both ordinary and extraordinary times, prayers, charms, and incantations were a part of life: blessings at meals, charms for fertility spoken at planting, prayers at childbirth, love spells, curses.

Given this worldview and given a world overflowing with practices meant to deal with the spirit world, whether those practices were church sanctioned, customary, or occult, the medieval world can be imagined as a place in which everyone, from bishop to peasant, queen to fishwife, interacted with the spirit world: "Flying about everywhere, demons were full of power, and their evil persistence needed to be resisted, their targets rescued by all possible means."[11] Taking action, doing things that resisted the demons and rescued oneself and those close to one from their influence, was both a need and an obligation.

This discussion has taken us squarely into a realm where the function and purpose of religious and secular badges could overlap. All might function as objects that sought to converse with invisible forces, that is to say, as amulets or talismans. The technical difference between these two terms is that amulets protect the bearer against danger, harm, and evil, while talismans bring the bearer good luck. These definitions are centered on the bearer, such that the object either repels hostile spirit forces (amulet) or attracts beneficent ones (talisman). When examining medieval charms and prayers as well as objects such as badges, however, this neat, bidirectional definition breaks down. Often a single object or charm could accomplish repelling the bad and attracting the good at the same time. Take as an example tiny lead vessels known as ampullae that held holy water or oil and were made to be suspended from a chain. Numerous ampullae survive, many of them with clear signs of wear. These objects can be understood as amulets because they were thought to protect the bearer from harmful forces, and they can also be understood as talismans because they were thought to attract the attention of the beneficent saint from whose holy site they came. Because of this overlap in function, the term *amulet* is used in this chapter to cover both meanings.

Religious badges functioning as amulets were intended for many viewers: the human beings, the demons and other malevolent forces, and the divine forces such as saints. Badges carried with them and radiated, as it were, the divine power of the saint or holy event whose image they bore, not really or only as representations but rather more as extensions of them. The divine power of the saint was not fragmented as more and more images (badges, statues, paintings) were produced; rather, it multiplied. Even a humble lead badge participated in this augmentation of divine power.

It makes sense to the modern mind to think of religious badges as dual-functioning amulets, both attracting the virtue of the saint to the wearer while simultaneously scaring off the demons. But could secular badges have functioned in a similar way? The answer is yes. To understand this process, I draw on Ruth Mellinkoff's study of grotesque figures in medieval art.[12] Mellinkoff makes a fundamental and critical point about grotesque images, which also appear on a number of badges. Most speculations about the purpose of these badges assume that the intended audience is human. But what if, following Mellinkoff's lead, we ask if that assumption is wrong? What if the intended audience is not other human beings but rather the spirit world? An amulet was intended to communicate with the world of the demons by providing protection from it, and grotesque images were especially well suited to this purpose. Mellinkoff articulates five ways in which grotesque images communicate with the spirit world to achieve protection from demonic harm: fight fire with fire, distract the demons, confuse the demons, fool the demons, and frighten the demons. These categories can all be illustrated with badges.

Fighting fire with fire means using one form of demonic force to frighten away another. Because demons are themselves always fighting with and raging at one another, they can be used to frighten away other demons. Examples of this are the numerous badges of monsters and fable creatures who will aid the wearer by fighting off other, worse spirits, such as the many-headed, furry demon shown in figure 4.5.

Distracting the demons meant neutralizing their evil by diverting them and fixing their attention elsewhere. Demons were believed to be notoriously distractible, and they were attracted to virtually anything unusual, that is to say, anything that is fierce, funny, or grotesque. They were easily diverted through ordinary activities, entertainment, or deformities, and "so guile and tricks were utilized to distract the demons from their evil purpose and thereby prevent their gazing on, and attempting to harm, whatever needed protection."[13] Many of the sexual badges fall into this category. A belled, walking penis badge, which in plate 7a is being ridden by a person playing a stringed instrument, might have betokened camaraderie and fun times in the brothel, as I suggested in the opening fictional sketch of Chapter 1. It also could have been understood to distract the demons, entertaining them and diverting them from the sexual organs of human beings.

While demons were believed to enjoy entertainment and distractions at all times, they were also believed to dislike confusion. Artists may have used knots, interlaces, mazes, labyrinths, braided work—anything indefinite, with no determinable end—in part because images such as these were considered

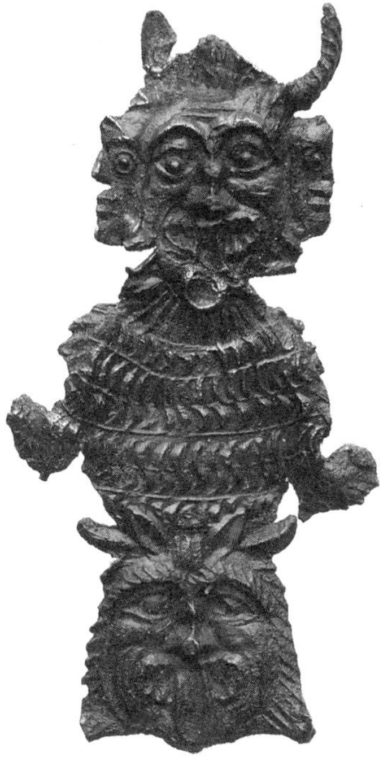

Figure 4.5. Pewter badge, many-headed, fur-covered, horned demon sticking out tongues, pin, origin unknown, 1375–1424, found in Valkenisse, Netherlands, 62 × 31 mm. Langbroek, Netherlands, Family Van Beuningen Collection, inv. 2770 (Kunera 06829). Photograph courtesy of Family Van Beuningen Collection.

to be superb protection against the demons who lurked everywhere; once the demons were lured in, they might never find their way out.[14] Into this category might well fall the star on the ampulla in figure 4.6 or circular badges and pins, which could trap the demon.

Believing demons could be fooled required faith in the beneficial effect of curses and vituperation. If you stand up to the demons and abuse them, you will ward them off. (This action is rather like the advice given to hikers should they encounter a mountain lion: make yourself big and loud and the animal will probably leave you alone.) There are badges that show a human face sticking out its tongue: bugger off, demons! The sexual badges showing men or women exposing their genitals while fixing a full front gaze on the viewer, the demon, could fall into this category, because this posture is not so much about sex as it is about power (see plate 7b and figure 8.11). A single badge can combine different categories, of course; the monstrous demon in figure 4.5, for example, both repels through greater demonic power and attracts or diverts by inviting closer study (just how many heads does it have, anyway?).

Finally, the demons can be frightened. One of the fundamental principles of all prophylactic methods is to place yourself or whatever you want to protect under a powerful god's protection, thereby using the natural dread associated with the deity to repel evil forces.[15] In other words, repel anything evil by calling on the power of your god. The badges cast into bells could be considered an example of this; their audience is the spirit world, which the bell and its badges frighten away. All religious badges possess the potential to fall into this category (whether or not they were actually used in this manner). A Saint Michael badge such as the fragmentary one in figure 4.7 would not only

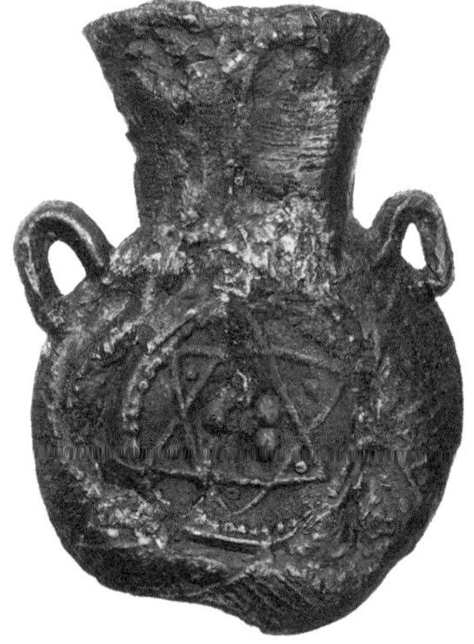

Figure 4.6. Pewter ampulla, five-pointed star in circle, eyelets, origin unknown, 1375–1424, found in Vissingen, Netherlands, 47 × 34 mm. Langbroek, Netherlands, Family Van Beuningen Collection, inv. 4200 (Kunera 16892v). Photograph courtesy of Family Van Beuningen Collection.

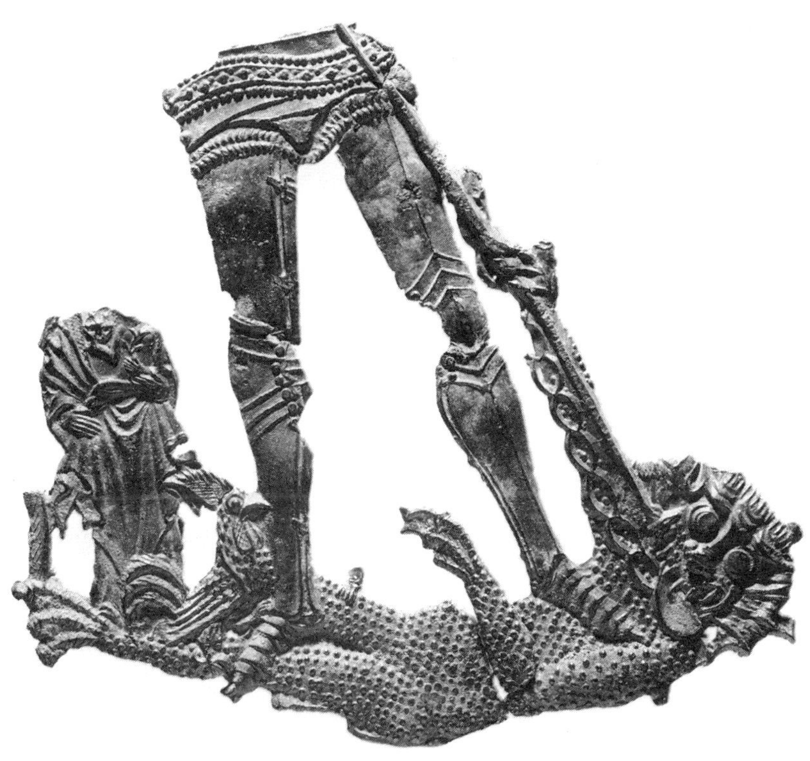

Figure 4.7. Pewter badge, fragment of Saint Michael as knight pressing lance into demon at his feet, attachment unknown, Tombelaine, Mont-Saint-Michel, France, 1400–1499, found in France, 72 × 77 mm. Paris, Musée de Cluny–Musée national du Moyen Âge, inv. CL4690 (Kunera 01318). Photographer: Gérard Blot. Photograph and permission from © RMN-Grand Palais/Art Resource, New York.

signal to the wearer's fellow travelers that one was a devotee of this saint; it would also show the demons that the wearer was protected by Saint Michael and so frighten them away. These badges (see also figures 1.1 and 3.5) even give the demons a vivid reminder of the humiliation, pain, and terror that beset demons who presume to tangle with the likes of Saint Michael.

Insignia

The word *insignia* is derived from the Latin word *insigne*, meaning emblem or symbol. Insignia are objects that are symbols of status or office and are used by religious or secular authorities to signal their legal and customary right to wield the power of their office. Often used ceremonially, they legitimate the bearer's right to the office, to the honor or rank held, and to the considerable powers devolving from it. A crown symbolizing royal power is an example of insignia. A bishop's crosier is another.

In the Middle Ages, the display of power was coterminous with exercising power. Power and identity had to be made visible, and so insignia proliferated as visible markers of power and identity. A crown made of gold and encrusted with precious stones signaled the wealth, power, influence, and might of the wearer, and linked him or her both concretely and abstractly to those who held this office in the past. Insignia physically transfered authority to the holder, transforming that person into a representative of a greater power—in the case of a bishop or a king, God, or in the case of a baron, the king.

By the late Middle Ages, insignia had long ceased to be (if they ever were) the sole domain of royalty and clerical elites. Groups of all kinds used insignia as a sign of membership. The Order of the Golden Fleece, for example, founded by Philip the Good, Duke of Burgundy, in 1430, was an elite circle to which originally twenty-five members of the highest nobility belonged (see plate 10). A few of their costly insignia survive, for example, in the Imperial Treasury in Vienna (though most of these objects are early modern). Many more examples of Golden Fleece insignia can be seen in medieval paintings of the order's illustrious members, who agreed always to wear the order's insignia. The Order of the Golden Fleece was the most exclusive of such lay orders, which were commonly religious, had social and cultural rather than political goals, and aimed to be stable over generations. Such orders, also known as confraternities or religious guilds, proliferated in the High Middle Ages.

Whether lowly pewter badges ever functioned as insignia is open to debate; perhaps ornate Saint Michael badges, for example, might have been insignia that indicated the office and authority of the wearer in lay orders of Saint Michael. There can be no doubt, however, that badges functioned often and everywhere as devices.

Devices: A Visible Sign of a Political Belonging

The modern world knows many practices in which social groups, institutional structures, political allegiances, rank, and office are made visible through signs worn on an individual's body. The police, the military, and members of such corporate groups as airlines wear uniforms; some, such as the military, also have an elaborate code of signs showing rank and merit. Members of a voluntary association sometimes wear a lapel pin associated with it. Some modern religious groups adopt distinct clothing and hair practices: some Orthodox Jewish men wear a yarmulke; some Muslim women wear a headscarf; some Catholic women cover their heads in church; ministers and priests wear robes; fundamentalist men in some religions wear beards, and so on. Such signs make something that is cultural and constructed (role, legitimacy, rank, allegiance, belonging, religion) immediately legible to anyone, regardless of rank, gender, and belonging, who is familiar with the practices.

The medieval European world also plainly and openly visualized social and religious group belonging, institutional structures, political allegiances, and hierarchical ranks by various means. These included dress, hair, and signs worn on the person. Some of these identity markers were identifiable across great geographical distances and ethnic or linguistic boundaries; others were local, specific, and mutable. Clothing, for example, could be a key indication of the wearer's "status, self-representation, and social and political allegiances."[16] All across Europe married women covered their hair with a kerchief (called a wimple). Ordained clerics and monks were tonsured, in which the top of the head is shaved and the hair becomes fringe. The robes or habits of specific religious orders were internationally recognizable because of the habit's color: black for Benedictines, gray for Franciscans, white for Dominicans, and so on.

Beginning the first decades of the fourteenth century a fashion revolution took place, in which young men began to dress quite differently from older men. While older, established men, such as merchants and lords, continued to wear long robes, it became fashionable for young men to wear short tunics and tight leggings or trousers, prominently fronted by a codpiece, a decorative covering of the penis. This youthful style of clothing symbolically and visibly highlighted virility as a marker of youthful, secular masculinity. Local and more mutable identity markers can be found, for example, in the clothing worn by mercenaries from the southern regions of Germany. In the fifteenth century, creative tailoring adapted to limitations on the display of costly fabric by slashing overgarments such as sleeves so that the underlying bits of expensive fabric could show through.[17] Mercenaries wore garments that were slashed in distinctive ways based on the locality of their origins. Someone who could read the fashionable slashing would have been able to see before the soldier spoke (since dialect would also have announced origins to a knowledgeable speaker of German) whether he was, for example, Swabian (from southern Germany) or Swiss.

The late medieval proliferation of visible systems of signification displayed on the body is represented normatively in another body of the evidence: the vast body of sumptuary law surviving from the Middle Ages. These laws set out rules aimed at regulating and controlling what people wore, seeking to bring a person's known social status and profession in line with the way they presented themselves to the world and to curb what municipal authorities deemed excessive or frivolous display. In the ideal polities envisioned by medieval authorities, a wide variety of social, economic, and religious differences would be stable and immediately visible from a distance.[18] This discussion must set aside the vexed issue of the relationship between theory and practice regarding these laws, which may have been largely symbolic statements that were regarded by their writers as normative but not intended for actual implementation. In any case, people manipulate visible systems of belonging, thus changing those meanings in intended and unintended ways. Sumptuary laws can also be understood as arguments promulgated from a place of power that were also examples (often reactive) of the cultural push and pull around what visual signs meant. Sumptuary laws tried to contain the inherent mutability and slipperiness of visible systems of identity representation; their repetitiveness and commonness suggests that they often failed to do so.

Sumptuary law's focus on an entire, clothed body encompassed a larger visual scale, as it were, than badges, which were casual signs, normally only a tiny part of a larger signifying ensemble and so small that they required proximity to be read. Clothing and fabric were very costly in the Middle Ages and represented a considerable investment of resources (when authorities attempted to regulate dress, they were also attempting to regulate how people managed their household finances). Cloth was a highly valued commodity; badges, on the other hand, were cheap, disposable, and had little inherent value. For these and other reasons (for example, religious badges acquired while on pilgrimage indicated piety, not excess), badges appear to have largely flown under the radar of sumptuary laws and clothing regulation. Important exceptions are discussed later in this chapter under "Compelled Badges."

Heraldry is another language of symbols and signs that is essentially a rule-based visual system for signifying identity by selecting and combining motifs, shapes, and colors. It was used for creating coats of arms, typically, but by no means exclusively, for members of elite families.[19] This visually based system of communication was mutable (it changed in each generation), yet legible across linguistic and political borders. Heraldry originated in the High Middle Ages and by the late Middle Ages it was used widely by elites to signal genealogical connections and by medieval associations to mark presence. Coats of arms were a kind of code that could be read by the initiated. Heralds, whose trained proficiency in reading these codes was much in demand in the late Middle Ages, worked as diplomats and, for example, on battlefields, identifying the elites gathered there, whether living or dead, by the coats of arms on their clothing and accoutrements.

Heraldry and modes of dress are examples of the ways in which symbols and images were employed across a wide spectrum of medieval social and political structures to speak a visual language of personhood, belonging, and power. Badges partook in these visual systems of identity formation; they were, as their name in German, Dutch, and French clearly says, signs, indicating that they referred to another layer of meaning. Worn to be visible and legible to others, many secular badges signified politically, and in English such political badges are often called devices.[20] They were worn as visible signs of institutional, political, and hierarchical relationships that made social categories of group identity visible on the body of an individual. We can think of these group identities as being corporate identities, which in the Middle Ages meant belonging to a specific social, civic, political, religious, or professional group.[21] Such devices represented, in historian Simona Slanicka's words, a "bond between different members of that group, presupposing the existence of a common programme, convictions, and aims," and they "imparted a corporate identity to a group and expressed it through a collective name."[22] Corporate identity, which is a fundamental and ordinary part of late medieval life, could be made visible by political badges.

What Was a Device?

A device was a kind of sign consisting of an image, at times (but not always) together with a set combination of colors and sometimes a motto that was chosen freely by an individual or a group to refer to themselves. Although sometimes derived from one element of a family's heraldic coat of arms, such as a Lancastrian red rose or a Yorkist white rose, the device offered great flexibility for the wearer for modification. Devices could be created to mark specific special occasions, such as a marriage, the signing of a peace treaty, or a carnival, and then distributed to friends and guests. Devices could be and sometimes were handed down from generation to generation as insignia or heraldry were, but they could also be invented anew. Devices could be worn by a person or applied to objects, from harness gear, tents, and weapons to paintings, dishes, and furniture.[23] Because political devices were intended to be easily legible in a public space, in terms of design they were not complex, instead featuring minimal framing and simple, clear images.

When rendered as badges, devices could be gifted to friends as a sign of political allegiance and distributed to the members of the household, a term used here in the expansive medieval sense meaning everyone from family to servants to clientele who lived with and served the great family. Given the size of these great households, the number of people displaying such a device could be large. Devices could be manufactured from many materials, from precious materials, such as gold and silver, to the ubiquitous lead-tin alloy of the badge, to perishable materials, such as cloth, parchment, paper, and leather. The device could be worn by anyone with a connection to the household, from the bishop allied with it to the kitchen maid sent to market to purchase fish, though the bishop's device might be of gold and the kitchen maid's of pewter or painted paper. Devices were a key component of the household's livery, that is to say, the uniform, colors, and badges worn by the household's members. The livery "created a social group of seemingly equal individuals—seemingly only, for while they all wore the same device or the same colors, they were however differentiated through the worth of the material and the finesse and quality of the workmanship. Such differences made it possible to express, with a fair degree of precision, differences of rank as well as the degree of proximity or distance to the leading members of a group."[24] Devices were not simply functional distinguishing marks. Servants, clientele, and followers who wore livery and devices on their persons created a living, moving representation of a household's size, scope, affluence, and power. Because devices were wearable signs of allegiance that (in theory at least) marked a close relationship to the giver, the process of acquiring one was an essential part of the way they functioned. Devices carried the identity of the giver with them, and this indexicality was retained in the device, or sign, as part of its meaning.[25]

Religious badges could function as devices, as they apparently did in the case of Louis XI mentioned at the beginning of this chapter, whose devotion was so well known that it earned him the moniker "the pious." It seems plausible that the forty-odd religious badges he acquired while on pilgrimage were distributed to function as both religious and political devices, given the widespread knowledge of his devotion to the Virgin Mary's shrine at Embrun in France.[26] Such an act was apparently not unusual, as a German nobleman's account book from a pilgrimage to Wilsnack suggests.[27]

Many of the surviving secular badges with nonreligious images were probably devices. These include flowers, such as the rose, which as a device for two warring dynasties gave its name to the English War of the Roses. The white and red roses associated with that war were combined by Henry VIII to create the Tudor rose. Animals were in common use as heraldic devices. The eagle and the lion feature as heraldic animals in national symbols to this day. In the late Middle Ages other animals were also frequently used in heraldic devices. These included the dolphin (a punning visual symbol for the

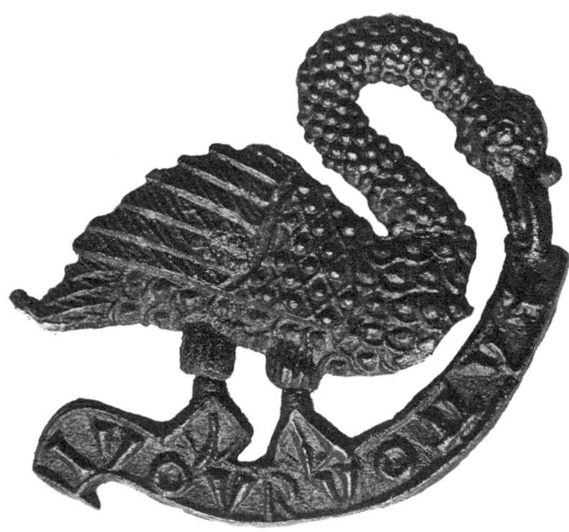

Figure 4.8. Pewter badge, swan standing on banderole that it holds in its beak, inscription IVOVRVONV, pin, origin unknown, 1400–1449, found in Nieuwlande, Netherlands, 27 × 32 mm. Langbroek, Netherlands, Family Van Beuningen Collection, inv. 1154 (Kunera 00704). Photograph courtesy of Family Van Beuningen Collection.

French crown prince, known as the Dauphin), the ram, the boar, the bear, and the hart or stag. The swan, for example, was a favorite personal emblem or device of the Lancastrian kings and was used by Henry V of England (r. 1413–1422). Simple pewter swan badges recovered in Great Britain such as the one in figure 4.8 may be Lancastrian devices. The geographic range of the political alliances of the Lancastrian barons and princes corresponds well with the find sites of the pewter swan badges.

The famous Dunstable Swan jewel, an ornate, priceless pendant found in the ruins of the Dunstable friary, might also have functioned as a Lancastrian device (figure 4.9). This costly treasure, made around 1400, was found in 1965 during the archaeological excavation of the site. The Dunstable swan may be a rare survivor of a kind of costly device that was once widely used, to judge by numerous portraits of the nobility from the late Middle Ages in which they wear valuable devices that proclaim their high standing and their political allegiances.

All across Europe, the late medieval world was awash in visible signs of status and group identity. The use of badges and other visible markers of identity ranged up and down the entire social ladder, from the highest to the lowest echelons of society, from bishop to prostitute. From the mid-fourteenth century onward, the number of badges, chivalric orders, political devices, and household liveries invented and used grew exponentially. Yet the way badges function as political devices to communicate meaning and political identity is not simple. Complexities demanding local knowledge and interpretation arose in every context in which badges worn as political devices were employed. Badges functioning as political devices told stories about shifting po-

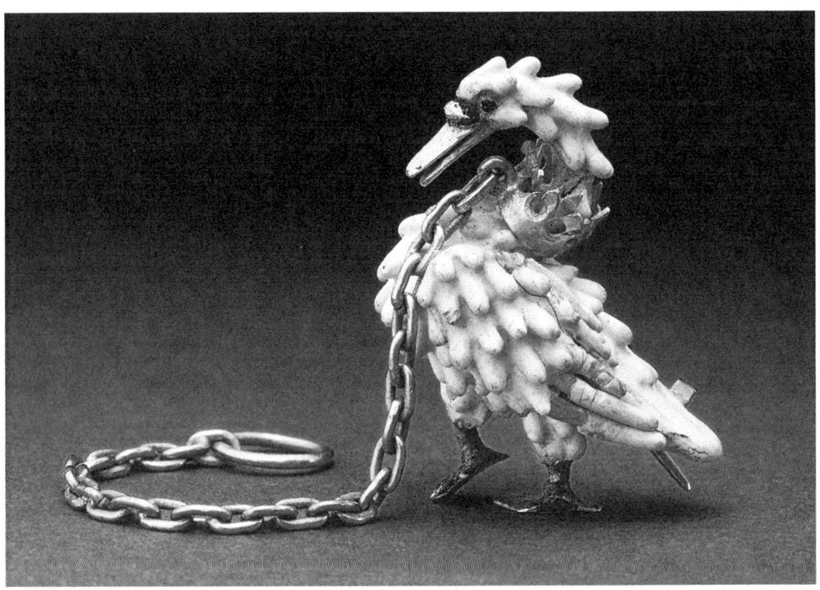

Figure 4.9. Dunstable Swan Jewel, gold and enamel ware and majolica, made in France/made in England (possibly), c. 1400, found in Dunstable, Dominican Priory, United Kingdom, 34 × 84 mm. London, British Museum, inv. PY 1996,0703.1. Photograph and permission from © The Trustees of the British Museum/Art Resource, New York.

litical allegiances and moral character, as is shown by this story from a late fifteenth-century German source about power politics in Bavaria.

Political Devices in Bavaria, 1466–1467: The Böckler League

The Bavarian Chronicle, written in German by the Munich poet and painter Ulrich Fuetrer (ca. 1430–d. between 1493 and 1502) in 1481, narrates the history of the Bavarian dukes from their putatively mythological beginnings to 1480.[28] A small incident in the interminable political conflicts between Bavaria's nobility and its dukes tells a great deal about the political meaning and value of badge devices.[29]

In the summer of 1466, the nobility of the northern reaches of the Bavarian duchy created a league or association that according to historians traced its origins to a tournament association. The 1466 league, called the Böckler League (*Bock* is the German word for a male ram, goat, or stag), used a badge, or political device, of the animal as a sign of belonging. Here is Fuetrer's description of the league's origins: "1466 30. August. And . . . at the same time, a league came into being among the nobles in Lower Bavaria and along the Bohemian Forest, who banded together in an association in which each one wore a Bock device, the knights a golden one and others a silver one, and whoever was a member of the league had to wear the Bock on his person."[30] Fuetrer goes on to name the most important members of the league before saying that they were called the Bock Men (*Böckler*).

Fuetrer selects interesting details to share with his readers. Writing some twelve years after the events, he does not call the political league a manifestation of a conspiracy, plot, or rebellion. His terms are neutral ones. *Bündnis,* which I have translated as *league,* implies a union for political purposes; *Gesellschaft,* which I have translated as *association,* is even more open, meaning more generally a guild or society of some sort. The neutrality of the language suggests how common it was for late medieval people to band together for various, sometimes overlapping purposes, whether religious, political, economic, or social.

Fuetrer does not describe the image on the device (and it is interesting to recall that he was a painter as well as a writer) or say how big they were. Perhaps such things were common knowledge. Rather, he tells two things. First, some of the Bock devices were manufactured out of gold and the rest of silver. We have seen elsewhere devices fashioned out of rare and precious materials for the elite, alongside similar devices fashioned out of pewter, for a much larger group of followers. Fuetrer makes a point of explaining that the badges made out of gold and silver were distributed according to a political hierarchy; the knights at the top of the local political hierarchy wear the golden Bock; all others wear silver. While in many cases the political hierarchy may have coincided with wealth, it need not have done so. A precious material, silver, and an even more precious material, gold, were used to make visible rank and hierarchy. In this way, traditional order is maintained in the Böckler League.

Second, Fuetrer explains that members of the league had to wear the device on their persons. Literally translated, Fuetrer writes that the league member, i.e. the Bock man, had to wear the device on himself (*an im*). I take this to mean that a league member could not give the device to a household member to wear, or put it away in his saddlebags, or leave it at home in a box and still claim to be a league member. Belonging to the group meant being willing to announce this political identity openly, to proclaim one's allegiance to the Bock Men. In other words, the league was not a secret rebellion or a conspiracy. By openly announcing itself, the league legitimized its political aims.

The Böckler League was seeking to present a united political front against their newest overlord, who, as the story continues one year later, was the young Duke Albert IV (1447–1508), known as Albert the Wise.[31] In order to settle political differences between the ducal house and the Böckler League, the opposing parties agreed to meet and negotiate in the city of Regensburg. In his retelling of what happened next, Fuetrer focused not on political grievances or strategies, as a modern reader might expect, but rather on the Bock devices.

> Then these Dukes [Duke Albert and his ally, Duke Ludwig IX of Bavaria-Landshut] and the Bock Men found a suitable meeting day and an agreement was reached that the Bock Men had to set aside their league and their Bocks [i.e., their devices]. And when the Bock Men arrived in Regensburg for the meeting, there were those who hid their Bocks, some under the tips of their hoods, some in the folds of their voluminous cloaks or mantles, because they were ashamed to wear it in front of Duke Albert, especially those whom he did not trust. But others wore it openly and in defiance.[32]

Fuetrer, whose Bavarian chronicle is in any case decidedly pro-Albert, goes on to say that the duke's eloquence and wisdom that day garnered widespread praise and approbation, especially because he was so young. Germane to this discussion are the details that Fuetrer shares regarding the devices. While Duke Albert's moral qualities are commended openly, Fuetrer uses the Bock devices symbolically to tell a story about the moral qualities of the members of the Böckler League. One group of the Bock Men are fence-straddling, back-stabbing sneaks. They follow the letter of their league's agreement and wear the device "on their person." At the same time, they do not wear the badge openly but conceal it in their clothing, thus undercutting the devices' intended symbolic claim that the league is not a conspiracy. The manner in which these Bock Men wear their devices betrays that they lack the courage of their convictions. Secretly wearing the device at the meeting proclaims their political illegitimacy. These Bock Men have become conspirators. Perhaps mentioning the shame that these Bock Men are said to have felt is intended to rehabilitate them somewhat for the reader. The other group of Bock Men, however, are fractious oath breakers. They wear the device openly and, as the text says, in defiance not only of the agreement made between the league and the dukes but above all, I believe, in defiance of Duke Albert himself. Openly wearing the device at the meeting proclaims, in effect, their political illegitimacy. These Bock Men have become rebels.

In Fuetrer's *Bavarian Chronicle*, the meeting, its preconditions, and the manner in which the Bock Men behave combine to change the meaning of their device. Intended as a device signaling an honorable alliance among well-born men with legitimate grievances against their overlords, it turned into a sign of a divided and conspiratorial group of unprincipled, disloyal, and dishonorable men. It is important to remember that the aim of the *Bavarian Chronicle* was to glorify the dukes of Bavaria. If the meaning of the device can shift so dramatically within the perspective of one partisan work, it is possible that the Bock device both assumed and shed other, divergent meanings as well, ones that are no longer accessible. The significance of devices for creating and transporting meaning stands at the heart of the episode. So sure is Fuetrer that his audience will understand that devices participate in the moral character of those who wear them that he does not bother to spell out the implications of the story he is telling. As the *Bavarian Chronicle* illustrates, devices were a ubiquitous and an ordinary aspect of medieval political life. Yet they were not about the surface. They were about the core. They participated actively in the hearts and minds of those who wore them and those who saw them. They were not symbols of fixed, unchanging meaning but agents marking fluid and dynamic changes in meaning that could be read by anyone who took the time to observe.

Outward Signs of Private Quarrels

The conditions of use for political devices were complex. Secular devices that claimed and created corporate identities could be self-invented, and they were self-chosen, negotiable, transferable, and retirable. "Self-invented" and "self-chosen" mean that an individual or an association was free to make their own new device and that they wore them voluntarily. "Negotiable" suggests that the meaning of the device, as we have seen with the Bavarian Bock Men, was unstable and open to interpretation; it also suggests that badges could and did acquire new meanings. "Transferable" means that they could be given away to express personal affiliations. "Retirable" means that a device could become outdated and be set aside, that is, retired. If the nature of the political bonds between people is always changing, then devices can become obsolete and even unreliable; it is possible to lie with a device.[33] To read a device properly, a person had to have up-to-date information about the political situation of the badge wearer and giver. Intended to suggest a mutually beneficial relationship, devices provided those who wore them, whether legitimately or not, with opportunities that they otherwise would not have had.

In a word, devices were not harmless. Rather, they were partisan displays that were adopted and adapted strategically; one medieval Parisian chronicler and observer, Jean Juvénal des Ursins, called political devices "outward signs of private quarrels."[34] Historian Simone Slanicka provides an example of the way in which devices were understood to create and broadcast political identities in her study of the role played by political devices in Paris between 1410 and 1420 during the violent civil war between the factions known as the Armagnacs and the Burgundians, as they struggled for possession of the French throne. The device of the Armagnac was a white band worn diagonally from one shoulder to the opposite hip. The device of the Burgundians was a diagonal cross formed by crossing two white bands diagonally known as the *saltire*, also called Saint Andrew's Cross. Both sides chose white because it was the royal color.

The badge in figure 4.10 shows a *saltire*. On the right stands Saint Andrew, who is touching the cross; above it is a mason's level and above that, a fleur-de-lis, both political devices; and in the lower left-hand corner is a carpenter's plane, which was the personal political device of John the Fearless, Duke of Burgundy and leader of the Burgundian faction. Pewter badges with the Burgundian device, crossed bands with a shield in the middle, have been found in the Seine. A famous member of the Armagnac party, the Duc de Berry, is shown in the month of May in his famous illuminated manuscript *Très Riches Heures*, wearing the white, diagonal band, while Christ's tormenters in the manuscript's passion scene wear the saltire. Slanicka points out the contemporary political significance of this representational choice: "There could hardly be a more serious accusation with which an Armagnac document could indict its enemies: through their positions and actions during the civil war, the Burgundians crucified Christ a second time."[35] The

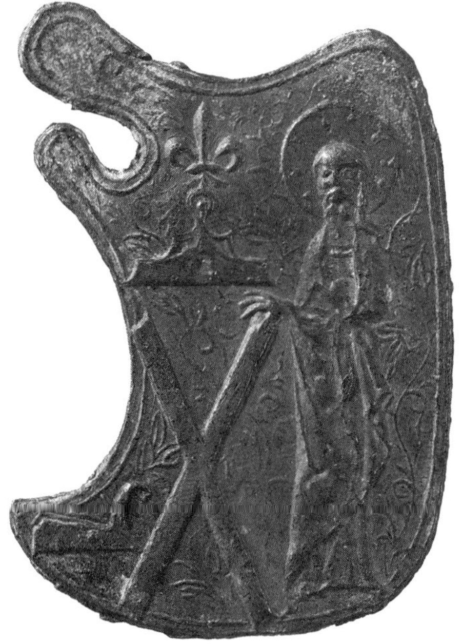

Figure 4.10. Pewter badge in shape of a tournament shield; on left from top to bottom, fleur-de-lis, mason's level, Saint Andrew's cross, carpenter's plane; on right, Saint Andrew; the political devices of John the Fearless (1371–1419), Duke of Burgundy (after 1409), attachment unknown, France, 1409, found in Paris, 52 × 36 mm. Paris, Musée de Cluny–Musée national du Moyen Âge, inv. CL18064 (Kunera 01579). Photographer: Jean-Gilles Berizzi. Photograph and permission from © RMN-Grand Palais/Art Resource, New York.

image of Christ's passion in *Très Riches Heures* participates in and makes a partisan statement about the most intense political strife of its time.

Originally, these devices may have been military signs, but by mid–civil war, they were being worn by the entire population, clerics and laymen, young and old, men and women alike. When the Armagnac party took over the city of Paris in 1414, even statues of the saints were decorated with the diagonal white band. The king himself was forced to wear the Armagnac band, which according to Slanicka was widely perceived as wrong and confusing because the king, as a peacemaker and mediator, was supposed to be above such signs.

In 1418 the Burgundian party retook Paris. Having succeeded, the Burgundian victors launched a wholesale massacre of the Armagnac faction, mutilating the corpses of Armagnac sympathizers in a gruesome, yet distinctive way: a strip of flesh was torn out, diagonally, from shoulder to hip across their chests, imitating the shape of the Armagnac device, the white band. Political identity was made visible in death, indelibly marked on the bodies of the defeated.

What might such brutal acts tell us about political devices and identity formation in the late medieval world? According to Slanicka, wearing the device legitimately transformed the status of the wearer because it was linked to high authority, in this case to the king or to those elites with a claim to kingship widely perceived as being legitimate. This authority authorized the transformation of the device bearer from peasant, laborer, cleric, or woman into a partisan fighter for a political cause. Perceived by some as having much the same status as an oath, the device enabled wearers to legitimately defend themselves, their goods, their town, and their king. Adopting the device allowed bearers to act to their own advantage. In other words, in the context of civil war, the device bestowed the authority to act, and at times even to kill without fear of punishment. Devices could be, in effect, instruments of warfare.

The Burgundian party's acts of mutilation take on further significance. To them, wearing the white band of the Armagnac party was a grave act of treason. Marking the bodies of the massacred announced visibly to all that the murdered person was a traitor and that (from the Burgundian perspective) their death was justified. Although the white band began as a device voluntarily adopted by its bearers as a sign of political allegiance with the Armagnac party, the victorious, rival Burgundians imposed the sign on the corpses of their fallen enemies to indicate their status as treasonous outsiders. The white band of the Armagnac became, in the hands of the Burgundians, a compelled sign of treason.

Compelled Badges

Beginning in the second half of the fourteenth century, many cities in northern Europe sporadically began to require beggars to wear visibly on their clothing a device made of lead, leather, or some other material that declared that the wearer had the legal status to beg. The device was compulsory (presumably one was not supposed to beg without it), and it functioned as a kind of identity card. In Nuremberg, these devices were called *Spangen*, and they were handed out not by a municipal office but rather by the beggar's confessor. Beggars' devices come into common use in the sixteenth century, when as historian Valentin Groebner notes, attempts increased to regulate their illegal production. (Such, as Groebner points out, was the risk of all such devices: they serve as identity markers and proclaim authenticity, and yet like all mass-produced objects, they can be counterfeited.)[36]

In late medieval England, there was a well-established and highly controversial system in which churches and religious houses provided asylum, or sanctuary, originally to felons and accused criminals, and over time also to debtors, alien craftsmen, and political refugees. Originally providing only temporary sanctuary, by the fifteenth century many sanctuary precincts had been granted immunities and rights by royal charter, supported permanent populations, and had discrete territorial boundaries (however permeable or even invisible these might become at times).[37] Male and female sanctuary seekers and dwellers were often compelled by statute to wear large, and hence highly visible, badges when outside their lodgings.[38]

Compelled signs and practices existed in the religious world as well. Pilgrimage could be compelled as required penance for sin, a practice known as penitential pilgrimage. In southern France, heretics undertaking penitential pilgrimage might also be compelled to wear a specific sign, in their case, a cross sewn onto their clothing as an outward sign of spiritual failings. Leigh Ann Craig discusses cases of female heretics (known as the Albigensians) sentenced to pilgrimage during the first decades of the fourteenth century in Toulouse by the inquisitor Bernard Gui (1261/62–1331).[39] He required them to wear either a single cross or a double cross, which was reserved for stubborn heretics who would not cooperate. In Gui's words, "We impose on you and enjoin you to wear two felt crosses of a yellow color, one in front on the chest, and the other in back between the shoulders, on all your clothing, without which prominently displayed you shall not go about either inside your home or outside of it; the length of one branch shall be two and a half palms, and the other, that is to say the transverse branch, two palms' length, and three fingers for the width of each branch. And you will repair or replace them if they tear off or if they wear off from age."[40] Gui is meticulous in setting out the color, number, placement, and size of these crosses; they must be large, clearly visible, worn on all clothing and at all times, even in one's own domestic space. For Gui, the compelled wearing of this cross was standard penance for heretics, a punishment that could be lifted if all conditions had been fulfilled.

For Christians, the cross symbolizes the suffering Christ undertook on behalf of humankind. Many surviving religious badges from holy sites in northern Germany and southern Denmark feature a crucifixion or a cross, each with distinct iconographical features. The penitential crosses described above that were worn by heretics in the Middle Ages functioned differently; they were, in Craig's words, "a most unwelcome stigma."[41] Widely recognized as a badge, or sign, of heresy, they elicited not mercy but scorn, not fellow feeling but harassment. Even as orthodox a sign as a cross could take on other meanings; wearing a penitential cross was an act of public humiliation. It made publicly visible the bearer's status as a heretic and as a compelled pilgrim. Such a cross invited harsh treatment when a heretical pilgrim undertook her or his penitential journey: beatings, ostracism, harassment. From an orthodox perspective, heretics constituted a threat not just to social order but also to cosmic or divine order. The heretic's status as a compulsory pilgrim had to be made visible to others if the penitential pilgrimage was to accomplish its work. The heretic's shaming cross demonstrated that the otherwise invisible threat heretics were believed to represent (since heretics generally look and act no differently than their neighbors) had been found, contained, and dealt with. From this perspective, even the harsh treatment such crosses elicited might have been understood as aiding a necessary correction.

Perhaps the best-known compelled badges from the late medieval world, however, were badges and devices that Jews were compelled to wear.[42] References to compelling Jews to wear devices or clothing distinguishing them from Christians appear in the constitutions (also called canons), which were the outcome of the Fourth Council of the Lateran in 1215. The final document issued from this gathering of church prelates and elites comprises seventy-one sometimes lengthy rules or principles that responded to contemporary political and religious dilemmas and problems within the Church by outlining institutional processes and standards, by demanding moral reform of the clergy, and by taking an emphatic stand on Christian heresies. Four short constitutions at the end of the document deal with interactions between Christians, on the one hand, and Jews and Saracens on the other. Canon 68 states that "we decree that such persons [Jews and Saracens] of either sex, in every Christian province and at all times, are to be distinguished in public from other people by the character of their dress."[43] The reason given was that because in many places Christians, Jews, and Saracens dressed alike, Christians had sex with Jews and Saracens by mistake, a practice that had to be stopped.

The requirement that Jews wear a distinguishing device appeared sporadically in other documents from various regions in medieval Europe. In 1269, for instance, Louis IX ordered the Jews of France to wear "a wheel made of yellow cloth or rag sewn on their outer garment on chest and back to insure their visibility. The wheel, which has to be four fingers wide, has to be large enough to contain a palm [of a hand]."[44] These compelled signs were used anachronistically in a French historical chronicle written in the 1320s to illustrate the expulsion of Jews from the royal domains of France in 1182 (figure 4.11).

Only men are shown in the image, and some of them have been marked by the yellow wheel. It is not clear why the artist places the cloth sign of a yellow wheel at the waist, which does not correspond with any other depictions of badges in use. Other symbols and stereotypes indicating Jewishness appear in the image. The bony, hooked nose of the man wearing a short gown in the front (who does not have a wheel on his clothing) summons up the anti-Jewish caricature of the "Jewish" face that emerged in the mid-thirteenth century.[45] The faces of the other men bear no stereotypically coded traits, and their clothing is similarly unmarked and ordinary. Some of them, however, appear to have tefillin or phylacteries on their foreheads, which are worn by observant Jewish men during weekday morning prayers. This object, central to the practice of the Jewish faith, marks them as Jews. The wheel signs, which appear to have been added last to the image, may be trying to spell out an identity because the other identity markers, which were critical to understanding what is happening in the image, were obscure to the manuscript's users.

The authoritative tone of a document such as the Constitutions of the Fourth Lateran Council can be misleading; in the late medieval world, the relationship between authoritatively asserted decrees and their implementation was changeable and complex. The Constitutions of the Fourth Lateran Council provided directives concerning ecclesiastical affairs; when it came to civil and criminal matters that fell in the secular realm, however, religious authorities had no independent and direct means of enforcement. (The heretic's cross is different because the investigation and correction of heresy falls within Church jurisdiction.) Instead, they were dependent on secular authorities—kings, princes, local lords, and city councils. In other words, the enforcement of any matter outside the immediate jurisdiction of Church law

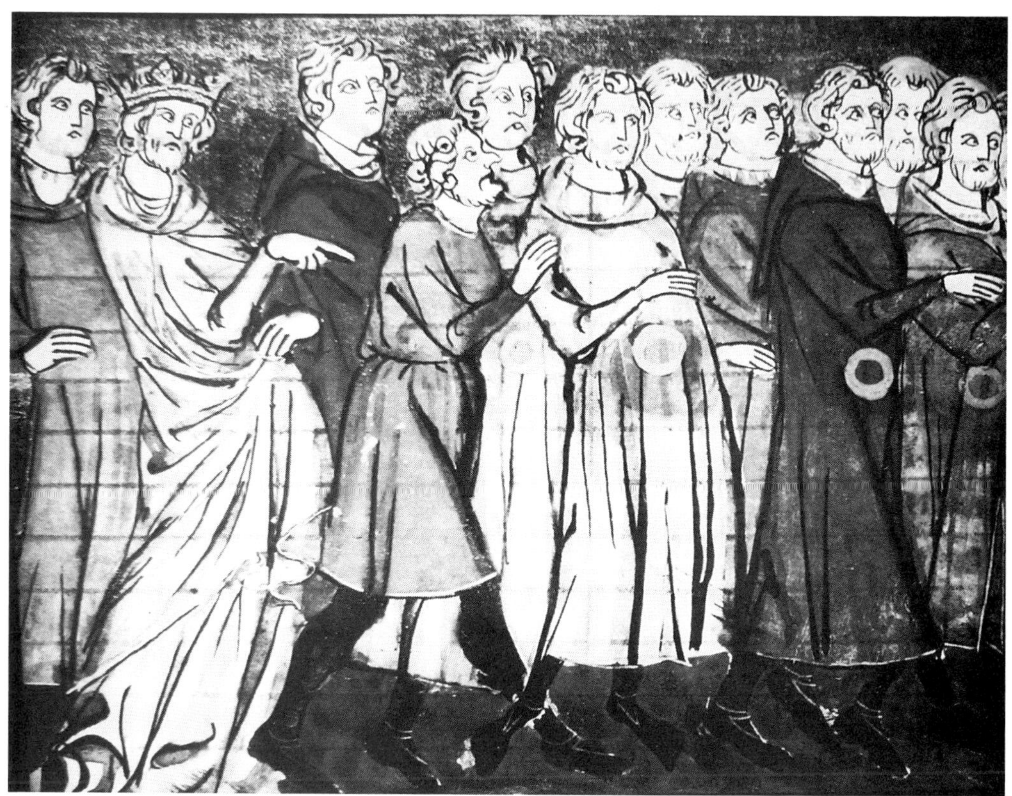

Figure 4.11. Expulsion of Jews from France, 1182, miniature from *Grandes Chroniques de France*, 1320s. Paris, Bibliothèque nationale de France. Photograph and permission: HIP/Art Resource, New York.

and the enforcement of any criminal punishments decreed by Church law had to be negotiated with the secular authorities. Now the picture becomes murkier still, for the overwhelming evidence from late medieval Europe is that far from working hand in glove, ecclesiastical and secular authorities all across Europe were often at odds with one another; their political aims and interests did not always coincide.

Anti-Judaism was omnipresent in medieval Europe. Both its violent excesses, such as the massacres in the Rhineland incited by the first Crusade, and its day-to-day hostility and discrimination made precarious the lives of medieval Jews. Yet Christians and Jews also interacted and lived alongside one another peaceably, and Jewish communities were often protected by one lord against the interventions of another. Even though these actions often amounted to one Christian lordship reserving to itself the right to exploit

Jews, they nevertheless created some of the conditions under which ordinary, peaceful interactions and cultural exchange between medieval Christians and Jews also took place.[46]

Within the context of late medieval Europe, the practice of displaying clothing and such features as haircuts and coverings that indicated profession, social rank, and status was normal for everyone. Everyone in late medieval Europe was wearing some kind of clothing that fashioned their personhood within the context of specific groups or collectives, whether those be short-term associations, personal affiliations, kinship structures, religious orders, marital status, regional identity, or professional status. Badges belong in this general context. Religious badges, most secular badges, and the political devices discussed in this chapter were voluntary. They were not solely passive statements of affiliation but rather also reflected the agency and intentions of the wearer. Jewish badges, the penitential cross, the sanctuary man's badge, and the beggar's device, on the other hand, were promulgated as being compulsory. Here agency resides more firmly with authorities. There may have been different reasons for secular authorities to force the wearing of such a device on Jews: to raise money, to incite persecution, to mark out religious difference. Forced by an authority on a wearer, compelled badges such as Jewish badges must have produced a stigma for the wearer. The fluidity of agency and mobility of identity that underwrote the voluntary wearing and discarding of political devices were lost.

In the medieval world, badges were not merely representative objects or superficial, functional, distinguishing marks. Rather, they were powerful instruments of group formation that expressed bonds between group members, implied shared beliefs and convictions, bestowed the right to take action, and demonstrated inclusion or exclusion. The relationships created by such badges, whether religious or secular in origin, were political in the broadest sense of the term. They created and maintained relations of power between individuals and groups, institutions, and movements. They could precisely signify rank, office, marital or sexual status, political allegiance, or position close to or far from a specific power. They created opportunities for their wearers to act and negotiate. Political badges heralded group formation and the creation of collective identities. The interactions between compelled and voluntary badges is under-researched. Perhaps that research could begin with the knowledge that badges were never neutral or passive. They were like words in a primarily oral world: they took a stand. This stance of power unites the compelled and the voluntary badges; what separates them is whether they assign or claim belonging.

Multiple Contexts, Multiple Meanings

This chapter has discussed badges as representatives of different functional categories of objects: personal adornments, amulets, and political devices. Thinking about badges through these categories has provided valuable lessons about badges and the multiple functions they might have had. For both religious and secular badges these categories provide concrete paths to imagining answers to the question of how the badge might have been used.

Take the badges of Saint Servatius. Were they gifts? Was the folded one an amulet? Might a Saint Servatius badge have signaled membership in, for example, a confraternity? Were they discarded or lost? These functions do not necessarily cancel one another out. The lines are fluid between these functions and can shade into one another. A single badge or object could have had more than one function and more than one meaning.[47]

To think about the multiple meanings that potentially inhere in one badge, I turn to one of the few medieval images I have been able to find showing someone wearing something that looks like a secular badge. Figure 4.12 shows a drawing from around 1505, at the very end of the period in which badges were in vogue. The artist is Urs Graf, a Swiss goldsmith, engraver, mercenary, and rogue, whose monogram, a short sword resting inside the letter G, graces the lower right-hand corner.[48]

The drawing shows a woman smiling coyly at the viewer. Shown in half-figure, her body facing left and turned slightly toward the viewer, she is dressed in ornate garb: a worked belt of cloth or leather angles down her skirt and off frame; the waistband of her full skirt is gathered into ruffles by a finely woven band; her lower torso is tightly encircled by a smocked or woven cummerbund; a brocade capelet stretches as it is pinned closed over a richly pleated shift in order to conceal yet also frame an ample cleavage. A fine, studded chain encircles her neck. On it hangs a large round ornament depicting what appears to be a crowned initial and from which dangle three small gems or bells. The woman's long hair is bundled on the back of her head in an ornate hair wrap typical of the times, though a few loose strands artfully frame her face. Her head is tilted to the side while she glances up, sideways, artfully, at the viewer, the right eye engaging the viewer with a look of seduction, while the left eye, in shadow, holds a veiled glance of sadness and exhaustion. For all of her finery, the woman is not pretty. The engraving shows us a double chin; thin lips; a high, thick, and large nose; small and beady eyes. Her face gives off a vague yet unmistakable air of illness, created by the shadows across her face, the minute spots on her skin, the puffiness under her eyes and their

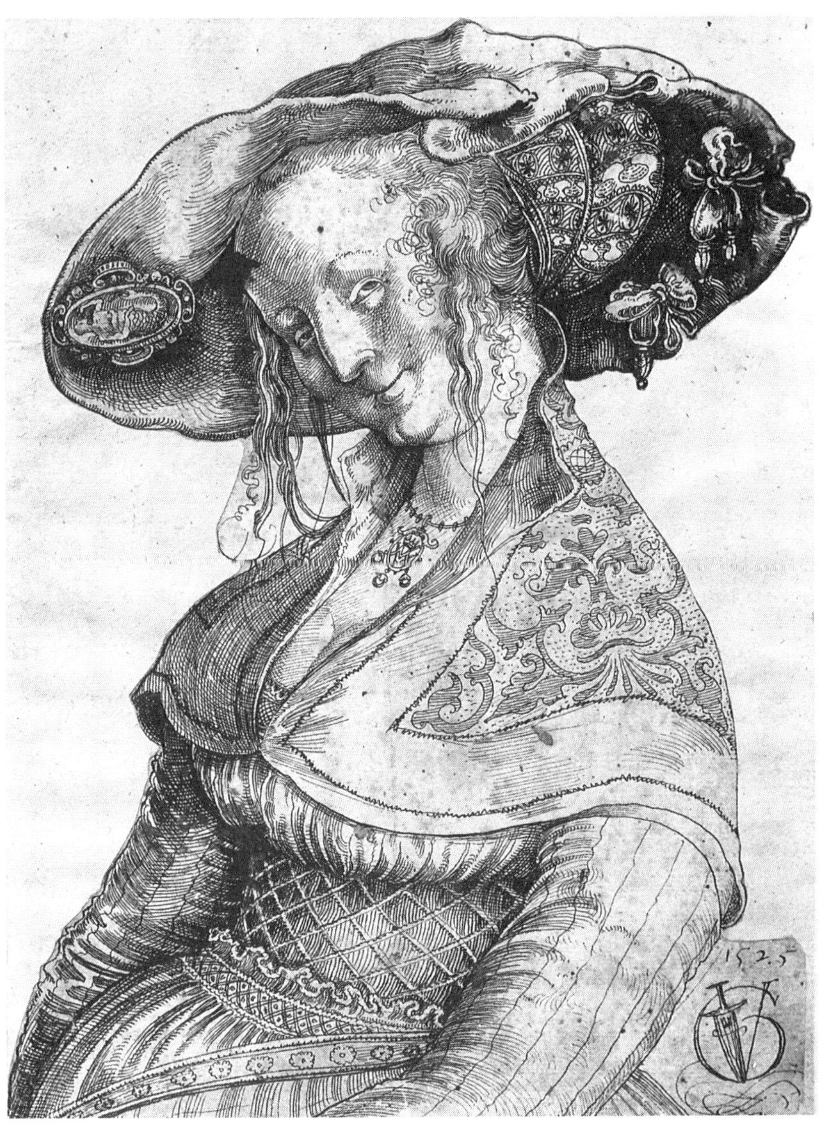

Figure 4.12. Urs Graf, *Simpering Harlot*, pen with black ink, 27.8 × 20.4 cm, 1525. Dessau, Germany, Anhaltische Gemäldegallerie, inv. Nr. B.IV.19. Photograph courtesy of Christiane Andersson.

contrasting glances. She is wearing a wonderful, huge hat. Part of the hat's brim is fixed or rolled back to reveal her face. The hat's brim is ornamented as well. At the back are two bows, which may well be functional parts of the hat, ribbons or ties to hold it on when fully opened up. On the hat's front brim is pinned a true ornament, a large and ornate brooch or badge of a mermaid, a creature half fish, half woman.

What are we to make of the portrait? Before returning to the pendant and the mermaid brooch, some background information on the artist may be helpful. Well known to the Basel authorities for his violent ways, which drew him repeated jail sentences, Graf was a gifted goldsmith who also worked in the field of design (typical for medieval goldsmiths) and who also, less typically, regularly strove to increase his wealth by working as a mercenary soldier for Basel, taking part in several battles. These two aspects of Graf's professional life came together in a series of engravings and drawings that engage the late medieval world of the professional soldier in what to us appears as naturalistic detail: scenes of gallows or the gory aftermath of battle; handsome, brawny young soldiers strutting in finery and weapons; and figures from the lowest strata of society whose lives were intertwined with the business of war—grizzled, disfigured veterans; the crippled and the sick; whores, soldiers' wives, and camp followers. The woman belongs to this sphere of life. Her fine clothes, beckoning gaze, coy smile, and above all the indefinable pall of poor health characterizing her features suggest that she is a prostitute.

The mermaid brooch and the pendant can be thought about by using the categories developed in this chapter, for while both are depicted as being a bit larger and more ornate than many of the badges with which this book is concerned, they nevertheless share key features with them. The hat brooch is worn on the upturned, inner hat brim and its depiction of a mermaid is also known from badges, as was shown on plate 6b; the initial, too, is known from many surviving badges. The mermaid brooch could be both an adornment and a visible sign of a personal relationship. The brooch, like the pendant medallion, is large and well made. The drawing is in black and white so it is impossible to know whether the mermaid brooch was painted, or how its color harmonized with the hat and the rest of her clothing, or whether the woman is dressed in an ensemble of harmonic colors or clashing ones, or if her garb consists of faded, used ribbon, trim, and cloth or new garments. The brooch is not worn under the bodice or on a chain, but rather it adorns the hat, displayed for all to see. Perhaps the mermaid brooch suggests a gift signifying an established relationship in which the wearer is cherished and adored. The same could be true of the pendant. The pendant brooch consists of a crowned initial that looks very much like an M. Does the letter refer to the woman's name? To the name of a husband or lover? More likely it refers to the Blessed Virgin Mary, as do so many medieval badges with the initial M. If that is the case, then the pendant might be signaling personal piety.

Or is the mermaid brooch an amulet? After all a mermaid is a kind of monster or demonic creature, so the ornament might have a magical function.

It would fight fire with fire, repelling lesser demons who fear the mermaid. It might confuse the demons, for who has ever seen a two-tailed fish-woman, one whose beginning and ending are indefinable and unknowable? Repelled, distracted, and confused, the demons are diverted away from the woman wearing the brooch, away from attacking her business, her good fortune, and her well-being, allowing good luck, prosperity, and health to make their way to her. Similarly, if the pendant signals devotion to the Virgin Mary, then it, too, could have an apotropaic function. It would not be far-fetched for a medieval woman to seek protection from a powerful deity, the Virgin Mary, whose enormous power will scare away the demons.

Might the mermaid brooch be a device? It announces itself on the hat, prominent for all to see. Might it be a widely recognized sign or symbol of a corporate or group identity, for example, prostitution? At the same time, the pendant might announce not only piety but membership in a guild or confraternity devoted to the Virgin Mary.

I hope to have made my point. A badge is not a simple object. It need not function in one simple way. Rather, a badge can have multiple meanings and multiple functions, which can shift depending on the viewer, on time and place, and on context. Because it suggests meanings, not simply one meaning, a badge sets the stage for the shared negotiation of meaning between the bearer and the viewer. For example, are you, woman in the engraving, a prostitute or a widow, and which do you want me to believe you are? Every badge is potentially an agent or a trigger for stories. A badge can gesture toward a shared world of story, whether miracles performed by the Virgin Mary or tales of mermaids. It can start conversations while suggesting potential outcomes. Or quite simply, it can provide an occasion to talk: I wonder who gave you that pendant, that brooch? I once saw one like that, oh, but not nearly so fine, when I was down south, where they mostly speak Italian. Badges can be adornment, signify social and political status, or signal any part of a complex web of relationships that can include the deceased, supernatural forces, or the living. Badges communicate and connect.

5
Badges and Pilgrimage

Sweden, a village
near Vadstena, 1385

The middle-aged woman kneels alone in the church on the stone floor. The icy cold sends its tentacles through the layers of woolen skirts and the cloak bunched beneath her knees to ease her aching bones. She prays. The remaining candles flicker.

Her mind and spirit, raw with sorrow and anger, cannot settle. The phrases and chants known and repeated endlessly since childhood come easily, but the peace that they should bring does not. A familiar state. Was it not so when her husband died and left her, a widow with three small children, to manage the manor on her own? Was it not so when his half-brother tried first with fair words and then with threats and blows to claim the manor and the trade rights, to sire his own bastards on her heedless of right or affection; failing that, he tried to grind them like dung under his heels on her husband's, his brother's, own manor and to turn her and the children, the rightful heirs, out onto the road like common beggars? Was it not so when she and her brothers fought him in court, agreeing reluctantly at her kinsmen's behest that she give him the best pasture by the creek to settle the dispute?

The old bitterness shadows everything—behind it, the old loss.

And now the dark spirits that inhabit the world, huddling in dark corners, hissing their threats, have gained entrance. They have set her little grandson's body on fire and sickened the cow whose milk sustained this sweet, quick child. Sensing victory near, they whisper in the ear of his poor, docile mother, who lacks the wit and the strength to stand against them, keeping her from sleep and driving her near madness.

If only her son had lived. His face rises unbidden in her mind, giving her that special blue-eyed look of his that mixed tenderness and resolve, gentler than his father, yet no less stalwart and proud. But without her son and his son, the end is near for all of them. They hold this manor for the little boy, and if he dies, their right to live here dies with him. Then that wretched weasel, that misbegotten nephew, like his father a terror to honest folk and an insult to the righteous, will call upon the law to take possession and throw them out.

Her son. She senses his hand resting on her shoulder. She must stop such thoughts. She must fight, and she needs allies who will wage war with the demons, who can chase them, catch them, punish them, frighten them away from the child, bringing the peace that allows healing to enter.

Of their own accord, her frozen fingers close around the sign of the great, strong holy man dangling from a string around her neck. It was her son's secret gift after he returned from the last trip to the rich trading cities to the south. He said that he touched the sign to the saint's shrine to carry its holy powers home to her, since she was unable to travel. He told her stories about the holy man. Servatius is no church lord like these fat flatterers and fornicators who surround them now, weaklings all. No, Servatius is a true warrior, a stalwart defender who shelters the weak and righteous, a fearless persecutor of false prophets, whose power and strength work God's wrath on evildoers everywhere. She will place her trust in him.

She rises slowly and moves toward the altar. The church is deserted yet alive; she senses it. The saints who abide in this place fill it with such power and holiness that the dark spirits cower and dare not enter. Holding the image-amulet high as she walks, she prays out loud.

Figure 5.1. Pewter badge, Saint Servatius flanked by angel on left holding key and angel on right impaling prone dragon with crosier, eyelets, Maastricht, Netherlands, 1403–1449, found in Dordrecht, Netherlands. Langbroek, Netherlands, Family Van Beuningen Collection, inv. 4040 (Kunera 04525). Photograph courtesy of Family Van Beuningen Collection.

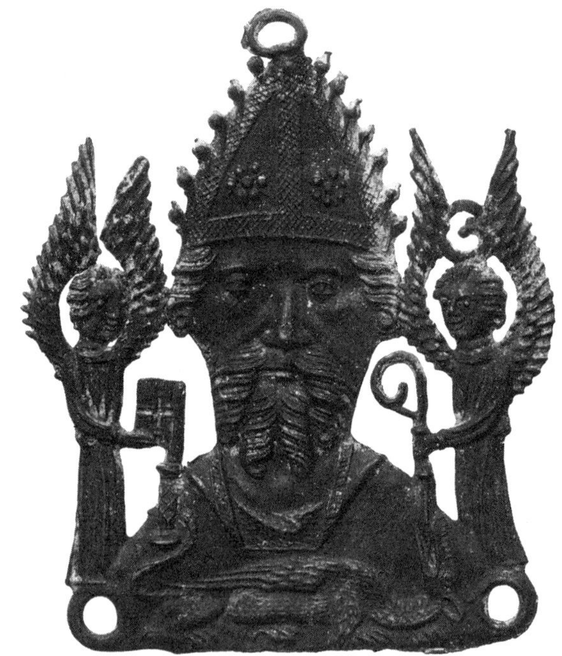

"Servatius, blessed Father, save the boy. In return I promise I will share our milk and cheese with the priest of this place as though he were of our kin, and I will do this with a humble heart, dear Father."

She stands now beside the shiny, newly painted altarpiece. Some of the saints look away, beyond her to the heavens perhaps. But others meet her eye with gazes alive with compassion and love. Servatius belongs here, with them, a host to stand behind his already strong blessings and power.

Holding the badge before her, she kneels, repeating her prayers. When she stands again, she examines closely the side and back of the new altar painting and its frame. Yes, just as her grandson told her, there is a place, almost imperceptible unless one looks closely, where the frame and board have begun to come apart. Carefully she pries it open and slips the Servatius amulet in the flat space between, as far as it can go. Carefully she smooths the pieces together, concealing the split. Retreating to the nave again, she kneels one last time to pray.

"Bless us, dear Father Servatius, with your protection, for we have great need of it. We beg you, dear Father, save the child."

Medieval religious badges featuring an image indelibly linked to a specific religious holy site compose, roughly speaking, about 75 percent of the surviving badges. Manufactured and sold at those holy sites, these badges may have performed any of the functions discussed in the previous chapter. A religious badge could have been an amulet; it could have been a visible sign of a relationship between the saint whose holy site the badge referenced and the wearer. It might also have functioned as a political device, both in the metaphorical sense that the wearer identified herself or himself as a member of the saint's household and in the practical sense that great lords on pilgrimage to their favored holy site might distribute religious badges from that site to members of their household, thus transforming the religious badge into a kind of livery. It might seem far-fetched to think of religious badges as having functioned at times as compulsory devices, yet as we saw previously in Chapter 4, the practice of penitential pilgrimage might have transformed an ordinary religious badge into something like a compulsory device. Above all, encompassing some or all the previous functions, the badge indexed and broadcast its bearer's claim to religious piety.[1]

The phenomena of the mass manufacture and use of religious badges in the Middle Ages was bound up inextricably with one of the most important medieval expressions of popular piety: pilgrimage.[2] Yet pilgrimage and religious badges did not emerge at the same time. Rather, pilgrimage was already an old and venerable practice when the surviving sources show the first glimpses of religious badges being sold at pilgrimage sites in the late twelfth century. Nor are badges made of the cheap metal, pewter, the only objects associated with pilgrimage. Over the three hundred years in which badge use flourished, religious badges were but one kind of object associated with pilgrimage and piety. Expensive religious badges were manufactured out of precious materials, such as silver and gold. Although few survive, late medieval paintings sometimes show elites wearing a single, costly religious badge on their hats. Many members of the Hapsburg dynasty, for example, were shown in portraits wearing badges of Saint Mary of Hal (Brabant) (see plate 10 for an example of a hat badge).

At the other end of the cost spectrum were a plethora of simple, badge-like objects that were imbued with salvific power and that never or rarely survived: simple strips of painted leather or parchment that are sometimes called scrips; cloth; painted paper; pipe clay; papier-mâché; and even ingestibles such as bread dough, cheese, dirt, and water.[3] Rare examples of scrip, cloth, and paper badges survive in a few manuscripts, such as the embroidery and paper Vera icon in the manuscript Paris, Bibliothèque de l'Arsenal MS 1176 rés (plate 5).[4]

The portability of religious badges means that they can be considered in the context of another category of late medieval objects: distinctive, small, mass-produced, cheap objects, often made of pewter, that were widely available for private devotional use in domestic spaces. Examples include small foldable reliquaries and altars; hollow-cast or flat-cast tiny statues that can be base mounted; and noisemakers, such as rattles, whistles, and bells, that were an integral part of the pilgrimage soundscape.[5] These objects testify to an increase of devotional interactions outside of clerically controlled spaces that was a key component of the rise in late medieval popular piety.[6] The small, carved oak plank with Holy Blood badges from Wilsnack and Blomberg, Germany, affixed (see figure 2.1) participated in this trend, being a small, portable, handmade assemblage that appears to have been designed for private devotional use.

Sanctity was intensely localized in the Middle Ages. It flourished in specific holy sites and places whose number and density increased over the course of the High and late Middle Ages. Pilgrimage brought ever-increasing numbers of people to these sites. In turn, badges and other small objects rendered the holy site's sanctity mobile, so that it could be brought back with the pilgrim and in turn sanctify private spaces.[7]

Pilgrimage in the early and High Middle Ages was characterized by long-distance travel, in which elites traveled quite far to visit one of a few holy sites (the later Middle Ages saw a rise in local and regional pilgrimage, as will be discussed later in this chapter). Fundamental for the sanctity of any holy site was the belief that the patron saint was a tangible presence at the site. The majority of the early holy sites were tomb shrines where the remains of the saint were buried. These underwrote the most ancient form of pilgrimage, to pray in the presence of the earthly remains of the holy person. Saint Peter is buried under the great cathedral of his name in Rome. Saint James's shrine at Santiago de Compostela was believed to hold his remains. The tomb of Saint Servatius, who was historically a fourth-century bishop in what was then a remote outpost of the Roman Empire, around Maastricht in Belgium, was interred in the Basilica of Saint Servatius in Maastricht; the remains of Saint Martin of Tours were entombed at the Marmoutier Abbey just outside of Tours, France. These venerable sites of sanctity remained significant pilgrimage sites throughout the Middle Ages; early on, the greatest of them developed unique, distinctive badge images.

Compostela, Spain: The Shrine of Saint James

We start with a little-remarked-upon passage from one of the most famous stories of thirteenth-century medieval German literature. A noble youth, abducted by seafarers and then abandoned by them on a foreign shore, makes his way through a forest and at length finds a road, where he sits, crying, until two people appear. The youth is in luck; they are not highwaymen or ruffians who approach. Rather, their attire proclaims them to be men of God, pilgrims, to be precise, wearing the scallop-shell badge of Saint James on their garments: "Meanwhile, as he sat there and lamented, as I have said, he caught sight of two old pilgrims approaching in the distance. They were of godly aspect, advanced in days and years, hairy and bearded, as God's true children and pilgrims often are. Those wayfarers wore cloaks of linen and such other clothing as is appropriate to pilgrims, and on the outside of their clothes there were sewn-on sea-shells and many other badges [Hatto: tokens] from distant lands. Each bore a staff in his hand."[8] A brief moment in the first great adventure of the life of the protagonist, Tristan, which will bring him to the

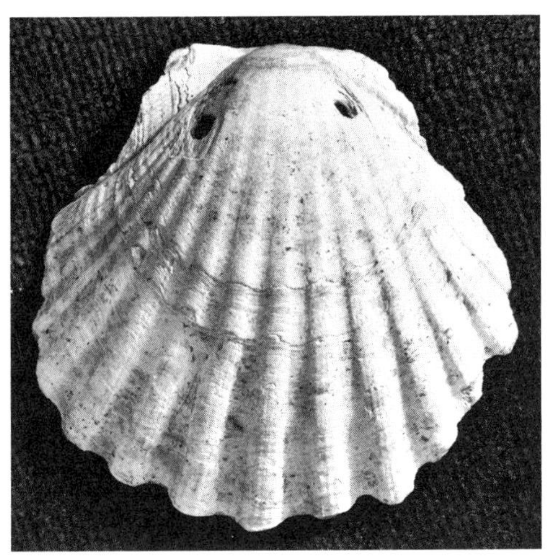

Figure 5.2. Scallop shell, attribute of Saint James the Great, holes, Santiago de Compostela, Spain, 1000–1599, found in Lund, Sweden, 53–54 × 55 mm. Lund, Kulturen, inv. KM 69 023:263a (Kunera 04000). Photograph and permission from Kulturen.

court of his uncle, King Mark, the episode prefigures Tristan's fate as a noble wanderer, destined to seek but never to arrive in safe haven, his formidable talents and virtues as a lord steered instead to sustaining a great yet forbidden love. The episode appears in this book because the description of the pilgrims suggests that their customary attire was widely familiar by the time *Tristan* was written around 1210. By the first decade of the thirteenth century, a German writer such as Gottfried could count on his audience recognizing the seashell badge, which referred, then as now, to the shrine to Saint James the Greater in Santiago de Compostela, Spain, and which is probably the most famous pilgrim badge in the western world.[9]

Often the badge was a real seashell, collected perhaps on the Atlantic beaches surrounding Compostela and drilled with tiny holes so that it could be affixed to a hat or cloak as seen in figure 5.2, which was found in Lund, Sweden.

Saint James shell badges turn up in many contexts. They have been found in medieval graves, an interesting context because Christians did not follow the practice of placing goods in the grave or coffin of the deceased.[10] These finds suggest that the Saint James shell badges were not perceived as grave goods per se; rather, the deceased was being buried as a pilgrim.[11]

The scallop-shell shape of the Saint James badge is its distinguishing feature. Besides using actual shells, these badges were also manufactured out of lead-tin alloy and other materials such as jet, a minor gemstone.[12] Over time new design elements were used to embellish the badge, for example, an image of Saint James in pilgrim's garb superimposed on the familiar scallop shell (figure 5.3); only in the late Middle Ages do badges appear featuring only Saint James (figure 5.4).

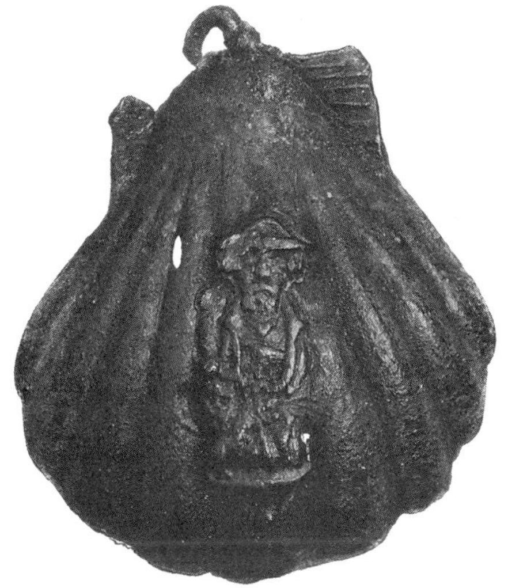

Figure 5.3. Pewter badge, scallop shell with superimposed figure of Saint James the Great, pendant, Santiago de Compostela, Spain, 1450–1499, found in Arnemuiden, Netherlands, 31 × 27 mm. Langbroek, Netherlands, Family Van Beuningen Collection, inv. 4504 (Kunera 16422). Photograph courtesy of Family Van Beuningen Collection.

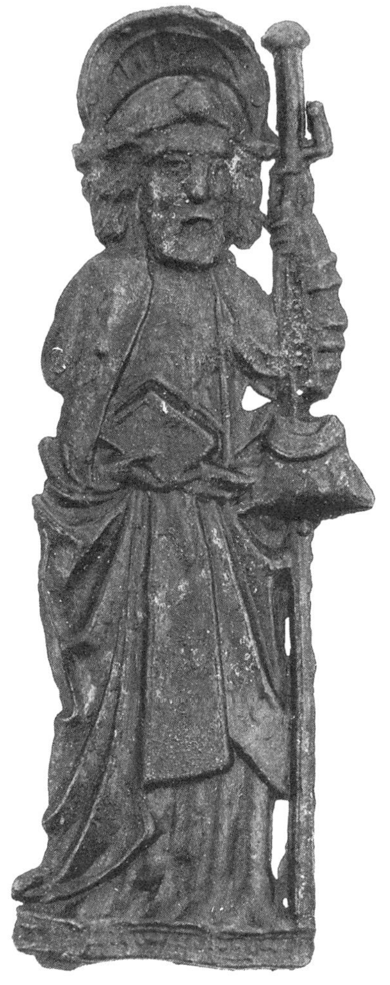

Figure 5.4. Pewter badge, Saint James the Great as a pilgrim holding book, staff, and purse, eyelet on back, Santiago de Compostela, Spain, 1400–1499, found in Vlissingen, Netherlands, 55 × 18 mm. Langbroek, Netherlands, Family Van Beuningen Collection, inv. 3691 (Kunera 06259). Photograph courtesy of Family Van Beuningen Collection.

Saint James badges appear across the entire period studied in this book. Recognizable across vast expanses of time and space, the seashell was an iconic design that spoke (and still speaks) to its origins unmistakably.

The Badges of Rocamadour

During the early and High Middle Ages, powerful elites became saints themselves. These included, for example, the three kings, or three wise men (Magi)—Balthasar, Caspar, and Melchior—who feature prominently in the New Testament story of Jesus's birth and whose traditional resting place since the twelfth century has been Cologne Cathedral. Olaf II Haraldsson (c. 995–1030) of Norway was canonized as Saint Olaf in 1031. Bishops, who in the early and High Middle Ages are best thought of as lords or princes of the Church, were often canonized, as we have seen. Many canonized bishops lived during the turbulent early centuries of European Christianization and had also acted as secular defenders of their embattled cities (Saint Servatius in Maastricht, Saint Martin in Tours). Even New Testament divinities, such as the Blessed Virgin Mary, Christ, and the apostles, though hardly elites in the world of the New Testament, were represented at their sites as elites, that is to say, as lordly or regal beings, in keeping with the majesty of their spiritual power.

The badges from Rocamadour, a city in southwestern France, which feature the Blessed Virgin Mary holding her son on her lap, provide a good example of this imagery of majesty and power in an early pilgrim badge. At first, Rocamadour appears to have been a tomb shrine site, where the hermit, Saint Amadour, was believed to be buried, as is implied by the place name Amadour's rock. In the twelfth century, this veneration seems to have merged into a new kind of holy site, one where a miraculous, wonder-working image or statue (nearly always associated with the Blessed Virgin Mary or with Christ) was venerated. At Rocamadour, monks from the Benedictine monastery of Tulle managed a wonder-working statue of the Blessed Virgin Mary, a representation of which is also found on the distinctive Rocamadour badge, the one in figure 5.5 having been recovered from Schleswig in northern Germany.

On an almond-shaped, lead-tin alloy object that is about seven-by-five centimeters in size, with a ribbon of lettering running around the edge and from which protrude six small eyelets to sew the object to clothing, sits a powerful, lordly woman of regal bearing. Crowned, wearing sumptuous garments, and seated on a throne, the woman holds in her right hand a scepter, an ancient sign of power, while on her left knee she also holds a boy prince, who appears to be grasping the scepter as well. (It is impossible to tell from the photograph alone whether the square hole at the center of the badge is deliberate or reflects damage.) Both figures level their gaze at the viewer. This lady is, of course, the most powerful woman of the celestial realm: the Blessed Virgin Mary, Mother of God and Queen of Heaven, bearing on her knee the Christ Child. A Latin inscription running around the edge confirms the identification: SIGILLVM:BEATE MARIE:DE ROCAMADOR (the Seal of the Blessed Mary of Rocamadour). Sitting in majesty, the Blessed Virgin Mary's posture and attitude are typical of Romanesque statues of the Virgin Mary, which do not emphasize her sweetness or youth but rather her overawing force and majesty.[13] Note that the object does not call itself a badge (*signa* in Latin) but rather a seal (*sigillum* in Latin), a form of authentication that had become widespread among elites by the eleventh century. Its form imitates that of a seal as well. In the twelfth century, seals were not thought to represent their absent owner but rather were understood to be an extension of her or him.[14] The seal's owner thus traveled and was present wherever the seal is seen. The pact that the medieval pilgrim made with this great lady is a powerful one indeed.

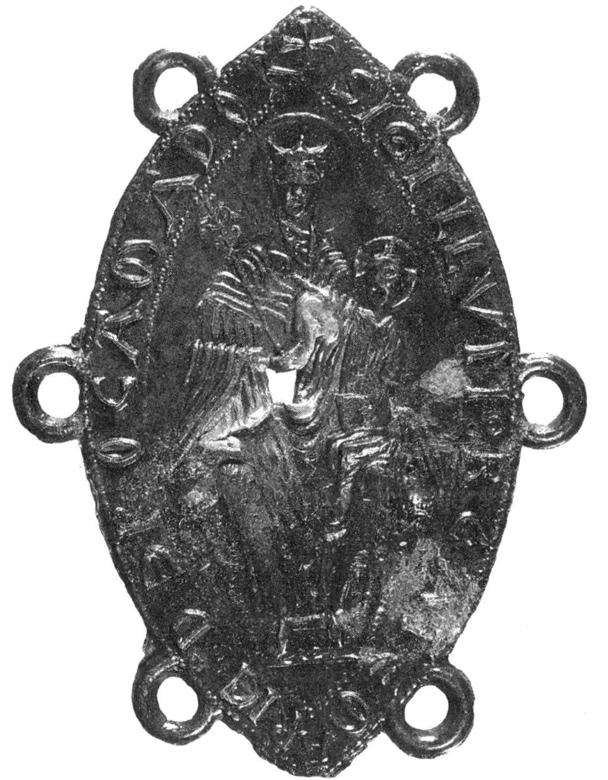

Figure 5.5. Pewter badge, Blessed Virgin Mary enthroned and holding scepter with Christ Child on her left knee, eyelets, Rocamadour, France, 1270–1299, found in Schleswig, Germany, 74 × 55.5 × 1.5 mm. Schleswig, Schleswig-Holsteinisches Landesmuseum, inv. KSD 375 325 (Kunera 04244). Photograph and permission from Schleswig-Holsteinisches Landesmuseum.

Saint Amadour and other saints were also venerated by pilgrims at Rocamadour, but the Marian devotion with its wonder-working statue quickly surpassed or, perhaps better said, engulfed them, pulling them into the Virgin Mary's orbit. The new holy site dedicated to the Virgin Mary intensified the already-existing sanctity of Rocamadour.

The evidence of twelfth-century pilgrim badge production introduced in Chapter 1 from Guernes de Pont-Saint-Maxence's *Life of St. Thomas of Becket* mentioned "Rocamadour lead figures of the Virgin."[15] The kind of badge to which Guernes refers probably looked much like the Rocamadour badge in figure 5.5, which is from the same period. Rocamadour badges of this design have been found in excavations in Denmark, Norway, and northern German cities, such as Schleswig, which is some 1,500 transalpine kilometers distant. Over time, new badge designs also appeared at Rocamadour. For example, in the fifteenth century, double-sided badges were sold that had an image of the Blessed Virgin Mary on one side and either Saint Amadour or Saint Veronica (also revered at Rocamadour) on the other. Nevertheless, the iconic almond-shaped badge with the seated Virgin Mary and the Christ Child appeared throughout the entire medieval period. The stability of the image defied or perhaps blissfully ignored artistic changes in style that influenced depictions of the Virgin Mary from the thirteenth century onward. An expression of new artistic trends in the twelfth century, by the fifteenth century, the Rocamadour badge with the enthroned Queen of Heaven was a venerable, old-fashioned, even conservative image that proclaimed tradition.

The Ampullae of Canterbury

The rapid canonization and immense popular veneration of Saint Thomas Becket demonstrated the dynamism of the medieval landscape of sanctity, as many new holy sites emerged over time and space.[16] One of the greatest pilgrimage sites of the thirteenth and fourteenth centuries was the tomb of the martyred Saint Thomas of Becket, archbishop of Canterbury, who was assassinated in December 1170 by knights loyal to his erstwhile friend and overlord King Henry II, and deified by Pope Alexander III a little more than two years later, in 1173.[17] The veneration of Saint Thomas followed two of the oldest and most venerable models for sainthood: Thomas was a bishop, and his remains were buried in the cathedral of his bishopric.

Yet the veneration of Saint Thomas was new and its rise rapid. When Guernes wrote of the French life of Saint Thomas, close to the time of the saint's death, he knew people who had known Becket and may even have met the saint himself. Guernes put the new saint within the context of older, established pilgrimage sites. Guernes argued, in effect, that the fervor of the pilgrims and miracles wrought at Canterbury had catapulted Saint Thomas's site and his martyrdom, though very new, into a similar status of venerability and holiness as enjoyed by older holy sites. (If Henry II at first rued having played into the scripted roles of the age-old, Christian story of martyrdom, which cast him as the godless villain and his old friend and adversary Thomas Becket as a saint, his family nonetheless quickly embraced and furthered Becket's veneration.)

From its inception, zealously promoted by Saint Thomas's clerical contemporaries such as Guernes, the shrine of Saint Thomas at Canterbury drew crowds of pilgrims, counted many miracles, and became one of the wealthiest pilgrimage sites in Europe. This state of affairs lasted into the 1530s when, as part of the English Reformation, reformers removed and destroyed Saint Thomas's remains and his shrine, a fate suffered by the other holy places and charismatic centers in England.

Over seven hundred Saint Thomas Becket badges survive (figure 5.6). They have been found throughout northwestern Christendom, concentrated in England and those territories directly across the channel from the island (the Netherlands, Belgium, and northern France).[18] Between trade and warfare, the English were everywhere in these regions for most of the High and late Middle Ages, politically controlling huge swaths of northern France dur-

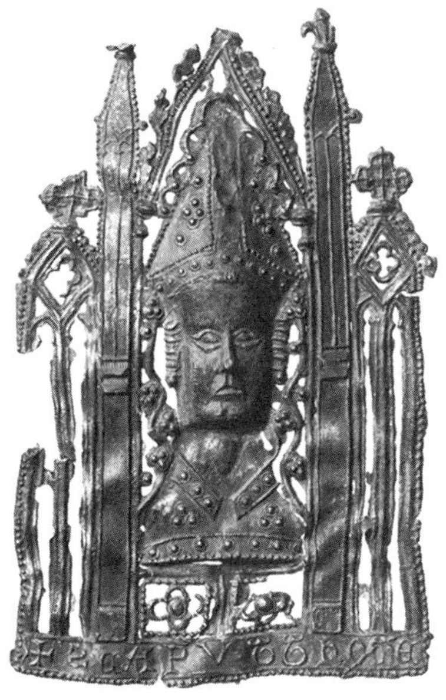

Figure 5.6. Pewter badge, head of Saint Thomas Becket wearing a bishop's miter, around his head a church-like architectural frame, inscription + S CAPVT THOME [the head of Saint Thomas], pin, origin unknown, date unknown, found in London, 80 × 51 mm. London, Museum of London, inv. 86.202/3. Photograph and permission from © Museum of London.

ing the Hundred Years' War. Most Saint Thomas badges show the bust of the saint wearing the miter.

As was discussed in Chapter 3 (see also plate 6a), a special kind of badge was produced for Saint Thomas's holy site, a small lead-tin alloy flask called an ampulla, or phial, that when pinched shut could hold a few drops of liquid. The Becket ampulla in figure 5.7 is one of the most artistically arresting to survive and illustrates well the potential of a badge to become a mobile sculpture. The figures on the front of the phial are three-dimensional. They press outward through space toward the viewer, paused in the last seconds of Becket's earthly life, the saint gazing solemnly at the viewer while the assassins behind him raise their swords to strike their deadly blows. Showing this moment in Becket's martyrdom is not unusual on Becket ampullae. It enjoins the viewer to remember and continue the narrative both backward and forward in time: how did it come to this moment and what will follow from it? What makes the ampulla stand apart is the saint's frontal gaze (note that the assassins look down or to the side), which unites the authority of the living bishop—calm, although he is seconds from a violent death—and of the sainted man, whose power lives forever.

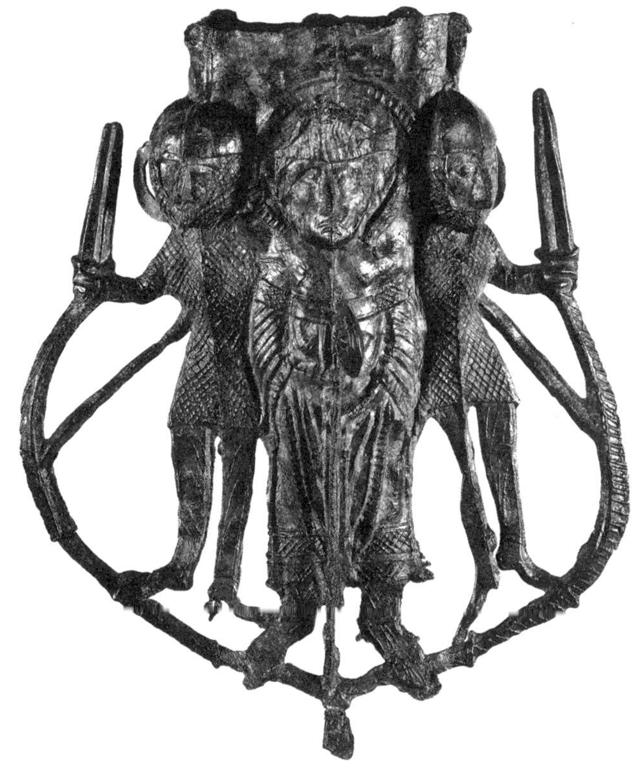

Figure 5.7. Pewter ampulla, knights assassinate Saint Thomas Becket, on back (not shown) pointed oval panel with the martyrdom, inscribed + OPTIM EGROR MEDIC FIT TOMA BONOR [Thomas is the best doctor for the worthy sick], pendant, made in England, 1170–1200, 100 × 87 × 28 mm. London, British Museum. Photograph and permission from © The Trustees of the British Museum.

Ampullae associated with the Canterbury shrine for Saint Thomas are mentioned by Guernes in his biography: "Now God has given St. Thomas this phial, which is loved and honoured all over the world, to save souls; in water and in phials he has the martyr's blood taken all over the world, to cure the sick. It is doubly honoured, for health and as a sign."[19] Guernes specifically mentions the liquid and its divine properties. Water from the holy site, poured into a holy container, and blessed in some fashion by the priests at the site (whether through prayer, or by touching the object to the shrine, or both) was transformed into a kind of divinely charged object.

Late Medieval Pilgrimage

The saints and divinities shown on religious badges appeared as members of a divine elite who used the copious material, social, spiritual, and symbolic resources at their disposal to smite the wicked, fend off demons, convert heathens, and better the lot of pious Christians, whether rich or poor, well connected or orphaned, whole or infirm, in this world and the next. Elites remained in the pantheon of powerful divinities to whom the needy of all stations could appeal for help, but over time new saints, many of them women, and new kinds of holy sites joined them. The growing number of late medieval holy sites was fueled by these new forms of venerated sanctity. The Blessed Virgin Mary at Rocamadour is an example of a holy site that grew up around a wonder-working image, more of which emerged in the late Middle Ages. There came into being so-called holy place shrines and sites, which possessed no physical remains of a saint at all, neither tomb, relics, nor image. Rather, a specific locale relied on legends asserting the saint's patronage of that place. Most of these sites did not produce and sell badges (although Rocamadour is an exception).

Relic sites are critically important for any discussion of religious badges.[20] Relics are usually pieces or body parts of a holy person, but special kinds of relics were associated with Jerusalem, the site of Christ's crucifixion and resurrection and his tomb. By the late Middle Ages, travel to Jerusalem was expensive, arduous, and dangerous. Spiritual travelers who survived the journey brought back relics such as earth relics, bits of stone or earth made holy by Christ having trodden on them.[21] They also returned with what are called metric or measurement relics. These are measurements of the True Cross, of Christ's body, or of the instruments of torture used during Christ's crucifixion, or of the distances between holy places in Jerusalem. These metric relics could then be remapped onto local places (see the cloister wall at Bebenhausen in Germany), where they functioned primarily to allow all those who could not travel to Jerusalem to nevertheless undertake and experience a pilgrimage virtually.[22]

The number of relic sites increased in the High and late Middle Ages. The shrine of the Magi in Cologne is a relic site, established in 1164 when the German emperor Frederick Barbarossa caused the relics of the Three Kings to be brought to Cologne from Milan (see figure 4.2). Some of the most important late medieval holy sites were associated with so-called contact relics, articles, such as a piece of clothing, that had been in contact with the body of a saint or divinity.

Examples of contact relics included the tunic worn by the Blessed Virgin Mary, revered at both Aachen and Chartres, and the veil of Veronica revered at Rome, as was briefly discussed in Chapter 2. The veil of Veronica (Latin *sudarium*) was a piece of cloth bearing an image of Christ's face purportedly not made by human hands. According to the legend, a widow, Veronica, encountered Jesus bearing the cross on the Via Dolorosa in Jerusalem on His way to the site of His crucifixion.[23] Using her veil to wipe the blood and sweat from His face, she found that His image had been imprinted on it. The presence of the relic in Rome is first mentioned in the 1190s. In 1207, Pope Innocent III encouraged its veneration by having it publicly paraded and displayed and by granting indulgences to those praying to it.[24]

Images of the Holy Face as it appeared on the Vera icon were widespread in the late Middle Ages; one need not have been on pilgrimages to Rome to know or use the images. As plates 3 and 5 suggest, the Vera icon was created in many modalities and materials, and these included pewter badges such as the one in figure 5.8, which was found in Nieuwlande in the Netherlands.

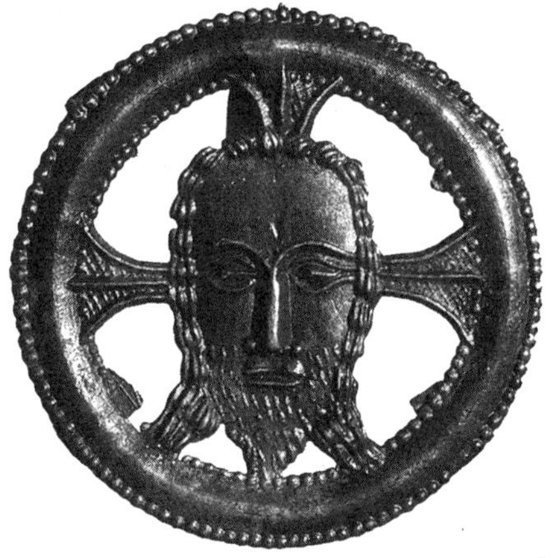

Figure 5.8. Pewter badge, Vera icon or Holy Face with nimbus in round frame with double pearl border, pin, origin unknown, 1400–1449, found in Nieuwlande, Netherlands, 31 mm (diameter). Langbroek, Netherlands, Family Van Beuningen Collection, inv. 1716 (Kunera 00074). Photograph courtesy of Family Van Beuningen Collection.

Relics possessed a charisma of their own. In the late Middle Ages, the sites where they were revered developed special forms of veneration, called in German *Heiligtumsweisung*, or the showing of the relic, that broadcast its power. In these religious ceremonies that ordinarily took place no more than once a year, and often only every seven to ten years, the holy relic would be removed from the treasury where it was stored and shown or revealed to the gathered masses. Medieval understandings of the divine power transmitted by the relic and of the mobility of relics are especially relevant to religious badges because, as we shall see in the discussion of the badges from Aachen, badges were absorbed into the same conceptual frameworks, functioning at times and in their own way as minor relics, or perhaps better said, as relic-like objects themselves.

By the second half of the fifteenth century, the landscape of holy sites in Europe had grown crowded as new sites emerged alongside old ones.[25] While long-distance pilgrimage did not cease, over the course of the fourteenth and fifteenth centuries pilgrims increasingly directed their devotions to the shrines of regional and local saints, as the increasing geographical density of holy sites made pilgrimage accessible to people from all walks of life.[26] There was an explosion in medium-distance and short-distance pilgrimage in the late Middle Ages, and those who undertook these pilgrimage journeys must have represented a large proportion of those who bought and used the millions of religious badges manufactured and sold during the late Middle Ages.

It is possible to understand with some detail the changing nature of late medieval pilgrimage and the reasons ordinary people undertook it because a fair amount of textual evidence about various kinds of such pilgrimages has survived. Yet the textual evidence only occasionally mentions badges. To put it another way, it is as though we have two parallel streams of evidence. One stream consists of the surviving badges and of images of pilgrims wearing badges, demonstrating that badges were mass-produced, ubiquitous, and legible expressions of piety; the other stream consists of a wide variety of texts, including but not limited to legal documents, miracle books, and late medieval wills, that talk in some fashion about pilgrimage. These two streams of evidence only rarely intersect. The surviving image-based sources are mute as to who undertook pilgrimage and why; the text-based sources are (largely) mute on the topic of badges. Yet these two streams of evidence must have originated from a single stream of pious practice and belief, in which the presence and use of badges was commonplace. Considering them together allows a fuller picture of late medieval pilgrimage to emerge.

Exploring late medieval textual evidence offers an opportunity to glimpse the people who undertook pilgrimage and some of their reasons for doing so. It is impossible to show that the people who will be discussed in the next pages of this book purchased badges. What can be said for certain is that they traveled to holy sites where badges were being sold and that they lived in and presumably returned to places where badges have been found that are from the sites they visited and that date to the era when their names appear in the historical record.

Who went on pilgrimage in Europe during its peak, the period between about 1350 to 1520, and why did they go?[27] Pilgrimage was an uncertain undertaking, and so wills were sometimes made before setting out. In the last decades of the 1300s, two inhabitants of Hamburg from different social strata wrote (or had written) wills using similar, formulaic language to record that they undertook journeys to holy places "to comfort [their] soul[s]."[28] Johann Vleteman was a burgher and presumably well-to-do, while Arnold, who has no last name, was identified as a stone breaker (a mason perhaps), someone who in modern terms worked in a quarry or in construction, in any case in one of the trades feeding the construction of stone building in northern Europe's urban centers in the fourteenth and fifteenth centuries.

There were many reasons to undertake pilgrimage. Pilgrims arrived at shrines to give thanks for miracles. They were keeping their side of a contract or bargain made when they prayed to a specific saint for relief and help and the saint listened and acted, for example, miraculously reviving a child who had drowned, engineering a release from jail, bringing a ship foundering in a storm to safe harbor, or lifting a debilitating physical affliction, such as blindness, deafness, crippling disability, or madness. Such reasons and more for completing a pilgrimage were compiled in the late Middle Ages by the religious authorities in charge of holy sites, who kept track of the miracle narratives performed by their saint as told to them by the arriving, grateful pilgrims.[29] The miracles and thanks recorded in these books offer a sobering view of the calamities, infirmities, and diseases with which medieval people struggled and for which divine intervention offered the only hope of relief. Badges acquired on journeys might have traveled home again as curative devices, which were believed, as we have seen, to transport the healing power of the shrine and saint; the previously discussed ampullae of holy water from Saint Thomas's shrine in Canterbury are but one example of this belief. Two things are important to keep in mind: first, that the miracles did not have to happen at the shrine; and second, that the pilgrimage fulfilled a contract between the saint and the supplicant-pilgrim. The supplicant prayed to the saint for relief, promising to undertake the difficult and costly journey of pilgrimage to the saint's holy site if the relief was granted; the saint granted the relief, and the supplicant kept her or his promise.

In the late Middle Ages, the increase in pilgrimage also intersected with the growth of indulgences.[30] Indulgences were part of what might be called the "sin economy." Medieval Christians expected to be punished for their sins, usually after death in Purgatory, before going to Heaven. The sinner's debts are these purgatorial punishments, measured in units of time spent in Purgatory. In this life one could accrue credits, that is, time excused from Purgatory, and such credits were indulgences—in late medieval sources usually called something like a remission or a blessing, or in Middle English, a pardon. Civic acts, such as charitable giving or hospital building, and religious acts, such as prayer or pilgrimages, were rewarded with indulgences, which thus shortened the sinner's time of suffering in Purgatory. (Recall the altarpieces in plate 1 and figure 1.4, in which the good burghers of Alkmaar are undertaking acts of charity by caring for pilgrims.) By the late Middle Ages, indulgences could in essence be purchased, with commissaries collecting alms in return for an indulgence or secular lords and various ecclesiastical institutions, with the permission of the Church, using the sale of indulgences to fund expensive projects.

Theologians might have distinguished between the sinner's guilt before God (Latin *culpa*) and punishment for sin (Latin *pena*), insisting that indulgences remit penance only, while for *culpa*, contrition and confession followed by absolution were absolutely necessary. But it would appear that many ordinary Christians largely ignored what might have seemed to many of them a technical or formal distinction. Indulgences were widely believed to expiate one's guilt before God, and the act of pilgrimage and the prayers said along the way allowed the pilgrim to accumulate spiritual credit, whether for oneself or for another. In other words, not only could indulgences be acquired for someone other than the person earning (or purchasing) them; pilgrimage, too, could be undertaken by a representative, its spiritual benefits being understood to be transferable to the sponsor.

The late medieval growth of pilgrimages and rise of indulgences went hand in hand. Holy sites appealed to the papacy for the privilege of selling indulgences, usually for the specific holy day or set of holy days of their patron saint or holy object, such as a contact relic. The ability to acquire an indulgence increased the spiritual power of the site and attracted more pilgrims. New holy sites emerged along established pilgrim routes. Responding to the ever-rising numbers of pilgrims, regionally proximate holy sites new and old began coordinating their celebrations and venerations, especially around the showing of relics that happened only once every decade or so, so that all the showings took place around the same time (but not overlapping!) in the same year. These anniversary years in turn often received the privilege of granting special indulgences. Pilgrimage had become accessible and desirable to many, many people.

Pilgrimage was good work that could be performed vicariously; as was mentioned above, the indulgences could be received on behalf of another. (Something like this is what is imagined in the story that opens this chapter; the son has brought back a relic-like badge for his mother.) It became common for testators to leave money for others to undertake pilgrimage on the testator's behalf. A spectacular example of this practice comes from the will of Queen Margaret of Denmark from 1410 (she died in 1412).[31] Two Danish abbots and their convents agreed to raise 3,000 Lübeck marks over two years and in that time to send no less than eighty-five pilgrims, often in groups of three, to specific named holy sites (virtually every pilgrimage site near and far) sometimes with specific itineraries and specific instructions for the prayers and masses to be said, all done on the queen's behalf. That is to say, the salvific force of these good works accrued primarily to her.

Ordinary wills reflected similar practices, though on nowhere near so grand a scale, of leaving a bequest for a pilgrimage to be carried out by an unnamed person. In a 1346 will from the northern German city of Lübeck, for example, Tale, widow of master Erpo, required that her three best overgarments, with linings, be sold and the proceeds spent on a pilgrimage to Aachen.[32] The 1352 will of Thomas de Ware, a London fishmonger, specified that someone be found to go on pilgrimage in his name to Saint James (i.e., Compostela) on funds to be raised by the sale of his goods on a ship "if she shall come safely to port, otherwise said bequest to be null and void."[33] In other cases, the testators name specific people, usually kin, to undertake pilgrimage on their behalf. In 1360, one Heinrich Sasse of Hamburg gives his niece, Beke, "forty marks of ready money and all his greater and lesser household goods in consideration of the eleven years she has served him" and stipulates as well that "the aforesaid Beke for the salvation of my soul shall make two pilgrimages, one to Trier and the other to Aachen. And my executors shall give her sufficient of my money for her expenses."[34] Figure 5.9 is an example of a religious badge from Trier that dates from the same period as Beke's pilgrimage. The pilgrimage sites of Trier and Aachen are not too far from Hamburg (about six hundred and five hundred kilometers distant, respectively), and so a journey there falls within the definition of regional pilgrimage.

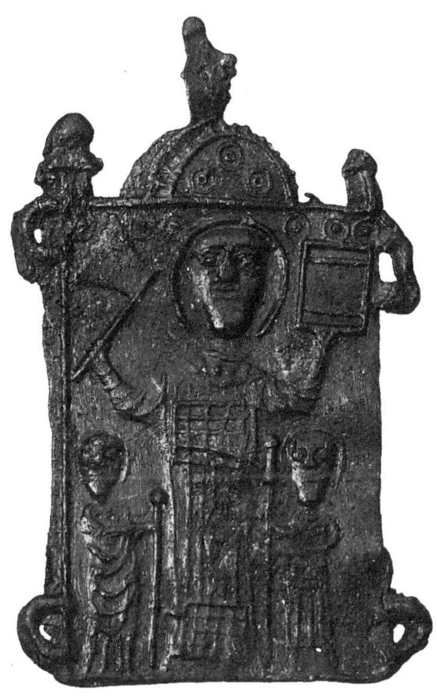

Figure 5.9. Pewter badge, Saint Matthew of Trier with axe, book, flanked by two figures with staffs, eyelets, Trier, Germany, 1325–1374, found in Dordrecht, Netherlands, 44 × 28 mm. Langbroek, Netherlands, Family Van Beuningen Collection, inv. 4115 (Kunera 06316). Photograph courtesy of Family Van Beuningen Collection.

It may have been understood that Beke's pilgrimages to Trier and Aachen on Heinrich Sasse's behalf were a precondition to inheriting. Many surviving late medieval wills from the same region require an heir to undertake a pilgrimage before inheriting, suggesting that inheritance as well can participate in the late medieval practices of compulsory pilgrimages discussed in Chapter 4. In a 1332 will, again from Lübeck, Meynekin van Vlenseborg (Flensborg, a northern German city on the border of Denmark) sent his son Adam to Saint Peter's in Rome "before he inherits," while his younger son is to go to Rocamadour "if he is able."[35] Meynekin's sons' journeys are long-distance pilgrimages, which, as has been said before, continued throughout the High and late Middle Ages. Why did Meynekin lay a lighter burden on his younger son? It is tempting to speculate that at the time the will was written, the younger son might not have been old enough or physically strong enough to be expected to survive the hardships of medieval travel. Whatever the case, such written evidence, though determined by the formal and legal requirements of the instrument in which it has come down to us, allows a small glimpse into the imbrication of religious and legal life for city dwellers of some means in late medieval German-speaking lands.

Meynekin's will seems to have created an "exit strategy" for the younger son, but none for Adam, the older. His journey to Rome was a precondition of inheritance, and one of the many distinctive badges from there might also

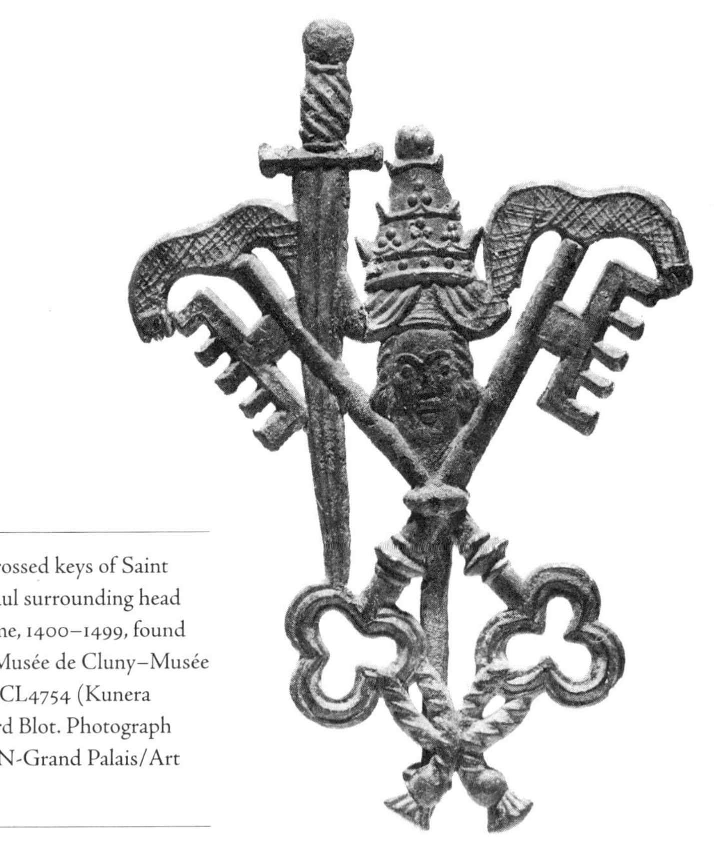

Figure 5.10. Pewter badge, crossed keys of Saint Peter with sword of Saint Paul surrounding head wearing papal tiara, pin, Rome, 1400–1499, found in Paris, 51 × 37 mm. Paris, Musée de Cluny–Musée national du Moyen Âge, inv. CL4754 (Kunera 01342). Photographer: Gérard Blot. Photograph and permission from © RMN-Grand Palais/Art Resource, New York.

have traveled with him back to Hamburg. A pilgrim in Rome in the 1330s would have had a choice of badges, each drawing on a different aspect of the core iconography that united them as belonging to Rome, among them, Saint Peter and Saint Paul (see discussion and figure 5.11 below), the Vera icon, and the distinctive papal insignia of crossed keys, as in figure 5.10.[36]

In this badge from Rome, the papal keys and sword surround a head wearing the papal tiara. Keys and tiara belong also to the coat of arms of the Holy See, a heraldic device of the papacy that originated in the early fourteenth century. Papal key badges blur the boundary between secular and religious badges. In some cases, they were probably not religious badges but rather heraldic signs, that is to say, political devices worn by members of the papal household. After all, beyond his religious authority, the pope was an ecclesiastical prince who headed a large and powerful administration. Papal key badges have turned up primarily in Paris and elsewhere in France, key political centers and hotbeds of political controversy during the many decades of the late fourteenth century when there were two, even three, popes at the same time fighting for ascendancy.

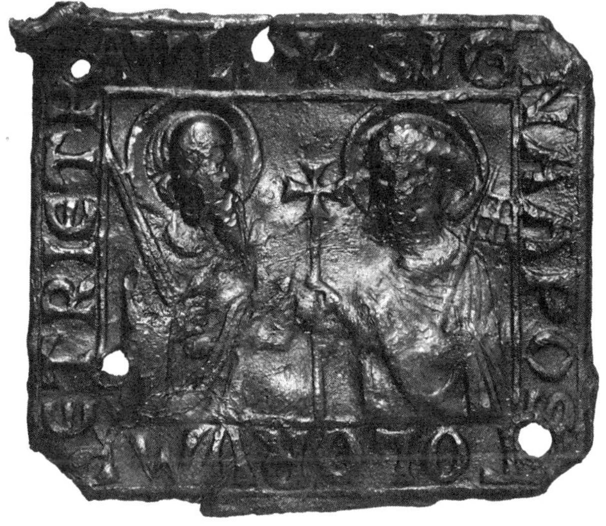

Figure 5.11. Pewter badge, rectangle with inscription enclosing Saint Peter with key and Saint Paul with sword, damaged eyelets and holes, Rome, 1250–1349, found in Dordrecht, Netherlands, 32 × 37 mm. Langbroek, Netherlands, Family Van Beuningen Collection, inv. 1907 (Kunera 00299). Photograph courtesy of Family Van Beuningen Collection.

Numerous badges from Rome show Saint Peter, recognizable because he is holding a bundle of keys, alone or with Saint Paul. There survive a number of flat, plaque-like, rectangular badges depicting these two foundational Christian figures who were both buried in Rome: Saint Peter in a tomb under the altar in the basilica bearing his name in the Vatican, and Saint Paul in a tomb above which Constantine founded the first Basilica of Saint Paul outside the walls in the fourth century. Figure 5.11 is a fine example of such a badge, which was found in Dordrecht.

The bearded, venerable saints stand side by side, Peter with his key and Paul with a sword, the instrument of his martyrdom (tradition holds he was beheaded), and between them a Maltese cross on a staff. Around the badge's rim runs a Latin text. A smaller Greek or perhaps Maltese cross in the inscription directly above the staff tells the viewer where to begin reading. (The Maltese cross is doing double duty here, because it also signifies pilgrimage and came to stand for a unit of indulgence called a careen, which is "a lent," or roughly forty days.) Two dots one over the other (a kind of colon) signal the inscription's end: + SIGNA APOSTOLORVMPETRIETPAVL: (the sign [*signa*] of the apostles Peter [*Petri*] and [*et*] Paul). Here the badge names itself, *signa*, using the Latin word meaning symbol or sign.

Side by side, these two badges from Rome have little in common with one another visually. One highlights heraldic symbols; the other the iconography of saints. Although these badges are different from one another, to those immersed in the image-based language of late medieval Catholicism, they would have been instantly recognizable as belonging to the same holy site.

Diversity and Recognition: The Badges of Aachen

The badges that pilgrims brought back from holy sites were multifunctional. Above all, when worn, they were understood to be an outward sign of the bearer's identity as a pilgrim and as a devotee of the saint depicted or alluded to on the badge. For religious badges to function, they could not be meaningful only to the person wearing them, and so their symbolism could not be esoteric or obscure.[37] Rather, for a pilgrim badge to do its work of broadcasting identity, it had to be widely and immediately intelligible. It had to draw on an already established language of visual signs, symbols, and formulas to communicate clearly, quickly, and well. While religious badges share this communicative function with secular badges, the visual language of religious badges was often more varied and complex, inviting not only instant recognition but also narrative entanglement.

Given that badges are intended to be intelligible and quickly recognizable, it would be reasonable to imagine that the badges associated with specific holy sites would have very stable designs. This is indeed the case with the Wilsnack badges (see figures 1.5, 2.1, 2.4, 3.10, and 3.20), whose three-holy-wafer design never changed. This stability may be due in part to the fact that the manufacture and sale of badges in Wilsnack were strictly controlled by the local clerical authorities. As was discussed in Chapter 3, the Wilsnack badge design is so nearly perfect that it seems impossible to improve upon or vary. Yet the extreme stability of imagery that is shown by the Wilsnack badges is the exception, not the rule. As was just discussed regarding the badges from Rome, most badges from holy sites drew on a range or set of images, symbols, and formula that were associated with the site. The design problem to be solved was a different one: how to design a badge that combined these preexisting elements in new ways while retaining the instant intelligibility and recognizability that broadcast a pilgrim badge's identity-making function. The wide variety of badges from the city of Aachen is ideal for showing how a communicatively focused design process worked. As the Aachen badges changed over time, they drew on old iconographies and introduced new ones, combining and recombining elements from the various shrines and holy sites and saints that were clustered in the city, and responding to new practices and pieties of the pilgrims themselves, all the while remaining recognizable as Aachen badges. These changing designs always indicate "Aachen," yet their complexity drew the viewer into the image, inviting her or him to decipher and decode the images and by reading them to immerse her- or himself in the divine stories and miracles to which the images allude.

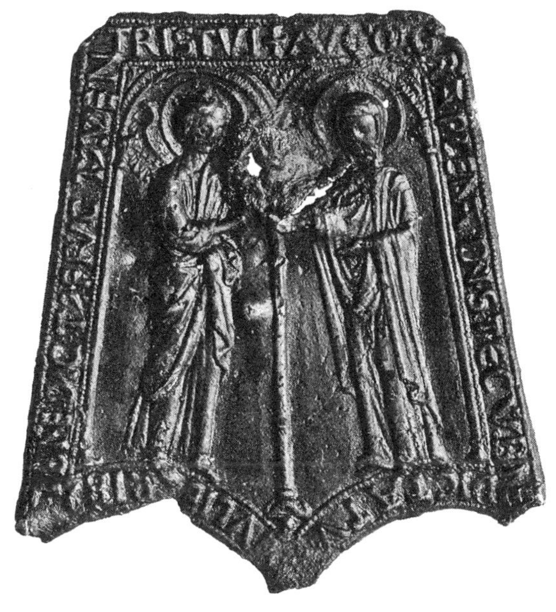

Figure 5.12. Pewter badge, in trapezoid shape and under round arcades stand Mary and the archangel Gabriel with inscription around edge AVE M GRA PLENA DNS TECV BNEDICTA TV MVLIERIS FRVCT'VENTRIS TVI, attachment unknown, Aachen, Germany, 1250–1299, found in Middleburg, Netherlands, 50 × 46 mm. Langbroek, Netherlands, Family Van Beuningen Collection, inv. 3093 (Kunera 04924). Photograph courtesy of Family Van Beuningen Collection.

By the mid-thirteenth century, the city of Aachen was one of the largest and most important pilgrimage sites in northern Europe and remained so throughout the Middle Ages.[38] Aachen boasted a venerable and ancient complex of buildings that had been expanded by Charlemagne in the 800s to serve as his residence, and included the Palatine Chapel consecrated in honor of the Virgin Mary in 805, the most important work of Carolingian architecture to survive to this day. Charlemagne's remains were buried under the chapel's floor. The Palatine Chapel was expanded and remodeled throughout the ages. There the shrine of the Blessed Virgin Mary was housed, built around 1230, which contained the four great Aachen relics, all contact relics, reputedly brought to Aachen by Charlemagne himself: a shift or tunic belonging to the Blessed Virgin Mary; the swaddling clothes or diapers of the Infant Christ; the loincloth worn by Jesus on the cross; and the cloth on which the head of John the Baptist lay after his beheading.[39]

The veneration of the Blessed Virgin Mary played the central role in Aachen pilgrimage. Early Aachen badges depicted the Annunciation. They placed the well-known, venerable image of the archangel Gabriel revealing to the Virgin Mary that she is pregnant with Christ on a badge with a distinct, trapezoid shape (figure 5.12).

Other designs that focused on the image of the seated Virgin Mary with the Christ Child on her lap appear to have largely displaced the trapezoid Annunciation badge. In the flat-cast badge shown in figure 5.13, the Virgin Mary sits enthroned in majesty, regal and powerful, holding a lily scepter in her right hand, with the Christ Child sitting or standing on her knee, on a rectangular badge featuring the squat, square twin towers that characterized the Aachen cathedral.

Similarly shaped badges featuring an edicula surmounted by a pitched, gable roof and with tiny eyelets for fastening were widely used starting in

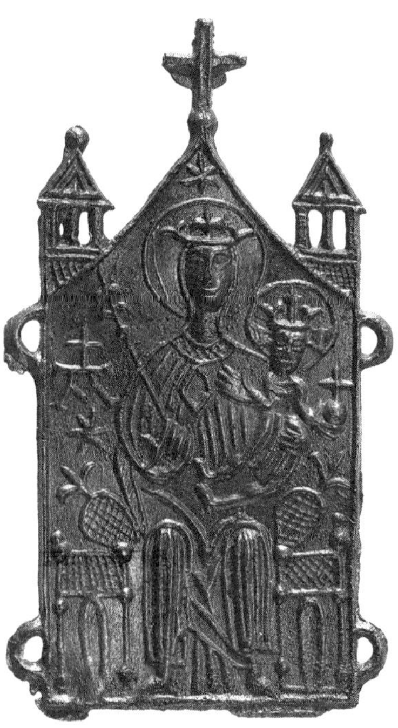

Figure 5.13. Pewter badge, in rectangular shape, Blessed Virgin Mary holding scepter with Christ Child on lap, eyelets, Aachen, Germany, 1300–1349, found in Amsterdam, 47 × 27 mm. Langbroek, Netherlands, Family Van Beuningen Collection, inv. 3385 (Kunera 06423). Photograph courtesy of Family Van Beuningen Collection.

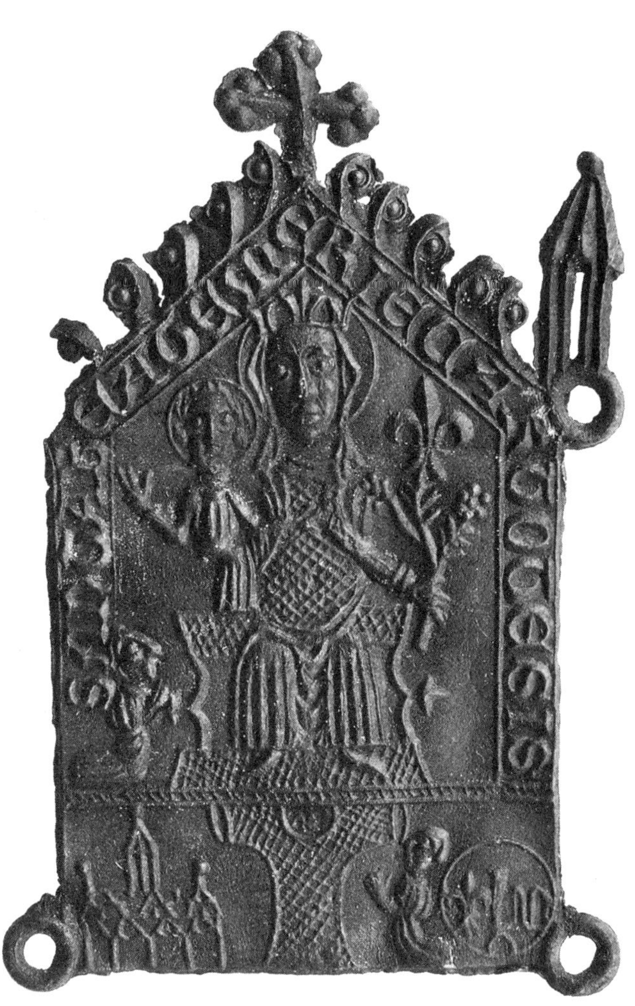

Figure 5.14. Pewter badge, Virgin Mary enthroned with Christ Child with kneeling figures and sacred tunic, enclosed in turreted architectural frame with inscription SAINTE BEATE MERIE CARTOTESIS, eyelets, Chartres, France, 1350–1399, found in Nieuwlande, Netherlands, 67 × 44 mm. Langbroek, Netherlands, Family Van Beuningen Collection, inv. 2130 (Kunera 00445). Photograph courtesy of Family Van Beuningen Collection.

the thirteenth century (see for example figure 3.11, in which the architectural features are also employed to help create an immediately recognizable image). It was also used for the holy site at Chartres where, similar to Aachen, a tunic belonging to the Virgin Mary was revered. The Marian badge from Chartres in figure 5.14 distinguishes itself from Aachen stylistically in a number of ways, and it includes a Latin inscription announcing the place from which it comes: CARTOTESIS.

For the Aachen badges, the rectangular, flat-cast shape was simple to design, to make as a mold, and to cast. Aachen plaque badges repeated their elements across a range of artistically more or less ornate designs, producing an array of badges similar to the Servatius badges discussed in Chapter 3. The Aachen badges in figures 5.15 and 5.16 portray the Virgin Mary seated on a stool throne with the Christ Child on her lap, rendered here in simple line drawings shown in descending order of craftsmanship.[40] The badge in figure 5.16, which also employs the iconic towers in its design, is a poorly made object; its figures are only schematically sketched, and it shows many casting flaws.

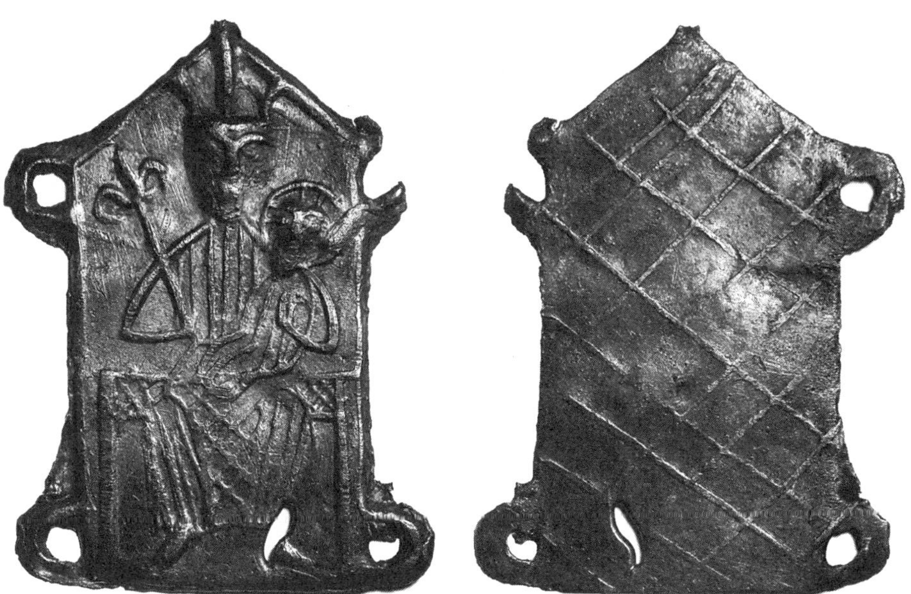

Figure 5.15. Pewter badge, Virgin Mary enthroned with Christ Child, eyelets, Aachen, Germany, 1300–1325, deposited around 1327 in a well in Stralsund, Germany. Schwerin, Germany, Archäologisches Landesmuseum Mecklenburg-Vorpommern, inv. ALM 2007/100, 447. Photograph courtesy of photographer: Dr. Jörg Ansorge, Horst, Germany.

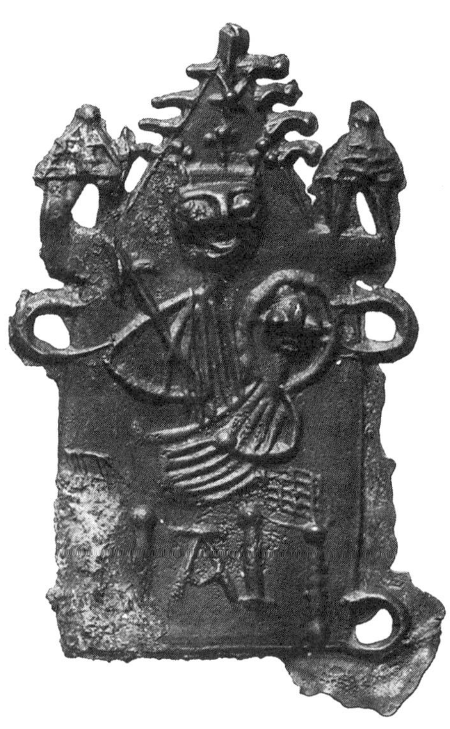

Figure 5.16. Pewter badge, Virgin Mary enthroned with Christ Child, eyelets, Aachen, Germany, 1300–1349, found in Dordrecht, Netherlands, 44 × 29 mm. Langbroek, Netherlands, Family Van Beuningen Collection, inv. 3368 (Kunera 06424). Photograph courtesy of Family Van Beuningen Collection.

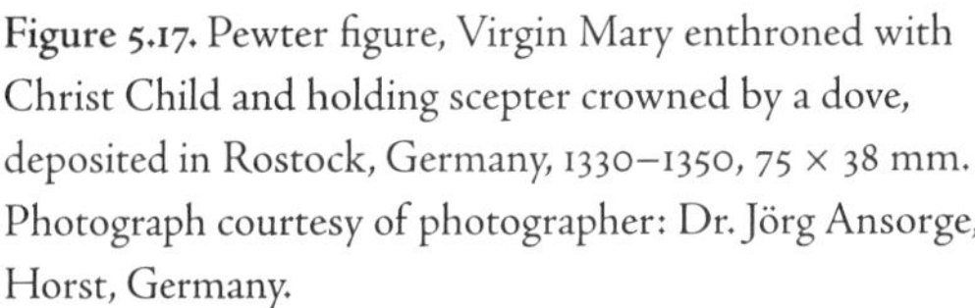

Figure 5.17. Pewter figure, Virgin Mary enthroned with Christ Child and holding scepter crowned by a dove, deposited in Rostock, Germany, 1330–1350, 75 × 38 mm. Photograph courtesy of photographer: Dr. Jörg Ansorge, Horst, Germany.

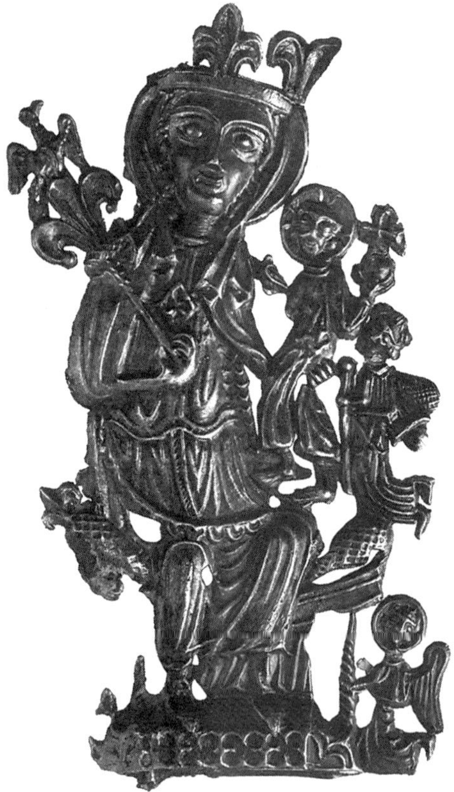

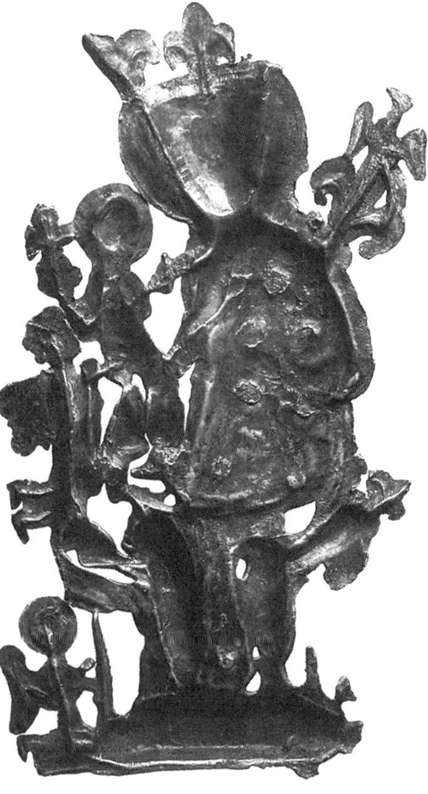

Design diversity remained a feature of Aachen badges throughout their long production life.[41] An unusual Aachen-related pewter object was found in Rostock, Germany (figure 5.17). It depicts the seated Virgin and Child as a miniature statue and appears to lack a means of being attached to clothing. It is possible that it, like similar figurines, was intended to stand on its own and to be deployed by its owner in some kind of devotional array.[42]

In the 1300s a new element became prominent in the Aachen badge repertoire: mirrors. Sometimes these badges consisted only of a frame, usually square, that originally held a small mirror. The three-dimensionality of the square mirror badge in figure 5.18 can be glimpsed, with its thick rim made to hold the now lost mirror in place. Soon mirrors, sometimes square and sometimes round, were being included routinely in iconographically rich Aachen badges. These mirrors are probably the single most important innovation in the Aachen badge iconography; they became arguably the identifying mark of an Aachen badge.

The badge in figure 5.19 exemplifies one common form of the Aachen mirror badges from the late Middle Ages. The badge is circular; embedded in

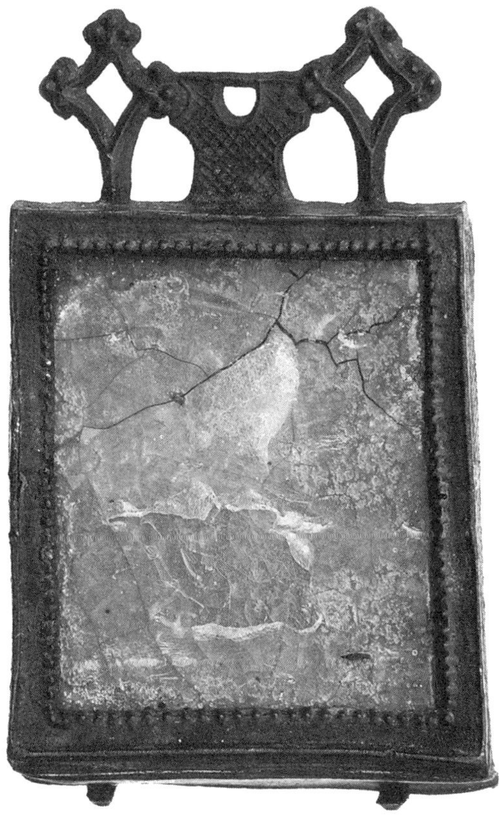

Figure 5.18. Pewter badge, square frame intended to hold a mirror surmounted by tunic on rod supported on either side by posts topped with decorated diamond, eyelets, Aachen, Germany, 1475–1524, found in Nieuwlande, Netherlands, 45 × 29 mm. Langbroek, Netherlands, Family Van Beuningen Collection, inv. 0674 (Kunera 00430). Photograph courtesy of Family Van Beuningen Collection.

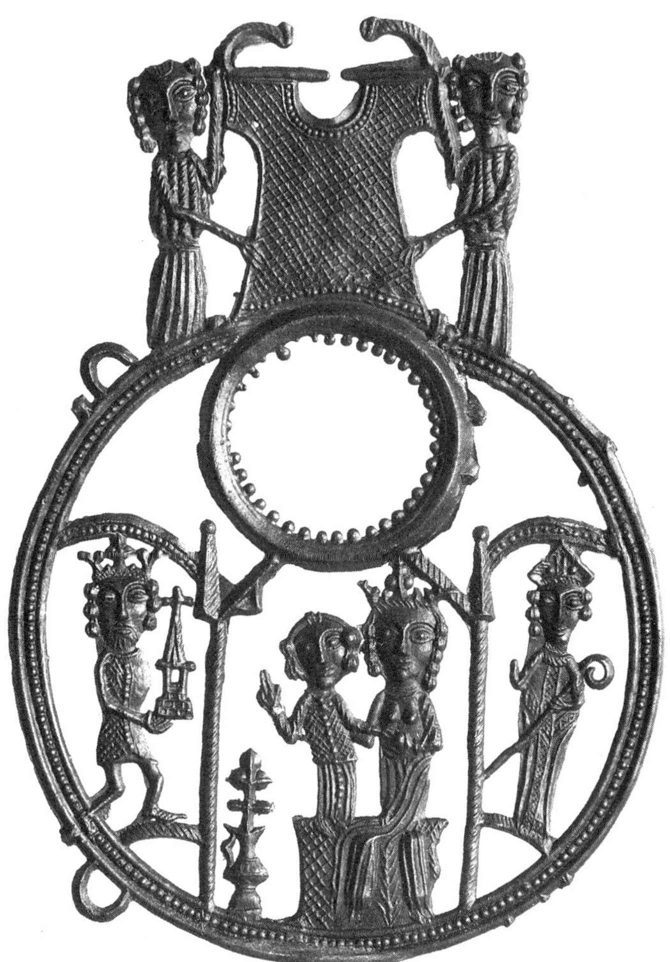

Figure 5.19. Round pewter badge, seated Virgin Mary with Christ Child and lily on the left flanked in left-hand niche by king holding a tower and in right-hand niche by a standing bishop with two figures in long garments displaying the holy tunic above, eyelets, Aachen, Germany, 1350–1399, found in Tholen, Netherlands, 85 × 61 mm. Langbroek, Netherlands, Family Van Beuningen Collection, inv. 3492 (Kunera 06476). Photograph courtesy of Family Van Beuningen Collection.

and echoing the larger circle is the circular frame that held the mirror itself. Directly below the mirror the Virgin Mary sits on a throne, her Son standing at her side. The Annunciation is alluded to on the badge by the lily in a vase that stands to their right. On either side of the Holy Mother and Son and in their own niches are the figures of bishop and secular ruler familiar from other Aachen images. The secular ruler offers Mary a distinctive tower whose shape alludes to the Palatine Chapel itself, which makes the king no less than Charlemagne himself. Above the mirror is Mary's tunic or shift, stretched on and suspended from a pole held by figures, depicting the way the contact relic was displayed for veneration. This badge recombines many of the iconic objects and saints associated with the pilgrimage site of Aachen—the Blessed Virgin Mary's garment, Mary herself, and the Christ Child, and other familiar components of the Aachen shrines—along with the mirror itself.

What Use Is a Mirror?

As was mentioned earlier, relic veneration increased in the High and late Middle Ages, and the surviving religious badges are often associated with holy sites where pilgrims and the devout revered relics. By 1400, it had become customary that such fragile relics were only rarely removed from their shrines or from the treasury for public displays. At Aachen the showing of contact relics took place every seven years. The close geographical proximity of Aachen to other venerable pilgrimage sites; the administrators at these sites timing their displays of precious relics so that pilgrims could visit a circuit of regional sites, including Aachen, within a short, prescribed time period; special jubilee indulgences—all of these meant throngs and throngs of pilgrims, and these masses produced an unexpected problem. Medieval pilgrims did not merely seek to participate in a liturgy or to cast a glance at a tomb shrine, a reliquary, a wonder-working image, or a contact relic. Touch, meaning direct contact with the shrine, relic, or miracle-working object, transferred the divine properties inherent in the holy object to the pilgrim. For this reason, pilgrims sought physical contact with these holy material remains.

The spiritual work of medieval pilgrimage required physical contact (kissing, for example) with the shrine or object. Sarah Blick has written extensively on late medieval renovations and remodelings of holy tombs, which added hollows and niches and other features so that the pious might get as close to the saintly remains as possible.[43] Similarly, for a pewter badge to work as an agent of holiness, its owner had to touch it to the saint's tomb or to the relic shrine. Contact transferred holiness from the shrine into the badge, which only then became an agent of divinity. Touch is what mattered, but the dimensions of mass pilgrimage sketched above made such touch nearly impossible. There were simply too many people. It was not possible for each individual to spend even a few seconds with contact relics, such as the Virgin Mary's tunic or shift, which in any case were too fragile to long withstand the hard use of so much touching, even if it took place only every seven years.

The solution to this dilemma came via a different sense, that of sight.[44] In the Middle Ages, sight was conceived of differently than in the modern, western world. In a nutshell, sight was thought of as a form of touch. Medieval understandings of the power of sight and medieval theories or hypotheses of how vision and objects worked differed from modern western ones. This statement implies that medieval objects were made with different beliefs about looking in mind. For medieval people, vision left the viewer changed; it was not possible to look at something and not to be affected by that encounter. The historian of science Katherine Park writes that "medieval understandings of vision placed the seer and the seen in a relationship not of opposition or of domination and subordination but of reciprocity and mimesis. Sight was simultaneously active and passive, and the eye was both an instrument of penetration and a point of vulnerability. . . . Looking was understood as a physical encounter, in which the subject reached out and touched the object, while the object . . . impressed its form on the viewer's body like a seal on soft wax."[45] Because seeing was a form of touching for medieval people, a mirror on a badge could perform the action of touch.

How was this understood to work? The mirror on the badge was understood to function in essence as a kind of proto camera. It would be exposed to the shrine or object by being held up by someone standing in the throng of worshippers so that the mirror reflected the shown relic. The mirror badge had not only captured a reflection of the holy object; it had touched it, just as powerfully as if it had been physically in contact with the relic. The act of combined seeing and touching had the same effect as physical contact. It transferred the divine power and holiness inherent in the holy object to the mirror badge itself. An Aachen mirror badge that had touched the holy relic via the power of its sight participated in the immensely powerful, transcendent divinity of the holy object, which it stored and emanated. The mirror badge became a kind of minor relic or relic-like object itself.

By the beginning of the fifteenth century the popularity of mirror badges was secure; mirrors had become the most common shared feature of Aachen badges. Enabled perhaps by a single, distinguishing feature, the wider iconography of the Aachen badges was characterized by variation and invention.

A Miniature Diptych from Aachen

This chapter closes with a detailed description of a remarkable mirrored badge-like object from Aachen that brings together all the elements discussed so far: mode of fastening, embellishment, memorability, theology, pious practice, storytelling potential, instant recognizability, pilgrimage, and popular piety. Not only is it a complex and elaborate object of exceptional beauty (though made of lead), it also retains some of its original embellishments.

This object was found in Dordrecht in the Netherlands, but it originated in the German city of Aachen, where it was made between 1375 and 1425. These dates can be established by its complex program of images of saints and holy objects focused on the veneration of the Blessed Virgin Mary, which was cultivated in Aachen from the late twelfth century onward and changed greatly over the course of three centuries.[46] Made to be suspended as a pendant, it is a diptych: two flat plates attached by a hinge. When closed, the object is about 11 by 5.5 centimeters, and when opened, about 11 by 11.5 centimeters.

Plate 8 shows the outside of the badge, with its two, symmetrical pieces joined by a hinge whose long sides emerge as four spires, each ending in a ring. When the diptych was closed, these four rings would have lain on top of one another and so formed a sturdy eyelet for suspending the badge. When opened, the outside resembles an altarpiece; it is organized as an arcade divided into narrow niches on either side, each enclosing a figure. On the left stand three women. In the middle niche, the Blessed Virgin Mary holds the Christ Child on her arm. She is flanked by two female saints, Saint Catherine of Alexandria and Saint Barbara of Nicomedia, two early Christian virgin martyr saints who were revered throughout the Middle Ages. Each saint stands in her own niche and holds her attribute: Catherine the wheel and Barbara the three-windowed tower. The three niches end in a kind of masonry tower crenulation, which provides a transition to the tympanum space. The rectangle of the right wing is organized in a similarly symmetrical manner. It contains male figures. In the center niche stands an image of Christ as Savior of the World, in which Christ is represented as a mature man, bearded and solemn, raising his right hand in blessing and holding in his left the world orb. He is flanked by two male early Christian martyr saints: Saint Cornelius, a third-century Roman priest who was an early pope, and Saint Anthony of Egypt, one of the Desert Fathers who was revered throughout medieval Christendom.

Each arcaded rectangle is surmounted by a triangular arcade resembling a tympanum, a common feature of monumental buildings, nearly universal in medieval stone-built churches and cathedrals, that was situated over a portal and always decorated. Here, each tympanum displays an iconic holy object. On the left, a round shape in the middle of the tympanum encircles an image of the shift believed to have been worn by the Virgin Mary; on the right-hand tympanum is depicted an image of the Holy Face. Each tympanum ends in a steeple-like peak on which, crowning the badge, stands a tiny statue of the Blessed Virgin Mary, flanked by kneeling angels and a little further out by the spire-like finials bearing the eyelets described above.

When opened, as is shown in figure 5.20, the inside displays two rectangles that originally held mirrors, surmounted by tympani repeating the images associated with contact relics (the Holy Face on the left and Mary's tunic on the right). Protected in this closed space were the images of the holy icons that this badgelike object, functioning in its capacity as a mirror-camera, had captured when exposed to the contact relics themselves. The

Figure 5.20. Inside of hinged pewter badge, rectangles of glass surmounted by tympani with the veil of Veronica or Holy Face (left) and the Virgin Mary's tunic (right), pendant, Aachen, Germany, 1375–1424, found in Dordrecht, Netherlands, 111 × 114 mm. Langbroek, Netherlands, Family Van Beuningen Collection, inv. 3753 (Kunera 06497v). Photograph courtesy of Family Van Beuningen Collection.

miniature dyptych's design mimics distinctive architectural features of the magnificent Gothic cathedrals that were going up all over Europe (including Aachen) during the High Middle Ages. The design signals that the object is itself a little cathedral, participating in the holiness and grandeur indicated by the building and its style. The statues, images, and objects that would have adorned cathedrals inside and out were also meticulously selected and organized to tell specific stories about specific holy figures and to narrate key moments in the belief system of Christianity by visual means. The miniature Aachen diptych follows this pattern of meaning-making as well.

Exceptionally, the badge preserves many features of its original embellishments. Traces of red paint are preserved on the tunic and traces of gold paint appear on the Veronica nimbus. Combined with the original bright and shiny silvery gleam of the lead-tin alloy, the miniature diptych would have been something like a little symphony of bright, rich colors. Its original vivid colorfulness imitated high Gothic cathedrals, from their brilliantly colored stained-glass windows to the original vibrantly painted interiors. So, too, the badge, originally detailed, colorful, and festive, and even, delightfully, made to be opened and closed, represents key Christian beliefs about the faith.

Birth, maturity, and death (all experienced and overcome) mingle in ordered and solemn processions on the badge. The saints and objects here are not chosen or placed randomly. They were selected and organized to tell a story of a faith world that negates worldly time and celebrates Christian concepts of time whose fulfillment begins with Christ and the Blessed Virgin Mary, mother and son, bringing redemption into the world. Each appears twice, in different guises. Christ, who alone appears on both sides of the diptych, is shown at two life stages: as a baby on his mother's arm and as a mature, bearded, adult male ruler. Mary stands tall in her diptych niche, regal in her guise as mother of God. On the steeple, however, she kneels in prayer, a merciful intercessor pleading for frail human souls. Time progresses with the saints who accompany the Virgin Mary and Christ in the inner diptych. They are all early martyr saints from what one might call the "heroic" age of Christendom: the first centuries of the Common Era that for the Church marked its time of struggle as a new faith. The martyr's overcoming of pain and death embodies the faith's ultimate promise of resurrection and the Church's ultimate triumph. Finally, fulfilled time persists in the present undimmed via the contact relics, a tunic worn by Mary and the Veil of Veronica that touched Christ's face, objects that were revered precisely because they miraculously offered to medieval Christians direct contact with the physical bodies of these holiest of figures. Past and present relinquish their linearity. In their third mediated appearance via the contact relics that were understood to have survived uncorrupted into the present age, Christ and Mary cause past and present to meet and coexist.

Order is created in this idealized version of a Christian faith world. Gender, for one thing, is ordered: men stand on one side, women and babies on the other. Power is another: the figures in the niche are dressed in the raiment of the elite, their spiritual power symbolized through worldly signs. There is order in the idea of ascension, of rising upward—the higher, the closer to the divine—and so the crowning figure, closest to divine power, kneels in awe and supplication.

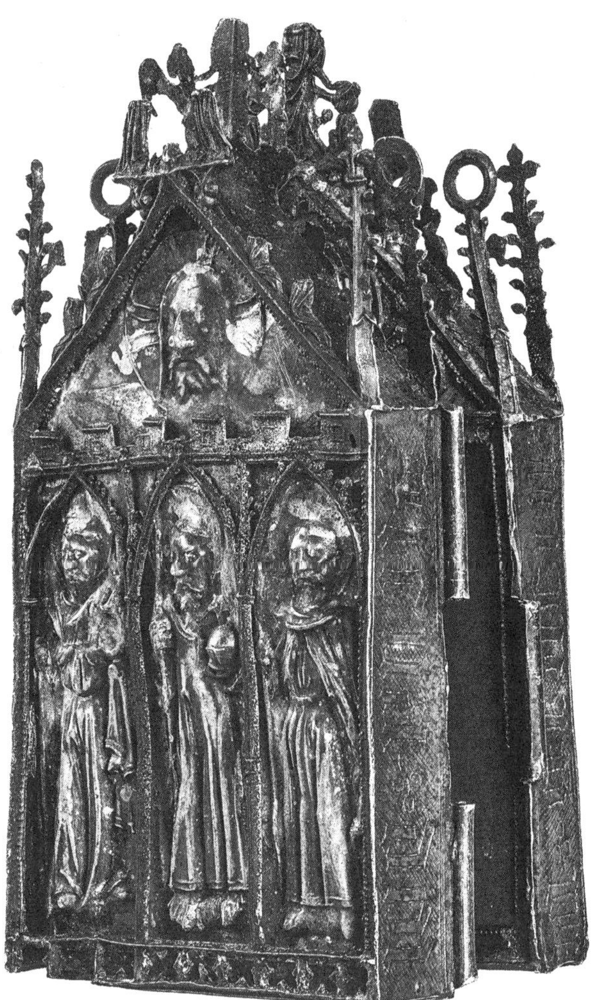

Figure 5.21. Detail of hinged pewter badge, right side showing side of frame with inscription, pendant, Aachen, Germany, 1375–1424, found in Dordrecht, Netherlands, 111 × 114 mm. Langbroek, Netherlands, Family Van Beuningen Collection, inv. 3753 (Kunera 06497r). Photograph courtesy of Family Van Beuningen Collection.

The final image of the miniature diptych offers a clear image of the inscription that is part of the frame (figure 5.21).[47] It reads, beginning in the bottom-right corner and proceeding left around the badge, AVE MARIA GRACIA PLENA DO(min)I (Hail, Mary, Full of the Lord's Grace).

Each side of the diptych features this inscription so that the prayer is repeated twice. Who speaks these words? The figure kneeling on the top of the badge, identified by experts as Mary herself, does not speak her own prayer. Nor are these words intended as a script for the wearer or owner, who would have known the prayer by heart and in any case may not have been able to read the Latin. Perhaps the prayer is spoken by the badge itself. By speaking, the badge would be taking action and participating in the worship of the Blessed Virgin Mary.

The Aachen diptych badge did more than remind its erstwhile owner of a pilgrimage to Aachen. It did more than represent the spiritual forces of Christianity by showing an ensemble of divine persons. Through its mirror and its prayer, the badge itself accessed, contained, and shared in the supernatural forces emanating from these divine figures, transmitting them for the protection, guidance, and well-being of the badge's wearer.

Elaborate and relatively costly as this remarkable badge-like object might have been, it was not a one-of-a-kind product. Fragments from similar diptych badges have been found, some from as far away as Gdánsk, Poland, indicating that even such elaborate badges were mass-produced at Aachen and traveled far with the pilgrims who purchased them.[48]

Aachen badges were produced over hundreds of years. They changed as pilgrim practices changed over the course of the Middle Ages. Originally an endeavor undertaken only by the upper classes and involving arduous travel over long distances to new, select shrines, pilgrimages had evolved by the fourteenth century, when developments such as the emergence of new holy sites made pilgrimages an act of piety undertaken by people from many social strata that usually involved only regional or local travel. The Aachen badges varied through a distinct, yet changing set of elements, images, and symbols revolving around the Virgin Mary, the Christ Child, contact relics associated with them, other saints such as Charlemagne who were venerated at the site, and the Palatine Chapel itself. Early forms, such as the trapezoid Annunciation badge, disappeared. New formal elements, chief among them the mirror badge, emerged to become standard, distinctive components of these badges that immediately identified them as belonging to Aachen. Badges were made and sold by both authorized and nonauthorized vendors, the latter coming to Aachen during the huge jubilee year showings to help meet the demand for badges created by the thousands of arriving pilgrims.[49] Different qualities of badge were available, from simple flat-cast badges to ornate and elaborate diptych badges that might also have functioned as tiny portable altarpieces. Different badges would have been produced for different occasions and to appeal to different, site-specific aspects of worship and veneration related to a pilgrim's religious affinities.

The different badges at Aachen document change over time in late medieval religious belief and practice that insisted on and continually created new continuities. In the case of Aachen, certain specific symbols and images (the Virgin Mary and Christ Child, a garment, a lily, the bust of Charlemagne) recurred again and again. They were combined differently or functioned as elements in new designs, but they were always there, persistently signaling their origin from the holy sites of Aachen. The new Aachen mirror badges responded to new practices and problems. Most pressing was the precipitous rise in piety among the laity of all classes and estates that led, among other things, to a huge increase in pilgrimage, especially of regional and local pilgrimage to sites less than four hundred kilometers away. Drawing a circle around the city of Aachen measuring four hundred kilometers in all directions encompasses some of the most prosperous, populous, and thriving regions of Europe. Add the fact that Aachen was a venerable city with a long Christian tradition and that it housed the remains of a medieval emperor whose exploits had become legendary and were retold in story and song. Then consider that it also housed no less than three major contact relics of Mary, Christ, and John the Baptist and had ecclesiastical institutions that managed the religious and logistical business of mass pilgrimage. One can then grasp the significance of Aachen as a holy site of pilgrimage in the late Middle Ages that was able to change with the times while maintaining a tradition of stability and permanence.

6

Badges and Chivalry

Ypres, 1382

The shiny, painted crown is a fine gift, far too fine for a woman like herself, born and affianced into a family of laborers. Her kin's knowledge of sheep breeding, disease, and care goes back generations and has earned them an honored place in this cloth-making city. So Pa says. Only in moments like this one, when her brothers and father are well and far away, can she remove the flat strip from its hiding place, carefully bending the pliable metal into a circlet, turning it this way and that, admiring it. Are the man and the woman lovers? Separated by a lily, they are not touching as lovers do. They are so well dressed. Perhaps the highborn save their caresses for times and places where there are no prying eyes, as she and her beloved do. Not like her brothers and father, with their women in the corners and in the barns. And what to make of the two little dogs, each sitting so prettily and staring so sweetly at their human friends, gentle, loving, and faithful to their human friends as the man and woman are to one another?

She must remember to ask if there are such dogs in the homes of the highborn. Her brothers' dogs are faithful, that is true, but in a manner that is fierce and terrifying. They do not dote on anything. No, they lope toward whatever they see, teeth bared, ready to go for the throat. They trust no one except for her brothers.

Why has her beloved given her this gift? Does he not understand the danger it represents to her? She has hidden it behind the carding tools under the bed. Her brothers and father would never bother with women's tools; they do not know or care where she stows hers. In any case, she never lets anyone else touch them, taking them out and putting them away herself. Hard-won knowledge when living in a household of men! When she was younger, after Mother died, how often did she hear from them, "Oh, let me help you, Little Sister"?

And then they would rummage carelessly through her small store of tools, and the fine teasels she had bloodied her hands and arms to gather would disappear, suddenly they would be a gift into the

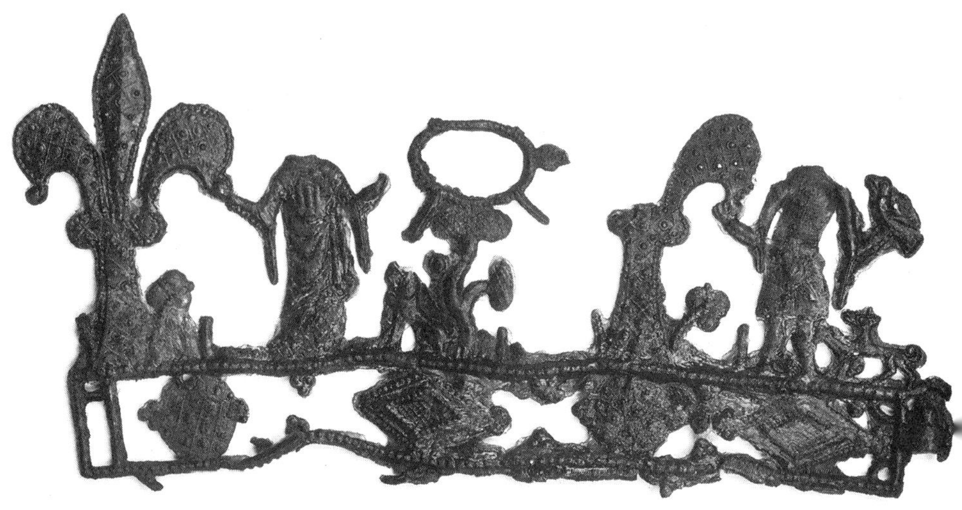

Figure 6.1. Fragment of pewter crown (front), reading from left to right, in the upper register large fleur-de-lis, female figure (now headless) and seated dog gazing up at her, in center a stylized plant topped by a circle, to its left fleur-de-lis (fragmentary) and male figure (now headless) holding falcon and with small dog touching his leg; in lower register space for a hinge?, decorations in round and lozenge shapes and on right remnants of clasp, origin unknown, before 1324, found in Ypres, Belgium. Yper Museum, inv. SM005237. Photographer: Els Deroo. Photograph courtesy of Yper Museum.

Figure 6.2. Fragment of pewter crown (back), origin unknown, before 1324, found in Ypres, Belgium. Yper Museum, inv. SM005237. Photographer: Els Deroo. Photograph courtesy of Yper Museum.

neighbor girl's apron pockets in return for a kiss. Or the wire carding combs, irreplaceable tools from Mother that make the work go faster, were whipped around and returned bent and broken. Still, times have changed. Now she cooks and cleans for them, and they let her be.

The crown is safe, but it is dangerous to take it out and admire it as she is doing now. She must wait for those rare moments when she can be certain that she will be left alone. And then, well, those are usually the times when she might just as well slip away and meet him. His handsome face floats into her mind, the sweetness of his kisses, the strength of his embrace, the spiced smell of his body, so different from the reek of sweat and barnyard that overwhelms the room when the men gather to eat.

He is tender and kind. He transports her far away with his fine, strange tales of tender love and devotion, old tales from France so he says, and sometimes he even sings them to her in that language. Yet he is a little naive, too trusting of his standing as a knight (so untested! so young!), of the influence of his position as a son of the great lord whose family has held land for so long. Yes, those things go far, but they meet their match and limits among those whose lives have been tied up with theirs through decades and generations of work on the land. He cannot buy these laboring men, her father, her brothers, who have worked the land for his father and his father's father before him and who own rights to their labor and their place. It is a matter of honor. He is a fool if he thinks he can win her from them at any price. And she is a fool if she thinks they will let her dispose of her honor herself, without a fight.

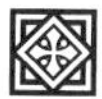

There are surprises that should not be surprising when studying badges. I experienced such a revelation while studying badges and other small lead objects owned by the Yper Museum (Ypres, Belgium). Knights, knights, armored knights on horseback everywhere! Shown in profile, armed and mounted on a stallion, the motif is always the same, yet no two are alike. The badges of knights were expected. The surprise was that the knight badges were outnumbered by pewter toys representing knights: mounted, helmeted, armed knights of the same material, design, size, and shape as the badges but welded to a small flat base so that they could stand upright. (These mounted knights were so alike that it seemed to me that, for

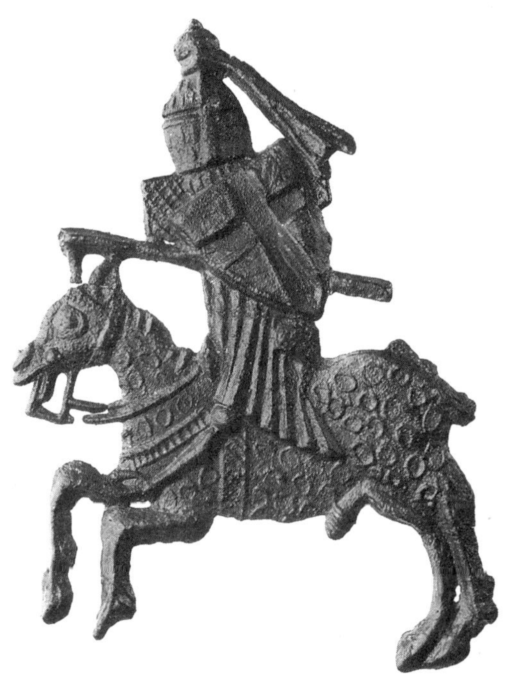

Figure 6.3. Pewter badge, jousting knight wearing plume-crested tournament helmet and holding lance and shield, pin, origin unknown, 1300–1349, found in London. London, Museum of London, inv. 86.384 (Kunera 03611). Photograph and permission from © Museum of London.

example, a mounted knight badge, its pin removed, could be welded onto a base and turned into a toy.) The Yper Museum had about ten of them, most recovered from the "drowned meadows" archaeological site that was discussed in Chapter 2; in 2005 an archaeological excavation in the city of Magdeburg, Germany, turned up a cache of molds for casting small pewter objects and dated to the thirteenth century that included one for a toy knight with a detachable sword and shield.[1]

Realistic details are typical for both knight badges and the knight toys. Like the knight badge shown in figure 6.3, many of the lead knight toys had authentic details: a plumed helmet, a shield with a heraldic image, lance balanced forward, saddle blanket just so, harness and stirrup drawn precisely, the horse's hooves raised in a gallop, tail and helmet banner flying. The lead alloy materials used for badges were also used to make toys in the Middle Ages.[2] The Yper Museum exhibited play kitchen utensils, a tiny cradle, and a little chair, traditional girls' toys alongside the toy knights. I thought of the toy soldiers made out of lead of which entire armies survive from the eighteenth and nineteenth centuries and that are still made today. The mounted knight toys suggest that such martial toys had a long history.

But perhaps the comparison was wrong. Among the surviving medieval soldier and army toys that I have seen, there were no toy foot soldiers, toy archers, or toy pack-mule drivers. The great variety and diversity of occupations, professions, and peoples who made up medieval armies—more mobile villages than modern organized military units—were largely missing. Perhaps the toy knights, whom I had first thought of as the officers of these complex medieval armies, should be compared not to modern toy soldiers but to Matchbox cars.[3] Perhaps the allure of knighthood included mobility: the trained, elite soldier who owned and rode intelligent, highly trained horses. The horse was an integral part of the knight's identity. Strength, speed, agility, courage—these attributes were not distributed across man and beast but rather united them. We do not know whether the children who played with the toy knights found in Ypres belonged to noble families; the toys were in suburban homes, in spaces where artisans also worked and lived. Yet much as children in the modern world play soccer, imagining themselves to be great soccer stars, so perhaps these faraway children from another time and place imagined themselves knights.

In the Middle Ages, knights came from the secular nobility and were by definition both political administrators and warriors. The knight badges remind us that the simplest definition of a knight was a warrior mounted on a horse. The German word for knight, *Ritter*, derives from the verb *reiten* ("to ride" in German) and means simply rider; the French word for knight, *chevalier*, derives from the word *cheval* ("horse" in French) and means simply horseman. These derivations make clear that the warhorse was an integral part of the knightly identity. Knighthood demanded access to substantial economic resources; the mounted soldier was by definition a man born into the upper classes and an officer.

By the High Middle Ages, knighthood had accumulated ideals and prestige that went far beyond its origins concerned with armed and trained military riders on warhorses. This unsystematic discourse of beliefs and values defined a true knight as one who was brave, just, generous, and loyal, protective of the weak and the distressed, literate and decorous, faithful and loving toward women.[4] These knightly virtues were and still are called chivalry (a word derived from the French *cheval*). Saints could be chivalric knights, too, as we saw in Chapter 3 with the badges and badge matrices from Mont-Saint-Michel. Another chivalric warrior saint is Saint George, shown on the badge in figure 6.4, who freed a maiden by stabbing a dragon with a lance and who wears contemporary military armor in many badges. The Saint George badge in figure 6.4 transported the ideals and the garb of chivalry into the religious realm.

That there was a huge gap between chivalric ideals and the brutal realities of medieval rulership and warfare did not escape the notice of the medieval world. Figure 6.5 features an elaborate image from the *Codex Manesse*, a huge,

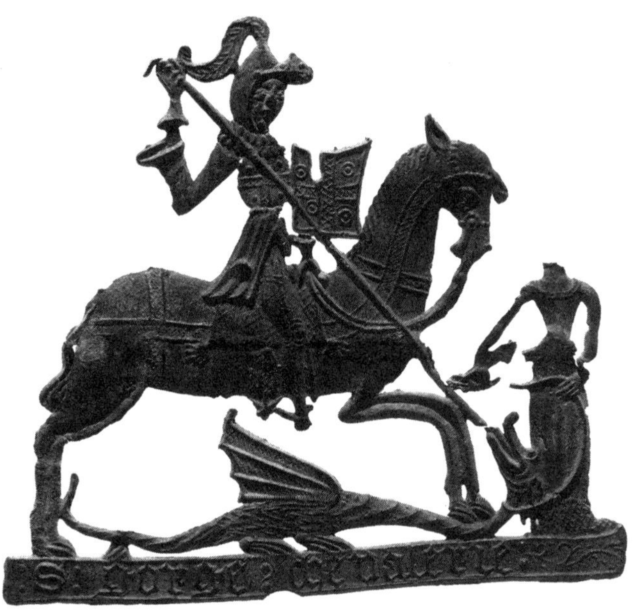

Figure 6.4. Pewter badge, Saint George armed as a medieval knight thrusting lance into mouth of prone dragon on which his mount treads and viewed by female figure on the right, attachment unknown, origin unknown, 1350–1450, found in Paris, 40 × 37 mm. Paris, Musée de Cluny–Musée national du Moyen Âge, inv. CL18004. Photographer: Gérard Blot. Photograph and permission from © RMN-Grand Palais/Art Resource, New York.

lavish early fourteenth-century compilation manuscript containing medieval German love poetry.[5] While courtly ladies watch from above and wring their hands in anguish, the mounted knights in heraldic dress engage in brutal, fierce battle.

The presence of the distressed ladies gazing onto the battlefield, the heraldic splendor of the knights, not to mention the *Codex Manesse*'s foundational assumption that the composition of love poetry is an appropriate pastime for chivalric knights, which will be discussed later in this chapter, place the viewer in the realm of chivalry; the blood splattering the wounded and dying knights and running down from the upraised sword that dominates the center of the image tells us that men are killing and dying on the battlefield.[6] Figure 6.5 presents the viewer with an image commingling chivalry and battle.

Chivalric discourse was present everywhere in medieval Europe.[7] It was pan-European, uniting a class of people, the secular nobility, across linguistic and national boundaries. One analogy is to think of chivalry as a kind of shared language, with recognizable regional variants that were fully comprehensible across political and geographical borders. It taught that a knight was expected to be just, courteous, literate, and refined and to pursue that which was good. The ideals of chivalry proliferated in vernacular texts and practices. There was poetry in every vernacular language celebrating courtly, or chivalric, love of women. There were treatises exploring chivalric virtue. There were stories celebrating the trials and triumphs of young men seeking to embody

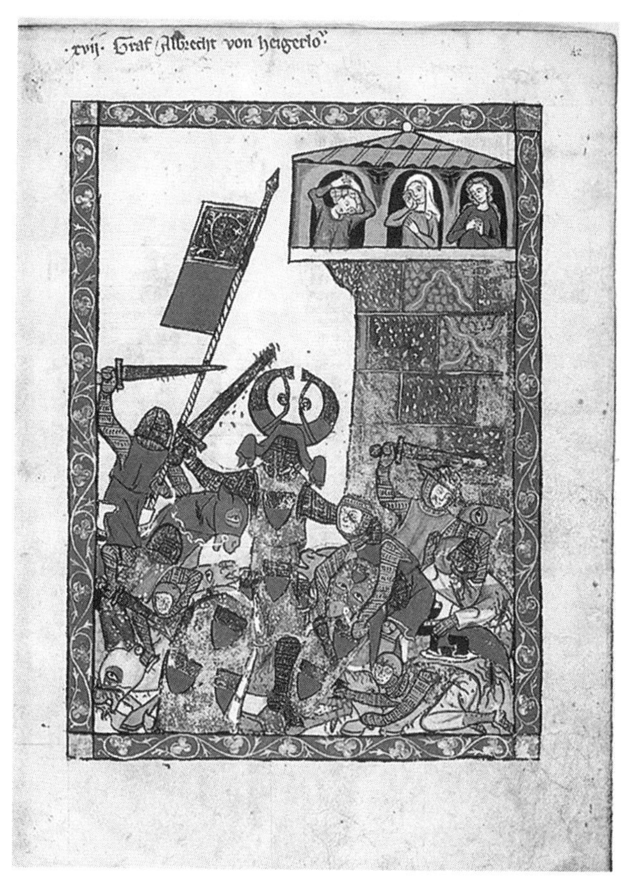

Figure 6.5. Manuscript illumination on parchment, Graf Albrecht II von Haigerloch (Albrecht II von Hohenburg und Haigerloch, 1235–1298), wearing heraldic devices and holding bloody sword aloft in a combat scene watched from a tower by three ladies, Zurich, 1300–1340, 35.5 × 25 cm. Heidelberg, Universitätsbibliothek Heidelberg, cod. pal. germ. 848 (Grosse Heidelberger Liederhandschrift or *Codex Manesse*), folio 42r. Photograph courtesy of Universitätsbibliothek Heidelberg.

chivalry, many of them embedded in a rich and complex fictional universe still known today, that of King Arthur and the Knights of the Round Table. Found in manuscripts, on wall paintings and frescoes, floor tiles, tapestries, and more, the image of the mounted, chivalric knight was ubiquitous across Europe.

Knights at Play: Tournaments

The toy knight, standing on its base, was a child's toy that was made to be moved and manipulated by a child in imaginary scenarios of play. The knight badge was made to be fastened onto clothing, a marker that moved with its bearer and that interacted with the bearer to signal something about him or her. Perhaps the child playing with the mounted knight becomes the knight in his or her imagination, taking on that identity in the space and time of play. What might the badge of the mounted knight signal about the identity of its bearer?

A first question: did real knights wear knight badges? Did they add a shiny badge of a mounted knight to their distinctive clothing? Let's take a moment to imagine that potential use. A mounted knight comes to town. He is not alone. Even a poor knight comes with two horses, a pack mule, and a servant or two to tend the animals and his instruments of trade, the weapons of war. The knight's clothing, bearing, and body are distinctive. He has the posture and movements of an athlete; his body is scarred, signs of battles survived; his clothing, no matter how worn and frayed, is that of his class, its materials and cut fashioned to allow him to ply his trade and to signal his noble origins. His weapons, too, are distinctive: his sword perhaps old and fine, his daggers and lances new and wicked, and all, including his armor, in top-notch condition. I try to imagine the melancholic, aging knight in Geoffrey Chaucer's "Knight's Tale" from the *Canterbury Tales* wearing a badge of a knight, and I fail. Nor do I have any more success imagining the knight's son, who also appears in the story as a knight, doing so. The real knight has no need of such a badge, although he may well have worn a religious badge had he been on pilgrimage or a secular badge signaling belonging to a noble household. Everything about him signaled his status and his occupation. The association with play that the knight badges evoke seems out of keeping with the gravity of the officer-knight's occupation.

But did real knights play? Yes, they did, and they called their play tournaments. These tournaments were fighting contests in which teams of knights would compete in various forms of armed combat.[8] The best known of these competitions is probably the joust, in which a mounted knight armed with a lance attempted to unseat his opponent. Many of the surviving knight badges, such as the one in figure 6.3, show knights holding jousting lances and wearing tournament helmets. Known both from literary texts and from historical evidence, tournaments were regular occurrences throughout the High and late Middle Ages that attracted participants and spectators from near and far. Tournaments might be organized by a great noble household solely as a sporting event, but they were usually integrated into other celebrations, such as weddings, knighting ceremonies, or diplomatic visits. Nor were such activities the exclusive domain of the nobility. In the fourteenth century, the urban elite of the cities of northern France, Flanders, and the Netherlands, for example, held civic festivals once or twice a year that besides feasts, performances, and a variety of civic rituals, included jousts and tournaments, often with teams from the different cities competing with one another. Carnival festivities and city festivals featured tournaments as well. Special grounds would be set up, with playing fields, different games, viewing stands, market booths, and vendor stands. To compare with our times, medieval tournaments resembled organized sports competitions, public festivals, and fairs.

But let's return to the jousting competitors, the knights.

Don a protective covering of metal weighing about fifty pounds; seat yourself on the back of a headstrong, impudent stallion weighing a ton; tuck a ten-foot lance weighing fifteen pounds under your right arm. Hold your shield in front of your heart with your left hand, and then charge! Gallop full speed toward your opponent and unhorse him by smacking his shield with your lance so forcefully that he topples, while surviving his blow to your shield without being unseated yourself. In this sport, there is no defense; there is only offense.

It is plausible to imagine knight badges in a tournament setting. The combatant knights and their retinues would probably have been wearing heraldic insignia and livery, discussed later in this chapter. Knight badges, such as the one in figure 6.3, were perhaps sold and gifted at the tournament as trinkets, to be worn not by the knights but by various spectators: city dwellers, laborers, servants, artisans, women, children. Displayed in this way, the badge would have been saying, "I was there; I watched the knights at play."

Tournaments often included team events, known as melees. What might a melee have been like? Below is an extended passage from a thirteenth-century French story, *The Tournament of Chauvency*, that gives the reader a vivid impression of watching one's favorite team fight their way to victory. The text tells the story of a specific tournament: which teams were present, who fought, who won, and who lost. It is hard for a modern reader to discern one team from the other; doubtless, names and titles hold specific clues about allegiances and alliances now obscure or lost. Nevertheless, we catch glimpses of the tournament team collecting their teammates and riding to the contest field. The depicted action is typical for a tournament, that quintessential nobleman's activity, but in the original medieval French text, the fighting, mounted knights are not men but women.

> During that year when the knights were powerless, and those bold men performed no feats of arms, the ladies went tourneying in Ligny. The tournament having been announced, they said that they wanted to know what kind of blows their sweethearts were always giving for their sakes. The ladies had the Countess of Crépy sought everywhere, as well as Madame de Coucy, for they meant to take them both along with them. When they got to the fields they had themselves armed; They met before Torcy. Yolande of Cailli went forward to fight first; Marguerite

of Oisy bore down on her for a joust; Amesse the bold went to seize her bridle.

When Marguerite saw that she was being blocked, she cried, "Cambrai!" and grabbed her bridle back. You should have seen her defend herself and skirmish when Catherine of the lovely face began to beat her back and cry "Onward!" You should have seen her pulling on the reins and giving and sharing out great blows, shattering great lances [and making iron hauberks] ring and resound, and making the iron coifs in the helms cave in and fall to pieces!

From behind came a great help, Isabelle, who came alongside to strike them now; The senescal's wife also didn't spare them at all.

Then the Countess of Champagne came quickly on a piebald Spanish horse; She didn't feint at her enemies for long; She went at them and struck them, and fought very fiercely there, with more than a hundred against her. Aëlis reached out for her, seizing her bridle. Crying "Montfort," noble Aëlis, along with her company, took Yolande hostage very courteously. Yolande didn't resent this at all—She is no German. Isabeau, whom we know well, came spurring over the plain, attacking them fiercely, shouting her rallying-cry of "At them, Châtillon!"[9]

Many medieval texts survive in which women are imagined as warriors or knights. *Knighton's Chronicle* (1348, England) describes an urban legend in which a troop of women (forty or fifty, it is claimed) would appear at tournaments dressed as men.[10] Stories of the Amazons are part of the adaptations of the tales of Troy and of Alexander that proliferated across Europe in every language. There are short, rhymed couplet texts in medieval German and medieval French about women fighting in tournaments, whether cross-dressed or not.[11] *The Tournament of Chauvency* belongs in this category of writing. Yet it does not present a burlesque of knightly combat; the noblewomen can fight as well as noblemen. Rather, the text suggests that while noblewomen could do the fighting, they take on this occupation only when the noblemen fail. This "compromise" position on gender relations—that noblewomen could do noblemen's work but chose not to—may be part of the text's humor. It might also suggest that gendered divisions of labor were understood as being primarily not biological but based on social agreements. The story of *The Tournament of Chauvency*, in which noble ladies take the place of noble lords on the tournament field and put on a darned good show, shows a playful vision of chivalry that included playing with conventional gender roles.

Chivalry and Courtly Love

There is no chivalry without women. Through its notion of courtly love, chivalry scripts a key role for noblewomen that is fundamental for its imagining of elite masculinity.[12] A young knight falls in love with a beautiful, highborn woman. He is faithful, cultivating his sentiments through refined, courtly entertainments, such as poetry and song, as well as tournaments. His love inspires him on the battlefield as well, where he displays courage, valor, and daring. Chivalric love is called "love service" because the knight is thought to be serving his lady in a way that is analogous to the way that a vassal serves his lord. As the fictional, female speaker in a short text treating courtly love that circulated widely in German-speaking lands during the middle of the fifteenth century sums it up, "For knight and squire are emboldened by the goodness of pure ladies, and they strive for their favor, sparing neither goods, nor body, nor life in their service."[13]

Plate 9 depicts this kind of love, as a woman, the knight's beloved, publicly presents him with a simple yet highly meaningful gift, a garland, as a symbolic token of her affection. Across the top of the image, four ladies with their hair artfully dressed gaze down from a battlement to a scene below. Their hands are raised in a rich variety of gestures indicating speech. The two women in the middle reach down from their raised positions, their right arms and hands stretching below the battlement into the space below. The young woman on the left holds a garland in her hand; the young woman on her right points at it. Below them, filling the middle two-thirds of the page, eight men crowd around five horses. The group is riding and moving toward the left. They are of varying sizes; three tiny men can be seen, two in the center ground facing one another, the third nearly hidden in the group all the way on the left. Two slightly larger male figures clothed in red tights and purple robes lead the way on horseback: one appears to be beating a drum; a second holds high a jousting lance. The action is focused on the young man in the center, blond, dressed in mail, and holding a shield with an eagle, yet bareheaded. He is flanked by two more riders. Just in front of him a man in red holds his amazing, blue-bescarfed helmet with its heraldic crest, while behind him, a man wearing a blue, conical hat holds high some kind of small, hammer-like tool or instrument. The young man is reaching up to touch the garland preferred by the young woman.

The crowded scene, full of noise and action, represents a knight victorious in a tournament receiving a garland as a token of affection from his beloved.

Decorous, chivalric love between the knight and his lady is the focus of the image. The message is carried by no less an actor than the young man's horse, which fills nearly half of the lower register. It is draped in a sumptuous blanket woven in a pattern of alternating green and white squares, each square emblazoned with a single letter that together spells out AMORS. In the *Codex Manesse*, a manuscript produced in Zurich, a German-speaking city, for German-speaking patrons, and representing in its nearly nine hundred pages the herculean effort of as near an exhaustive compilation of 150 years worth of German-language poetry as was possible at the time, the chivalric image uses not the medieval German word for love, *minne*, but the French word for love in its medieval spelling, *amors*.

The manuscript illumination conjures up the role of courtly love in late medieval ideals of chivalry. A single word, *amors*, a foreign word in the German, Dutch, or Flemish vernaculars of the places where many badges and manuscripts using it were produced, represents a way of thinking about human attachment and affection that came into being in the elite, secular culture of France in the High Middle Ages and that rapidly spread among elites across Europe. In our world, we would probably call such an attachment romantic love, but in the Middle Ages, it would have been understood as a related, yet different form of attachment, known as chivalric, or courtly, love. Although by the fourteenth century all vernacular languages had their own well-developed vocabularies for love, *amors* retained pan-European presence and recognizability, acting as a signal for courtly love (the modern stereotype of French as the language of love is an old one indeed).

Chivalric love represented both a set of elite beliefs and a set of elite practices, from the tournament with its prizes and audience of fine ladies shown in plate 9, to hunting and falconry, to literary pastimes such as reading secular texts in the vernacular (Arthurian romance, for example), to composing and performing poetry and song. In the chivalric world, the activities of poetry and diplomacy were closely linked. A courtly knight should be neither coarse nor brusque. Rather, he should have a pleasing way with words, devoting time to cultivating this art and to sharing it, and if possible, he should be able to compose and sing as well. Courtly music and courtly literature, with its stories and poems about love and chivalric knighthood, were pursuits that united members of the secular elite across the many linguistic and national boundaries of late medieval Europe. A gift with words, the ability to sway others with language, to persuade them toward a point of view favorable to the outcome you desire, seduction one might call it, was a quality shared by chivalric poets and knightly diplomats alike.

Chivalric love was fundamentally an ideal of virtue that was performed. The heart of these performances was the public cultivation of tender feelings of attachment, both toward elite women and toward one's fellow knights as well. A wide range of human attachment and affection was encompassed in medieval notions of chivalric love. The knight in plate 9 is accepting the garland from a young woman, who to judge by her uncovered head and the long hair that flows over her shoulders is unmarried. The young noblemen and noblewomen who experience courtly love in much medieval Arthurian romance, for example, usually marry. Medieval love poetry, however, often imagined a poet or knight adoring and serving in faithful love service a married lady, creating situations that were used to explore discretion as another facet of chivalric, courtly love. Chivalric love between men was understood as a bond of friendship that could underwrite political relationships. The strong, peer-to-peer male bonds of chivalric love might also have fostered cohesion among a group of knights.[14]

By the mid-fourteenth century, knighthood and chivalry had created a professional identity that also cut across linguistic and national identities, a pan-European, shared, elite social identity that was universally recognized both by those who claimed that identity and those who did not (witness clergy railing against knights!) as formative, meaningful, and real.

The contrast between the brutal facts of medieval warfare and the delicate calibrations of feeling and action in chivalric love and friendship may present an unresolvable conflict, and yet chivalry was not brought down because of what might be perceived as an unbridgeable large rift between its theory of love and its practice of killing. Rather, it thrived. By the time the word *amors* makes its way onto the manuscript page of plate 9, around 1320, chivalry is 150 years old, and by the time it appears on badges, another fifty-some years have passed. By the fifteenth century, when the use of chivalric badges was at its height, chivalry had become common currency among prosperous elites across Europe, and the watchword of chivalry was *amors*.

Chivalric love concerned elites. In the fictional sketch that opens this chapter, the beautiful young woman from the laboring class knows this, too. She holds in her hands a different kind of gift from her knightly lover: a tiny strip of lead-tin some four centimeters high that might have been intended to be bent into a circlet held in place by the small hinge on the side. It is decorated with the figures of a well-dressed man and woman, each attended by a dog and turned toward one another, yet separated by large fleur-de-lis. Some twenty-odd examples of such objects survive, most fragmentary and most showing religious scenes, such as the Three Kings.[15] The fragment found in

Ypres, however, uses the iconography of courtly love, signified by the dress and postures of the couple and by the attending dogs symbolizing fidelity. Who or what wore such an exquisite, tiny object, small enough to be held in the palm of one's hand? Perhaps it is truly a *bibelot*, a small trinket or object made to be gazed at, without value beyond its signifying function, which is unambiguous enough to be dangerous to the young woman of the sketch should her family discover it. Her brothers would put a different spin on their shared understanding that those who participate in the practices of courtly love are elite men and women. For them, the gift of such a symbolically freighted object from a knight to a girl from lower estate would represent one stage in a highborn rogue's attempt to debauch their sister.

Over time the ideals and symbols of chivalry and courtly love crossed many social boundaries. They became intelligible, as the sketch suggests, far beyond those social circles in which they first emerged and later were widely practiced. They rapidly moved beyond the nobility by the middle of the thirteenth century and came to designate an idealizing form of self-fashioning that was enthusiastically adopted by the wealthy merchants and elites in cities as far apart as London and Nuremberg and most in between. These circles adopted the pastimes and manners of chivalric, courtly love alongside the gentry and nobles from Berne to Stockholm, from Vienna to Carlisle. The ideology of knighthood and love survived and thrived for such a long time because it came to signal a pan-European elite status.

Homage and Love

The images and symbols that belong unmistakably to the world of chivalry and courtly love appear on badges as well. The word *amors* appears on badges often, as we have seen in plate 9. The symbolic action of the lady presenting the victor knight with a garland is similarly present in badges.

The badge in figure 6.6 is tiny, a little more than two-and-a-half centimeters high and less than two centimeters wide. A man and a woman face one another; both are elite, judging by their clothing and hairstyles. The man kneels on one leg, his clasped hands raised and extended at chest height toward the lady in a still recognizable gesture of entreaty. The lady's left arm is bent and raised. The place where her left hand should be disappears behind the knight's clasped hands. Clearly the image suggests that her left hand embraces his. The woman's right hand is clearly visible. It is poised in the approximate center of the badge and at approximately waist height, well below the

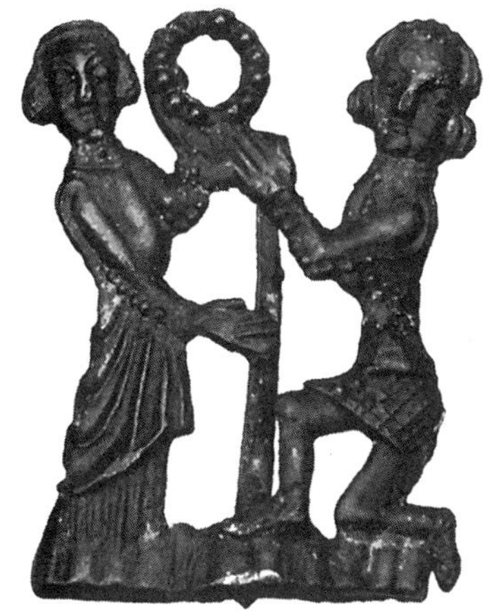

Figure 6.6. Pewter badge, scene of courtly love with woman bestowing a garland on kneeling man, pin, origin unknown, 1350–1399, found in 's-Hertogenbosch, Netherlands, 25 × 20 mm. Langbroek, Netherlands, Family Van Beuningen Collection, inv. 3324 (Kunera 06773). Photograph courtesy of Family Van Beuningen Collection.

clasped hands yet in a direct line with them. The eye rises along it, from the woman's right hand to the three hands above it, and finally to a circular object balancing just above the conjoined hands, a rim decorated with tiny, raised dots. A garland is changing hands between a man and woman, symbolizing the attachment or conjoining of the couple who grasp it.

The gesture shown in the badge and other images like it would be intelligible to a modern viewer: a man kneeling in front of a woman is proposing marriage to her. The medieval badges are probably saying something similar; garlands are worn by unmarried women (and men), for example, and so the presence of the garland on the badge suggests that love is in play, while the solemn gesture suggests marriage or some other form of binding relationship based on mutual consent. Yet these medieval badges have another layer of meaning as a political act. They were circulating at a time and place when an elite man kneeling before another elite person was a venerable and immediately recognizable political gesture. It was the nearly universal enactment of political vassalage known as swearing homage. In front of witnesses, one lord knelt before another, raising his clasped hands. The standing lord surrounded the kneeling lord's hands with his own. Both swore an oath. The deed was done; a new political relationship had been sealed.

Although the gesture of vassalage staged a hierarchy—the standing lord is the overlord, the kneeling lord is the vassal—the gesture was not one of submission or defeat (for which the medieval world also had a gesture, which involved stretching oneself out, prone on the ground before the victor). It signaled rather that a political relationship involving mutual support had been formed and that loyalty and promises of mutual support were being exchanged. Each was swearing an oath of fealty to the other, even as the political hierarchy of their relationship was clear. Each had put some kind of resources on the table (for example, the vassal receiving from the overlord financial and juridical privileges—i.e., the privilege of exacting taxes and hearing cases—for specific villages, towns, or areas in exchange for military service, that is to say, arming a group of followers and showing up with them if summoned by the overlord). The concrete terms of a vassalage agreement varied according to local and regional customs and law. Yet the near-universal gesture of vassalage, carried out in front of witnesses by the lords themselves (whether man or woman), should not be understood as merely representing a previously reached bargain. The gestures performed (and often tokens exchanged) made the vassalage memorable and binding. The performance of vassalage created the relationship in the eyes of the world.

The political context of the gesture on the badge under discussion would have been immediately obvious to medieval people; it may even have been the dominant understanding of the gesture. The badge in figure 6.6 must carve out its own sphere of meaning. It must find a way to say unambiguously "I am about courtly love," or it risks being misunderstood as a political badge. That a woman is present does not guarantee this understanding, because elite women could be lords and so, both in theory and practice, receive homage from vassals. The garland makes clear that the badge refers to the world of courtly love. Yet at the same time, our badge is transferring the meanings associated with lordship and vassalage, the political, economic, and social world of the court, into the realm of love. The lady stands. She is the overlord and the kneeling man, the vassal. The homage that he swears to her is, we surmise, undying love, and the fealty she swears to him in turn is, we surmise, the same.

The examples of courtly love discussed in this chapter up until now are in their own way serious ones, in the sense that they are decorous and refined. Such was the nature of chivalric, courtly love, according to its own conventions. Does courtly love seem a humorless pursuit? Perhaps my presentation has made it so. In fact, the presence of wit was a defining characteristic of the literature and imagery of courtly love. Sophisticated, urbane, and witty, the poetry and stories concerning courtly love are often complex, refined works that invite the reader to reflect on or take pleasure in the impossible dilemmas in which courtly lovers find themselves. There are examples of courtly love poetry in which a lovesick person is gently mocked; jokes are exchanged in treatises on courtly love; and audience laughter is provoked by many scenes in stories of courtly love.

The delight in comic play and wit characterizing so much courtly love literature appears in the badges as well. Take figure 6.7, for example. Here, the

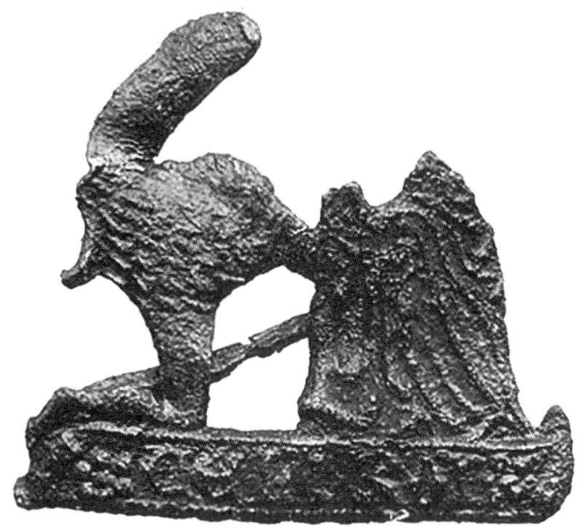

Figure 6.7. Pewter badge fragment, phallic creature kneels before figure wearing a long robe, inscription CES ROI, pin, origin unknown, 1375–1424, found in 's-Hertogenbosch, Netherlands, 30 × 33 mm. Langbroek, Netherlands, Family Van Beuningen Collection, inv. 4544 (Kunera 17072). Photograph courtesy of Family Van Beuningen Collection.

classic gesture of the knight-vassal kneeling in liege homage before his lord or his lady is given a comic, ribald turn. All the elements are present, allowing the viewer to identify the image as the classic gesture of homage. Only one element has changed: the knight has been transformed into a penis creature, which offers homage to another figure (the damage to the badge makes it impossible to tell for sure whether the figure is male or female). A broken scroll bears legible words in French: CES ROI.

As a send-up of chivalry and courtly love, it would have been funny enough to transform the knight into a phallus creature, showing unmistakably love's physical side. But the badge does not stop at that. It has a French caption that says CES ROI, which means this is the king. Who is the king? Which one is the king? If the phallus creature is the king (and kings could be vassals), then the badge is perhaps saying that sex is king. If the king is the now-fragmented figure whose sex is indeterminable, the potential jokes and meanings multiply. It is hard to find a precise meaning, but what is clear is that the badge mocks courtly love twice over: first, visually, by transforming the knight into a penis creature, reducing the courtly knight to his physical, sexual organ; and second, linguistically, with a caption that creates a challenge and parodies discourses of courtly love.

Heraldic Devices

Mounted knight badges were probably not worn by real knights, but real knights did fashion and wear heraldic devices of all kinds, including badges. So did their wives, children, relatives, servants, squires, and political allies.

When worn by members of the great knightly households, such badges are called livery. As was explored in Chapter 4, badges were used as devices by many kinds of other medieval groups as well, such as members of religious confraternities, guild associations, and civic officials of all kinds.

Badges relating to knighthood participated in the complex world of medieval heraldry and heraldic devices, a historically distinct universe of medieval signs and symbols used to indicate identity and belonging. As the historian Michel Pastoureau writes in his elegant introduction, heraldry is "the science that studies armorial bearings, the coloured emblems pertaining to an individual, a family, or a community. Their composition is governed by the specific rules of blazon that distinguish the medieval European heraldic system from all other systems of emblems, whether earlier or later, military or civil."[16]

Heraldry is "a social code and a system of signs."[17] It is a visual language that communicates via color, shape, and symbol and that is intelligible to anyone who takes the time to learn its descriptive and routinized verbal descriptions called blazon.[18] Shared conventions establishing heraldry were quickly established and were in widespread use by the thirteenth century, having been taken up by medieval institutions such as cities and towns, confraternities, guilds, and universities. Heraldic signs were created in many materials and placed on all kinds of objects, for example, wall paintings, books, clothing, furnishings, and personal adornments.[19] The heraldic signs most widely known in the modern world are coats of arms, or family crests, whose use, although much changed since medieval times, survives into our times. When used by noble families, heraldic coats of arms created a visual system that encoded the specifics of an individual's status, rank, and identity. An individual knight bore on his shield and standard (and probably on other elements of his equipment as well) a unique coat of arms composed of heraldic symbols drawn from the families of his father and his mother. The coat of arms identified the bearer and the bearer's retainers uniquely. Thus, knightly brothers would have slightly different coats of arms; duplicates would be borne not by a blood relative but by a dependent member of the household. Noblewomen had coats of arms as well, designed according to the same principles as those of men.[20]

A coat of arms was put together using specific symbols and patterns and following a complex, specific set of rules. Among the necessary ingredients were specific symbols, which were called charges in the language of heraldry (for example, a flower such as the fleur-de-lis); colors, called tinctures; shapes, such as circles or crosses, which also have specific names; and the manner in which the lines of partition were drawn on a shield. The little clasp badge in figure 6.8 features six basic shapes.

Imagine the badge is a clock. Look first to two o'clock, where there is a shield pale, which has a band running vertically down the center of the shield; at four o'clock there is a crossed shield, which is divided vertically into an even number of equal parts; at six o'clock there is a shield bar or barry, which has one or more bars running horizontally across it; at eight o'clock, a saltire or diagonal cross; at ten o'clock, a shield bendy or bend, a strap or band running diagonally; and at twelve o'clock, a pall, which is a Y-shaped charge rising from the base point of the shield. Could such objects (a second one survives) have had a purpose beyond adornment? The badge is very small, not even three centimeters across, which means that even when new and shiny, it would still have to be viewed close up to be decoded or read. Might each shield have represented the individual member of a tournament team? Might it have been a teaching object, offering a helpful mnemonic device for learning the basics of heraldry? Might it be a discrete sign of office, worn by a herald, for example, as a token of his office? Might each small device have been part of a larger garment or adornment, such as a belt, that together encoded a network of relationships from a specific time and place?[21] Further research is needed to propose answers to these questions.

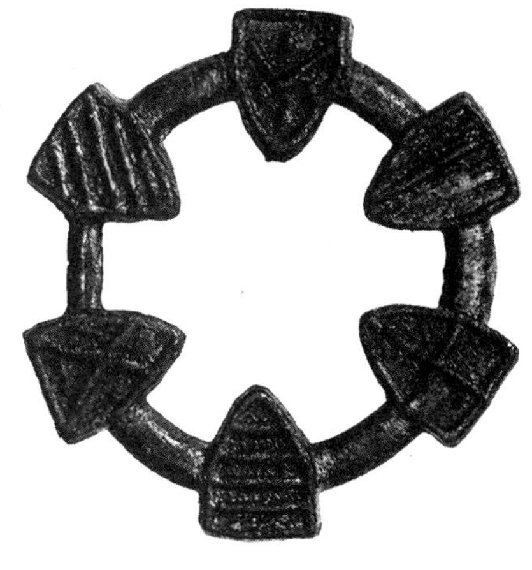

Figure 6.8. Pewter badge, round clasp with six shields, clasp, origin unknown, 1375–1424, found in Rotterdam, Netherlands, 25 × 25 mm. Langbroek, Netherlands, Family Van Beuningen Collection, inv. 2367 (Kunera 00889). Photograph courtesy of Family Van Beuningen Collection.

The use and meaning of the various signs composing a coat of arms came to be fixed early on. Heraldry would not have been widely intelligible otherwise, and as a visual system of signaling identity, it was not intended to be secret or esoteric (however much it may seem so today) but rather to communicate widely and well genealogical information and the bearer's identity. As time went on, the visual system of communication became complex, in large part because of its wide adoption. Men known as heralds mastered the history and language of heraldry.[22] They were a fixture at late medieval courts and in city governments, where they were tasked with both reading existing devices and creating new ones; a few late medieval, illustrated manuscripts from them have come down to us. The ubiquitous presence of heralds in high places reminds us that chivalry was pursued by the governing classes, and so it intersected in fundamental ways with their political aims and ambitions. In the matter of coats of arms, heralds provided a huge body of important knowledge that mattered politically. The more knowledge one had about great families, their genealogies, their marriages and ever-shifting political alliances, the deeds of their most illustrious members, and the great events in which they had participated, the more one could read from the displayed coats of arms and devices, that is to say, the more stories one could tell about the kin networks of the individual who bore them. Being able to read and understand these signs and symbols of knighthood meant more than identifying the political players on the field; it meant conjuring up the world of chivalry and the chivalric system of ideals and beliefs that gave meaning to their actions.

Heraldry participated in the universe and performance of chivalry. Heraldic devices and coats of arms proliferated from the thirteenth century on, appearing across Europe in a wide variety of surviving evidence. Its language was used in simplified forms, especially charges, that is, such images as flowers or animals, and other devices, which were used in many contexts, including but not limited to armor, helmet, shield, clothing worn by a knight and his retinue, horse trappings, tents, banner, and so on. Heraldic devices were created out of such materials as embroidery and cloth and appliqued to clothing.[23] They are shown and described in texts: in Wolfram von Eschenbach's Arthurian romance *Parzival,* the charge of Parzival's noble knight father, Gahmuret, for example, is an anchor. Devices using charges could be found in nearly all realms of elite life, appearing on illuminated manuscripts, portraits, tombstones, sculptures, and household objects. The people represented in the *Codex Manesse* (see figure 6.5 and plate 9) are equipped not just with weapons but also with heraldic devices that lend color, design, pattern, and pomp to their displays of prowess and warfare and that allow those who can read the symbolic language (and we should probably imagine that the onlooking ladies excelled in this art) to identify the men on the field of battle and the networks of allegiance in which they act.

Using heraldic symbols in these ways makes them devices of the kind introduced in Chapter 4. They signaled the bearer's identity as belonging to a specific group, whether family, profession, guild, confraternity, city, or household. For the members of the knightly, noble class, a device displayed to the world the bearer's participation in the culture and social status of knighthood. Such identity markers extended beyond the visual into other sensory realms as well. The rallying cries of the ladies in the excerpt from *The Tournament of Chauvency* discussed at the beginning of this chapter are a kind of aural device, one made of language, voice, and sound, and a familiar feature of medieval warfare. Each battle cry is a shout that names a great household, whose image-based devices and coats of arms must have been present everywhere on the battlefield as well: on the knights' shields and clothing; on the implements, tack, and gear; on the clothing of their retinue. Coats of arms and devices were critically important claims of belonging. All of these devices, symbols, and signals were legible. They conveyed information about the bearer and the bearer's family, lineage, rank, and allegiances. Plainly displayed, they were meant to be deciphered, to be read.

Badges added their small voice to the chorus of material objects surviving from the Middle Ages that are marked with heraldic devices. The badge shown front and back in figures 6.9 and 6.10 is an "in the round" object featuring fully realized images, here heraldic ones, on both sides. It has two nubs at the top of the shield and an eyelet at the bottom, suggesting that it was originally made to be part of a larger ensemble of some sort.

Sometimes badges associated with knighthood used heraldry and charges in decorative ways designed to enhance the reality effect of an object. For example, many mounted knight badges and toys discussed in this chapter's opening paragraphs show the knight holding a shield etched with something like a heraldic device or a charge.[24] The knight in figure 6.11 holds a shield with six fleurs-de-lis, a widely known charge announcing association with French royalty or the Virgin Mary.

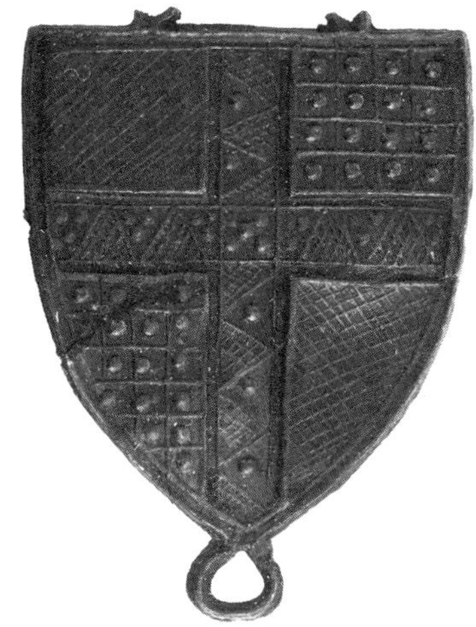

Figure 6.9. Pewter badge (front), shield quartered by a cross with field and cross decorated with dots and hatches, unknown attachment, origin unknown, 1350–1399, found in 's-Hertogenbosch, Netherlands, 42 × 31 mm. Langbroek, Netherlands, Family Van Beuningen Collection, inv. 3886 (Kunera 01918r). Photograph courtesy of Family Van Beuningen Collection.

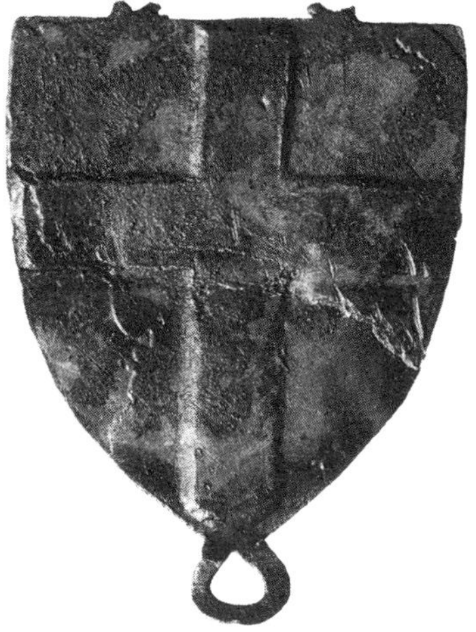

Figure 6.10. Pewter badge (back), shield with Latin cross, attachment unknown, origin unknown, 1350–1399, found in 's-Hertogenbosch, Netherlands, 42 × 31 mm. Langbroek, Netherlands, Family Van Beuningen Collection, inv. 3886 (Kunera 01918v). Photograph courtesy of Family Van Beuningen Collection.

The shield of the knight in figure 6.3 features a huge cross; common on badges and elsewhere are also the lion and the eagle, widely regarded animal symbols of power that persist to the present day.[25] Note the eagle that is prominently displayed in plate 9. Even knight badges with shields now blank and lacking any sign of heraldic symbolism could have been painted in specific heraldic colors and with a specific heraldic device or charge.

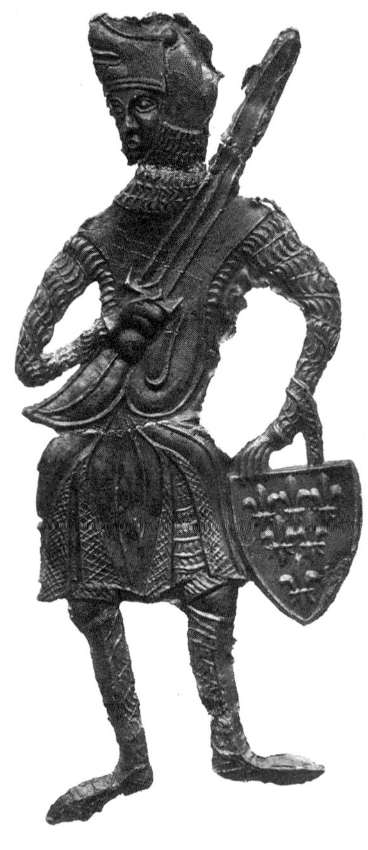

Figure 6.11. Pewter badge, knight with helmet and sword and holding shield with six fleurs-de-lis, pin, origin unknown, 1350–1399, found in Tholen, Netherlands, 85 × 37 mm. Langbroek, Netherlands, Family Van Beuningen Collection, inv. 3491 (Kunera 06782). Photograph courtesy of Family Van Beuningen Collection.

The Knight of the Swan

The visual language of heraldry animated hearts and minds across medieval Europe. Sometimes its most powerful symbols were brought to life. One example of such a medieval fictional character who balances between human and symbolic forms is the knight of the swan (in German, *Swannritter*), Lohengrin.[26] In the French and German tales about him, the swan knight embodies all chivalric virtues. Handsome and strong, he is a fearless warrior who wins battles for his lord and who champions the innocent and abused for the sake of justice. German versions even connect him to the story universe of the Grail, making Lohengrin a scion of that magical realm.

Various versions of the story of the knight of the swan linked the character explicitly to real noble families in northwestern France and Belgium, especially the dukes of Brabrant, who used the swan in their heraldic arms, making it a story about their noble origins. The knight arrives and leaves in the story sailing on or in a swan boat. The heraldic device, the swan, also becomes a dynamic element of storytelling. The knight is called the swan knight throughout the story because his true name, Lohengrin, is secret. He even forbids his wife (the heiress whose champion he was) to ask him his true name, a familiar literary device (think Cupid and Psyche) that usually ends the same way: the hapless spouse, in time overcome by doubt and anxiety, asks the forbidden question, gains an answer, and loses her or his beloved. It is tempting to read figure 6.12 as an image of Lohengrin's abandoned wife who maintains a semblance of her husband's presence by holding a shield with his heraldic device.

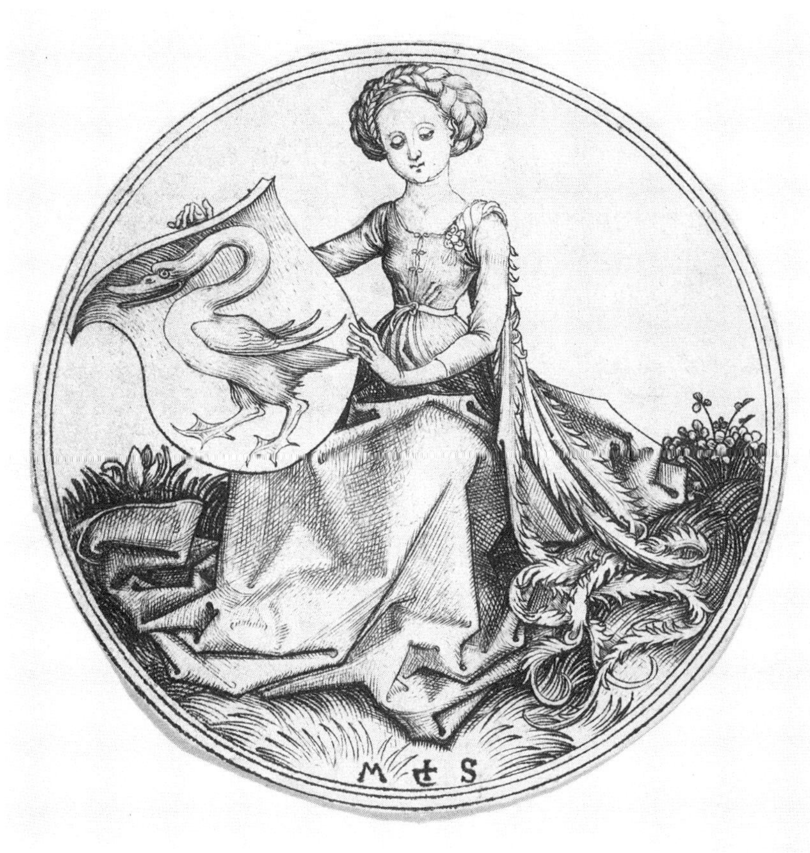

Figure 6.12. Martin Schongauer (c. 1435/50–1491), *Young Woman Holding a Shield with a Swan*, burin engraving, 7.8 cm (diameter). Colmar, France, Musée d'Unterlinden, inv. 82.3.2. Photographer: Christian Kempf. Photograph and permission from © RMN-Grand Palais/ Art Resource, New York.

Many badges featuring swans survive. The Parisian swan badge in figure 6.13 is one example. The caption on the badge, J'ATENS DE VOUS MERCI (I am looking for your mercy), suggests that the swan itself might be speaking. In the swan knight stories, the swan badges also seem to come alive.[27] These tales embody the charisma of heraldic devices as emblems of chivalry. At the same time, they hint at their mystery. A heraldic badge presents the knowledgeable viewer with an immediate, unmediated statement of identity: I am the swan knight. And yet, as the story unfolds, the reader is asked to contemplate an unsettling enigma: who is the person, really, who bears this device? The heraldic device, the swan, is both identity and mask, and the

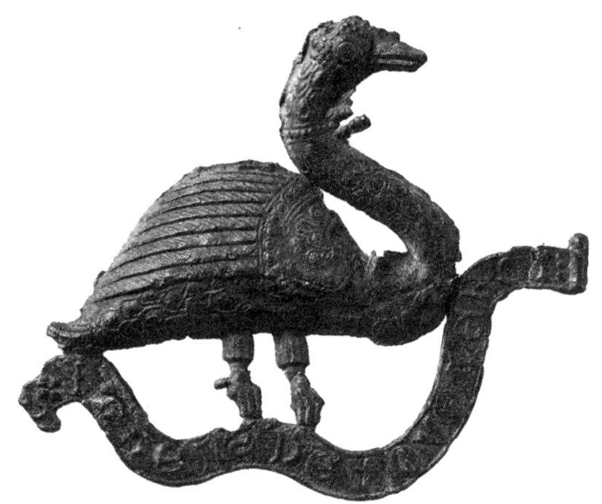

Figure 6.13. Pewter badge, swan with inscription, origin unknown, 1400–1449, found in Paris, 51 × 62 mm. Paris, Musée de Cluny–Musée national du Moyen Âge, inv. CL4725. Photographer: Jean-Gilles Berizzi. Photograph and permission from © RMN-Grand Palais/Art Resource, New York.

growing tension between those two things drives the story forward. Heraldic devices proclaim an obvious chivalric identity for all to see, yet their very tangibility and lack of ambiguity open up a very modern question: who is the person who bears this identity? The story of the swan knight grapples with the porosity and instability of what was ultimately an enigmatic boundary between symbolic and social identities.

Chivalric Orders

The demands of rapid visual communication that were met by heraldry in both its highly differentiated (coats of arms) and simple (badges) forms shaped another aspect of chivalric identity in the late Middle Ages: chivalric orders.[28] Confraternities, guilds, lay orders, and other kinds of societies and organizations were not the domain of bourgeois elites alone. At the highest level of society, noble elites created highly exclusive and prestigious guilds or military brotherhoods known as chivalric orders. Among the most famous of these are the Order of the Garter in England, founded in 1348 by Edward III and to which noblewomen also belonged, and the Order of the Golden Fleece, founded in Bruges by Philip, Duke of Burgundy, in 1430. Such orders had distinctive devices that at times blur into the category of insignia, meaning an object that confers on or embodies the bearer's political authority and power (examples are the crown and the bishop's staff). In the case of the Order of the Garter, the symbol (heraldically speaking, a charge) is a short, buckled belt or garter that is shown in a circle; in the case of the Order of the Golden Fleece, it is a golden sheepskin or fleece usually worn suspended from a jeweled collar. Late medieval and early modern portraits of the noblemen who were members of such orders often show them wearing these insignia, as in plate 10, a portrait of the Dutch nobleman and general Jan II van Wassenaer (1483–1523), burgrave of Leiden.[29]

Many European museums own late medieval or early modern examples of lavish insignia fashioned out of gold and gems for members of these prestigious chivalric orders. Among the surviving badges can also be found images and charges associated with some chivalric orders.

One fundamental goal of chivalric orders was to fashion shared ideals that transcended regional boundaries, local politics, and any putative divide between secular and religious power. The late medieval badge shown in figure 6.14 was created for a new holy site focused on a wonder-working statue of the Blessed Virgin Mary in the cathedral of Aarschot, Belgium, merged secular and religious symbols of power.[30] On the badge, the Virgin sits enthroned between two heraldic shields bearing the crests of members of the

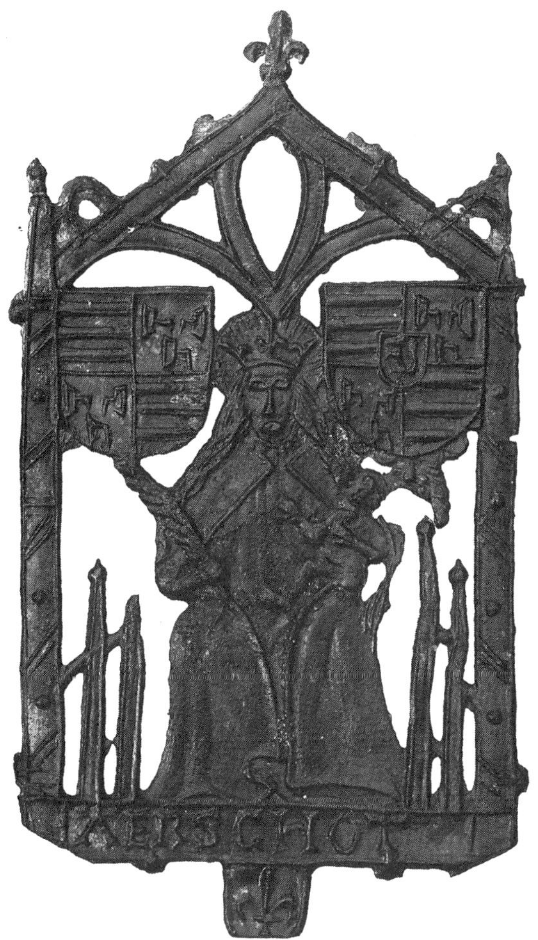

Figure 6.14. Pewter badge, Virgin Mary seated with Child under arch on either side of her lilies and heraldic shields of Croÿ family, suspended from right-hand shield the Order of the Golden Fleece, at bottom of badge the inscription AERSCHOT and shield of city of Aarschot, eyelets, Aarschot, Belgium, 1475–1524, found in Nieuwlande, Netherlands, 75 × 41 mm. Langbroek, Netherlands, Family Van Beuningen Collection, inv. 1228 (Kunera 00412). Photograph courtesy of Family Van Beuningen Collection.

Croÿ family, who had rebuilt the cathedral after its destruction (together with large parts of the city) in a siege in 1489 and who strongly promoted the new holy site. Below the Virgin Mary is the heraldic shield of the city of Aarschot. From the right-hand shield is suspended the Golden Fleece, to which order its most powerful member, William of Croÿ (1458–1521), belonged. On the badge, secular and religious imagery and symbolism seamlessly intertwine; as Hanneke van Asperen remarks, "Those who bore these religious badges away from Aarschot spread the image of authority and power that the Croÿ family wanted to project."[31]

Oswald von Wolkenstein

Belonging to a prestigious chivalric order bestowed social goods: honor, worth, and connections. Wearing the device of such an order, whether that device was made of gold or of pewter, claimed and announced its wearer's belonging to an elite, knightly brotherhood that was transcultural and translinguistic. An unusual work of late medieval art illustrates these points. It is one of the first authentic portraits of a German poet and depicts the Austrian nobleman, diplomat, and composer Oswald von Wolkenstein (1376/1377–1445), shown in plate 11.

Oswald's portrait was made sometime between 1432 and 1438, when he was about fifty-five years old.[32] Probably made under his direct supervision, the portrait shows Oswald wearing distinctive badges. What do the badges signify and what kind of identity is the nobleman seeking to fashion with them? Answering these questions leads us to survey some of Oswald's achievements, which encapsulate chivalric self-fashioning in the late Middle Ages.

Oswald's long and eventful life was spent maneuvering in, around, and through never-ending crises. There were variously calibrated combinations of political turmoil at the local, regional, and national levels, from bitter, decades-long, feud-like, often violent legal quarrels both in and outside of court with neighbors and relatives, to taking part in major battle campaigns across Europe (the anti-Arab wars in Portugal and Spain, the anti-Hussite campaigns in eastern Europe, the Baltic crusades). There was the ongoing business of making and breaking political alliances with overlords, peers, and subordinates. Embroiled in politics, Oswald appears to have sought throughout his life to outmaneuver his immediate overlord, Duke Frederick IV of Austria (1382–1439, r. from 1402) by seeking alliances with their shared overlord, Sigismund of Luxembourg (1368–1437), who was king of Hungary and

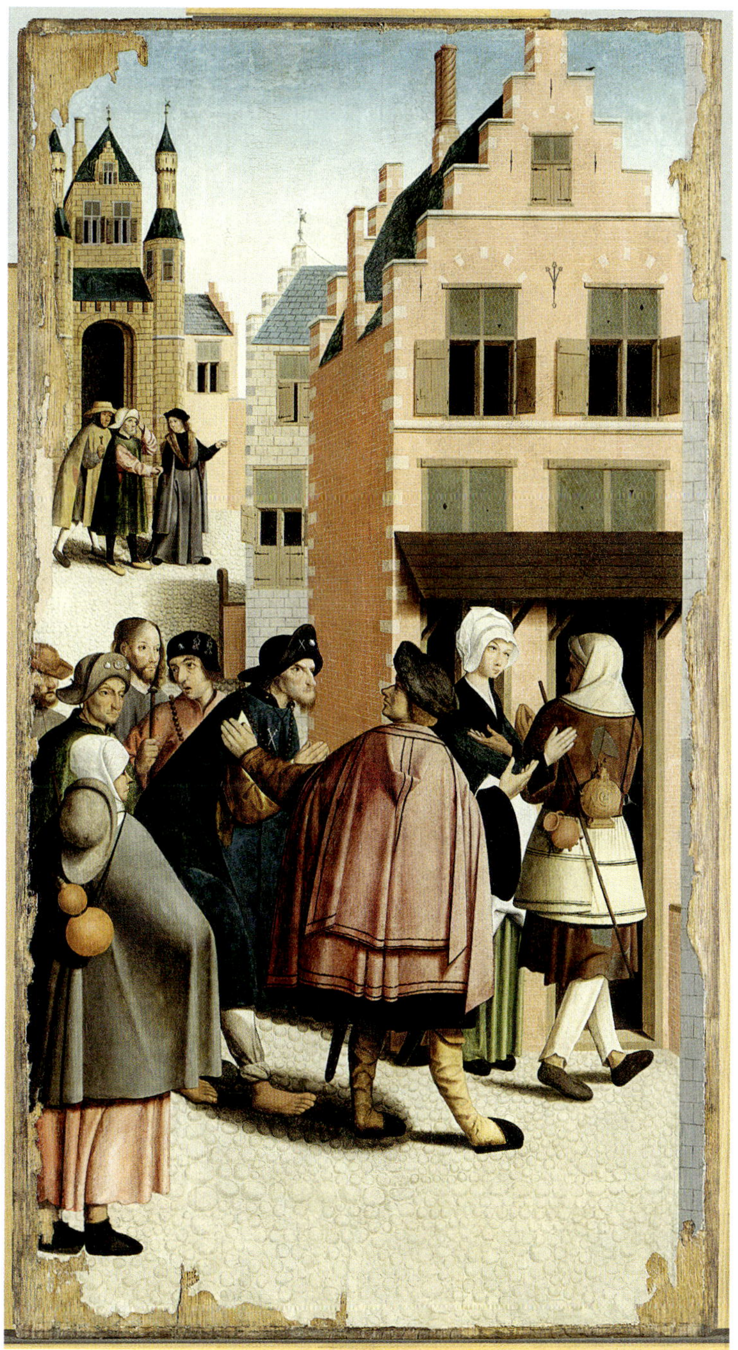

Plate 1. The Master of Alkmaar, *The Seven Works of Mercy*, oil painting on panel, 1504, detail from panel five of six, 103.5 × 56.8 cm. Amsterdam, Rijksmuseum, inv. SK-A-2815-5. Photograph courtesy of Rijksmuseum, Amsterdam.

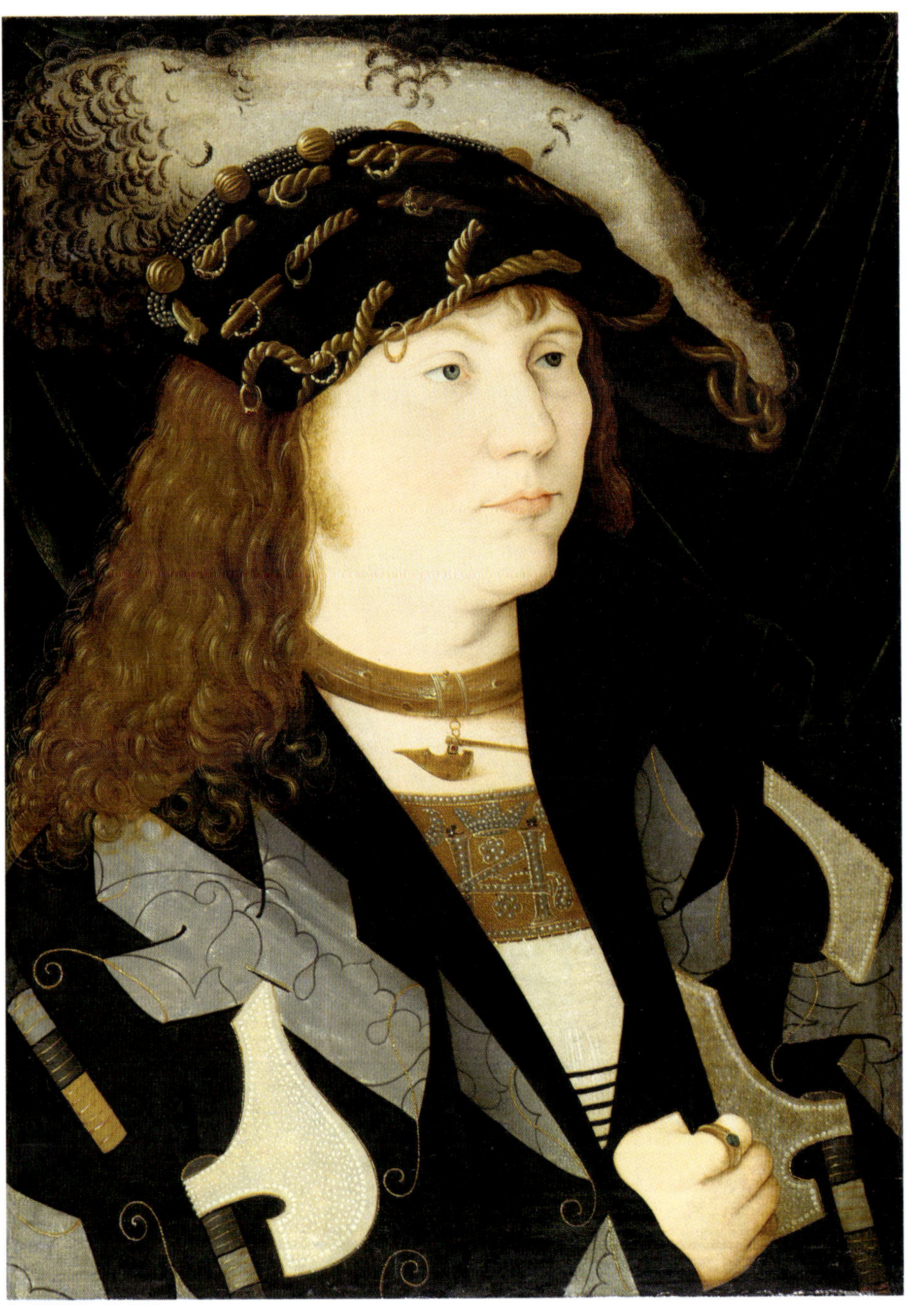

Plate 2. After Jacopo de' Barbari, *Portrait of Henry V of Mecklenburg, The Peaceful* (1479–1552), oil on wood panel (with tempura?), after 1507, 18 × 12.75 in. (45.7 × 32.4 cm). Raleigh, North Carolina, North Carolina Museum of Art, purchased with funds from the North Carolina State Art Society (Robert F. Phifer Bequest) in honor of Robert Lee Humber, G.69.33.1. Photograph and permission from North Carolina Museum of Art.

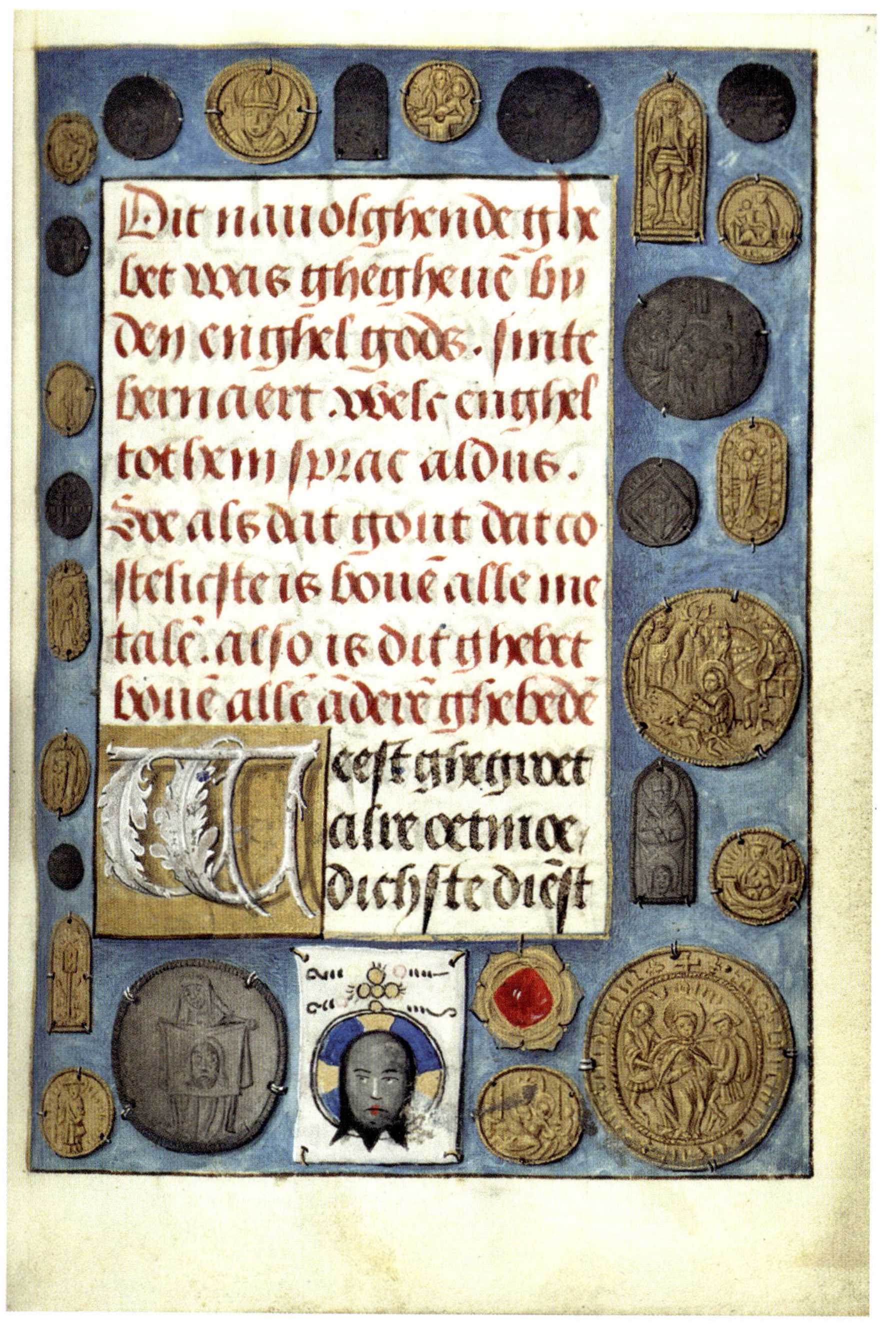

Plate 3. Master of the Dresden Prayerbook, detail of Book of Hours, illumination with images of pilgrim badges, parchment, Bruges, Belgium, c. 1500, 14.5 × 10.5 cm. Berlin, Kupferstichkabinett, Staatliche Museen zu Berlin Preussischer Kulturbesitz, inv. 78 B 14, fol. 19r. Photographer: Jörg P. Anders. Photograph and permission from Art Resource, New York.

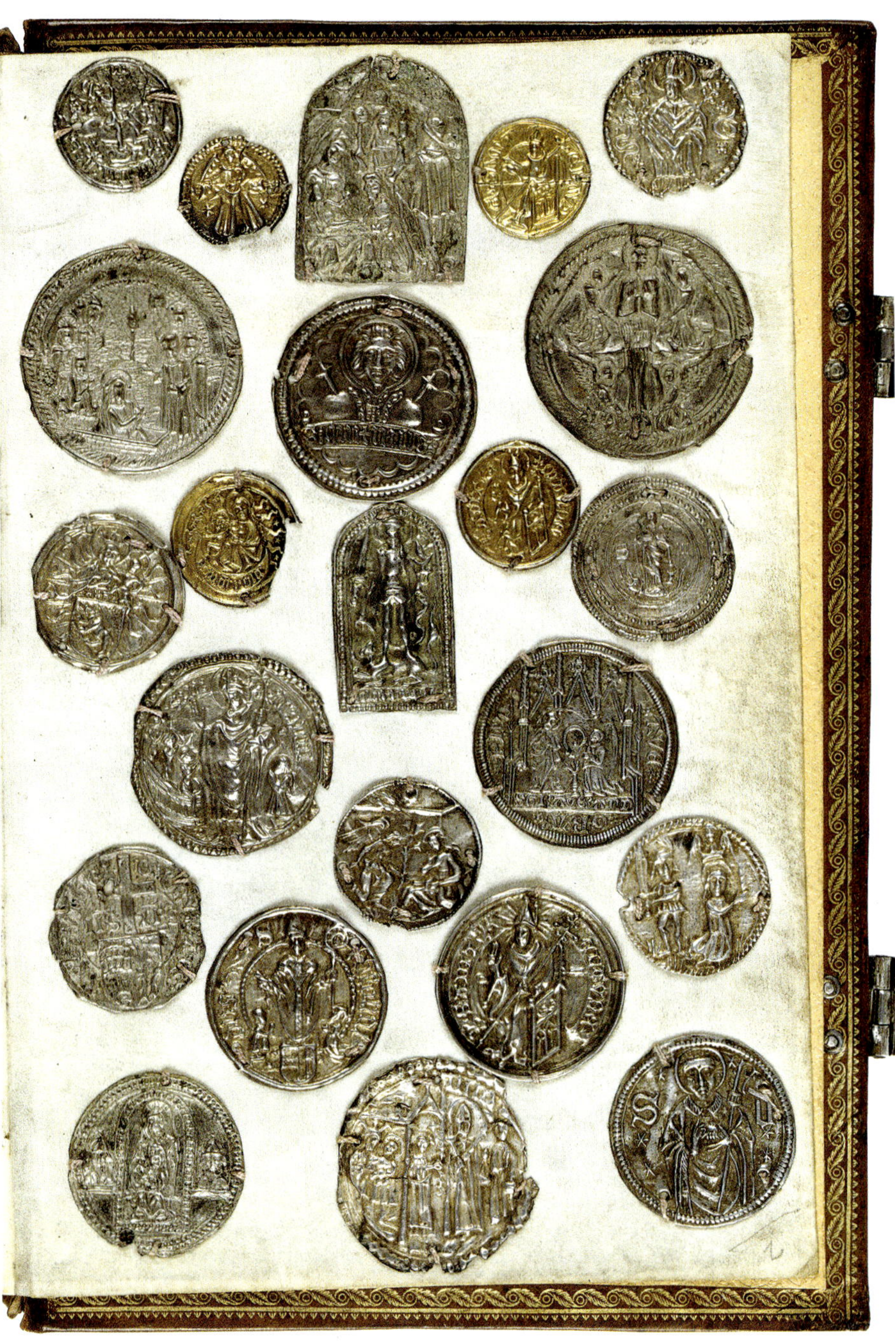

Plate 4. Master of the Small Eyes, detail of Book of Hours, twenty-three silver and gilt pilgrim badges sewn on empty page, vellum, Bruges, Belgium, c. 1440–1460, 19.6 × 13.4 cm. The Hague, Nationale Bibliotheek van Nederland–Koninklijke Bibliotheek, 77 L 60, fol. 98r. Photograph courtesy of photographer: Hanneke van Asperen. Source: Museum Meermanno/Huis van het Boek & National Library of the Netherlands, The Hague.

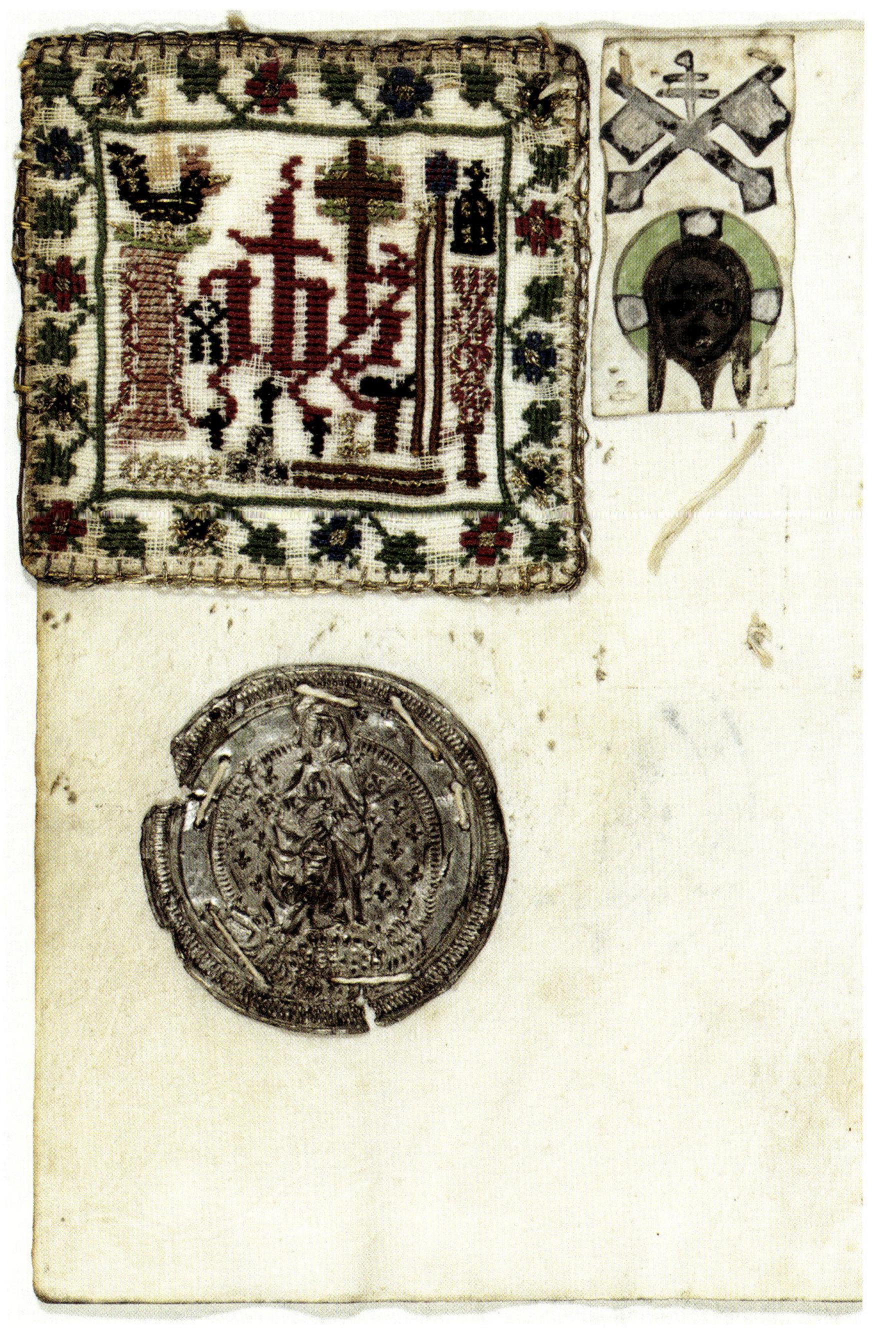

Plate 5. Manuscript page of Book of Hours, sewn-in embroidery of Holy Initials, paper badge featuring Saint Peter's keys and the veil of Veronica and pilgrim badge, Paris, 1450–1500, 130 × 80 mm. Paris, Bibliothèque de l'Arsenal, inv. MS 1176 rés, fol. Av-Br. Photograph courtesy of photographer: Hanneke van Asperen. Source: Bibliothèque nationale de France.

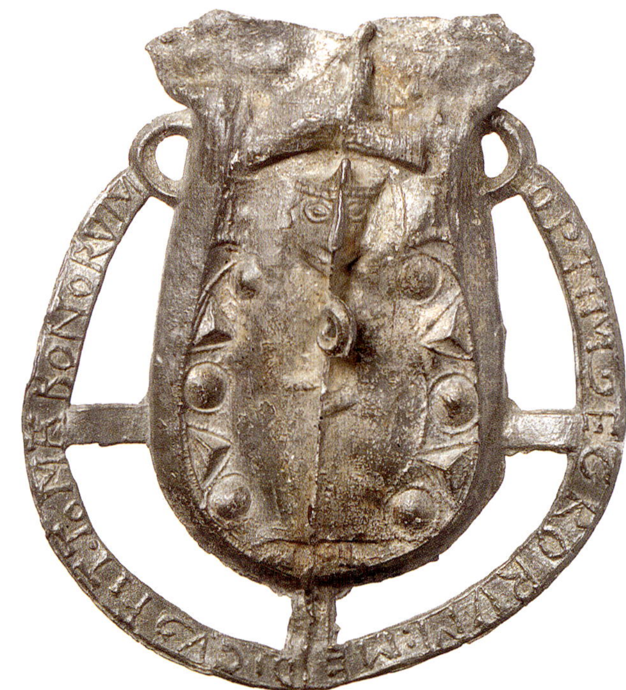

Plate 6a. Pewter ampulla, Saint Thomas Becket, inscription OPTIMUS EGRORUM MEDICUS FIT TOMA BONORUM [Thomas is the best doctor for the worthy sick], origin unknown, 1300–1400, found in London, 85 × 77 mm. London, Museum of London, inv. 8778. Photograph and permission from © Museum of London.

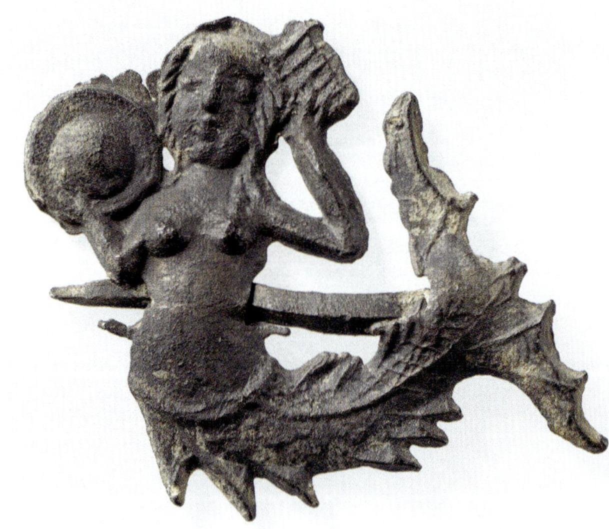

Plate 6b. Pewter badge, mermaid holding mirror in right hand and comb in left, pin, origin unknown, 1400–1449, found in Paris, 24 × 25 mm. Paris, Musée de Cluny–Musée national du Moyen Âge, inv. CL18074 (Kunera 01652). Photographer: Jean-Giles Berizzi. Photograph and permission from © RMN-Grand Palais/Art Resource, New York.

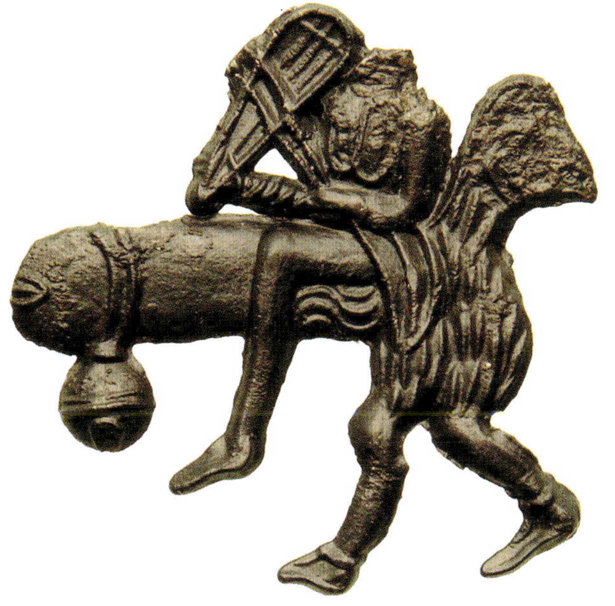

Plate 7a. Pewter badge, walking, shod, belled penis creature ridden by a viol-playing, bare-legged human figure, pin, origin unknown, 1375–1424, found in Nieuwlande, Netherlands, 27 × 27 × 13 mm. Langbroek, Netherlands, Family Van Beuningen Collection, inv. 1845 (Kunera 00645). Photograph courtesy of Family Van Beuningen Collection.

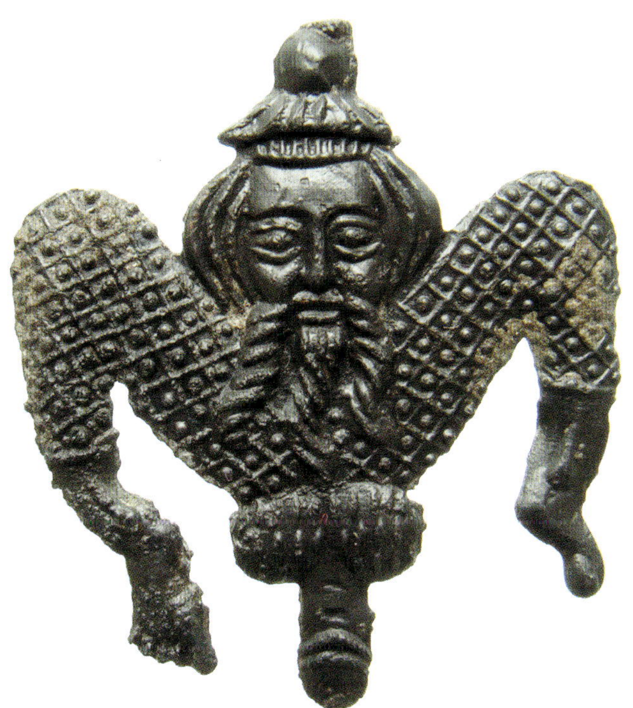

Plate 7b. Pewter badge, squatting man with long beard and bare feet wearing fancy leggings and exposing genitals, pin, 1400–1449, found in Nieuwlande, Netherlands, 39 × 33 mm. Langbroek, Netherlands, Family Van Beuningen Collection, inv. 0785 (Kunera 00618). Photograph courtesy of Family Van Beuningen Collection.

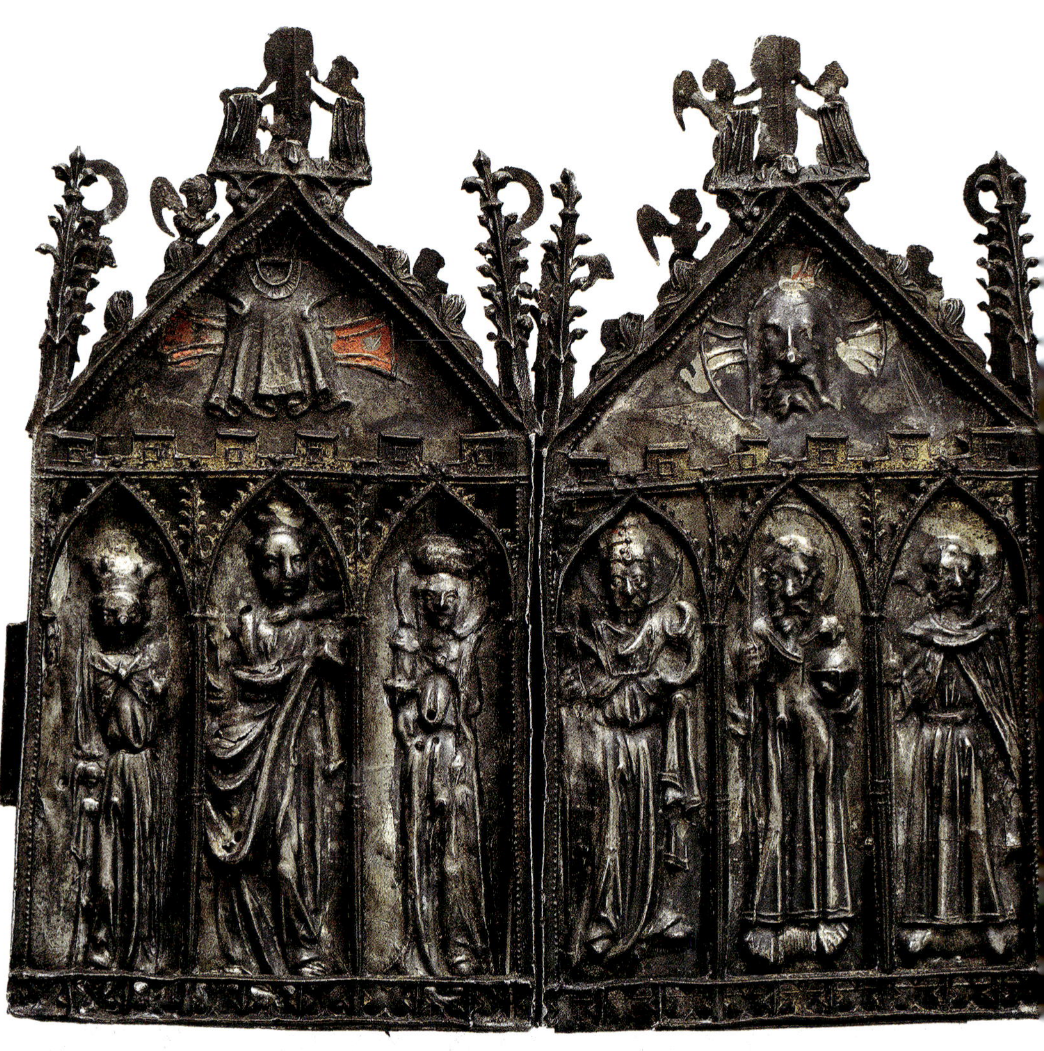

Plate 8. Outside of hinged pewter badge, saints in arcaded niches, three male saints on right under tympanum with Holy Face and three female saints on left under tympanum with Virgin Mary's tunic, pendant, Aachen, Germany, 1375–1424, found in Dordrecht, Netherlands, 111 × 114 mm. Langbroek, Netherlands, Family Van Beuningen Collection, inv. 3753 (Kunera 06497r). Photograph courtesy of Family Van Beuningen Collection.

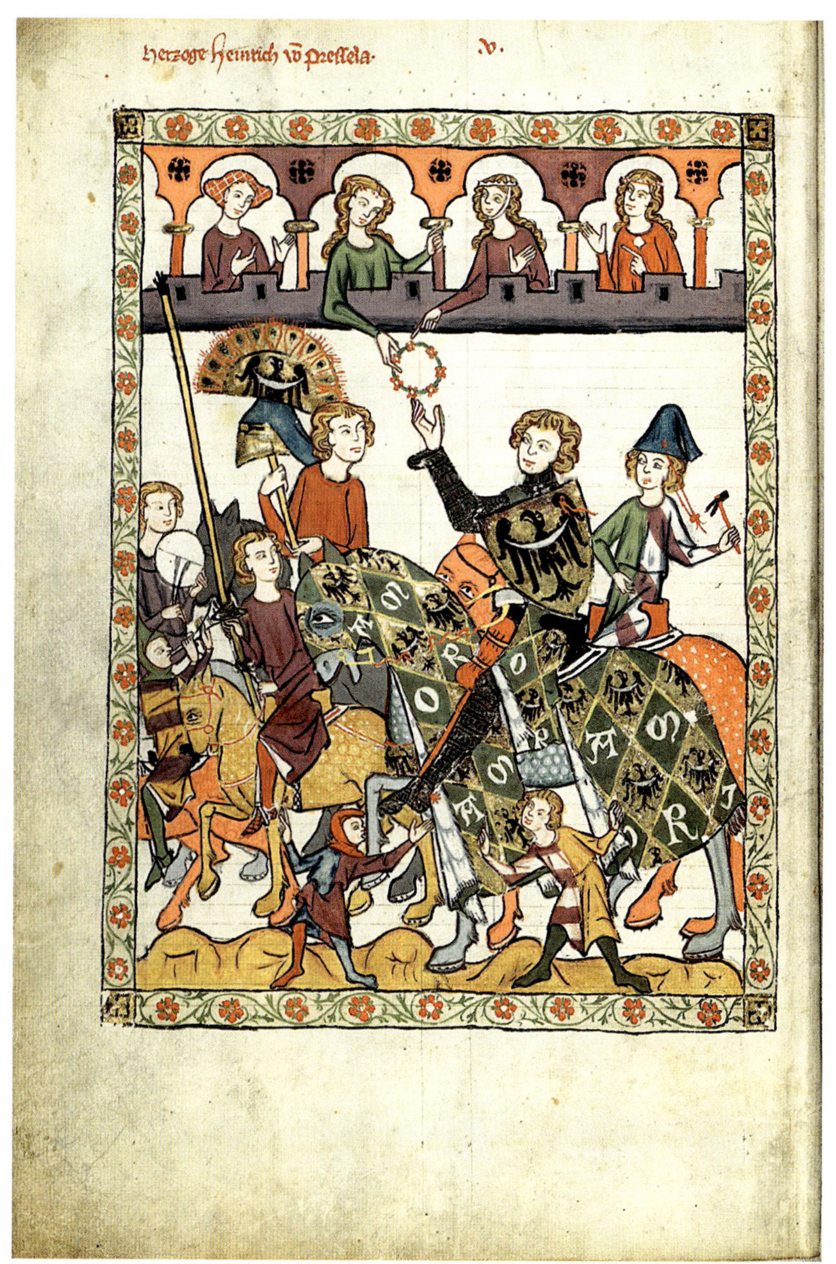

Plate 9. Manuscript illumination on parchment, Herzog Heinrich von Breslau (probably Duke Henry VI of Silesia-Breslau, c. 1253–1290) receives a garland from a young noblewoman in a festive scene, Zürich, 1300–1340, 35.5 × 25 cm. Heidelberg, Universitätsbibliothek Heidelberg, cod. pal. germ. 848 (Grosse Heidelberger Liederhandschrift or *Codex Manesse*), folio 11r. Photograph courtesy of Universitätsbibliothek Heidelberg.

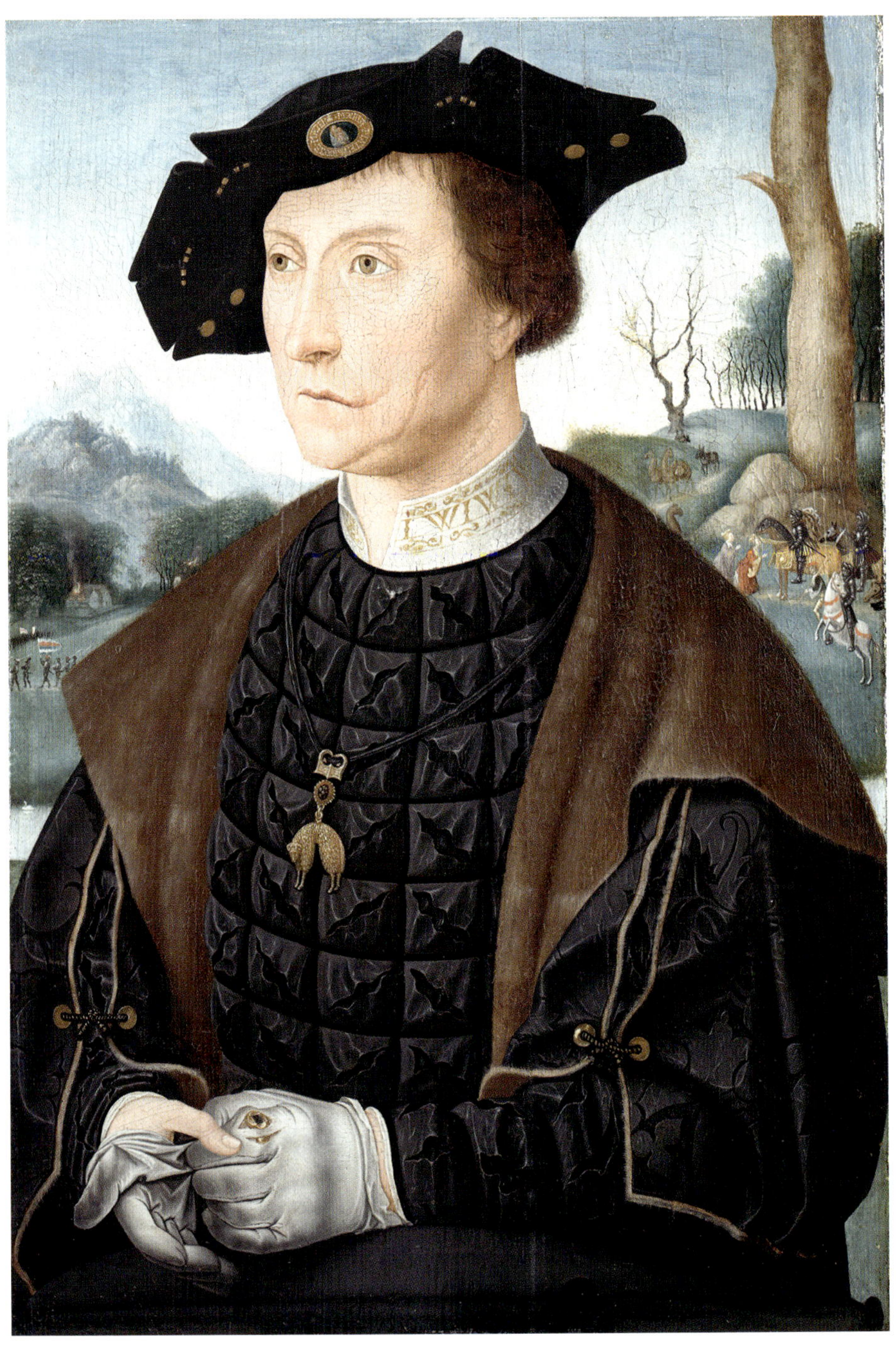

Plate 10. Jan Mostaert, workshop, *Jan van Wassenaer* (1483–1523), oil on wood, 1520–1522, 47 × 33 cm. Paris, Musée du Louvre, inv. MI802. Photographer: Tony Querrec. Photograph and permission from © RMN-Grand Palais/Art Resource, New York.

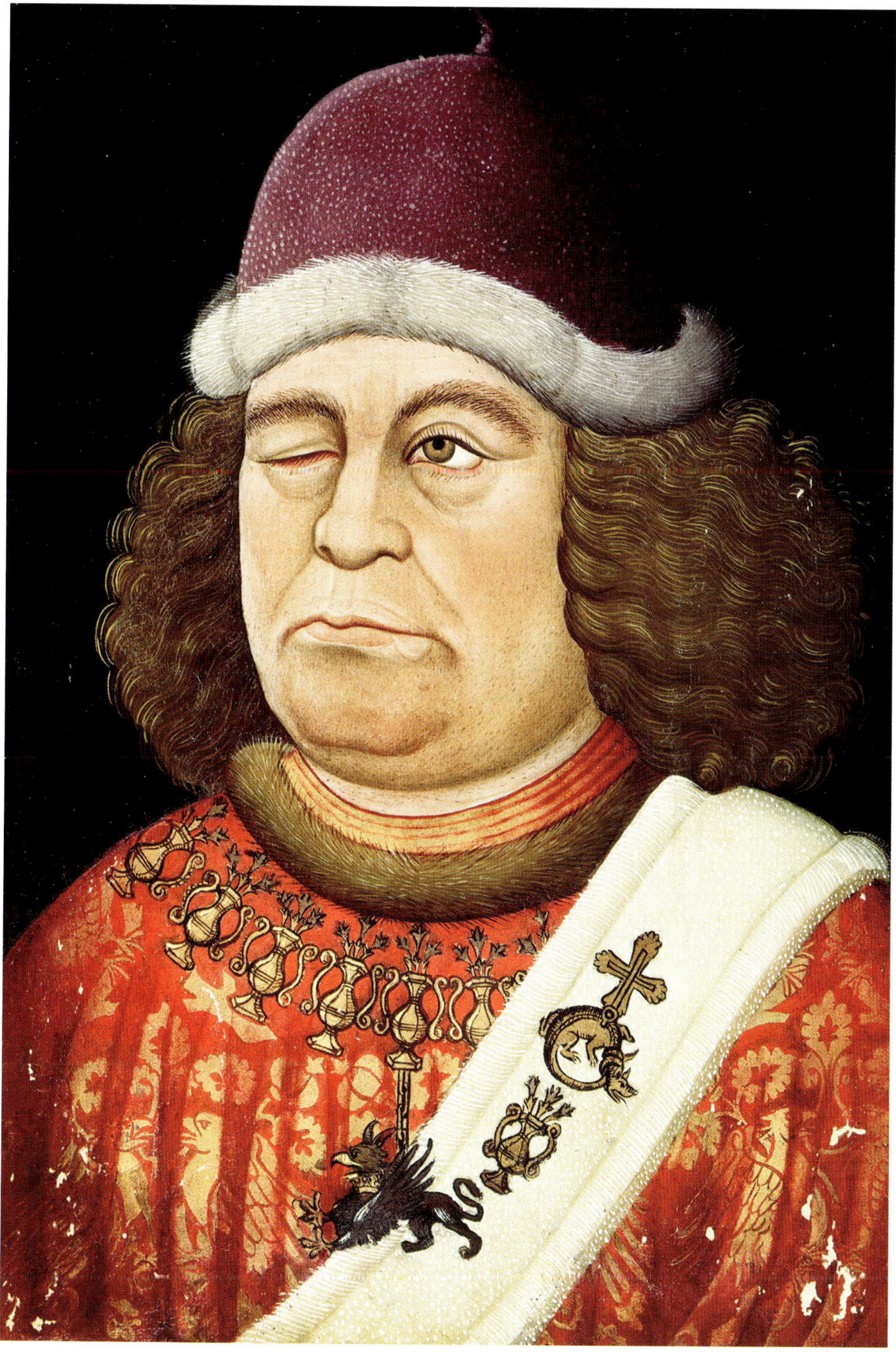

Plate 11. Manuscript illumination, portrait of Oswald von Wolkenstein, Austria, 1432–1438. Innsbruck, Austria, Universitäts- und Landesbibliothek Tirol, no signature (Innsbrucker Liederhandschrift B), folio 1. Photograph and permission from INTERFOTO/Alamy Stock Photo.

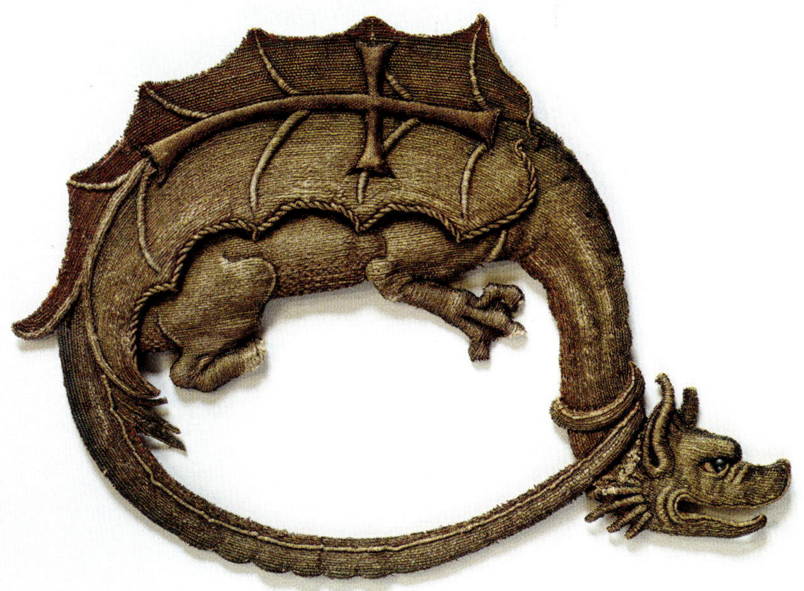

Plate 12a. Cloth badge, raised embroidery in gold and silk thread on linen, device of the Order of the Dragon founded 1387 by King Sigismund, southern Germany, c. 1430, 27 × 39 cm. Munich, Bayerisches Nationalmuseum München, acquired in 1860 with the collection of Martin von Reider, Bamberg, inv. T 3792. Photographer: Bastian Krack. Photograph and permission from © Bayerisches Nationalmuseum München.

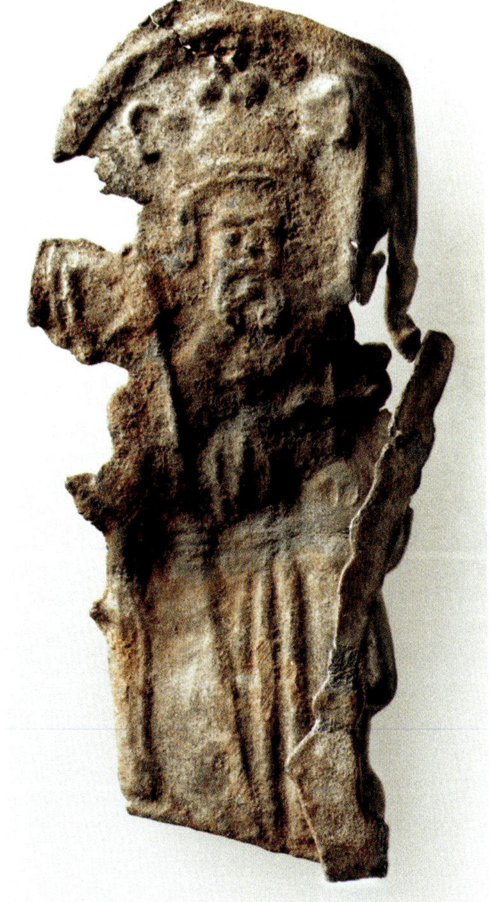

Plate 12b. Pewter badge, Saint Olaf. Oslo, Museum of Cultural History, inv. C51657. Photographer: Mårten Teigen/CC BY-SA 4.1. Photograph courtesy of Museum of Cultural History, University of Oslo.

Croatia (1387–1437), king of Bohemia (1419–1437), and Holy Roman Emperor (1433–1437). There were never-ending financial difficulties, sometimes calamities (apparently Oswald even tried his hand as a shipping merchant at one point; the ship sank with its cargo and he barely survived). All this was accompanied, on a personal level and throughout his life, by a full and wholehearted participation in chivalric practices.

The outline of such a biography is run-of-the-mill for the late medieval nobility. Political strife and financial turmoil cloaked in chivalric identity were the norm. Two things are extraordinary about Oswald. First, perhaps more extraordinary to us than to his contemporaries, Oswald von Wolkenstein often acted as a diplomat and was repeatedly elected by his fellow nobles to act as a trusted mediator and negotiator on their behalf. Second, he was a gifted and prolific poet and composer who was recognized as such in his own time. More than one hundred poems, many with musical notation, have come down to us.

Oswald himself cultivated the identities of knight, politician, and poet as though they were one. Not only did he compose poetry; he devoted attention and resources to preserving his own poetic work by having it collected into manuscripts. Three of these compilation manuscripts survive, named for the cities where they are now housed.[33] Two were created during Oswald's lifetime. They contain (more or less) his entire oeuvre of some 110 songs, most with notations of melodies. Without his effort, we would know next to nothing of Oswald's work as a poet-songwriter, and our knowledge of late medieval German literature would be immeasurably poorer.

Oswald's oeuvre was wide-ranging. He composed traditional, monophonic melodies as well as polyphonic ones, which in the context of their own time were more modern. He tried his hand at nearly every kind of traditional poem or song; the only genre noticeably missing is political poetry (perhaps a lifetime spent in the brutal realities of medieval politics made the prospect of creating art about it less than appealing). Oswald wrote religious and devotional lyrics of many kinds. He wrote worldly poetry, such as courtly love laments, dialogues, female-voiced poems, pastourelles, and a few didactic works. He wrote a number of erotic and obscene poems. Finally, there are a few highly innovative autobiographical songs on which his modern reputation largely rests. Devoting time and resources to compiling his work into manuscripts shows that Oswald could command the considerable resources necessary to accomplish the task: funds for the manufacture or purchase of expensive writing materials (quills, inks, parchment for two of the manuscripts, paper for the third) and to support the scribes (there are at least eight hands in the surviving manuscripts) undertaking the time-consuming work of compiling and copying. Oswald must have been very proud of his accomplishments as a poet and as a songwriter.

And then there is the portrait in which Oswald stages himself as a wealthy, mature, politically well-connected lord. Made during Oswald's lifetime and probably under his supervision, it has been sewn in place at the beginning of the Innsbruck manuscript (the Vienna manuscript also opens with an Oswald portrait, now badly damaged). This portrait of chivalric self-fashioning and political dignity was designed to be the first thing the reader saw when she or he began to read Oswald's collected poems. It set the stage for everything that follows. What kind of texts does it lead one to expect? The fervent devotional poems, the allegories, the declarations of courtly love—all fit the manner of the dignified man draped in gold badges shown here. But the collection contains other kinds of poems, too. There are witty and sarcastic poems, erotic ones, and even obscene poems that might seem unsuitable in the august framework of these chivalric orders. Yet as with badges, distinctions between the sacred and the profane, between the decorous and the obscene, do not map easily onto social status or station in life in the Middle Ages, nor did they map neatly onto an imagined divide between religious and secular ways of being. Rather, the sacred and the erotic, the proper and the ribald, coexisted, assigned apparently according to their respective places and moments by criteria different than those we use today.

Poet and chivalrous knight were one. Two of the three surviving compilation manuscripts open with the author portrait that must have been, like the poetic compilation itself, designed by Oswald for the express purpose of presenting a chivalric identity to posterity. The small, bust-length portrait depicts a heavy-set man whose copious, brown curls are capped by a sumptuous and expensive fur-lined hat of purple cloth. His right eye is closed, apparently reflecting a real physical impairment. Staring solemnly into the near distance, the man is dressed in a robe-like garment with a fur collar and made of exquisite red-and-gold brocade in whose pattern griffins and bouquets of leaves intertwine. Such long robes were worn by mature, elite noblemen and seen in many images from the fourteenth and early fifteenth centuries, when such conservative attire contrasted with the fashion for courtly youths, who wore tunics and tights, and with the fashion for fighting men, who wore doublets, tights, and codpieces. These contrasts mean that the choice of garments staged the subject sartorially as a noble lord of mature years whose primary roles were those of political negotiator, diplomat, and arbiter.

To successful lordship belonged the art and craft of maintaining and claiming alliances. These networks of alliances showed a lord's reach and reputation and were an integral part of his political stature. In Oswald's portrait, the badges are heraldic devices signaling political alliances. Selected by Oswald to be part of this portrait, they were probably the highest honors that he received in his life. Draped below his neck and across his shoulders is a magnificent chain of gold, vase-like objects, each holding three long stalks, which represent jars containing lilies.[34] From the chain there dangles a large, bronze-colored griffin. These objects fashioned from precious metals—jar, lily, and griffin—represent Oswald's membership in the chivalric Order of the Jar, which was founded by the kings of Aragon (in Spain) around 1400. Oswald was made a member of the order in 1415–16 by Margaret of Prades (1387–1429), queen of Aragon, during the winter that he spent at her court. These symbols represent Oswald as widely traveled and connected by virtue of his accomplishments to one of the great royal houses of Europe. The symbols of jar, lily, and griffin are repeated in the image. Directly above the griffin there is a second badge, another jar with lilies. Oswald's examples appear to be fashioned out of precious metals, but pewter badges survive using these symbols, such as the one in figure 6.15, which is similar to those shown on Oswald's portrait.

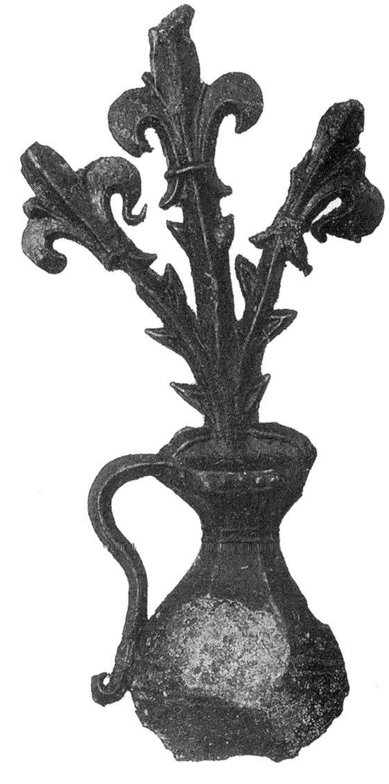

Figure 6.15. Pewter badge, three lilies in a vessel, attachment unknown, origin unknown, 1450–1499, found in The Hague, 47 × 23 mm. Langbroek, Netherlands, Family Van Beuningen Collection, inv. 3982 (Kunera 17258). Photograph courtesy of Family Van Beuningen Collection.

Images of griffin, jar, and lily have also been woven into the cloth of the robe that Oswald is shown wearing, transforming it into a veritable tapestry or backdrop of chivalric identity for the gold objects floating on top. Oswald is also wearing a white, thickly fringed sash that drapes diagonally across his body. The griffin hovers above the sash, set off by its whiteness. Pinned above it, as we have said, is another jar with three lilies. Above it in turn is an object consisting of two equal-sized parts: a cross with four arms of equal length sitting on top of a circle across whose top rim rests a large and ungainly creature—a resting dragon, much like the one shown on plate 12a. This badge is the device of the Order of the Dragon, founded by King Sigismund of Luxembourg. Oswald was made a member of the order in 1431, not long before the portrait was made. The white, fringed sash is similarly part of the heraldic device of the Order of the Dragon.

In the portrait, these devices function as a kind of objective measure of Oswald's chivalric worth and international reputation. They have been bestowed on him by two of the greatest lords of his time, validating his status as a chivalric nobleman. The badges assert that two powerful rulers have honored the chivalric virtue they found in him. The portrait claims an identity. Oswald chose to have displayed the badges that proudly announce his pan-European political allegiances and alliances. Oswald's decision to compile his poetic oeuvre and to open that compilation manuscript with a self-portrait featuring political badges and devices presents the modern viewer with a magnificent piece of late medieval, elite, chivalric self-fashioning.

The rapid proliferation of heraldry and badges in the High and late Middle Ages coincided in time and place. Badges were an ideal medium for producing more and new signs associated with social institutions or a specific knightly household because they were cheap and easily mass-produced. Nor were badges the only kind of object used to make devices that signaled belonging. Rather, badges belonged to the cheap end of things. Devices were also fashioned out of precious materials, as was discussed in Chapter 4, and from cloth and thread, often embossed, embroidered, or appliqued onto fabric, as will be discussed again in Chapter 7. Lead-tin alloy badges were not pioneers in the art and practice of heraldry; as is so often the case with badges, their production took up, recycled, or repurposed an already existing practice of signification.

7
Badges in the Medieval City

Ypres, late May, 1383

The honor of joining the confraternity and wearing the golden crossbow is marred by the fact that his father, wife, and daughters take all his efforts for granted, when he deserves this honor much more than many others who wear it.

That brother-in-law of his, whose humble demeanor clashes with business cunning, who is so quiet in his presence yet jovial and open with others, overlooks and thwarts him, ignoring his business acumen and his excellent advice. How much time has he not sacrificed to do good work, teaching the poor schoolboys how to reckon and read because that benighted old fool of a schoolmaster does such a piss-poor job? How the pupils adore him and flock to him! He will order small rosette badges made of lead-tin from the leadsmith down the street, something to give the boys at Shrovetide so that as they run through the streets his name will run with them.

He hurries away from his fine home on the city square, reaches the old town gate, slowing so that the watchman can see the golden crossbow badge on his cloak and let him pass through the city walls and out into the derelict Rijselstraat suburb. It is growing dark. There are only a few souls about; the glimmerings of hearth fires are few and far between.

Over the years the yards in the Rijselstraat suburb have thinned. Where once the fullers and dyers jostled one another for a prime spot—his father still bores the snot out of anyone who will listen to his interminable tales of better days when there was more action and more money—now half the pits are empty, filled with mud and trash. The remaining weavers have grown insolent, emboldened by the likes of his brother-in-law, who has lured them back inside the city walls with promises of new looms and loom stalls.

A waste of money. As though the old looms aren't perfectly adequate! Who does his brother-in-law think he is fooling anyhow, with this prattling on about a new kind of cloth and a new market to the south? Better they should do what they know best.

Why should a member of an old merchant house such as himself have to justify his business and trade to these upstarts? People should understand the value of time-honored Ypres cloth. Ungrateful wretches the lot of them, taking advantage of the networks built by old merchant houses such as his own and not even acknowledging their debt. The wiser members of the confraternity agree when he whispers about his brother-in-law's base origins and baser betrayals. Old fools! They will thank him when they learn about the business he has transacted with the English bishop, Henry, on his last trip to Ghent. That will be the end of his brother-in-law and his allies. But all in good time.

Decay has effaced familiar landmarks, and he nearly rushes past the alley that leads to the crumbling warehouses and work yards still owned by his family. The going is slower now as he picks his way through the detritus of decay. What a mess! Who is in charge of collecting the rents here anyway? Isn't it that insolent old clerk who was his father's confidant, the one who used to humiliate him in front of everyone by correcting his French, the one who sent that impudent message yesterday that has brought him out at night into this dunghill in the first place?

Yesterday, on the Sabbath yet, the kitchen maid—barely human that one, barely speaks Flemish—stood trembling in the paneled chamber of his townhouse. She stammered out that the old clerk had come to the back door.

"Bad business," she stuttered. "He bring secret. For head of house. Bad business. With English. Big business."

The threat of such stories! As he raised his hand to cuff her, she held out a cheap, bent, tin crossbow badge, and whispered,

"He say, 'give to master.' He say, 'Rijselstraat yard.'"

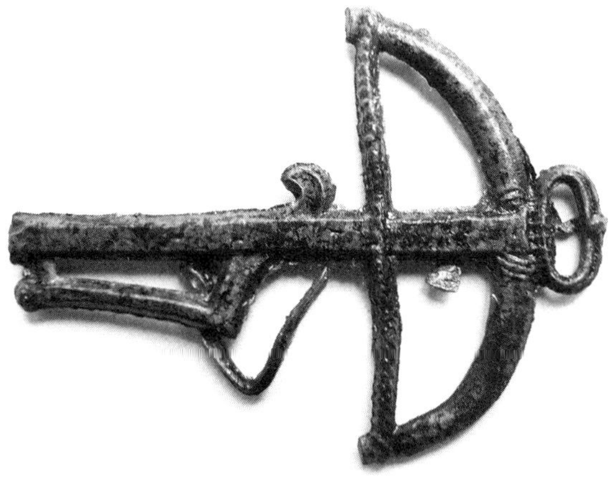

Figure 7.1. Pewter badge, crossbow with windlass and footrest, pin, origin unknown, 1275–1299, found in Ypres, Belgium, 55 × 40 mm. Yper Museum, inv. SM 005055 (Kunera 04992). Photographer: Els Deroo. Photograph courtesy of Yper Museum.

How he wishes he had landed that blow. A good whipping that girl has earned, pretending to know something of the affairs of her betters. And yet the incident has troubled his sleep. How came that old know-it-all to lay hands on a badge of the crossbow confraternity? How dare he pretend allegiance to a guild far above him in wealth and station? How dare he usurp a status to which he has no right? That weaselly old clerk is trading on the presumptuous overfamiliarity that has led his father, grown soft in his old age, to give him the outrageous gift of annual income from rents. He is draining the family coffers, neglecting his obligations to maintain the property, and now, on top of all that, the brazen effrontery of the crossbow sign! It must stop, and he is coming to Rijselstraat to stop it.

His eye is caught by firelight flickering from a hovel; a figure beckons from the doorway.

Enough of this! He is the head of house and master here! He pauses, frowns, arranges the golden crossbow on his cloak, and calls out as he steps over the threshold.

"You, clerk! Wretch! How dare you claim to belong to the crossbow?"

A peasant in a new red doublet? Another wearing new hose? The righteous speech sputters and dies. There are five of them. One leans against the wall, twirling a knife in his fingers. Two sit on stools by the fire warming their hands. A fourth stands in the middle of the room with his hand resting lightly on the hilt of a sword. A fifth man is a dark shadow in the darkest corner, a large bundle at his feet. The fire crackles. The men say nothing.

He retreats toward the door, but before he has taken three steps, one of the fellows at the fire has sprung up and blocked it and the other has pushed him forward, hard. He stumbles into the arms of the swordsman still poised, with a thoughtful expression on his face, in the middle of the room. The swordsman grabs and pins his body while the right hand, from nowhere, presses a knife to his throat.

"Cat got your tongue, I suppose. Or will get it soon enough. Show him the old servant whose loyalty he has repaid so graciously."

The man in the shadows kicks the bundle toward the firelight, and a familiar face stares out at him in death. It is the old clerk.

The swordsman steps in close and fingers the gold crossbow.

"He was trying to warn your father, you know, that we had learned of your betrayal. Oh, well, it's up to us to deal with you now. I think

I'll keep this trinket. Return it to your brother-in-law, perhaps. Bishop Henry will wonder what has happened to his trusty turncoat, but that can't be helped."

The swordsman rips the crossbow badge away, and in the same motion thrusts him toward the three men at the door, who jerk his arms behind him and, as he begins to cry out, shove a gag in his mouth.

As they drag him out of the hovel, away from the light, into the dark, toward marsh and river, the swordsman calls out the last words he hears before a blow to the head renders him senseless. "Remember, fellows, no blood on his clothes!"

Badges both religious and secular have been recovered overwhelmingly from cities that flourished during the High and late Middle Ages in northwestern Europe. Especially prominent for badges recovered up until this day are two great cities, London and Paris, flanking on the west and the south a geographically dense cluster network of rich, manufacturing cities in the United Kingdom, Low Countries and northern France (Flanders): Dordrecht and Amsterdam in the Netherlands; Ypres, Bruges, and Ghent in Belgium; Valenciennes in France; and more. The cities in this zone of highly developed urbanization were the engines of the economic, religious, and political changes out of which modern European culture arose.[1] Most surviving secular badges, as well as a large percentage of the surviving religious badges, have been found here, although more badges are steadily being found and studied from Baltic cities such as Gdańsk in Poland. The kinds of badges discussed in the previous chapters circulated in these cities: political devices, amulets, religious badges, pilgrim badges, badges of friendships, chivalric badges, heraldic badges, and so on. Understanding the symbolism, functions, and meanings attached to medieval badges means understanding the political and social structures of these medieval cities.

King and Bishop Flank a Tower

The symbolism of the badge shown on the cover of this book, found in the city of Ypres, expresses political ideals shared across the geographical region where badges are ubiquitous (for the original badge, see figure 3.14). Round, a little less than six centimeters in diameter, fastened with a pin, and surviving in an unusually complete state with its backing intact, the badge centers on an image of a stone building of some kind, a church or gateway tower, which is held up by two figures, recognizable by their attributes of office as a king (crown and scepter) on the tower's right and a bishop (miter and staff) on the left. Can one think of a better symbol of civic harmony? It is possible to imagine that the building represents a stone tower and gateway that is part of a city wall, protecting and sheltering the city's inhabitants while representing the city's prosperity and its political autonomy. The gateway tower and the city for which it would stand are supported by the highest human authorities from the religious and secular spheres, respectively, a king and a bishop, who kneel at its side. Of the same height and sharing the same posture yet separated by the building itself, these two rulers gaze out at the viewer in a tableau that skillfully suggests both the separation of their realms and their equality and cooperation. The image is encircled by a rondelle decorated with small greenish stones separated by small tree-like designs and by small human heads, whose hairstyles indicate both elite status and gender: the men have pageboy haircuts; the women wear nets over their coiffures. These onlookers add secular elites, including women, to the badge. They surround the bishop, the king, and the tower, creating an internal audience in the badge and at the same time expanding the badge's vision of civic harmony into potentially a series of concentric circles, of which the male and female human busts on the badge show only the first. The human faces in the badge all gaze out at the viewer as if to invite her or him to join the next ring of civic harmony.

In this reading of the badge, city, church, and kingdom present themselves as a harmonious whole. The badge envisions an orderly world, cooperatively organized, in which elites and their political and religious institutions willingly collaborate for the good of the whole. It is striking that the badge does not represent hierarchy, which was regarded the *sine qua non* of medieval political thought. The highest representatives of secular and religious power are imaged as being of similar size, and they are on the same plane. In the imagery, they are equals in raising up and supporting the urban sphere. The hierarchies and rivalries of estate, wealth, guild and trade organization, religious institutions, politics, and intellectual thought that were ubiquitous in late medieval life are banished. The badge symbolizes harmony, order, and balance, an ideal rarely realized in the politics of late medieval civic life.

The badge interpretation put forward here is deliberately open. The central image is in fact a variation of the dedication theme, familiar from medieval iconography, in which a highborn secular donor is shown giving a sacred building to a religious figure, sometimes a highly placed churchman such as a bishop, sometimes a saint, sometimes a divinity such as the Virgin Mary herself. Some surviving large openwork badges, such as the one shown in figure 1.3, share the imagery of the Ypres badge shown on the cover and in figure 3.14 and discussed above but create a subtle shift in meaning through a change in the postures of the king and bishop.[2] In figure 1.3, the king on the right kneels, a political gesture of fealty and submission, while the bishop on the left stands. A specific political hierarchy and ideology, namely, that secular power is subordinate to religious power, is here made concrete. The shift in posture makes asymmetrical the directionality of the two figures, so that the king's knees orient his body and gaze toward the bishop on the left, while the bishop, upright and fully frontal, seems to ignore the king and gazes instead solemnly out at the viewer. The image in figure 1.3 symbolizes hierarchy between bishop and king, which conforms well to the conventions of a dedication image.

The openwork badge in figure 1.3 also presents some intriguing suggestions about the ways in which badges like it might have been worn. Like other openwork badges, it lacks a pin. It rather has small eyelets at the outer top corners of the crossbar that would have allowed it to be sewn onto something, a feature often seen on openwork badges. Figure 1.3 sports a ring at its tip, another common feature that might be a further eyelet but might also have anchored a pendant. The eyelets indicate that badges such as figure 1.3 could have been, for example, sewn or attached in some fashion onto fabric, parchment, leather, or paper, which would have then shown through. Because the original pewter was bright and shiny, these ornate open frames would have stood out well against many backgrounds. Yet turning over an openwork badge such as figure 1.3 suggests a more complicated state of affairs because their backs are equipped with tiny, carefully placed clips meant to be pinched down to hold in place some kind of backing. Two of these clips can be glimpsed at the bottom of the badge in figure 1.3, symmetrically aligned behind tiny decorative triangles; a third is folded over the crossbar and just under the foot of the kneeling ruler holding the tower. Such clips indicate that a badge originally had its own backing, now usually lost.

Such an openwork badge was a complex ensemble in its own right, the silvery shine of the openwork contrasting with a differently colored, carefully chosen backing now long disintegrated, perhaps sporting even a small pendant of some kind dangling from it, the whole thing sewn onto something else. Further, in comparison to most badges openwork badges such as figure 1.3 are large objects, more than double the size of most badges and four times the size of some. The large size means that they are too large to be worn on a hat. Yet like all badges, they are clearly meant and made to be seen. Perhaps they were sewn onto a larger swath of cloth, such as a cape or cloak, a caparison (the cloth covering a horse), a tent, a banner, or draperies of some kind. They make sense in the context of city ceremonies and events, perhaps worn as a device marking the bearer as a member of a great household, whether clerical or secular, perhaps displayed in a procession marking a political visit or a peace treaty, commemorating a feast day, or used in some fashion in a local tournament sponsored by civic authorities or great lords.

In a 2013 article, Hanneke van Asperen argued that the dedication image shared by the badges on the cover, in figure 1.3, in figure 3.14, and others like them with the central image of king and bishop flanking a tower, belong to the vast and complex holy site of Aachen, which, as was discussed in Chapter 5, was one of the most popular and frequently visited pilgrimage sites in late medieval northern Europe.[3] She argues these badges represent the dedication of the Palatine Chapel, built by Emperor Charlemagne (who thus becomes the king shown on the badges) and consecrated in 815, which was experienced essentially as a kind of shrine of shrines after the installation of magnificent new reliquaries in the first decades of the thirteenth century.[4] Nevertheless, badges using this imagery have to date only been found in the politically turbulent, economically advanced urban landscapes of Flanders and the Low Countries.

Let's return to the round badge from Ypres shown on this book's cover, and its original, figure 3.14. It combines and varies existing design elements to create a striking, jewelry-like object that conveys a political message. King and bishop, here symmetrical and aligned, suggest an equitable balance of power. The tower or church they support suggests the stone edifices of real cities. The faces of the elite men and women gaze serenely at the viewer while encircling the central image of symmetrical power. These elements transform this badge into a symbol of civic harmony, a vision of a longed-for ideal that was rarely realized in practice.

The Complexity of Medieval Cities

The peace and harmony symbolized in the round Ypres badge was distinguished more by its absence than by its presence in the cities of northwestern Europe. Thriving, bustling centers of economic might and political power, most were organized in ways that differ from cities today.[5] Badges, whether religious or secular, made good sense in such a world. They were mobile markers of personhood and political belonging in urban worlds whose inhabitants—be they lords, merchants, religious women or men, citizens, resident aliens, migrants and transients whose status ranged from high to low, the laboring poor, or the indigent—encountered and crossed multiple, shifting, and often invisible boundaries every day. To explain the complexities of belonging in a medieval city, historian Miri Rubin employs the concept of a continuum of strangers, ranging from unstrange citizens at one end through a variety of desirable and familiar strangers to excluded, undesirable aliens at the other end.[6] Her exploration highlights the diverse ways in which medieval cities sought to manage and control the transitions between categories (stranger to neighbor, for instance) that happened when people's status on the stranger continuum changed over time. Rubin writes that "townspeople as a whole lived together—settled and familiar—while retaining marks of difference that occasionally justified their exclusion from some aspects of political and civic life."[7] As we shall explore in this chapter, simple, mass-produced pewter badges may have played a role in making visible this embedded difference by allowing city dwellers to claim and display their place.

Medieval cities in the Low Countries and in German-speaking lands generally owed nominal allegiance to a noble overlord (the higher up and farther away, the better) whose retainers, servants, and officials were present in the city, as were the aristocrats and nobles of their regions, who maintained great houses and held politically important events of all kinds in cities. Nevertheless, these cities were, in practice, independent, self-governing entities.

There were exceptions, notably capital cities such as Paris, which were royal seats and hence extensions of royal power. The largest city in German-speaking lands, Cologne, was the capital of an ecclesiastical prince and so fits the model of capital cities. These capitals functioned in a way that resembles how cities are understood today. But when one scans the cityscape of the late medieval European continent, with its thriving and complex network of hundreds of cities, in Flanders, northern France, Belgium, the Netherlands, and across German-speaking lands, the picture changes. Here the landscape was covered by municipalities large and small that functioned largely as independent entities, with their own, unique systems of governance, defense, taxation, coinage, law, citizenship, and custom, and their wealth amassed via early capitalism through the organized manufacture and sale of goods, through trade and trade monopolies, and through banking. The largest of these—Berne and Zurich in Switzerland, Nuremberg in Germany—were city-states governing large territories; other commercially important cities, such as Amsterdam in the Netherlands and Bruges, Ghent, Ypres, and Antwerp in Belgium, exercised enormous economic control through their trade alliances and their manufacturing monopolies.

In such cities, administrative units and different kinds of institutions enjoyed autonomy. Different districts, jurisdictions, and corporate structures represented in effect cities within cities, and conflicts within cities about boundaries, borders, and jurisdiction were omnipresent. City districts or sections were not administrative subunits but were rather autonomous and independent units, often with their own city halls, chapter houses, and governance structures. This independence was granted to the many religious establishments—parish churches, monastic foundations and churches, cathedrals—in cities as well, while the lords who lived in cities represented another layer of political and social complexity. At the same time, the citizens (or burghers) of these medieval cities demonstrated keen civic awareness and deep pride in local uniqueness. Another distinguishing characteristic shared by late medieval cities was that they teemed with civic organizations and societies of all kinds, such as guilds, confraternities, and sworn associations.

These civic corporations and associations, all of which demonstrated political personhood and civic belonging, took many forms. There were the municipal governments, which oversaw a plethora of city offices and officials, for example, tax collectors and coin and mint administrators. There were inspectors of every commodity and trade. There were judges, lawyers, city criers, messengers, and so on. Another form of civic organization were civic brotherhoods, some militia-like and organized around the city watch, for example, which will be discussed later in this chapter. There were merchant guilds and trade organizations, artisan guilds regulating crafts and production, and lay confraternities (also called guilds by some historians) of all kinds, often named after a saint.[8] Some lay confraternities were linked to a parish or a specific religious order; others were not. Many lay confraternities focused on performing good works, including providing public feasts at which alms were given to the poor. In the late Middle Ages, relief for the poor in the urban centers of northwestern Europe was carried out not by parish churches or by religious orders but rather by municipal governments and by confraternities, both lay and religious. Other confraternities were aimed at youth, both young men and young women, and provided informal religious education as well as various religious and civic activities. Finally, guilds, confraternities, and brotherhoods were often in charge of organizing the festivities and rituals at civic festivals. Nor were those at the lowest rungs of society excluded from these organizing structures. By the late Middle Ages, references appeared in city records across northern Europe to religious fraternities of beggars and the poor, *confraternitates pauperum*.

These confraternities, sworn associations, and guilds were corporate bodies, and as corporations they were not merely social organizations. Rather, corporate membership was an important defining feature of political life in late medieval cities. As the historian Franz-Josef Arlinghaus points out, "The smallest units of a medieval city were not individuals, but corporations. Not only was political participation linked to membership in guilds or other collectives, but these corporations united as such to form the city."[9] Medieval cities were not so much municipalities as they were agglomerations of different districts, associations, and corporate collectives. Far from the ideal of harmony projected in the round badge from Ypres, they were typically riven by long-standing animosities with roots in social difference and by political quarrels that erupted into violence. The Parisian civil war, which was discussed in Chapter 4, is but one, albeit spectacular example of such urban conflict. Arlinghaus gives a more mundane example from the German city of Hildesheim, in Lower Saxony, where in 1332 the inhabitants of one city district scaled the walls surrounding another district (note that the different city districts had their own walls), massacred everyone, and burned the buildings to the ground.[10] Intracity hostilities between the districts, communities, and corporations that made up the town or city were common, though eruptions into violence less so. Nor were relationships between the many independent cities and towns any less fractious. Intercity warfare helped to fuel the bricolage of smaller and larger regional wars grouped under the heading of the Hundred Years' War, and there was similar, small-scale violence in cities in German-speaking lands as well.

Yet in spite of it all, medieval European cities attracted huge numbers of migrants from the countryside, hung together successfully as political entities, and were the incubators of enduring economic, political, and social change. Let us leave it to the historians to explain how they managed to do so successfully for hundreds of years, and speculate instead on the role that the lowly badge might have played in that achievement.

Badges and Medieval Corporations

Medieval cities teemed with formal and semiformal corporate bodies of all kinds. To belong to one or many of these and to display that belonging were the fundamental expressions of civic pride, political power, and political belonging. The visual representation of these corporations was similarly an integral part of urban life. Badges participated in this way of being and belonging. The devices discussed in the preceding chapters, whether linked to knighthood, to noble identity, or to civic offices and corporations or collectives in the broadest sense, functioned as political badges. They were worn and seen in medieval cities, where they were an ordinary and ubiquitous part of city life. They made government, administration, and corporate identity visible for all to see. They created and demonstrated that the individual wearer belonged to a class of people who had access to or influence over political power, whether as a function of civic rule; as an associate of an influential, well-regarded, and well-connected confraternity; as a birth member of the ruling estate; or as someone living under the protection of a great household or a great lord. Such devices were visible claims to standing in the city. They asserted both personhood and belonging.

Medieval corporations (groups of people banded together in different ways and for different purposes) comprised, of course, vast differences of wealth and power.[11] The degree to which any one device partook in political meaning was dynamic and shifting, dependent on a wide variety of contextual factors. As was shown with the example of the Parisian civil war and the Bock Men devices worn by the nobility of Bavaria, personal devices could be seen as exceptionally strong political statements, powerful enough to transform the identity of the bearer. Heraldic devices were one object embedded in larger systems of signifying political belonging (clothing, livery, coats of arms) that confidently asserted access to powerful baronial families. Devices were so commonly understood as a statement of political power that, as Jennifer Lee has shown, medieval people worried about the criminal and misleading use of badges, for example, the circulation of counterfeit badges, the wrong people wearing badges (medieval confidence men or imposters, presumably), or the imposition of badges onto subordinates by their overlords.[12] On the other hand, wearing a badge of a mounted and armed knight might be a very weak statement of political power. Wearing such a badge might have been less about claiming power and more about participating, as a spectator, for example, in a noble pastime, about having been present at a great event. Wearing the badge of a religious confraternity might in some contexts signal one's status as a wealthy and influential local statesman or as being able to claim familiarity with and access to such people. It might also simply signal deep religious piety. Wearing a fixed heraldic device indicated one's birth status and kin. Embroidered on a wall hanging, it might be decorative; painted on a shield used on the battlefield, it could be a matter of life and death, indicating friend or foe.

Many of the badges found in cities represent or belong to the world of civic belonging. Although scholarship on linking specific badges to specific groups or collectives is still in its beginnings, the crossbow badge can illustrate the claims made in the previous paragraphs.

Crossbow Badges

Some twenty-six badges (a relatively large number) survive that show a tiny weapon, a crossbow. Meticulously modeled, these badges depict windlass crossbows; they show the crank used to wind the hemp string and the foot rest or stirrup at the bottom of the bow used to anchor the weapon as the string was wound. Most of the badges are furnished with a pin, and the majority are from the Low Countries, although a few have been found in the United Kingdom as well.

Crossbows were known from the eleventh century on. Although they were deadly weapons that were easy to use, their chief disadvantage was a slow reloading time; they could only fire about two bolts, as their ammunition is properly called, a minute. Modern popular lore about the Middle Ages sometimes claims that the crossbow was considered a dishonorable weapon because it required virtually no training and little strength to operate, and so was a weapon that could be used by fighters of nonmilitary status, for example, peasants, artisans, craftsmen, women, and city dwellers. But if the weapon was widely considered dishonorable, why make it into a badge? For late medieval city dwellers, at any rate, the crossbow was clearly a symbol of civic pride and virtue. Laura Crombie's 2016 study of the many archery and crossbow guilds in medieval Flanders (virtually every city and town had one) show that beyond their origins and role in military service, membership in crossbow and archery guilds included both "elite" (i.e., noble) and "bourgeois" members, as well as in some guilds youth, women, and priests; that these guilds were involved in a diverse array of urban activities and support networks; that they were important players in civic politics; and that their great urban competitions, which were featured in some of the most elaborate events in Flanders, "promoted regional unity and strengthened commercial networks."[13]

Dutch cities such as Amsterdam also had archery and crossbow guilds. A group portrait of the members of a crossbow guild, made in Amsterdam in 1533 by Cornelis Anthonisz (ca. 1505–1553), represents well the dignity and civic pride of such groups.

The image in figure 7.2 shows the left side of a painting whose full canvas depicts seventeen well-dressed young men wearing similar black caps and bipart robes and gathered around a banqueting table. Figure 7.2 shows nine of these men in postures similar to those in the rest of the painting. One man standing in the background holds a crossbow; three men wear affixed to

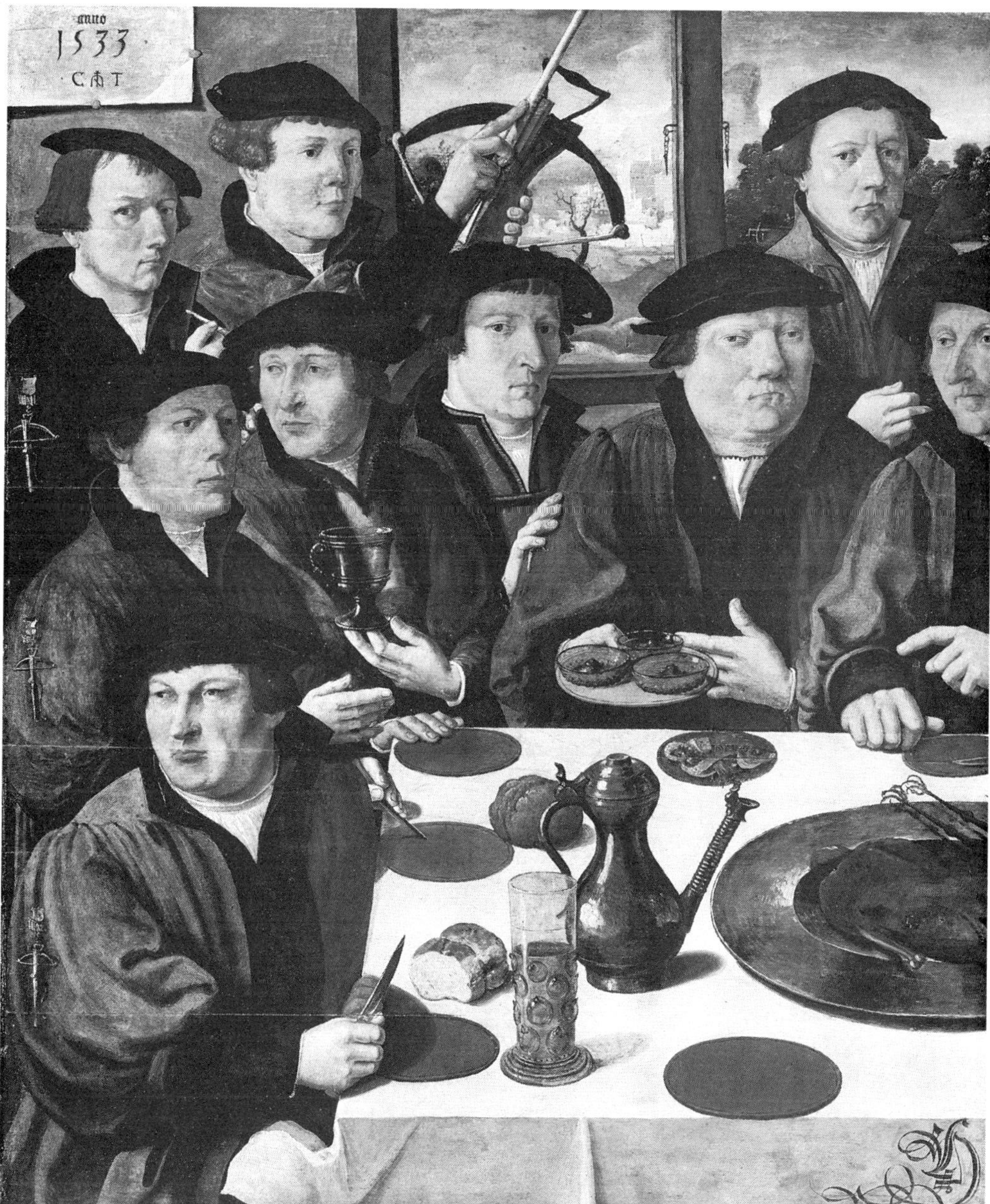

Figure 7.2. Detail, Cornelis Anthonisz, *Banquet of Members in Amsterdam's Crossbow Civic Guard*, oil painting on panel, 1533, 130 × 206.5 cm. Amsterdam, Amsterdam Museum, inv. K_SA_7279. Photograph courtesy of Amsterdam Museum.

their right sleeve a small crossbow topped by a small heraldic shield. These crossbows resemble the badge in figure 7.1 in size and shape, although it is possible that the painted crossbows were made of a more precious material. The painted, sleeve-pendant crossbows are devices, and they indicate that the men in the painting are civic militiamen, specifically members of the guild of the crossbow. In their fine matching robes and devices they have gathered for a guild feast. Perhaps they will also be singing; on the full painting, a seated man just to the right of the final seated man on figure 7.2 holds a sheet of paper with musical notation.

The painting is an early example of the kind of magnificent group portrait for which the Dutch were to become famous in the early modern period. These group portraits have their roots in the late Middle Ages and in the flourishing urban culture of the Low Countries, with its proliferation of municipal, religious, political, and social organizations, societies, and guilds. The group portrait exuded a form of civic pride that was grounded in a deep sense of corporate identity, of belonging to a group that was distinctly and uniquely bound up in a specific locality, that is to say, pride in being a member of a specific corporation belonging to a specific city. The attribute was profoundly medieval in the sense that it was the defining characteristic of late medieval city life. What the early modern era added to the mix in these paintings were the remarkable faces of the men portrayed, each one unique and compelling. These group portraits brilliantly stage individual identity as an attribute of local, civic, corporate culture. They offer unique and remarkable testimony to both the continuity between medieval and early modern culture in the Netherlands and to the radical changes of the early modern age.

What can be learned from this painting about badges? The lead crossbow badges pre-date the painting by more than one hundred years. Yet it is important to bear in mind that the men in the 1533 painting commissioned a painting that was intended to construct their corporate identity as old and venerable, which it was. They chose to be shown doing traditional things in a traditional way. The crossbow pendants pinned to their sleeves were a part of the staging of continuity with the past. Far from being dishonorable, the crossbows were worn with pride by members of the city elite who may well have been following in the footsteps of their fathers in being members of the elite guild. The crossbow seems a fitting symbol of civic pride, for it was a weapon that can be operated by the son of a merchant to defend the city in which his family has made a fortune in, say, the cloth trade. The son of a merchant, growing up in a city, would have been educated in reading, writing, arithmetic, bookkeeping, and business and trade practices, a very different education than the son of a noble knight, who would have been taught riding, jousting, fencing, horse breeding, weapon skills, battle tactics, farm and estate management, and diplomacy. The crossbow badge and the confraternities that chose it for decades as their symbol, their badge, may have felt that the weapon symbolized better than any other their difference from noble elites and their willingness to defend their achievements and identity militarily. Citizens and city dwellers held the militia members of such guilds in high esteem; the guild members wore their crossbow badges, whether made of lead or a precious material, with pride.

Badges and Friendship

In an intense, complex, and competitive social world characterized by overlapping, changing, and sometimes conflicting spheres of belonging and by a complex range of possible status positions on the continuum of strangers, notions of friendship became not less but more essential.[14] Many of the surviving secular badges whose symbolism is enigmatic and opaque to us may well belong in a large and elastic category of medieval friendship that includes or refers to a wider range of human attachments than we might consider friendship today. As will be explored in this section, the visual language used in these badges revolves around the symbolism of heart, hands, and crown. In the Middle Ages, the heart was considered the seat not just of affection but also of will and courage, qualities more commonly associated in the modern world with the mind. The symbolism here suggests that by joining hands in friendship, friends also joined their heart-minds to face the world together and that by crowning their friendship, they elevated a freely chosen relationship over others.

Many surviving badges testify to the power and the central importance of friendship in the late medieval world. Friendships are, in John M. Jeep's definition, "amicable interpersonal relationships."[15] A friend is a favored companion, someone to whom one is attached not because of kinship, marriage, or professional affiliation but because of affection and esteem. The word is found in all Germanic languages: Old English *freond*, Old High German and Middle High German *friunt* (variant spelling, *vriunt*), Norse *fraend*, Dutch *vriend*. The meanings and connotations of the concept of *friend* were wider in the ancient forms of the Germanic languages than they are today; *friend* was often used to mean "relative or kin who is favorably inclined," but the meaning of favored companion was widely used.[16] To understand the conceptual core of friendship as a relationship based primarily on some form of affection, it is important to recall the word's etymology. *Friend* is related to the adjective *free*. By the High and late Middle Ages, the notion of deep attachment to a companion whom one has chosen freely based on affection or esteem (which of course can but does not have to follow channels of socially established relationships, such as kinship, marriage, retinue groups, or political affiliations) was the dominant meaning of friendship. Contrasting with arranged marriages and with fixed political hierarchies, friendship is freely chosen, and it places affection and esteem first. Middle High German often uses the word *friunt* and its feminine version *friundinne* as synonyms for *lover*, meaning something like "beloved companion." Here, a sexual component is implied but never as the overriding connotation. What is at stake here is affection, the idea of a surplus of attachment and esteem that has arisen between two people independent of the social bonds that have brought them together. Romantic love and friendship in the Middle Ages might be understood not as different kinds of affection or emotion but rather as related terms residing at different points on a single continuum.

Badges participate in the world of friendship, although tracing the connection is not easy. Tokens of friendship exchanged between or given by friends need not bear any image or symbol directly related to friendship, because any image or object meaningful to the beloved companions can take on the function of memorializing the special bond. Badges that were political devices marking association or guild membership or religious badges that have been brought back from pilgrimage could have been gifted in friendship, which of course would not leave a trace on the badge. Contrast this with the situation when dealing with religious badges or with heraldic and political badges of all kinds. It is easier to suggest plausible contexts to guide interpretations of these badges because the badges themselves were embedded in the social, religious, and political order and used a widely shared and familiar set of symbols. If these badges were to work as they should, they had to convey their identity messages and claims quickly and reliably, and so they had to employ well-known and easily decipherable images. Like religious badges, political badges were not ultimately obscure, even though many things (legal documents, administrative records, paintings, and the like) that would have deepened their contextual intelligibility for us have disappeared over time.

Even though friendship is a category of badge use that is often invisible to us, the corpus of surviving badges suggests that there was a medieval iconography of friendship, a special and familiar set of images and symbols that was reliably and consistently employed to symbolize friendship in the larger sense detailed previously. The iconography combined and recombined images of heart, head, and hands, and it appeared in both religious and secular contexts.

Medieval people dwelling in religious communities used the word *friendship* to describe the close bonds that could arise between their members. To describe these relationships in modern English, the term *spiritual friendship* is used. A great deal is known about the spiritual friendships that arose among members of monastic communities, both male and female, and about the spiritual friendships that arose between nuns and beguines, on the one hand, and the male priests who were their spiritual guides and confessors, on the other. Members of these religious communities, both male and female, wrote about these friendships, and these communities valued their writings and therefore preserved them. Letters, religious tracts, spiritual biographies, and convent histories document the importance that was attached to the bonds of mutual affection and esteem, mediated through piety and shared quests for religious enlightenment.

The book narrating the spiritual life and teachings of the German Dominican mystic Henry Suso (German, Heinrich Seuse) (1295–1366) tells many stories about his lifelong service to the nuns under his spiritual care and the high esteem in which they held him. One anecdote provides valuable clues about the use of a badge-like object to memorialize and deepen the bonds in this circle of spiritual friends.[17] Henry Suso and the nuns under his spiritual care developed close bonds revolving around Suso's spiritual experiences and practices, which sometimes involved self-torture in emulation of Christ's suffering. A pious nun (other sources suggest that it was a holy woman named Elsbeth Stagel) received a vision of the Blessed Virgin Mary holding up for worship the name of Jesus Christ in the form of the IHS monogram and praising Suso's piety and his love of Christ.[18] The vision inspired action. Stagel embroidered the Christogram on a small piece of cloth (*tüchli*) with red silk. It was to be worn secretly or intimately (*heinlich*), perhaps meaning under clothing or directly next to the skin and therefore invisible to others. She made a number of these badge-like Christogram ribbons and had Suso place them on his naked heart (*uf sin herz bloss leit*) and bless them before they were given away. God revealed to Stagel that wearing the Christogram ribbon and saying the rosary (Paternoster) for it daily would bring to the bearer God's blessing in this life and His mercy in the next.

Inspired by Suso's spirituality, produced in many copies, and sanctified by direct contact with the body of the holy man Suso, the Christogram ribbons were saturated with the love of Christ that dwelt in Suso's heart, which they could continually titrate, as it were, into the body of the wearer when activated by prayer. Hands embroidered the Christogram ribbons, hearts were physically touched by them, and heads (if you will) had read them and spoken the holy words. These hands, hearts, and heads may not be represented per se in Suso's sanctified ribbons, but nonetheless they were intended to be present in the minds of those who made, blessed, gifted, and wore them. The hands, hearts, and heads conjured by the Christogram ribbon belonged not to a single body but to many, joined together in a collective body of spiritual friendship.

The Symbolism of the Heart

In the early part of 2012, the *Daily Mail* reported that a farmer in Cheshire, England, had found a lovely, fourteenth-century brooch made of gold by using a metal detector.[19] About two-and-a-half centimeters in size, its shape suggested a heart with, as reporter Nick Enoch put it, "two hands clasped together in decorative sleeves at its base."[20] According to the article, the brooch was valued at 25,000 pounds sterling, and the auctioneer was quoted as speculating that it was a betrothal gift "from a gentleman to his other half" and that "it is rare to find these two symbols [heart and hand] together on one brooch."[21]

The auctioneer and reporter believed that the symbolism of clasped hands at the base of a heart was rare, but if they had had occasion to study ordinary, mass-produced badges, brooches, and similar objects from the Middle Ages, they might have told a different story. Clasped hands were in fact a familiar visual symbol, as this chapter will make clear. The auctioneer who valued the item made an educated guess about its original function. He speculated that it was a betrothal gift from a gentleman to his fiancée. In this context, the term *gentleman* was probably intended to signal class; a giver who could afford such a costly item would have been wealthy and a member of the upper class. *Gentleman* works well because it avoids speculating on whether the wealthy giver came from a noble or a merchant family. One way or another, the giver had large financial resources at his or her disposal.

Yet there is nothing about the object per se that indicates whether it was commissioned or purchased by a man or a woman. Further, there is nothing about the object per se that indicates the sex of its recipient. It is an ornamental pin, a piece of jewelry. Medieval paintings show men wearing badges, devices, and ornaments of all kinds, including jewelry. Was the pin in fact a love gift? It is plausible that it could have been given and received as a token of a serious, romantic bond, but other kinds of tender attachment such as friendship between men or women are also possible.

Though cheap and mass-produced, pewter badges must also have been given and received as gifts and tokens of affection and love. In an anonymous, fifteenth-century middle English dance song, the unnamed speaker, a young woman, asks her boyfriend, Jack, for a pin or brooch, presumably wishing for a sign or token of his affection for her.

[Yc] Predele my kerchef undur my chyn;
Leve Jakke, lend me a pyn
To predele me this holiday.
I fasten my kerchief under my chin.
Dear Jack, give me a pin
For fastening this holiday.[22]

Could the pin the fictional speaker asks Jack to give her be what we now call a badge? English badges, as we have seen, were made with pin fasteners on the back, so they could hold a kerchief closed as is imagined in the poem. The context for wearing and receiving a badge seems right. The poem is staged in a holiday setting, which in late medieval England would have included dancing, flirting, and the possibility of sexual encounters. The girl desires to look her best (elsewhere in the poem she mentions shining her shoes) and to dress up by wearing finery. The poem suggests that she is a young girl (in modern terminology, a teenager), who might prize a shiny, perhaps painted, lead badge. Finally, badges, being cheap, seem a plausible gift in the imagined context, in which the girl probably belonged to the laboring class.[23]

The badge in figure 7.3 fulfills many of the criteria suggested by the ballad verse. It is English and has an image that suggests devotion but is not lewd: the

Figure 7.3. Pewter badge, heart-shaped frame with crown, pin, origin unknown, 1300–1499, found in London, 7 mm (height). London, Museum of London, inv. 80.69/2 (Kunera 03688). Photograph and permission from © Museum of London.

heart, crowned and adorned with flowers along its sides. Note the pin attachment visible in the center of the frame. Such a badge could easily have fulfilled a practical function (holding a kerchief closed) while proclaiming to the world that its wearer had a devoted sweetheart. Such an ornamented, heart-shaped, pinned badge seems a fitting sweetheart gift from a young man to a young woman, as is imagined in the ballad. The heart also recalls the great lovers of medieval lore. Lovers exchanging their hearts, metaphorically speaking of course, had been a popular trope in fictional texts since the 1180s. The heart-shaped badge implies not sexual lust but rather love based in such virtues as loyalty, trust, and devotion. Further, the heart is crowned, a motif that brings to mind a modern English phrase, "You are the king, or queen, of my heart."

A badge such as the heart-shaped one is in effect a brooch. When worn, the badge would have floated, as it were, on the backdrop of the fabric to which it was affixed, which would have been visible within the badge's frame. The framed, open space also offers the possibility of modifying the badge by adding small pieces of other materials (parchment, paper) as a backing, as can be seen in many openwork badges. The option to put a backing on a badge radically expanded the possibilities for personalizing them. Was it worn pinned to a fine piece of scarlet cloth, which became both the background and the center of the badge? Might the white, shiny frame have been filled with a ready-made image or piece of colored paper? Could the purchaser order a specific, miniature motif, perhaps an image of an object that had special meaning for the couple, or a name (his? hers? theirs together?), or a word, such as *amour*? The point is that these inexpensive and widely available objects could be and doubtless were personalized, adapted, and modified to contain and memorialize specific, existing, or desired relationships and outcomes. Our example, which imagines the ballad girl's boyfriend, Jack, gifting her with a heart-shaped badge framing, for example, a piece of bright gold paper, specifies that relationship as love between a man and a woman. Though pewter badges were mass-produced, they could be and were made personalized and individual.

These two examples of heart-shaped badges, one made of gold and one of pewter, use the heart as a symbol of passionate attachment to another individual, still standard fare in the symbolic language of romantic love, as it was in the Middle Ages. Another example of this symbolism is shown in figure 7.4, a crowned heart badge from France. The representation of a banner woven through the heart and spelling out the word *amours* echoes the textile Suso badges.

Heart symbolism appears in the twelfth-century blossoming of vernacular literature about love. "You are mine, I am yours, of this you can be sure.

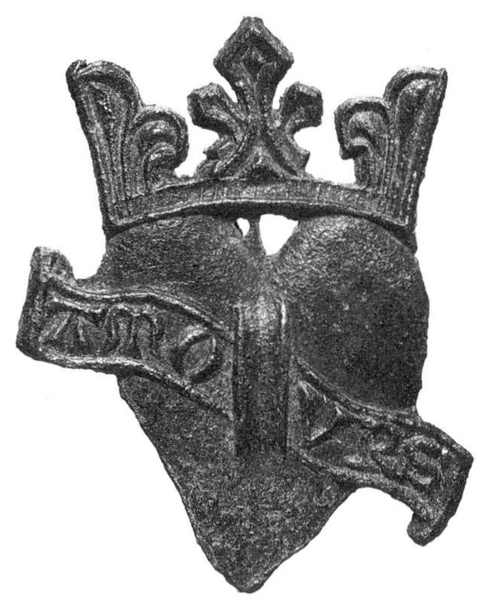

Figure 7.4. Pewter badge, crowned heart with inscription AMOVRS, pin, origin unknown, 1350–1424, Valenciennes, France, 26.5 × 22 × 2 mm. Valenciennes, Musée des Beaux-Arts, inv. 2005.4.152 (Kunera 10166). Photograph and permission from Musée des Beaux-Arts de Valenciennes.

You are locked in my heart, and the key is lost, and so you must stay there forever," say the lyrics of an anonymous ditty from around the mid-1100s, written in German and found in a Latin-language manuscript that originated in the 1180s in the monastery of Tegernsee, Germany.[24] "Your eyes have wounded my heart," sings the German poet Heinrich von Morungen, probably in the decade between 1190 and 1200, as he begs the woman he adores to return his feelings, using the image of his heart to stand for the locus of his passionate love for a woman. It appears in the earliest examples of Arthurian romance. The Old French story *Yvain: The Knight of the Lion*, written by Chrétien de Troyes around 1180, uses the symbolism of the heart to show the reader how sad the hero, Yvain, is when he leaves his beloved wife: "How hard it was for my lord Yvain to leave his wife! He rode off without his heart. His body might follow the king, but his heart could not be led. She who held it, joined to her own, was she who stayed home."[25] In this work, falling passionately in love means giving your heart to your beloved, and if your love is requited, then your heart will be joined to the heart of your beloved, who will tenderly safeguard them both.

Some decades later a German author, Hartmann von Aue, retold and adapted Chrétien's story in German; the hero's name, spelled as it would have been pronounced in German, was now Iwein. In Hartmann's version, Iwein and his wife, Laudine, symbolically exchange hearts when they part, an act that highlights the fervor and constancy of their attachment to one another: "They exchanged hearts between them, the lady and Sir Iwein. Her heart in Iwein's breast followed the king [Arthur], while Iwein's heart in her body remained behind."[26] Hartmann introduced a new variation on the symbolism of the gift of the heart by turning it into an exchange. This reciprocity creates a moment of equality of men and women, because they share both the effect of love (you lose your heart to your beloved) and the demand of love (love obliges you to safeguard the treasure, the beloved's heart, entrusted to you).

Hartmann also expanded the passage to include an explanation of the lover's exchange of hearts. The allegorical figure Lady Love (often depicted as Venus) speaks up and explains that such passionate attachment creates not weakness or fragility but rather virtue and strength: "I am Love and I often enable men and women to lose their hearts and be all the stronger because of it."[27]

The evidence related here (there is much more) attests to the fact that by the year 1200, the heart was a commonplace symbol for romantic love all across Europe. The heart is a locked box; the heart is a wounded part of the self; the heart is removed and given to the beloved; hearts are exchanged by lovers. There is imagination in the ways the symbol of the heart is varied, but the metaphorical ways the heart is used to think about love mentioned here do not contradict one another. For example, in the passage from Chrétien de Troyes, Yvain's wife safeguards his heart, which implies similar actions to those imagined in the German song: locking it up, keeping it safe and secure, treasuring it. Taken together, the symbolism of the heart tells a story about passionate attachment as a reciprocal state of emotional intimacy whose basis is constancy and fidelity—a form of deep and enduring companionship that includes erotic love. The notion of what we moderns call romantic love may be so familiar to modern readers that it seems to be a universal feature of human existence, but in fact, many of the features of romantic love arose among the aristocracy in France in the early twelfth century, from whence it conquered the western world.

The imagery of the heart as symbolizing passionate attachment is not confined to the secular sphere, as was shown in the discussion of the Christogram ribbons. By the late Middle Ages meditations on the heart of Christ have become a staple of pious devotional practice. Although there are other iconographical aspects of the heart, the badges discussed in this chapter clarify that they refer to worldly love or friendship; the heart symbolism itself is not confined to either the secular or the religious sphere of meaning but functions within both.

Head, Heart, and Clasped Hands

The heart-shaped badge made of gold that was found in Cheshire in 2012 incorporated a second, significant iconographical feature; the point of the heart was transformed into clasped hands emerging from two decorative sleeves.

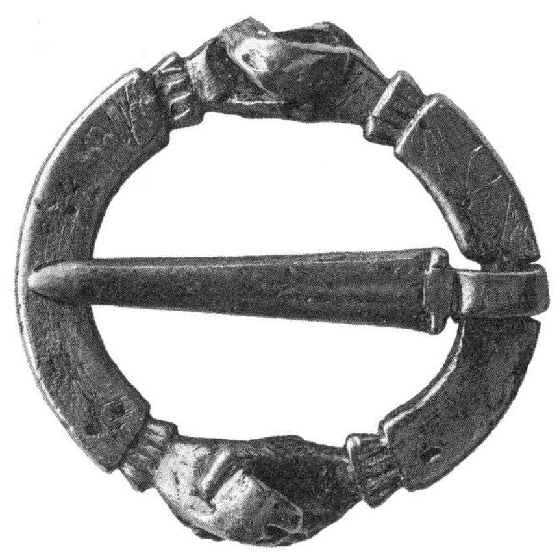

Figure 7.5. Pewter brooch, gilded hand troth. found in Hamburg-Harburg, Germany, ca. 20 mm in diameter. Hamburg-Harburg, Archäologisches Museum Hamburg (AMH). Photographer: Torsten Weise. Photograph courtesy of Archäologisches Museum Hamburg (AMH).

Clasped hands are a common symbol on late medieval badges (and beyond); museum collections often contain many small medieval finger rings made of inexpensive materials, for example, with clasped hands.[28] A small medieval brooch found in the Hamburg-Harburg excavations shows, top and bottom, two examples of a handshake (figure 7.5).

Shaking hands, also known as hand troth or hand plighting, was originally a symbolically freighted, performative legal gesture that was used in the Middle Ages to indicate the acceptance of an obligation or oath, for example, in marriage. The way the hands clasp on the object in figure 7.5 is sufficiently representational to take anatomical detail into account. While it is possible to cross one's hands, to interlace one's fingers, or to lay one hand on top of the other, it is not anatomically possible to shake hands with oneself, that is to say, to place one's hands together, palms facing, with fingers facing in opposite directions and with both thumbs on top. There are (at least) two actors represented on the badge; its gesture has a contractual or legal implication. The fashionable cuffs on the brooch or badge point to a common feature on clasped-hand badges: embellishments of some kind, buttons or button-like objects running down the side (such sleeves can be seen everywhere in late medieval artwork).

The repertoire of visual symbols for medieval friendship and love also includes heads and crowns, combined in figure 7.6 in an arresting manner. Crossed hands and circling arms appear in this badge in which a well-dressed woman stares solemnly at the viewer. Wearing a crown or headdress of some kind, her hair is neatly captured and covered by a net-like structure suggesting the intricate, bejeweled lace hairnets that late medieval artwork shows being worn by women of means. Forming the badge's circle, her arms are clothed in the double layer of sleeves of an elegant and expensive style

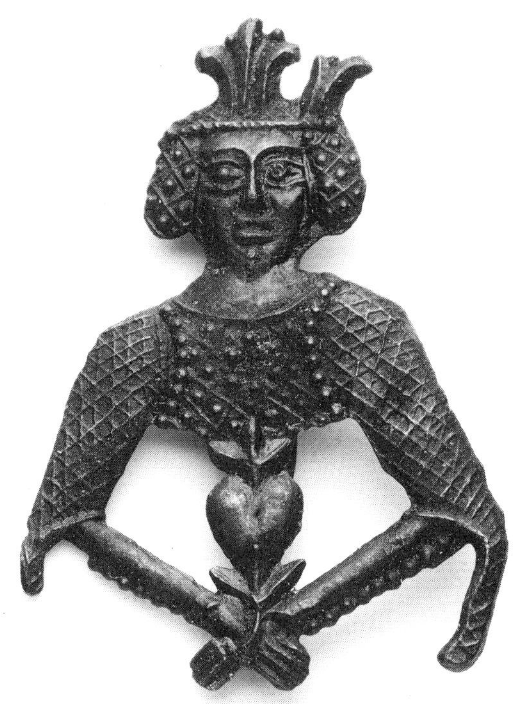

Figure 7.6. Pewter badge, crowned and elaborately coiffed woman balances on crossed hands emerging from sleeves of her sumptuous garment a heart pierced by an arrow, pin, origin unknown, 1325–1374, found in Ypres, Belgium, 37 × 33 mm. Yper Museum, inv. SM 003505 (Kunera 07055). Photographer: Els Deroo. Photograph courtesy of Yper Museum.

of dress. The fabric of the outer garment's torso and sleeves is damasked, or embroidered, in some way. The sleeves end at the elbow in long, decorative points. The forearms emerging from them are encased in a second, tightly fitting garment, or perhaps gloves, with a long row of buttons running on the outside from elbow to wrist. The hands belong, it is clear, to the single figure imagined here, who crosses her hands at the wrists as though they were bound together like a prisoner's hands. At the center of the badge is an arrow that is piercing a heart, which is placed, more or less anatomically correctly, in the imagined torso's center. The arrow rests on the crossed wrists, immobilizing them; the hands have become a base on which the pierced heart balances upright.

Another badge employing nearly identical imagery, though without a human face, conveys a similar message (figure 7.7). The Middle Ages knew the symbolism of Cupid's arrow, symbolizing deep, romantic attachment that strikes unexpectedly and embeds itself into the core of the self. Here is a heart, already pierced by the arrow of love, visible to the viewer. Is the wounded heart being offered up as a gift, or do the crowned arms balance the lover's heart?

Before deciding that the imagery of heart, hands, and crown refers unerringly and always to romantic or erotic love, as the badges in the previous figures might suggest, I would like to look at another badge that makes use of this visual symbolism (figure 7.8). The sides of the badge are sleeves out of which emerge at the top little hands that together support or clasp a crown (whether there is a heart under the crown cannot be discerned). The center of the badge is occupied by a young man, to judge by his long tunic, bobbed haircut, and lack of a beard. The youth reclines, legs crossed, across the entire horizontal plane of the enclosed space. He appears to be smiling, and in his

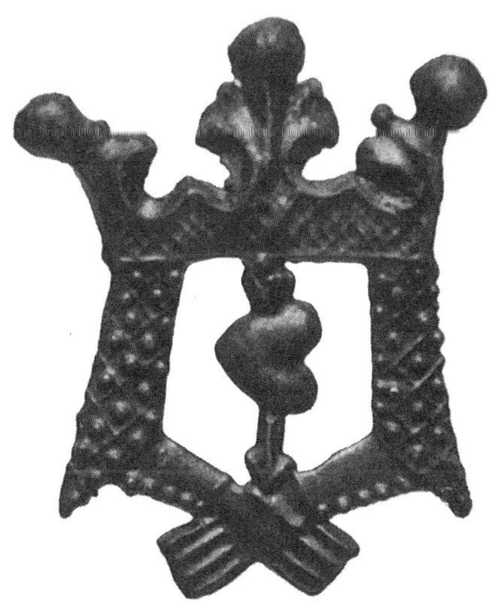

Figure 7.7. Pewter badge, crossed hands emerging from fleur-de-lis crown, heart pierced by arrow, pin, origin unknown, 1325–1375, found in 's-Hertogenbosch, Netherlands, 27 × 22 mm. Langbroek, Netherlands, Family Van Beuningen Collection, inv. 3887 (Kunera 17280). Photograph courtesy of Family Van Beuningen Collection.

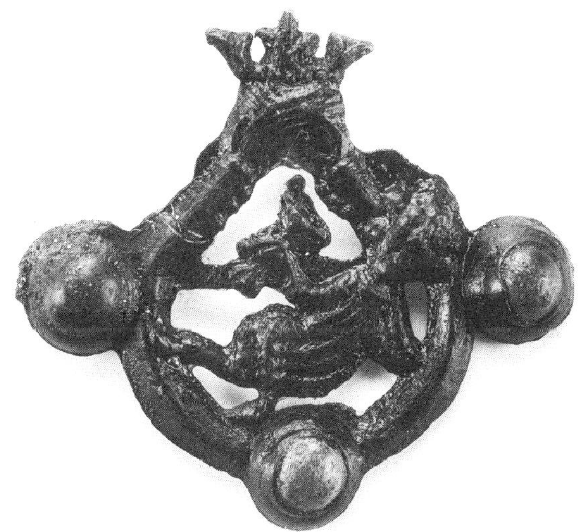

Figure 7.8. Pewter badge, reclining male figure holding a chalice in right hand in round frame decorated with three green glass beads, at top clasped hands emerging from buttoned sleeves and holding a crown, pin, origin unknown, 1325–1374, found in Ypres, Belgium, 28 × 30 mm. Yper Museum, inv. SM 004050 (Kunera 07245). Photographer: Els Deroo. Photograph courtesy of Yper Museum.

right hand he holds high an outsized chalice or drinking vessel. Surely, he is offering a toast: Santé! Proost! Prosit! Skaal! Cheers! Zum Wohl!

This cheery badge combines, perhaps surprisingly, the imagery of crown, heart, and hands, associated in other badges with romantic or erotic love, with a grinning young man drinking, a type associated then and now with boozy good times among friends. To judge by the drinking songs, bawdy stories, and administrative records of drunken behavior that have come down to us from the Middle Ages, modern youth have no historical monopoly on partying. Despite the disapproval of preachers, teachers, parents, and guardians (then and now), socializing with comrades, buddies, and friends over drink and food, with dancing, singing, gaming, and brawling thrown in, was a beloved pastime of medieval youth. The badge is about drinking as an inherently social act; the image of someone raising his glass implies an audience of fellow drinkers. The gesture signals comradeship. Whether or not the person viewing the badge is actually drinking, the badge suggests or, perhaps better said, anticipates a reciprocal gesture: that a glass be raised in return. The badge draws the viewer, then and now, into an established social ritual that makes drinking a part of the larger bond of camaraderie. The badge places the symbols of hands and crown in a new context in order to enact a specific notion of youthful fellow feeling and friendship.

Exploring badges that adopt, combine, and vary the symbols of heart, hands, and crown reveals a social world of friendship in which bonds of mutuality, reciprocity, companionship, tenderness, and romantic attachment were variously evoked to speak about a wide variety of freely chosen human relationships: drinking buddies, spiritual friendship, comradeship, romantic friendship. The symbolic elements of heart, head, and hands are selected, combined, and recombined in the surviving badges. The ways in which these badge designs play with these elements suggests the artistic freedom the medium afforded badge designers. It suggests a shared universe of symbolic language; the badge designers and their patrons knew that these elements signified friendship. Whoever purchased, commissioned, or gifted these objects was making a special and weighty gesture, seeking entrance into the world of friendship. In the medieval period the wide scope of freely chosen, tender human attachments could be symbolized, as we have seen, by clasped or crossed hands, by a heart, a crown, or a head. The badge designers' ingenuous and often witty combining and recombining of different elements of the shared symbolic language of friendship suggests how ubiquitous and comprehensible that language was and how widely and deeply friendship was valued in the Middle Ages.

Badges in Cities

Medieval cities were overflowing with performativity of all kinds. Some of this performativity was religious. Does the ubiquity of religious performance in the streets and the insistence on the rhythms of liturgical time suggest that medieval city dwellers were deeply pious? To this day there persists a general belief that medieval Christianity was characterized by an unparalleled unity of faith and piety based on shared belief. In this view, medieval Christianity is a religion of togetherness. A quick check of the historical record shows that nothing could be further from the truth, the institutions of the medieval church often enjoying substantial autonomy and being every bit as riven by political hostilities as medieval cities, though there is little outright warfare. For most medieval laypeople, the shared identity of medieval Christianity was a fact that depended not on shared doctrine but on the public profession of faith through simple, shared practices. It was a shared identity that transcended political divisions. And that is the point. It is not that the religious identity was strong and political identity was weak. Rather, religious identity became a kind of container or frame that could hold the others without erasing them. As historian Franz-Josef Arlinghaus states, "Religious processions are not designed to, and do not per se, establish togetherness. Rather, the importance of these performative acts is to be seen in their power to combine two potentially opposing phenomena typically found in European cities: on the one hand, to display the autonomy of groups and quarters and, on the other, to foster a certain cohesion among the players."[29] Arlinghaus speculates on the centrality of religious performativity in creating unity in medieval cities. He points out that alongside religious performances and rituals medieval cities had secular rituals as well: the public payment of taxes, for example, or the public dispensation of justice (trials, executions). His research shows that "when political administration as such is at the center of the ritual, the emphasis is on the autonomy of the individual districts, but when religion is at the center of the emphasis the whole population can participate, which allows political autonomy to recede into the background."[30]

Arlinghaus states that "it was not the content of the Christian religion but the specific forms of religious communication implemented during the High and late Middle Ages that contributed to the unity of the medieval city."[31] Badges mattered because they constituted a specific form of communication that was typical for and suited to the unique complexities of the many kinds of status claims—from citizen, neighbor, familiar stranger, or friend to excluded alien—that were characteristic features of medieval cities.[32] The fact that each badge displayed to the knowledgeable a specific, semi-autonomous communal identity was key to the badge's success. When great numbers of badges were on display, jostling, mixing, and mingling with one another on the days of public feasts, commemorations, or processions, they displayed multiple ways of belonging while demonstrating the peaceful coexistence of hostile factions. The badges communicated separateness and autonomy while fostering a diffuse yet powerful communal sense of shared identity. When this historical form of city identity ceased to exist, so too did the badges that made it visible.

8

Badges and Carnival

Ypres, after the first Sunday in August, 1410

The little blond dog has a long, soft coat and brown eyes like two pieces of dark amber wet from the sea, ears that stand straight up, a pink pointy nose and a grin on his face. A drunk whose breath reeks of cabbage swill pushes his way in ahead of his friends, glares at the dog, and then bellows in the general direction of the elderly woman next to whom the dog is sitting.

"Wadja name this one, Granny?"

"Bjorn," says Granny without looking up. She is stroking the dog's back, running her fingers through his fur and working out the knotted and tangled places, then rubbing the dog's chest while he sits, no more than two hands tall, proudly beside her. And quiet, too, for a change.

"Bjorn," she says again, louder.

"Bjorn, you dummy, its name is Bear!" Cabbage Breath and his companions roar with laughter. The dog joins in with a hail of ear-splitting, high-pitched, talk-stopping barks.

It is late afternoon. A sudden deluge of near-freezing rain has driven the carnival revelers to the shelter of tents, stables, homes, and inns. The makeshift tavern in the abandoned stable behind the convent smells of smoke, wet wool, drenched shoe leather, and sweat. Again, the door is thrown open. A young man blows in. Eager to warm his icy hands and dry out his sloshing shoes, he staggers through the packed bodies toward the crowded hearth and crashes into a drinker whose back is turned.

Stumbles and curses, an overturned chair, a flying elbow, and a full mug of ale crashes to the floor spraying sharp fragments of pottery. Before the young man can take two steps, a hand grabs the neck of his tunic, spinning him around with such force that the shoulder seams split open, and noxious, beery, cabbage breath bellows in his face.

"You rabid dog and son of a swine! You'll buy me another beer right now or you'll find yourself in pieces like that mug."

"But I don't have any money."

Simple and young, too ready with the truth and too trusting that it will save him. For a man far gone with drink, it is equal odds whether beer or brawl is more satisfying, and he has just made one man's decision easier. A fist lands in his stomach. As he doubles over, the other man smashes in close behind. As he goes down, the fist drags him back up.

"Cough up, you lying, leprous beggar!"

Cabbage Breath tears the money pouch off the young man's belt and dumps the contents on the table. Three items fall out, not coins but tiny pewter objects: a little square topped by something resembling a little shift; a walking penis creature being ridden by a woman playing an instrument; an odd sort of pilgrim that is, on closer inspection, a vulva. Cabbage Breath's face twists in disbelief.

"What the devil is this, you skinny-thighed, bat-eared coward?"

But before Cabbage Breath can again kick the young man, now prostrate on the floor and bleeding from crockery cuts, a woman's voice shouts "Stop!"

Granny and her dog stand over the moaning fellow on the floor and look Cabbage Breath full in the face.

"That's enough. You've shattered plenty of mugs yourself, and God knows, you've had enough beer. You behind the counter, get over here and clean up this mess. You there, hiding by the door, see to your friend before he passes out.

"Now, pay attention to me! Take a look. These things are not such a bad trade. Come, come. Pick them up. They belong to you now. Take

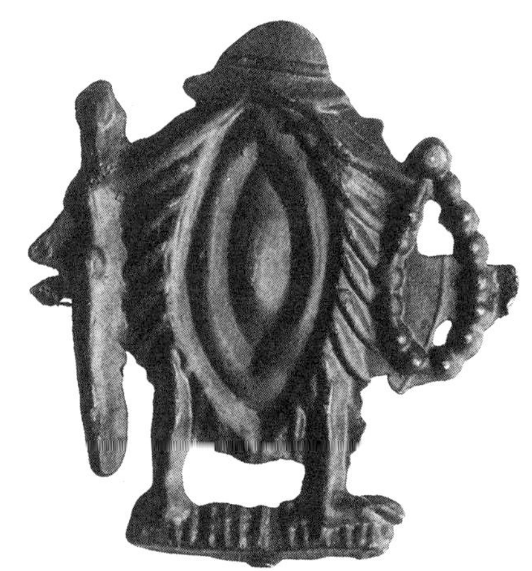

Figure 8.1. Pewter badge, vulva dressed as pilgrim and holding staff and rosary, pin, origin unknown, 1375–1424, found in Amsterdam, 23 × 21 mm. Langbroek, Netherlands, Family Van Beuningen Collection, inv. 1324 (Kunera 00665). Photograph courtesy of Family Van Beuningen Collection.

these dancing balls and female secrets to the house just outside the city walls by the southern town gate. You may find it is worth more fun than a mug of ale! And this little shift, well, you might have even greater need of it. It is from far away, and it once belonged to the Blessed Virgin Mary. It blesses and protects whoever holds it in good faith."

"Didn't do this fella any good, did it?" rumbles Cabbage Breath as he pockets the penis creature and the vulva pilgrim.

"Then give it back to him and get out."

The drama is over. The drinkers' attention has turned elsewhere. Cabbage Breath studies the little shift and laughs.

"Not even big enough to cover somebody's privates! Won't do me no good where I'm goin'. Take it back then, buddy, and say your prayers better next time."

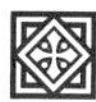

Public ritual and celebration marking important events were a ubiquitous and ordinary part of late medieval urban life.[1] Public processions wound their way along prescribed routes in the city. These often mixed secular and religious features, from plays and costumed parades to music, street games, dances, and liturgical and religious celebrations. Processions might be a part of public events as various as the public dispensation of justice in public trials, punishments, and executions; weddings and funerals of the great lords; diplomatic visits of the powerful, whether lords, ecclesiastical princes, or the representatives of other great cities; and the religious liturgies of the great holy days, annual commemorations of local saints, and new thanksgiving festivities, such as Ypres's annual Thundach, which gave thanks to Our Lady of the Ramparts for lifting the English siege of 1383. Processions were integrated into the liturgies of holy days, for example, Easter and its holy days including Palm Sunday, when in many cities processions included a *Palmesel* (a statue of Christ mounted on a donkey) being pulled through the streets to reenact Christ's entrance into Jerusalem.[2]

Surviving accounts from medieval cities across Europe demonstrate that these processions and practices represented shared traditions that were locally realized and replete with variation across time and space. The specifics, such as the liturgies and songs sung, the specific acts and rituals performed, the objects used, the propitious times of day and the season, would have differed depending on the holy day and on the locale, so that the ensemble and constellation of each religious festivity would have been unique. Processions, whether religious or profane, sought to transform an entire medieval cityscape into a performative space and the entire participating population into actors.

Every institution or household of means staged appropriate public rituals and festivities for momentous occasions, from the convents, monasteries, parish churches, and great cathedrals, to the noble and patrician houses great and small, to the urban guilds and civic rulers of the cities. Many of these festivities were private, of course, but depending on the occasion some included public-facing events, which ranged widely in size and scale. Some were integrated into the framework of larger, recurring urban festivities; some centered on the initiating institution or household alone; some were political actions that emerged in response to political pressures. Some took an afternoon, others a week; some fed fifty guests, others five thousand or more; some relied on "homegrown" entertainment, with song, plays, and pageantry being produced by those who staged the entertainment, while in other cases entire troupes of skilled artists were hired; some were solemn and serious while others were wild and ribald.

Such public political actions, rituals, and festivities were ubiquitous in the late medieval world.[3] They crossed all social categories of life, from the hovel to the castle, from the tavern to the guild hall, from the courtyard to the street and the open road. Artists of all kinds, from acrobats, jugglers, and dancers to singers, poets, and actors, moved from court to court and town to town to work. Skilled storytellers and reciters, such as heralds, were known everywhere. Public officials from high to low donned special garments and processed through the streets. So did the canons, clerics, choirboys, and priests of the churches great and small. Until the mid-fifteenth century even enclosed monks and nuns might have joined on truly momentous occasions. The confraternities were there along with representatives of the noble households. How could they not be? To be visible, to see and be seen on these occasions was an act that staked a claim to membership in corporate identities. It announced for all to see, "I belong here, I am a part of this place, my corporation belongs here." The identity being created in this manner was that of the civic entity, the city or town, in which the festivity took place. It demonstrated visibly and publicly the corporate identities that derived their legitimacy from the distinct, largely independent town or city where they belonged, just as the fact of these political and religious organizations created that town or city, not only symbolically but through building and planning in tangible and real ways. At the same time, public festivities and occasions showed in tangible ways that the civic structures were grounded in and connected to the divine order. Such public occasions did not represent the city; they were the city.

Badges fit well into this world. Some of the surviving badges that now seem enigmatic may have been made to commemorate or participate in such public occasions. Other badges whose sphere of meaning is easily established can be imagined in the world of public festivities. Devices and heraldic badges such as those discussed in Chapter 6 might have been worn on such occasions. How better to parade the size and influence of your household than during a political event, public festivity, or religious ritual at which your servants, retainers, and supporters wore the political device of your household? The same held true for showing membership in a corporate body of some kind, whether municipal or district government, guild, or confraternity. Surviving records from late medieval Lübeck, for example, tell us that members of the Confraternity of the Circle, which sponsored important theatrical activities during carnival, wore their circle badge during carnival season.[4] Political alliances could have been demonstrated in this way. Religious badges of all kinds (think of the pilgrim badges found far from their sites of origin) might have been deemed especially appropriate or efficacious when worn during liturgical festivities.

Festivals and processions, whether religious or secular, were embedded in liturgical time. This concept describes a way of thinking about time that was a fundamental part of medieval Catholicism.[5] Liturgical time is thought of as moving cyclically or seasonally rather than moving forward linearly. Liturgical time passes with a sequence of religious milestones that are marked by special rites and rituals. These celebrations constantly weave connections between past and present. In the Catholic mass, for example, connections between the Old Testament and New Testament are created through the notion of prefiguration, in which events in the Old Testament are seen to prefigure the birth, life, and death of the Christian savior, Jesus Christ. Readings are chosen from both the Old and New Testaments and accompanied by a sermon that elaborates the resonances between them.

The most fundamental framework for Christian liturgical time is, of course, the story of the death and resurrection of Jesus Christ, known as the Passion. It is commemorated and relived during the Holy Days that begin with Palm Sunday, in which Christ entered Jerusalem on a donkey, through the Last Supper, crucifixion, burial, and resurrection on Easter Sunday. (These are known as movable holy days because the date of Easter Sunday is not fixed but rather is calculated yearly according to the lunar calendar.)

Easter is the most solemn season in the Christian calendar. It marks Christianity's foundational belief: that Jesus Christ was the son of God and a savior who sacrificed Himself to atone for the sins of humankind, and that He was resurrected from the dead. His eternal life promises a similar eternal life for those who believe in Him. The season of Easter calls on Christians to meditate on the pain and torment suffered by Christ in His crucifixion, which He suffered through no cause of His own but on their behalf, and to celebrate the miracle of His resurrection and the promise of eternal life it holds out to the faithful.

Easter was and is for devout Christians a time of intense religious fervor; holy day processions are an integral part of Catholicism throughout the world today. The Easter holy days are preceded by six weeks of Lent, in which the believer prepares for the Easter holy days. During Lent, believers were traditionally expected to fast and to give up select activities. These sacrifices were understood as a form of penance that both purified the believer as well as harmonized her or him, as it were, with the suffering and death of Christ. Through sacrifice and renunciation, the participating believer incorporated liturgical time not only into her or his own emotional and religious universe but also into her or his physical experience. And every year, the liturgical season of Easter, which culminated in Easter Sunday, began not with Lent but rather in the week preceding Lent known as Shrovetide or Carnival, which in medieval times included public festivities and the performances of plays on topics ranging from morally edifying to obscene.

Carnival

Shrovetide carnival was a ubiquitous, ordinary part of life in pre-Reformation continental Europe.[6] What is known about medieval carnival comes chiefly from two unexpected sources. First, texts of plays or skits, both religious and secular, survive that were performed during the carnival season.[7] Second, there are administrative records from towns and cities where carnival happened. Taken together, these sources show that in many cities and towns, a bawdy and raucous side of carnival festivities coexisted with morally edifying aspects.

There was not a high and wide division between religion and the secular world, with Easter and Lent on one side and carnival on the other. Easter was the occasion across Europe for huge civically sponsored and publicly performed religious play cycles that had ribald, comic interludes; at the same time, religious rituals and plays were a part of Shrovetide festivities.[8]

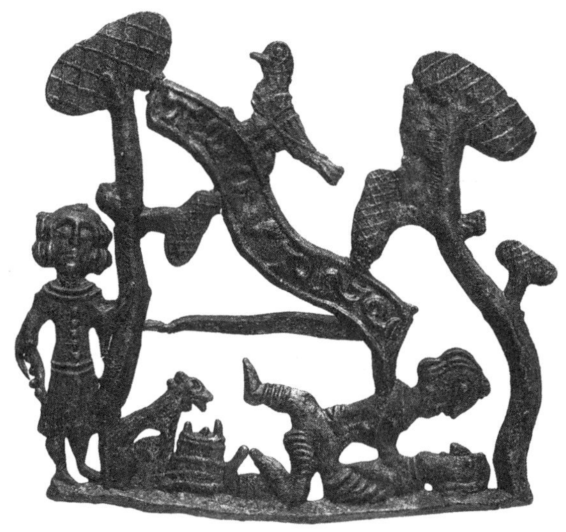

Figure 8.2. Pewter badge, Lady of Vergi, copulating couple between trees with inscription AMOVRS and watched by dog and man on left, pin, origin unknown, 1375–1424, found in Dordrecht, Netherlands, 44 × 50 mm. Langbroek, Netherlands, Family Van Beuningen Collection, inv. 1792 (Kunera 00610). Photograph courtesy of Family Van Beuningen Collection.

Obscene and ribald badges correspond well to the general tenor of ribald carnival activities, as this chapter will show, but they present interpretive challenges to modern scholars. Badges found in the Low Countries, for example, explicitly refer to the thirteenth-century Old French romance *The Chastelaine de Vergi*, which is a story of courtly love between a knight and a young, unmarried noblewoman who are betrayed. The badges, however, emphasize the physical side of the young couple's affair, showing them having sex in the garden, with the lady's dog, a key character in the story, standing guard, while a man, probably the young woman's uncle, watches or awaits (figure 8.2).

Why does the badge appear to create a comic or even obscene version of what the texts present as a sad story? I have not found answers to this question. Unlike political devices or religious badges, obscene badges are much harder to situate within the social and political matrices of medieval life. Badges are casual signs that recognize and pronounce affiliations and relationships, but what might these relationships of allegiance have been in the case of obscene badges? Who were the givers and who the wearers? Even though carnival practices and theatricals were also often of a morally edifying nature, carnival offers one plausible social framework in which comic, ribald, and obscene badges make sense.

Carnival was a politically complex event that involved negotiation and conflict among various urban actors, such as guilds, citizens, visitors, and individual artisans and merrymakers, with city councils organizing, funding, and permitting (or forbidding) various spectacles; mediating between opposing parties; and (attempting to) enforce orderly behavior or (seeking to) punish disorder and crime. Records of city councils rewarding groups of actors and performers with wine and coin allow glimpses of who might have performed some of these entertainments: schoolboys in the city of Arnhem in the Netherlands, members of the craft guilds and of the patrician class in Nuremberg, and so on. At times the documents show the councils deciding where and when which events would take place. They afford a glimpse of city councils wrestling with the thankless task of drawing a bright line between permissible and forbidden disorderly conduct. The Nuremberg city fathers officially permitted (or required) various guilds to perform their traditional carnival dances (at times they appear to be mediating between different groups); a council order from 1480 required a man, who had petitioned to be released from the carnival dance because of his age and infirmity, to walk alongside his guild brethren.[9] For a number of years in a row, the Basel city council forbade the practice of "running in the devil's guise" or "running in the devil's hide" in the streets, the frequent repetition of this ban suggesting that it had little effect.[10] "Running in the devil's hide" suggests both what the participants were wearing, that is, a costume that to judge by frequent references to it as "hide" (*haut*) might have used some kind of pelt (the many-headed demon badge in figure 4.5 is covered with some kind of fur or hide, for example). The phrase also encapsulates what the people wearing these costumes did: they moved or ran through the city streets, a frequently mentioned mode of participating in carnival.

The Nuremberg city council considered complaints about egregious misbehavior, for example, demanding that the leader in charge of a confraternity or guild group name to them the man who had carried a "shameful and immoral handcrafted member" (that is to say, some kind of penis statue) through the streets in Nuremberg.[11] Violence simmered under the surface; reports of brawls are not rare.

The administrative records also provide a tantalizing glimpse into the variegated world of carnival entertainment, for example, the large number of plays or skits that were performed on both religious and secular topics. Although only a small fraction of the actual texts survives, the administrative evidence, which often provides titles of plays when payments are recorded, demonstrates that performing plays on all kinds of topics was an ordinary and ubiquitous feature of carnival in German-speaking towns and cities. It is fortunate that these dry account books of the city fathers, listing payment after payment for play after play, have survived. Without them, modern people might still be arguing about whether or not medieval people actually participated in and witnessed performances of secular plays and spectacles.

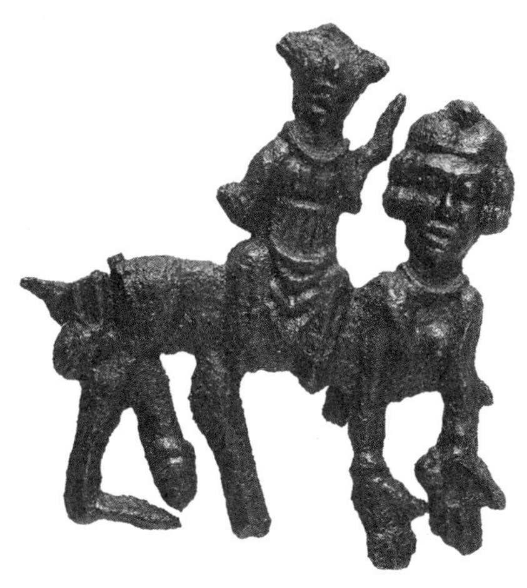

Figure 8.3. Pewter badge, Aristotle carrying Phyllis on his back, pin, origin unknown, 1400–1449, found in Nieuwlande, Netherlands, 28 × 20 mm. Langbroek, Netherlands, Family Van Beuningen Collection, inv. 1917 (Kunera 00539). Photograph courtesy of Family Van Beuningen Collection.

Plays were performed on topics ranging from Old Testament themes, such as Esther, and David and Goliath, to farces such as "the Neidhart play," in which a lovesick poet accidentally gifts his highborn lady with a turd instead of a flowering violet. The city of Lübeck, whose administrative records from the Middle Ages survive in great number, seems to have specialized in performances of morality plays during carnival. Many of the surviving carnival plays from Nuremberg, on the other hand, excel in creative verbal obscenity, a reminder that at carnival time both physical and verbal lewdness were tolerated.[12] Some surviving secular badges overlap thematically with surviving carnival plays, for example, the surviving carnival plays from Nuremberg featuring variations on the widely circulating medieval story of how the philosopher Aristotle fell prey to his own carnal desires and allowed himself to be ridden by a young woman. The badge shown in figure 8.3 sums up this story but differs in one key way from the majority of the written sources. It draws explicit attention to the sexual nature of Aristotle's love by highlighting his grotesquely enlarged penis, an image that resonates powerfully with the many phallic creatures populating the badge corpus.[13]

Entertainment during carnival included processions, parades, and dance entertainment or spectacles such as sword dances (called *morisk* or Moorish dances in Germany). In many medieval cities the various guilds, confraternities, and trade organizations each had a hallmark or traditional dance or spectacle that they performed at carnival. Surviving administrative records talk about scenes or tableaux enacted on some kind of movable conveyance, called in German *punten*, meaning ships on wheels, on which costumed people posed in all manner of biblical, mythical, legendary, ecclesiastical, and contemporary (pope, bishop, kaiser) tableaux. A visitor to Bergen op Zoom in the Netherlands on May 4, 1533, described such floats, which were interspersed with guild groups processing or performing traditional dances, for example: "After that followed Mary, John, and other disciples. After that came a big crowd all dressed as the evil spirit [i.e., the devil]. After that many crossbowmen."[14]

The gentry came to town during carnival, carrying out their tournaments and participating in carnival games. In his article on carnival in medieval German towns, Eckehard Simon relates various incidents from administrative records: when Duke Sigmund came to carnival in one city, he ran through the town with the women, that is to say, he took part in a carnival practice in which women were given license during carnival to be freed from the supervision of their husbands and fathers and to carry out carnival games of their own: "Held on Thursday before carnival Sunday, women's carnival [*Weiberfastnacht*] gave women license to storm male bastions like monasteries, invade inns to stage their own feasts and dances, and direct lewd words and gestures at men who dared to show themselves in the streets."[15]

Processing, moving, walking, or, as the administrative records put it, "running through the town" were standard tropes in carnival descriptions. The Nuremberg city council, for one, appears to have tried very hard to contain carnival disorder in the streets by regulating processions, forbidding disorderly conduct in the streets, and repeatedly enjoining revelers and actors to take their drinking, skits, and boisterous carnival practices indoors. But the urban streetscape remained the performative space of carnival.

People moved through the city districts at carnival, both in ordered processions and in what must have amounted to spontaneous street theater. They often did so wearing masks or costumes and disguises of many kinds: cross-dressing, dressing as peasants, and costuming themselves as animals, mythical creatures such as wild men, and demons and devils. In some cases, they apparently went nearly naked (streaking, as the practice is called today). They took part in traditional carnival games such as the hunt of the wild man in which children also participated. In a surviving administrative record from the city of Brugg, Switzerland, city officials admonished the schoolmaster and his wife to use the schoolboys' fees to care adequately for them, which includes, among other things, keeping their *tüfels kleidung*, or devil's clothing, in good repair.[16] Presumably it was the schoolboys' right and duty to "run in devil clothes" during specific feast days or during carnival. A pack of Brugg schoolboys on a saint's day, disguised in their devil costumes and running through the city streets, might have been a raucous sideshow to the piety of the singing, walking priests during Corpus Christi or one of the main acts in a Shrovetide carnival parade. Mischief seems an inadequate word for what they probably got up to.

Badges and Carnival

Badges seem made to order for the heightened performativity of carnival festivities, their mode of visual communication well suited to the mood of carnival and the movement of people through the city. Religious badges could have performed many functions during carnival time. Saint George was a popular saint, with myriad guilds and confraternities dedicated to him; the account from Bergen op Zoom, for example, lists a Saint George in the procession: "After that came someone dressed as Saint George riding on a large handsome stallion."[17] Religious badges showing Saint George could have been worn by guild members at carnival or in processions on other feast days, taking part in the mix of identities and allegiances conjured by badges. Perhaps carnival was a time for a pilgrim to display on his hat the religious badges acquired during his travels, for a pious woman to signal with a religious badge her devotion to a local saint while also marking her distance from the raucousness around her, or for the priests and canons to pin their saint's device on the hats of the choirboys before releasing them to stroll through the market or to attend family gatherings. Musician and acrobat badges might have been worn by those artisans to identify the troupe to which they belonged. Badges that denoted a public role, such as a badge featuring a town crier or a bannerman, might have functioned as a kind of device signaling the bearer's authority. Such badges could have been worn for many occasions, including carnival.

The iconography of carnival as it comes down to us from the administration of German-speaking lands overlaps with that of surviving secular badges, as the following discussions will demonstrate, and this is despite the fact that badge use is not well attested from the southern German towns that preserve a large amount of carnival-related texts and records. As is so often the case in the late Middle Ages, local and regional practices participate in, contribute to, and modify a widely shared, indeed near-universal, visual language.

Take the figure of the wild man, for example. A mythic creature well known from medieval literature and art, he appears in a wide variety of secular and religious contexts (there were wild women and children, too, though they rarely appear on badges).[18] Wild men were also traditional "guests" at carnival.[19] Every year in Nuremberg the butchers and upper-class youths dressed up as wild men (and wild women) to perform the Schembart run, called in German *Schembartlauf*. This processional event involved performing a grotesque dance in front of a woman, who would crown one of the dancers king. Simon discusses the widely practiced carnival game known as the wild man hunt: "First attested in 1338 in the Swiss town of Aarau, this ritual in-

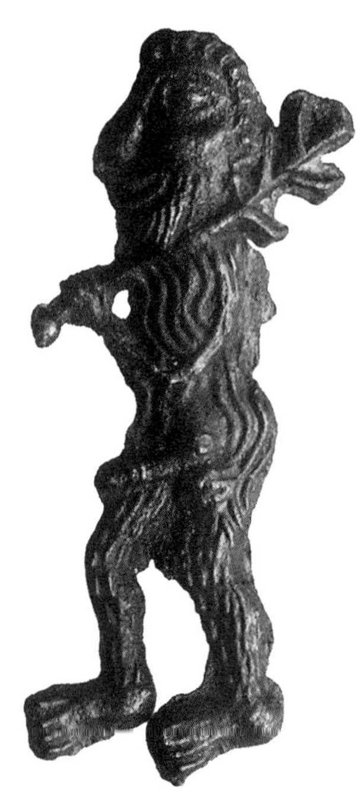

Figure 8.4. Pewter badge, wild man with branch-like club, pin, origin unknown, 1400–1449, found in Nieuwlande, Netherlands, 30 × 14 mm. Langbroek, Netherlands, Family Van Beuningen Collection, inv. 2522 (Kunera 00593). Photograph courtesy of Family Van Beuningen Collection.

volves revelers chasing after one of their own, who is covered only with ivy leaves, or hair, the mythical savage from the wood, and putting him in chains or mock-killing him. . . . In 1435, Basel entertained its church council with a wild-man dance. It featured twenty-three fellows with hair, half red, half green, falling to their feet, who danced while bashing each other with clubs stuffed with tow."[20]

The surviving wild man badges, often from the Low Countries, show a man whose body is covered with fur and who is usually clutching a cudgel while holding an odd or enigmatic posture that the textual evidence helps us to decode: it indicates movement of some kind, such as hopping or dancing, alluding to the ambulatory, performative practices of the wild men's appearance at carnival (figure 8.4).

Placing wild men badges within the context of carnival does not tell us who wore them, of course. We can speculate that wild man badges functioned as devices in some way for the brotherhoods, guilds, or confraternities who traditionally performed these dances. But perhaps such a badge could signal other things as well. Perhaps it could have functioned as a shaming gift, given to someone to say "you idiot, you savage, you wild man." Perhaps it was worn proudly, to show the world that one was a member or friend or fan of the guild that performed the wild man dance. Perhaps it was a token received at the end of a successful wild man hunt. In the late Middle Ages the wild man migrated into the escutcheons of European nobility, where he lives on today.[21]

Other badges of mythic creatures might have had their place in the world of carnival as well. A merman badge such as the one in figure 8.5 might have functioned in this context as a device signaling membership in a confraternity or guild that sponsored a carnival event. Mermaid badges, which often show the mermaid holding a mirror, may suggest vanity and may also be associated in some fashion with carnival (see plate 6b).

Perhaps many of the surviving secular badges that now appear so enigmatic belonged to the world of carnival, signaling membership in a carnival guild or participating in some fashion in carnival revelries. Take, for example, figure 8.6, the hybrid creature (a mythic creature? a monster?) that to judge from the dual bagpipes being played is capable of making a lot of noise.

That the imagery of the devil (another kind of monster) was closely associated with carnival has been made clear in the previous paragraphs. The demon badge in figure 4.5 harks back to the many mentions of devils and devil costumes that occur across the entire temporal and physical landscape of northern European carnival. There are many similar demon or devil badges,

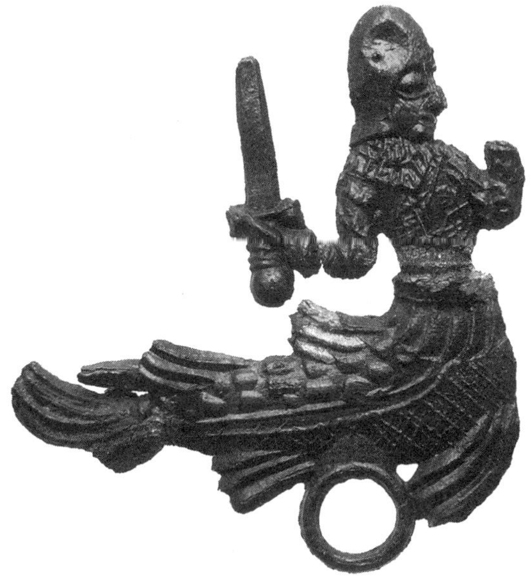

Figure 8.5. Pewter badge, merman, helmeted and holding sword in right hand, pin, origin unknown, 1400–1449, found in Valkenisse, Netherlands, 28 × 27 mm. Langbroek, Netherlands, Family Van Beuningen Collection, inv. 1906 (Kunera 00601). Photograph courtesy of Family Van Beuningen Collection.

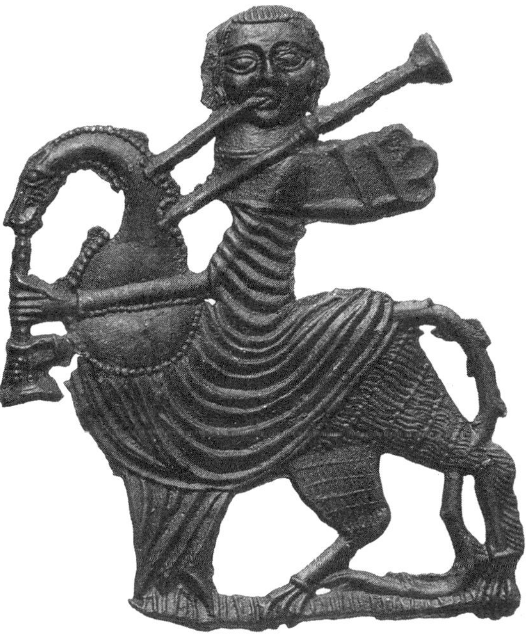

Figure 8.6. Pewter badge, human-like creature with wings and draped in cloth playing bagpipes while riding beast with serpent-like head and cat-like hindquarters and tail, pin, origin unknown, 1350–1399, found in 's-Hertogenbosch, Netherlands, 51 × 42 mm. Langbroek, Netherlands, Family Van Beuningen Collection, inv. 3122 (Kunera 06854). Photograph courtesy of Family Van Beuningen Collection.

sharing attributes such as being covered by fur or a pelt, having horns, and often, as in this image, having a second face or head in place of genitalia. Perhaps such badges shared features with the now-vanished devil clothes.

The wide, grimace-like smile on the face(s) of the devil badge in figure 4.5 takes us into a related iconographic world: the imagery of the fool. A face riven by a grimace-like smile and with the tongue sticking out belonged to the standard iconography of foolishness that was ubiquitous across medieval and early modern Europe and that was associated with carnival and with other festivities (figure 8.7).[22] Sometimes the fool is using his fingers to stretch his mouth even further; sometimes donkey ears (think of Puck in Shakespeare's *A Midsummer Night's Dream*) poke up out of his head covering.

The iconography of the fool was not limited to secular spaces or to carnival; it was found in sanctified settings throughout the Middle Ages. Fool's faces peer out from the misericords of countless medieval churches and grimace down from those buildings' waterspouts and spires. The Festival of Fools was a religious feast day celebrated by ecclesiastical orders and popular especially in medieval France, in which the choirboys impersonated the bishop and the pope. Still, the fool was definitely in his element at carnival. How might a fool badge have been used? Perhaps, as was suggested earlier, it was a device signaling membership in a jocular, season-specific guild or confraternity. Perhaps a fool badge was deemed a gift appropriate to carnival, a joke gift between friends or a shaming gift between enemies. All manner of games were played during carnival, including team sports noble and not so noble, from tournament to hostage-taking games. Does the loser receive as a consolation prize a fool badge, which betokens humiliation? Perhaps more simply, the fool badge signals license, as it were, to transgress accepted norms and conventions of behavior. Wearing the fool badge at carnival warns the man or woman standing next to you that you will do and say exactly as you please. If this were so, then wearing the fool badge would be a final act of social reciprocity because it would serve notice that accepted rules of conduct were about to be broken.

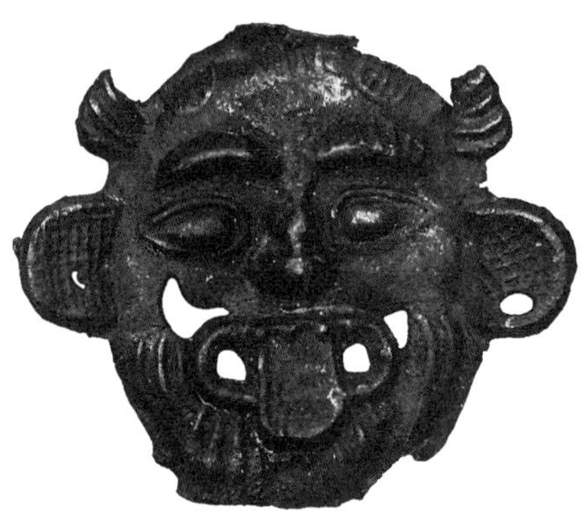

Figure 8.7. Pewter badge, fool or demon with tongue sticking out, pin, origin unknown, 1325–1374, found in Dordrecht, Netherlands, 28 × 35 mm. Langbroek, Netherlands, Family Van Beuningen Collection, inv. 3581 (Kunera 06850). Photograph courtesy of Family Van Beuningen Collection.

Finally, there are the various sexual badges, such as the penis creatures of figure 1.2 and plate 7a.[23] These include what I have elsewhere called the "wandering genitalia" badges that show penises or vulvas as auton-

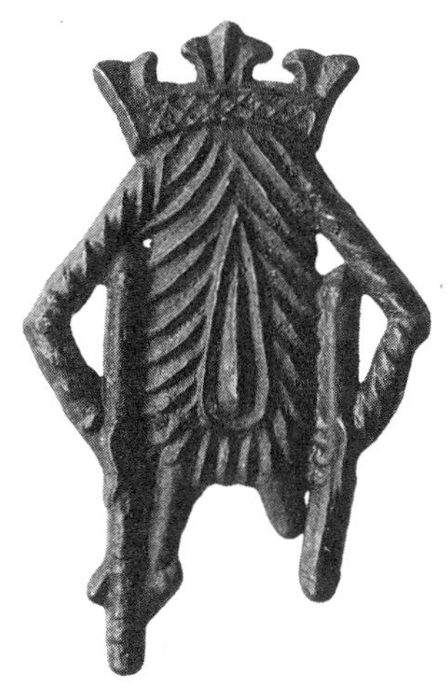

Figure 8.8. Pewter badge, crowned vulva walking on stilts, pin, origin unknown, 1375–1424, found in Nieuwlande, Netherlands, 25 × 16 mm. Langbroek, Netherlands, Family Van Beuningen Collection, inv. 2592 (Kunera 06482). Photograph courtesy of Family Van Beuningen Collection.

omous creatures, with legs and feet and sometimes wings, capable of making their way in the world, like the pilgrim vulva in figure 8.1. The crowned vulva shown in figure 8.8 is using stilts of some kind for mobility.

Other badges show intercourse and other sexual acts and include badges such as those in figures 8.2 and 8.3 that refer to well-known medieval stories with risqué or ribald content.[24] A badge from Valenciennes depicts a little house, its zones for drinking and for sex marked by drinking flagons on the right and a copulating couple on the left, overseen from the second floor by an outsized man holding a bulging purse in one hand and a flagon in the other (figure 8.9). The badge is inscribed with the sentence, SO [M]ENNEN SI IN MENNEN HUUSE (So they make love in love's house). The badge

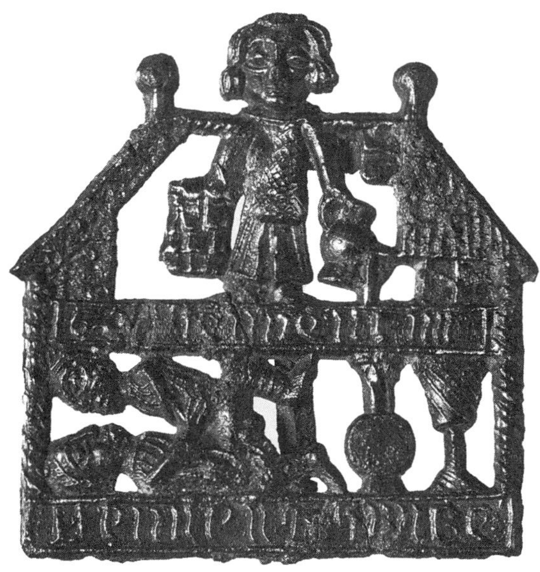

Figure 8.9. Pewter badge, brothel scene with inscription, pin, origin unknown, 1375–1424, found in Valenciennes, France, 31 × 30 × 4 mm. Valenciennes, Musée des Beaux-Arts, inv. 2005.4.263. Photograph and permission from Musée des Beaux-Arts de Valenciennes.

seems to show an inn or a brothel. There is a play on words in the inscription; *mennen* could mean either "love's house," which presumably means brothel, or "my" house, which leads to the question of who is imagined to be speaking: moneybags on the rooftop, whose posture and placement suggest ownership and who is facing the viewer, or perhaps (but less likely) the wearer of the badge. The former suggestion would keep the inscription within the frame of badge scenario, making it seem plausible, but the openness of the inscription may well be intended as a joke, too. Like the other badges discussed here, it seems especially well suited to carnival time to judge by the descriptions of bawdiness surviving in the carnival records.

Sexual badges are in many ways a kind of enigmatic badge, more so because they are hard for us to understand today in that they were deliberately designed to be mysterious; the contexts in which and for which they created meaning are largely lost to us. Some enigmatic badges deliberately undermine the medieval convention that badge images be easily intelligible. These enigmatic badges play with visual and sometimes textual elements in order to deliberately challenge the viewer's decoding abilities and to make a joke. Such badges might be called "riddling" badges and the badge in figure 8.10 is a good candidate. It uses reverse or mirror script to achieve a measure of obscurity, combines a religious allusion with secular imagery in a jocular way, and makes a bilingual pun. On the righthand side of the badge is a vulva (the squiggle that looks like a tail is probably a broken eyelet); the left is a placard with a single Dutch sentence written in mirror script: DIT.ES.CONTE. UNDE.AR.GHESELLE.KIN+DIE.VAN+ROMEN.COMMEN.SIN (This is cunt and her little companion, who are come from Rome).

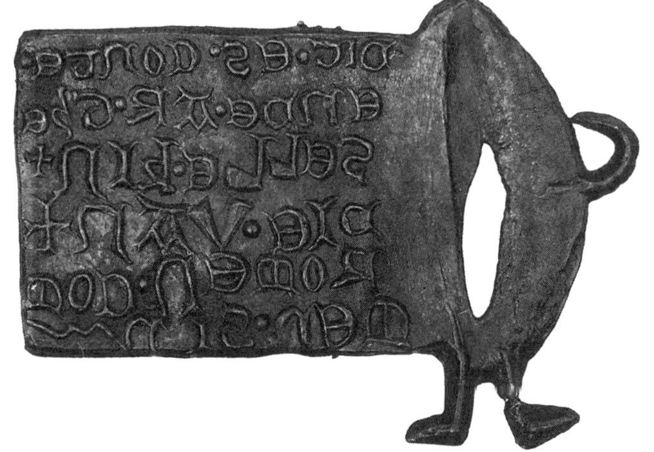

Figure 8.10. Pewter badge, walking vulva figure holding plaque with reverse script inscription, eyelets, origin unknown, 1325–1374, found in Sluis, Netherlands, 30 × 42 mm. Langbroek, Netherlands, Family Van Beuningen Collection, inv. 4225 (Kunera 17090). Photograph courtesy of Family Van Beuningen Collection.

This complex object requires multiple levels of knowledge and stages of decoding. Decoding the sentence requires a mirror, and the further step of holding the badge up to the mirror to read the sentence in it (at least, if the person decoding the badge is not able to read backwards). If the reader knows both Dutch and French (hardly an uncommon situation in the late medieval Low Countries) and speaks the sentence out loud, he or she will then discover that the spoken sentence includes a bilingual pun: in Dutch, *conte* means cunt, which in Old French sounds like the words for story or for ass.

Puns are funny, of course, and this bilingual play on words, often exploited in Old French comic literature, and the fact that the sentence is a third-person description (rather than, say, an utterance using an "I" form) takes us squarely into the realm of late medieval fabliaux and farce. Descriptive sentences like this one are a standard feature of medieval farces, where they are spoken by heralds to introduce new characters to an audience. Here is an example from a Nuremberg carnival play in which a herald is introducing the philosopher Aristotle, who is the play's chief comic protagonist: "Now be quiet, don't talk so much! Listen to what I'm telling you. Here stands a master of medicine who knows the art of master Pliny, and the high arts of master Origene, and comes from the highest school in Athens."[25]

I have let stand in the carnival play citation the herald's conventional address to the audience asking them to quiet down and pay attention. It conjures up the performative context of carnival plays, which for the sake of brevity I will call a stage but which in Nuremberg, for example, probably was simply a cleared space on the street or in a house or inn, and it implies that certain actions were expected by the audience before the main event. The preliminary actions implied here involved focus, understood in the case of the play as halting conversation in order to redirect attention to the staged performance, and in the case of the badge as finding a mirror to carefully focus in (the badge is after all only three-by-four centimeters in size) on the badge text. The similarities between the speech and the badge's placard text are also apparent. Each begins with a dietic pronoun (*dies* [this]; *hie* [here]) gesturing toward the actors or players. In the case of the play, this is the imagined actor (presumably costumed or with props) who has stepped into the performative space; in the case of the badge, it is both the badge itself and the "little companion," presumably the person wearing the badge. Just as the herald is imagined describing in words the person who is already onstage, so too the placard repeats in words what is already present in the image: the vulva. In both cases, the main figure being alluded to is accompanied, as it were, by others: Aristotle by the ancient philosophers whose lore he has mastered (Pliny, Origen); the vulva by the companion mentioned on the badge. The collective contexts imagined by the play and the badge are complex and characterized by imagined interactivity.

In the play the herald identifies the new character by profession (complete with references to other philosophers whose knowledge he has mastered) and by a geographical point of origin: Athens. The cunt and its companion, too, are identified by a geographical point of origin: they have come from Rome, which is a reference to pilgrimage. Other badges showing vulvas dressed as pilgrims make this context clear; figure 8.1 shows a badge of a vulva dressed in a pilgrim's hat and holding in each hand a religious attribute, rosary and pilgrim's staff, that are functioning simultaneously as symbols for female and male genitalia.

That a pious and ideally chaste activity such as pilgrimage should be mocked as a sexual activity—or alternatively, that a woman's sexual desire should be embodied as a pilgrim who wanders from shrine to shrine, which suggests promiscuity—may surprise modern readers. But by the late Middle Ages virtually every aspect of late medieval religion could be the subject of satire or comedy. Here, the suggestion is that the vulva (and her companion in figure 8.10) are vagabonds. Fabliaux and farce are replete with lecherous priests and monks and with vagabonding clerics and members of religious orders both male and female.[26] The reference to pilgrimage is part of the placard vulva badge's multilayered riddling, punning, and joking, which by design and intention (mirror script, the naming of a wearer on the badge) bring the visual and linguistic registers into debate with one another and assume excellent multimodal decoding skills on the part of the viewer.

More lewd, obscene, or simply strange badges survive. What about the torsoless, bearded grotesque with a big dangling penis (plate 7b) or the naked, squatting woman exposing her sex (figure 8.11)? Are such images that focus the gaze on human genitalia audacious or insolent? Harking back to Chapter 4, is their intended audience solely those who originally purchased, wore, or used them, or might an audience of evil spirits be intended as well? The answer must depend in part on the contexts in which the images were used, and even then there may have been debate about their acceptability.

Finally, the image of a wimple-wearing woman holding a digging implement in one hand while with the other touching a penis that is buried in the earth brings new coordinates of meaning into the interpretive matrix for sexual badges. Figure 8.12 suggests the season of spring and agricultural activities: soil and plants; the penis imagined as a seed waiting passively to sprout or as a tuber root waiting to be dug up; the married woman as the active agent cultivating this garden. Its imagery takes the viewer beyond the world of carnival and suggests a worldview in which the generative and reproductive potential of sex is equated with life-giving, necessary nourishment whose agents are women.[27]

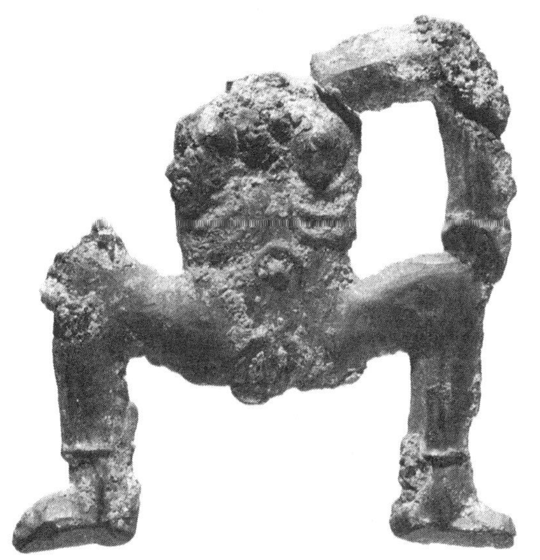

Figure 8.11. Pewter badge, squatting nude woman showing her sex, attachment unknown, origin unknown, 1400–1449, find site unknown, 21 × 21 mm. Paris, Musée de Cluny–Musée national du Moyen Âge, inv. CL2348 (Kunera 01650). Photographer: Gérard Blot. Photograph and permission from © RMN-Grand Palais/Art Resource, New York.

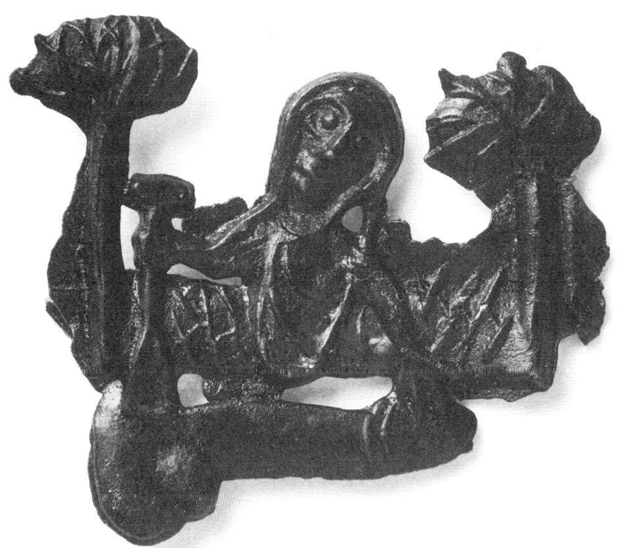

Figure 8.12. Pewter badge, woman with shovel touching buried phallus, pin, origin unknown, 1300–1349, found in Ypres, Belgium, 25 × 30 mm. Yper Museum, inv. 002954 (Kunera 06915). Photographer: Els Deroo. Photograph courtesy of Yper Museum.

With its plays and dramatic enactments, its sports, morality plays, traditional performances, processions, and displays, carnival may well have occasioned some of the most raucous and disorderly of the public events that were an integral part of the medieval city. Nevertheless, it was but one of a multitude of civic festivities and public celebrations and occasions in which the profane and the sacred rubbed shoulders as the city created a symbolic simulacrum of itself and the ever-shifting relationships of power and political allegiance that circulated in and through it.[28] Badges were an integral part of this self-fashioning. Badges must have been displayed often and widely in these tumultuous, heterogeneous, dynamic, market-driven cities: badges from near and far, badges familiar and strange, common and uncommon, religious and secular, decorous and unrestrained, solemn and joking, tender and aggressive; badges worn by rich and poor, high and low, pious and impious, neighbors and strangers. In the pageantry of the medieval city at carnival time, social groups and identities mingled, from the corporations and guilds that usually provided the entertainment, to the civic functionaries overseeing festivities and charged with keeping order, to the canons, priests, and choirboys in the procession, to the participants and spectators from near and far who took part in such a public occasion.

Concluding Remarks

Sweden, west of Vadstena,
winter, 1365

It is bitter cold. Falling snow, blown sideways by the savage wind, blinds the three men and obliterates the track. The horses are failing and night closes in. The men and horses are hungry, but what of that? It is the weakest of the three assassins stalking them. The grim reaper, Cold, will do them in before Hunger or Lord Albrecht's men catch up.

An icy gust of wind brings with it the faintest hint of the smell of hearth fire. They follow the trace westward, into the wind, into the forest, into a world of racing air that is white at bottom, top, and sides, moving slowly so the horses can feel their way. The hearth smell grows stronger and brings them to a hamlet of two, no three farmsteads blurring in and out of view. They almost miss the first house, hidden from view by a copse of trees and sheltered from the track, if track there be under the snow. While two move the horses leeside, one ducks under the thatched eave, raps on the wooden door, and calls out.

"Good people, we come in peace and on the King's errand. Good people, in God's name we beg you to grant shelter to us, wayfaring far from home on this terrible night. There are only three of us, with horses. We can pay."

A middle-aged widow opens the door and peers out in the blowing snow, her hand restraining a large, snarling dog, the scent of smoke, warmth, and shelter flowing around her and out into the gathering night. In the flickering light from the hearth, she peers closely at the man who speaks such a strangely accented Swedish. He is young. His pockmarked face is marred by a scar over his right cheek and nose, no looker in the best of times, though strong and well nourished, and now an ugly, bedraggled sight, gaunt with cold and wet. She assesses him again, quickly, taking the measure of the way he is clutching his cloak about his body. Is he hiding a sword?

But already she can see that the bareheaded, dark blond man standing behind him has just as quickly read her glance. He barks an order in a strange tongue, and then all three men fumble two-handed under their cloaks to unbuckle their sword belts. She opens the door wider and steps forward, receiving the swords still on the belts. Two swords are serviceable and worn, the third is old and magnificent, a downward-curving hilt ringed with silver and gold, edges of swirled steel and grim as a wolf's tooth. A woman knows these things. Without their swords, the daggers in their belts and boots are little danger. They do not come to rob on such a night, when snow makes stealth unneeded. They will move on.

But for now, they wait on her word at the door. The dark blond must be the lord. He is of middle height, in the prime of life, with a long, bent nose and an uneasy gaze. He pulls the riding glove off his hand and wearily rubs his tawny beard stubble. The seal ring on his right hand glints. He limps. He is sore from the saddle, but Scarface and the third man, who has huge hands and shoulders the size of tree trunks, are not.

The woman's grandson, curious as always, steps outside unbidden, his feet in the wooden shoes filled with fresh straw and a cape pinned over his shoulders. He and Tree Trunk lead the horses to the dwelling's entrance on the narrow end, to the stable where the animals are bedded down. They will have to stack the cart and tools on top of the sledge to make room for the horses, for thanks be to God the stable is full this winter and the loft above it groans under the weight of a full harvest. The boy knows horses. He will tend them. With a nod of her head, the woman steps to the side and the men enter her dwelling.

Drifting over the wattle half-wall to the human dwelling space comes the smell of wet horse and horse dung mingling with those of cow, goat, and sheep, the precious, warm scent of living abundance. By the hearth the wayfarers remove their wet clothing, draping it over the drying racks under the watchful eyes of the grandchildren and the aged laborer who is also part of the household. They crowd together on the widow's sleeping bench, making room for the lord and his men to sit.

The lord's black bodice stinks of sweat, the finely woven wool is no longer new, its weave is patched in places and worn thin. The delicate embroidery around cuffs and neck is coming apart, threads pulled and missing, broken, the pattern disrupted, the stitches unraveling. No woman's hand has tended this garment for a long time. He takes it off. The widow places it alone on the drying rack, where steam and the smell of wet wool and sweat rises from leg bindings, foot and hand wraps, and heavy cloaks. She tells her grandson to put the oak wood on the fire; it brings better light and heat and makes less smoke. He must fetch water too (a hard task, that, in this storm!) from the well. She sends her little granddaughter scrambling up and down the loft ladder, fetching dried grasses for sweetening the room, two measures of rye and one of lentils, and the half cheese. The travelers lean back and close their eyes.

Carefully cooking the porridges, the widow sits by the hearth and idly fingers the black bodice, its smooth and silky weave so unaccustomedly soft to the touch. A shame that this beautiful embroidery has been neglected; it is exquisite work. She turns it over. Yes, the embroideress has left long threads skillfully tucked and hidden, ready to be used for repair. The old laborer is telling stories now. Scarface and Tree Trunk laugh, and the old man, silenced by these last bitter years, is once again enjoying an audience. The children are quiet yet wide awake. Only the lord, lost in his thoughts, appears half-asleep. Well, the light is good enough. Perhaps the pattern will work itself into her hands? There is no learning a pattern without the doing of it, and there is time before the meal will be done. She takes the needle from its holder around her neck, threads, sews. Looking up, she sees that the brooding glance of the lord has fallen on her, no expression on his face.

Dawn promises a better day. The old man grooms and feeds the horses; the child scrambles up the ladder once again, for dried rye cakes and hard cheese; Scarface fills the felted water vessels from the well. The widow fetches the swords from her sleeping bench. Scarface counts silver coins into her hand. "Best for us that they were away quickly," the widow silently reflects, "before others learn of such wealth come to such a poor house. Best for them if they were away quickly." Their mutterings in the night have shown that for all their fine manners they stink of trouble in high places, big people trouble that harms the small. Her grandson will drive the sheep and goats eastward to forage in the water meadow; that and the fresh snow promised by the clouds should cover the tracks.

Tree Trunk swings onto his horse. The lord comes out, the cuffs of the black bodice peeping out from under his cloak. Sighing, he lifts himself onto the stone by the gate to mount. Scarface approaches the widow and presses a small object into her hand. A crowned, bearded man, seated on a throne and holding a huge axe, commands her gaze. The object is powerful.

Before she can ask, Scarface speaks.

"He says to tell you that he gives you this in thanks. He says that this is Saint Olaf, a great prince among our wayfaring ancestors of old, who fought to bring his pagan people to Christ and was martyred, as we all know, by the stubborn infidels among us, then as now, then as now.

"He says that he descends from the Saint on his mother's side, the mother who stitched this shirt for him, and who is no longer here to repair it. And as you have done mother's duty to him, freely and of your own will, so he chooses son's duty to you. As a son he asks the great father of his family, Saint Olaf, to bless you and to protect you and your kin always, as he himself promises to do.

"Send your boy to him in Vadstena with this, if you need help. He is a lord, my lady, though in a spot of trouble now. He will know you."

She turns and looks the lord in the eye and, bowing, speaks her thanks.

"Peace be with you and yours, my lord. Ride careful and hard. May the Saint shield us all from harm."

In the hard starlight of northern dawn, they wheel and ride away. The wind mingles snowdrift and cold mist. The riders are quickly lost from sight.

A badge of Saint Olaf unearthed in Norway in an archaeological excavation can be seen on plate 12b. Most of the medieval images pictured in photographs have been, if not restored, at least dusted off and cleaned up, rid of the grime that accrues with time. But not this one. Bent, corroded, broken, rusted, the lines that create its image fading away, the Saint Olaf badge displays not so much the patina of age as the material metamorphosis wrought by the passage of six hundred years. Time has remodeled it and will continue to do so.

In each chapter this book has moved from fiction, to objects and their images, and then to academic reflection. The objects, however, are the book's living structure, if you will, its dynamic inner frame. Objects and images do many things, as art historians have said far better than me. One of the things they do is make arguments; to paraphrase historian Kristen Neuschel, they appeal to *any* present, suggesting that recovering, as this book seeks to do, a range of claims that an object might have made in the past does not preclude them from making new arguments relevant to a present day.[1] When it was made, purchased, and worn, the Saint Olaf badge carried the kinds of social and religious meanings that have been explored in this book. In the contemporary world, its charisma as an object can also arise from the way in which it can embody symbolically the pastness of the medieval world in the present.

The approach to medieval badges in this book has been most profoundly shaped by my training as a literary scholar who is also a medievalist and as a teacher of the German language in its modern and medieval forms. This professional orientation shows in many ways: using storytelling to engage the reader; finding ready-to-hand examples and analogies from medieval literary texts; thinking in terms of comparative and contrastive structures, of motifs, and of adaptation. The deepest affinity that I found with the research of medieval art historians, as the research on this book transformed me into a student of their field, was an abiding and central focus on attending to form and to the materiality of objects. As a literary scholar, I have always perceived form (genre, for example) as a kind of argument, and I have always thought of language as something material that carries traces of its fleeting breath- and sound-based ways of making meaning into even those means of its expression, such as writing or sign language, that are far removed from its utterings and murmurs. I hope in this book to have listened well to the messages inherent in the multivalent materiality and form of badges.

In this book I have, I think, neglected to answer, or at least to answer thoroughly and well, a number of important historical questions. These I trace in the following paragraphs. In my defense, I will say that this neglect arises in part from my particular interdisciplinary lens, which favored the kind of approach outlined in the preceding paragraph, but also because, as I remarked in Chapter 1, I would not have been capable of writing a study answering these historical questions until I had written this book.

A plausible hypothesis worth exploring further is that badges were the first mass media in the western world. Millions were produced and used, meaning that ordinary people in the past, not just elites, knew how to "read" or decode them. The fact of badges' mass production suggests that more research needs to be done on visual literacy in the late medieval world, approached not from the presumption that the late medieval world suffered from a scarcity of images and from a widespread inability to comprehend and use images in sophisticated ways (the presumption of visual "illiteracy," as it were), but rather from a presumption of image-based plenitude and visual literacy that was widely shared.

It is time for scholars to rewrite our understanding of late medieval visual literacy as a fundamental and complex mode of communication. Hanneke van Asperen and I alluded to these ideas in our introduction to the special issue of the *Medieval Journal* when we wrote about placing "the study of medieval badges in a new frame of inquiry that is based on the overarching hypothesis that badges, whether secular or religious (or both), operated as a kind of pan-European, symbolic mode of communication that transcended the verbal, linguistic, political, and social boundaries across which they moved."[2] Badges show us that this late medieval visual mode of symbolic communication was semantically open, was worked with ambiguity, and depended on contextual knowledge.

The mass production and use of badges and the wide range and intelligibility of their images coincides in time and place with those parts of northern Europe where vernacular literacy was most widespread. In other words, again quoting Hanneke van Asperen and myself, "A growth in visual literacy went hand in hand with the growth of vernacular, linguistic literacy . . . [and] the role and function of visual literacy for communication in the High and late Middle Ages, and the interplay thereof with rising levels of linguistic and vernacular literacy, are still not adequately understood."[3] The modern boom in visual communication is often presented as something new, yet it has a long history. Understanding better medieval modes of visual communication and their imbrication in the rise of vernacular, linguistic literacy would extend our ability to reflect meaningfully on visual communication in the present day.

Medieval badges claimed belonging. Whether religious or profane, self-chosen or compelled, badges were used by medieval people to make communities visible to themselves and to outsiders, creating networks small and large within medieval society. Most badges were worn voluntarily and depending on context for longer or shorter periods, but sometimes they were compelled, and when this happened, the fluidity and mobility of identity that distinguished voluntarily worn badges were lost. New research is needed to tackle historical questions regarding the interactions between compelled badges and voluntary badges in the late Middle Ages; to date, the robust streams of scholarship treating compelled badges, religious badges, and secular (whether political or cultural) badges only rarely intersect. Perhaps part of the answer to the question of why badges seem to disappear from ordinary use in the early modern period may be found in the semantic narrowing, as it were, of the meaning of the badge, such that the wearing of a simple, secular badge is understood as having been compelled by an authority, as I hypothesized in Chapter 2.

Badges were intended to be public-facing objects, to be used and seen by everyone. Wearable, movable, malleable, and discardable in their own time yet robust enough to survive in large numbers into ours, medieval badges communicated visually in sophisticated ways that as their mass production suggests, had been mastered by medieval audiences regardless of gender, religion, language, region, station, status, or wealth. Medieval badges help to overturn modern notions of the Middle Ages as a dreary, monochrome image desert punctuated by occasional oases of light and color accessible only to elites. They can guide us into imagining a Middle Ages awash in visually communicated, complex systems of signification that were expressed in an astonishingly diverse and wide array of objects used by rich and poor and that demanded at least a modicum of interpretive knowledge and skill on the part of every viewer. Badges intersected with and participated in the complex and ambiguous visual systems for representing community that were fundamental to the Middle Ages. I hope that this book will contribute to bringing badges from the fringes to the center of medieval studies scholarship.

Notes

The following shortened forms appear in the notes:

HP	H. J. E. van Beuningen and A. M. Koldeweij, eds. *Heilig en Profaan*, 4 vols. Cothen and Langbroek, Netherlands: Stichting Middeleeuwse Religieuze en Profane Insignes, 1993, 2001, 2012, 2018.
HP1	*Heilig en Profaan 1*, edited by H. J. E. van Beuningen and A. M. Koldeweij. Rotterdam Papers 8. Cothen, Netherlands: Stichting Middeleeuwse Religieuze en Profane Insignes, 1993.
HP2	*Heilig en Profaan 2*, edited by H. J. E. van Beuningen, A. M. Koldeweij, and D. Kicken. Rotterdam Papers 12. Cothen, Netherlands: Stichting Middeleeuwse Religieuze en Profane Insignes, 2001.
HP3	*Heilig en Profaan 3*, edited by H. J. E. van Beuningen, A. M. Koldeweij, D. Kicken, and H. van Asperen. Rotterdam Papers 13. Langbroek, Netherlands: Stichting Middeleeuwse Religieuze en Profane Insignes, 2012.
HP4	*Heilig en Profaan 4*, edited by H. J. E. van Beuningen, H. van Asperen, A. M. Koldeweij, and H. W. J. Piron. Rotterdam Papers 14. Langbroek, Netherlands: Stichting Middeleeuwse Religieuze en Profane Insignes, 2018.
Kunera	Kunera: A Database of Late Medieval Badges and Ampullae. Nijmegen, Netherlands, Radboud Universiteit. https://www.kunera.nl/default.aspx
Matter of Faith	*Matter of Faith: An Interdisciplinary Study of Relics and Relic Veneration in the Medieval Period*, edited by James Robinson, Lloyd de Beer, and Anna Harnden. London: British Museum, 2014.
Mittelalterliche Tragezeichen	*Mittelalterliche Tragezeichen: Social Media des Mittelalters / Medieval Badges: Social Media of the Middle Ages*, edited by André Dubisch. Exhibition catalog. Lübeck, Germany: European Hansemuseum, 2020.
Das Zeichen am Hut	*Das Zeichen am Hut im Mittelalter: Europäische Reisemarkierungen. Symposion in Memoriam Kurt Köster (1912–1986) und Katalog der Pilgerzeichen im Kunstgewerbemuseum und im Museum für Byzantinische Kunst der Staatlichen Museen zu Berlin*, edited by H. Kühne, L. Lambacher, and K. Vanja. Frankfurt: Peter Lang, 2008.

Chapter 1

1. Denis Bruna discusses medieval French and Latin naming practices for badges in his study *Enseignes de plomb et autres menues chosettes du Moyen Âge* (Paris: Léopard d'Or, 2006), 74–75.
2. Some badges are three-dimensional. One could also say that these objects, such as tiny crowns or decorative plaques (figures 6.1 and 6.2), tiny folding diptychs wearable as a pendant (plate 8 and figures 5.20 and 5.21), or the toy knights discussed in Chapter 6, are badge-like.
3. For an introduction to the general topic of pilgrim souvenirs, see Diane Webb, "Remembering Pilgrimage: Souvenirs," in *Pilgrims and Pilgrimage in the Medieval West* (London: Tauris, 1999), 124–32.
4. On women as pilgrims see Leigh Ann Craig, *Wandering Women and Holy Matrons: Women as Pilgrims in the Later Middle Ages*, Studies in Medieval and Reformation Traditions, vol. 138 (Leiden: Brill, 2009).
5. Because pewter is an alloy, defined as a solid metal made from two or more chemical elements, it is also known as tin-alloy, lead-tin, copper-alloy, and so on, as is discussed in more detail in Chapter 3.
6. This rough estimate is based on the number of badge images in the Kunera database (currently about twenty thousand); these are largely photographs of still-existing badges or photographs of badge casts in medieval bells (more about that in Chapter 2). The Kunera database does include some images or drawings of medieval badges that have vanished, but many surviving medieval badges are not yet represented in the Kunera database.
7. Carina Brumme, "Pilgerzeichen: Erhaltungsbedingungen und Verbreitungsräume," in *Das Zeichen am Hut*, 127–42. In "Some Approaches to the Archaeology of Christian Pilgrimage," *World Archaeology* 26.1 (1994): 57–72, here page 57, J. Stopford discusses other aspects of the evidence for mass production, including the "infrequency with which these mass-produced products were made with the same moulds," the evidence for "lengthy disputes over rights to production," and staggering sales numbers such as "130,000 badges being sold in 14 days at Einsiedeln and at Regensburg in Germany, a less well-known pilgrimage site, 50,000 badges were sold at the official shop between 1519–1522."
8. On the communicative function of all badges, see A. M. Koldeweij, "The Wearing of Significative Badges, Religious and Secular: The Social Meaning of a Behavioral Pattern," in *Showing Status: Representations of Social Positions in the Late Middle Ages*, ed. Wim Blockmans and Antheun Janse (Turnhout, Belgium: Brepols, 1999) 307–28.
9. There are other historical questions that this book will not answer: the origins of the use of badges in western Europe (perhaps due to influences from Byzantium and the rise of indexical semiotics in the Latin West); the potentially sizable role played by the mass presence of sophisticated visual literacy (in which badges participate) in the preprint rise of vernacular linguistic literacy in the Latin West; and the many reasons for the demise of the use of badges in the sixteenth century. Sketched in the previous sentence is the outline of the book I have not written, which I would only have been able to write after the book you are now reading was finished and which I now hope to write collaboratively with an interdisciplinary team as the next phase of research into medieval badges.

10. On the beginnings of pilgrim badge production, see Jennifer M. Lee, "Signs of Affinity: Canterbury Pilgrims' Sign Contextualized, 1171–1538" (PhD diss., Emory University, 2003).
11. Paula Gerson, Annie Shaver-Crandell, and Alison Stones, eds., *The Pilgrim's Guide to Santiago de Compostela: Critical Edition*, vol. 2 (London: Harvey Miller, 1998), 72–73.
12. Ian Short, ed., trans., and intro., *A Life of Thomas Becket in Verse: La vie de saint Thomas Becket by Guernes de Pont-Sainte-Maxence* (Toronto: Pontifical Institute of Medieval Studies, 2013), 169. Guernes goes on to comment on the ampulla (phial) that was one of the first badges connected to the Becket shrine at Canterbury: "And now God has granted to St. Thomas a phial that is cherished and honoured throughout the world."
13. See Stopford, "Some Approaches"; and Brian Spencer, "Pilgrim Badge," Grove Art Online (Oxford: Oxford University Press, 2003).
14. Willy Piron, "Pilgrim Badges and GIS: A Northern Affair?" in *Wallfahrer aus dem Osten: Mittelalterliche Pilgerzeichen zwischen Ostsee, Donau und Seine*, ed. Hartmut Kühne, Lothar Lambacher, and Jan Hrdina (Frankfurt: Peter Lang, 2012), 475–86.
15. See Chapter 2. For an overview of trends in badges scholarship in Germany, see Hartmut Kühne and Jörg Ansorge, "'Holiness' from the Mud: Badges and Pilgrimage in German-Speaking Lands—A Case Study from the Northern German City of Stade (Lower Saxony) in the Former Diocese of Bremen," in *Mediæval Journal* 8.1 (2018): 11–56.
16. For scholarship on badges from these areas, see Denis Bruna, "Enseignes de pèlerinage de la *Vita Tolosana* Provence et Languedoc: Nouvelles découvertes et état de la question," in *Saint Jacques et la France: Actes du colloque des 18 et 19 janvier 2001*, ed. Adeline Rucquoi (Paris: CERF, 2003), 65–82; Jean Berger, "Les enseignes de pèlerinage du Puy," in *Jubilé et culte marial*, ed. Bruno Maes, Daniel Moulinet, and Catherine Vincent (Saint-Étienne, France: Publications de l'Université Saint-Étienne, 2009), 87–114; Michel Baudat, "La dévotion à saint Antoine abbé à travers des enseignes de pèlerinages récemment découvertes," *Bulletin des Amis du Vieil Arles* 111 (2001): 39–46; D. Carru and S. Gagnière, "Notes sur quelques objets de dévotion populaire, ampoules et enseignes de pèlerinage au Moyen-Âge tardif provenant d'Avignon," *Mémoires de l'Académie de Vaucluse*, 8.1 (1992): 55–92; Philip Ferrando, "Quatre enseignes de pèlerinage inédites pour Sainte-Croix de Montmajour," *Bulletin des Amis du Vieil Arles* 110 (March 2001): 5–13; J.-M. Lassure, "Enseignes de pèlerinage du XIVe siècle trouvées à Toulouse et au Pouget (Hérault)," *L'Auta* 35 (2002): 200–206.
17. On the meanings associated with lead in the Middle Ages, see Jennifer M. Lee, "Material and Meaning in Lead Pilgrim Signs," *Peregrinations: Journal of Medieval Art and Architecture* 2.3 (2009): 152–68.
18. For a wonderful short article distinguishing badges from other small pewter objects, such as tiny decorations that were used to embellish leather belts and straps, see Hanneke van Asperen and Willy Piron, "Het is geen insigne: Een korte verkenning van middeleeuwse objecten in lood-tin," in *HP4*, 23–34.
19. See Malcolm Jones, "The Secular Badges," in *HP1*, 99–109; and Jones, "Sacred and Profane: Reinforcement and Amuletic Ambiguity in the Late Medieval Lead Badge Corpus," *Amsterdamer Beiträge zur älteren Germanistik* 59 (2004): 111–37. See also

Richard Kieckhefer, "Erotic Magic," in *Sex in the Middle Ages: A Book of Essays*, ed. Joyce E. Salisbury (New York: Garland, 1991), 30–55.

20. For more information about this painting, the original of which hangs in the Mauritshuis, The Hague, the Netherlands, see Ann Marie Rasmussen, "Das Porträt von Herzog Heinrich V. von Mecklenburg in North Carolina (USA)," *Mecklenburgisches Jahrbuch* 135 (2020): 349–52.
21. This topic has now been treated in depth in a major study by Barbara Newman, *Medieval Crossover: Reading the Secular Against the Sacred* (Notre Dame, IN: University of Notre Dame Press, 2013). For badges, see, for example, A. M. Koldeweij, "Shameless and Naked Images: Obscene Badges as Parodies of Religious Devotion," in *Art and Architecture of Late Medieval Pilgrimage in Northern Europe and the British Isles*, ed. Sarah Blick and Rita Tekippe (Leiden: Brill, 2005), 493–510. For a fascinating study of the use of penis creatures in a political setting, see George Ferzoco, *The Massa Marittima Mural* (Florence: Consiglio Regionale della Toscana, 2004; Leicester: University of Leicester, 2004); for a revision of Ferzoco's argument, see Mathew Ryan Smith, "Reconsidering the 'Obscene': The Massa Marittima Mural," *SHIFT: Queen's Journal of Visual and Material Culture* 2 (2009): 1–27.
22. Subsequently published as Ann Marie Rasmussen, *Wandering Genitalia: Sexuality and the Body in German Culture Between the Late Middle Ages and Early Modernity*, King's College London Medieval Studies, Occasional Series 2 (London: Centre for Late Antique & Medieval Studies, King's College London, 2009).
23. Edith Wenzel, "*zers* und *fud* als literarische Helden: Zum 'Eigenleben' von Geschlechtsteilen in mittelalterlicher Literatur," in *Körperteile: Eine kulturelle Anatomie*, ed. Claudia Benthien and Christoph Wulf (Reinbek: Rowohlt, 2001), 274–93.
24. Barbara Hanawalt, *Growing Up in Medieval London* (New York: Oxford University Press, 1993).
25. On this point, see Sam Weinberg, *Historical Thinking and Other Unnatural Acts* (Philadelphia: Temple University Press, 2001), 5.

Chapter 2

1. Arthur Forgeais published catalogs of his collection as *Collection des plombs historiés trouvés dans la Seine*, 5 vols. (Paris: Chez l'Auteur, Quai d'Orfévres, 54, 1861–1865).
2. To learn more about the early history of badge collecting, see two articles in the exhibition catalog *Mittelalterliche Tragezeichen*: A. M. Koldeweij, "Die Sammlung H. J. E. van Beuningen und ihre Vorgänger / The H. J. E. van Beuningen Collection and its Predecessors," 132–49; and Carina Brumme and Hanneke van Asperen, "Kleine Objekte und große Kontexte: 170 Jahre Forschung zu mittelalterlichen Zeichen / Small Objects and Larger Contexts: 170 Years of Research into Medieval Badges," 150–77. See also Klaus Herbers and Hartmut Kühne, "Einführung: Mittelalterliche Pilgerzeichen—zur Geschichte und den gegenwärtigen Perspektiven ihrer Erforschung," in *Pilgerzeichen—Pilgerstrassen*, ed. K. Herbers and H. Kühne (Tübingen, Germany: Narr, 2013), 7–27.
3. For more information, visit the web page "Udbetaling af danefædusør," Museer og slotter Nationalmuseet, https://natmus.dk/salg-og-ydelser/museumsfaglige-ydelser/danefae/udbetaling-af-danefaedusoer/.
4. An overview of Köster's publications and contributions is provided by Jörg Poettgen, "Europäische Pilgerzeichenforschung: Die Zentrale Pilgerzeichenkartei (PZK) Kurt

Kösters (1986)," in *Jahrbuch für Glockenkunde* 7/8 (1995/96): 195–207, http://www.pilgerzeichen.de/html/poettgen-koester.html. On the study of badges in medieval bells, see Jörg Poettgen, "Pilgerzeichen auf Glocken: Studien zu Geschichte, Verbreitung und Motivation ihrer Verwendung," in *HP2*, 128–36. Poettgen also published extensively on medieval bells; for a list of Poettgen's publications see Konrad Bund and Rüdiger Pfeiffer-Rupp, eds., *Varia Campenologiae: Studia Cyclica—25 Jahre Deutsches Glockenmuseum auf Burg Greifenstein, Festschrift für Jörg Poettgen*, Schriften aus dem Deutschen Glockenmuseum 6 (Greifenstein, Germany, 2009), 215–20. See also Elly van Loon-van de Moosdijk, "Pelgrimsinsignes op 'Nederlandse' klokken," in *HP2*, 112–27.

5. *Medieval Pilgrim Badges from Norfolk* (Kings Lynn, UK: Norfolk Museums Service, 1980); *Pilgrim Souvenirs and Secular Badges: Medieval Finds from Excavations in London*, vol. 7. 2nd ed. (Woodbridge, UK: Boydell, 2010); *Salisbury Museum Medieval Catalogue* (Salisbury, UK: Salisbury and Wiltshire Museum, 1990). See also "Pilgrim Souvenirs," in *Age of Chivalry: Art in Plantagenet England, 1200–1400*, ed. Jonathan Alexander and Paul Binski (London: Royal Academy, 1987), 205–24.
6. *Pilgrimsmärken och vallfart: Medeltida pilgrimskultur i Skandinavien* (Lund, Sweden: Almqvist & Wiksell International, 1989).
7. *Enseignes de pèlerinage et enseignes profanes: Catalogue d'exposition* (Paris: Éditions de la Réunion des Musées Nationaux, 1996); *Enseignes de plomb et autres menues chosettes du Moyen Âge* (Paris: Léopard d'Or, 2006); and also *Saints et diables au chapeau: Bijoux oubliés du Moyen Âge* (Paris: Seuil, 2007).
8. Arnaud Tixador, *Enseignes sacrées et profanes médiévales découvertes à Valenciennes: Un peu plus d'un kilogramme d'histoire* (Valenciennes, France: Valenciennes Service Archéologique, 2004).
9. Henryk Paner, *Średniowteczne świadectwa Kultu Maryjnego: Pamiątki pielgrzymie w zbiorach Muzeum Archeologicznego w Gdańsku* (Gdańsk, Poland: Muzeum Archeologizne w Gdańsku, 2013) and *Gdańsk na pielgrzymkowych szlakach sredniowiecznej Europy* (Gdańsk, Poland: Muzeum Archeologiczne w Gdańsku, 2016).
10. On Hendrik-Jan van Beuningen's activities as a collector, see A. Ferrier, "A Collector and His Collections: Subject and Objects," in *Gevonden voorwerpen: Opstellen over middeleeuwse archeologie voor H. J. E. van Beuningen*, ed. D. Kicken, A. M. Koldeweij, and J. R. ter Molen, Rotterdam Papers, vol. 11 (Rotterdam: Boor, 2000), 8–11; and in the same volume J. R. ter Molen, "H. J. E. van Beuningen: Levensschets van een bevlogen verzamelaar," 12–28. See also A. M. Koldeweij, "De insigne collectie van H. J. E. van Beuningen en zijn zestig 'mooisten,'" in *HP4*, 7–22.
11. See Hanneke van Asperen, "Kunera: A Dutch Saint and a Database of Badges and Ampullae," *Peregrinations: International Society for the Study of Pilgrimage Art* 1.4 (2004), http://peregrinations.kenyon.edu/.
12. Badges may have been produced in workshops some distance from the holy site to which they belonged. It has been suggested that the Wilsnack badges were produced about twenty kilometers away in the cathedral city of Havelberg, the diocese in which Wilsnack is located. Antje Reichel, personal communication with Ann Marie Rasmussen, February 28, 2016.
13. The social and cultural connections between a pilgrim disposing of a badge and the place where she or he deposited it could be complex. Carina Brumme argues, for

example, that medieval badges of Saint Anthony found in the western Ukrainian city of Lviv (German, Lemberg) most likely belonged to Hanseatic merchants who were living and working in this important trading city. "Der heilige Antonius und die Hanse: Pilgerzeichen als Indikator für den Einfluss mittelalterlicher Handelsbündnisse auf den Wallfahrtsverkehr / Saint Anthony and the Hanse: Pilgrim Badges as Indicators for the Influence of Medieval Trading Alliances on Pilgrimage Traffic," in *Mittelalterliche Tragezeichen*, 326–63.

14. See Hartmut Kühne and Jörg Ansorge, "'Holiness' from the Mud: Badges and Pilgrimage in German-Speaking Lands—A Case Study from the North German City of Stade (Lower Saxony) in the Former Archdiocese of Bremen," *Mediæval Journal* 8.1 (2018): 11–56.
15. For an excellent introduction that weaves the evidence from medieval archaeology into a larger picture of medieval life, see Roberta Gilchrist, *Medieval Life: Archaeology and the Life Course* (Woodbridge, UK: Boydell, 2012). See also Geoff Egan and Justine Bayley, *The Medieval Household: Daily Living, c. 1150–1450* (Woodbridge, UK: Boydell, 2010).
16. This vibrant new field offers examples of many different approaches. To name but three examples: Zrinka Stahuljak studies the imbrication of medievalism, medieval archaeology, and medieval objects with the rise of the French nation-state in *Pornographic Archaeology: Medicine, Medievalism, and the Invention of the French Nation* (Philadelphia: University of Pennsylvania Press, 2012). Jeffrey J. Cohen's contributors explore the thought worlds of medieval objects in *Animal, Vegetable, Mineral: Ethics and Objects* (Washington, DC: Oliphaunt, 2012). On the beliefs and practices associated with medieval objects, see the essays in Laurent Feller and Ana Rodríguez, eds., *Objets sous contrainte: Circulation des richesses et valeur des choses au Moyen Âge* (Paris: Publications de la Sorbonne, 2013).
17. See Jennifer M. Lee, "Material and Meaning in Lead Pilgrim Signs," *Peregrinations: Journal of Medieval Art and Architecture* 2.3 (2009): 152–69.
18. On this object, see R. F. C. van der Lof, "Een plankje voor pelgrimsinsignes in Weesp en zijn verwanten," *Antiek* 25.6 (1990): 307–11.
19. On popular piety in the Middle Ages, see the work of art historian Sarah Blick, for example, "Common Ground: Reliquaries and the Lower Classes in Late Medieval Europe," in *Matter of Faith*, 110–15; and "Votives, Images, Interaction and Pilgrimage to the Tomb and Shrine of St. Thomas Becket, Canterbury Cathedral," in *Push Me, Pull You: Art and Devotional Interaction in Late Medieval and Renaissance Art*, ed. Sarah Blick and Laura Gelfand (Leiden: Brill Academic, 2011), 21–58.
20. See Françoise Labaune-Jean, *Le plomb et la pierre: Petits objets de dévotion pour les pèlerins du Mont-Saint-Michel de la conception à la production (XIVe–XVe siècles)* (Caen, France: Publications du Craham, Série antique et médiévale, 2016).
21. See Tixador, *Enseignes sacrées et profanes*.
22. For a fascinating and detailed exploration of the medieval cloth industry through the lens of medieval archaeology, see the essays in Marc Dewilde, Anton Ervynck, and Alexis Wielemans, eds., *Ypres and the Medieval Cloth Industry in Flanders: Archaeological and Historical Contributions*, Archeologie in Vlaanderen, vol. 2 (Zellik, Belgium: Instituut voor het Archeologisch Patrimonium, 1998).
23. See, for example, Martha Howell, "Credit Networks and Political Actors in Thirteenth-Century Ypres," *Past and Present* 242 (February 2019): 3–26.

24. See Lars Andersson, *Pilgrimsmärken och vallfart: Medeltida pilgrimskultur i Skandinavien* (Lund, Sweden: Almqvist och Wiksell, 1989), who mentions ten badges found in or near an altarpiece or its base in Scandinavia.
25. Cornelia Oefelein, "The Signs and Bells of Mass Pilgrimage," in *Mobs: An Interdisciplinary Inquiry*, ed. Nancy Van Deusen and Leonard Michael Koff (Leiden: Brill, 2012), 231–68, here p. 243; see also Hartmut Kühne, "Das Rheinland als Pilgerlandschaft im Spiegel von Pilgerzeichen auf Glocken des 14.–16. Jahrhunderts," in *Wallfahrt und Kulturbegegnung: Das Rheinland als Ausgangspunkt und Ziel spätmittelalterlicher Pilgerreisen*, ed. Helmut Brall-Tuchel (Erkelenz, Germany: Heimatverein der Erkelenzer Lande e V., 2012), 49–87.
26. Lars Andersson notes that about eighty medieval bells with traces of cast pilgrim badges survive from Scandinavia alone, in *Pilgrimsmärken och vallfart*, 20. In addition to the scholarship in note 4; see also Elly van Loon-van de Moosdijk, "Pilgrim Badges and Bells," in *Art and Symbolism in Medieval Europe: Papers of the "Medieval Europe Brugge 1997" Conference, Volume 5*, ed. G. de Boe and F. Verhaeghe (Zellik, Belgium: Instituut voor het Archeologisch Patrimonium, 1997), 149–54.
27. There is debate among specialists about how exactly pilgrim badges were cast into bells. "Using up" a badge by leaving it in the casting clay to melt away would suggest at the very least that badges were abundantly available. Reuse is suggested by the fact that some badge imprints in bells are so similar that it suggests that a single badge was repeatedly imprinted onto different casting bells and then removed. See, for example, Andersson, *Pilgrimsmärken och vallfart*, 20. And of course, these techniques could have coexisted.
28. Pioneering work on these painted badges was done by Kurt Köster. See his "Gemalte Kollektionen von Pilgerzeichen und religiösen Medaillen in flämischen Gebets- und Stundenbüchern des 15. und 16. Jahrhunderts: Neue Funde in Handschriften der Gent-Brügger Schule," in *Liber Amicorum Herman Liebaers*, ed. Frans Vanwijngaerden, Jean-Marie Duvosquel, Josette Mélard, and Lieve Viaene-Awouters (Brussels: Koninklijke Bibliotheek Albert I, 1984), 485–535; and "Religiöse Medaillen und Wallfahrts-Devotionalien in der flämischen Buchmalerei des 15. und frühen 16. Jahrhunderts: Zur Kenntnis gemalter und wirklicher Kollektionen in spät-mittelalterlichen Gebetbüchern," in *Buch und Welt: Gustav Hofmann zum 65. Geburtstag*, ed. Hans Striedl and Joachim Wieder (Wiesbaden, Germany: Harrassowitz, 1965), 459–504. See Denis Bruna, "Témoins de dévotions dans les livres d'heures à la fin du Moyen Âge," *Revue Mabillon* (1998): 127–36; and Hanneke van Asperen, "The Book as Shrine, the Badge as Bookmark: Religious Badges and Pilgrims' Souvenirs in Devotional Manuscripts," in *Domestic Devotions in the Early Modern World*, ed. Marco Faini and Alessia Meneghin (Leiden: Brill, 2018), 288–312, https://doi.org/10.1163/9789004375888_016.
29. Hanneke van Asperen, *Pelgrimstekens op perkament: Originele en nageschilderde bedevaartssouvenirs in religieuze boeken (ca. 1450–ca. 1530)* (Nijmegen, Netherlands: Stichting Nijmeegse Kunsthistorische Studies, 2009); an English translation is now available as *Silver Saints: Prayers and Badges in Late Medieval Books* (Turnhout, Belgium: Brepols, 2021). See also Hanneke van Asperen, "A Pilgrim's Additions: Traces of Pilgrimage in the Belles Heures of Jean de Berry," *Quaerendo* 38.2–3 (2008): 175–94, reprinted in *The Limbourg Brothers: Reflections on the Origins and the Legacy of*

Three Illuminators from Nijmegen, ed. R. Dückers and P. Roelofs (Leiden: Brill, 2009), 85–104. Megan Foster Campbell's dissertation discusses some of this evidence as well: "Pilgrimage Through the Pages: Pilgrim's Badges in Late Medieval Devotional Manuscripts" (PhD diss., University of Illinois, Urbana-Champaign, 2011).

30. Kathryn M. Rudy, "Sewing the Body of Christ: Eucharist Wafer Souvenirs Stitched into Fifteenth-Century Manuscripts, Primarily in the Netherlands," *Journal of Historians of Netherlandish Art* 8.1 (Winter 2016): DOI: 10.5092/jhna.2016.8.1.1
31. On the phenomenon of printed pictures being inserted into manuscripts, see Peter Schmidt, *Gedruckte Bilder in handgeschriebenen Büchern: Zum Gebrauch von Druckgraphik im 15. Jahrhundert*, Pictura et Poesis, vol. 16 (Cologne: Böhlau, 2003). For an example of a late medieval prayer book whose inserts include both badges and woodcuts, see the manuscript Vienna, Österreichische Nationalbibliothek, Cod. Series Nova 2624, f. 253r.
32. Loretta Vandi, "The Holy Land in Paris: Embroidering, Depicting, and Stamping the Passion in a Fifteenth Century Book of Hours (Paris, Bibliothèque de l'Arsenal, MS 1176 A rés.)," *Peregrinations: Journal of Medieval Art and Architecture* 7.1 (2019): 43–86, https://digital.kenyon.edu/perejournal/vol7/iss1/2.
33. There is another Vera icon on the image from the Dresden Prayerbook in plate 3; it is at the bottom of the page centered directly under the inscribed text. On images of the Vera icon in religious manuscripts, see Hanneke van Asperen, "Voor het aangezicht van God," chap. 4 of *Pelgrimstekens op perkament*, 155–86; van Asperen, "'Ou il y a une Véronique atachiée dedens': Images of the Veronica in Religious Manuscripts, with Special Attention for the Dukes of Burgundy and Their Family," in *The European Fortune of the Roman Veronica in the Middle Ages*, ed. Amanda Murphy, Herbert L. Kessler, Marco Petoletti, Eamon Duffy, and Guido Milanese, with the collaboration of Veronika Tvrzníková, Convivium Supplementum, vol. 2 (Turnhout, Belgium: Brepols, 2018), 232–48.
34. John Harthan, *The Book of Hours* (London: Thames and Hudson, 1977), 35.
35. See Kathryn M. Rudy, "Kissing Images, Unfurling Rolls, Measuring Wounds, Sewing Badges and Carrying Talismans: Considering Some Harley Manuscripts through the Physical Rituals they Reveal," *Electronic British Library Journal* (2011), Article 5. http://www.bl.uk/eblj/2011articles/article5.html.
36. Hanneke van Asperen, "Die Reliquienbüste der Anna: Abzeichen aus Düren in spätmittelalterlichen Handschriften / The Reliquary Bust of Saint Anne: Badges from Düren in Late Medieval Manuscripts," in *Mittelalterliche Tragezeichen*, 290–321.
37. Caroline Walker Bynum, "Are Things 'Indifferent'? How Objects Change Our Understanding of Religious History," *German History* 34.1 (2016): 88–112.
38. See Natasha Awais-Dean, *Bejewelled: Men and Jewellery in Tudor and Jacobean England* (London: British Museum, 2017).
39. On Jewish badges, see Flora Cassen, *Marking the Jews in Renaissance Italy: Politics, Religion, and the Power of Symbols* (Cambridge: Cambridge University Press, 2017); on sanctuary in medieval and early modern England, see Shannon McSheffrey, *Seeking Sanctuary: Crime, Mercy, and Politics in English Courts, 1400–1550* (Oxford: Oxford University Press, 2017), 153–56, here p. 156.
40. Ittai Weinryb, ed., *Agents of Faith: Votive Objects in Time and Place* (New Haven, CT: Yale University Press, 2018).

41. Anatol Stefanowitsch, "Emojis als Tragezeichen / Emojis as Badges," in *Mittelalterliche Tragezeichen*, 514–39.

Chapter 3

1. An exhaustive and beautifully illustrated study of these important excavations has been published: Françoise Labaune-Jean, *Le plomb et la pierre: Petits objets de dévotion pour les pèlerins du Mont-Saint-Michel de la conception à la production (XIV–XV*[e] *siècles)* (Caen, France: Publications du Craham, Série antique et médiévale, 2016). I am grateful to Françoise Labaune-Jean for sharing with me and granting publication permission to me for the images in figures 3.2 through 3.8, which were originally published in *Le plomb et la pierre*. For a discussion of similar finds uncovered during excavations in Zerbst, Germany, see Daniel Berger, "Frühe Belege mittelalterlicher Zinngiesser in Zerbst, Lkr. Anhalt-Bitterfeld," *Archäologie in Sachsen-Anhalt* 7 (2014): 88–134; also similar are the finds from Magdeburg, see Daniel Berger, "Gussform für Zeichen mit Kreuzigungsszene und Dreiecksspange," in *Aufbruch in die Gotik. Der Magdeburger Dom und die späte Stauferzeit*, vol. 2, ed. Mathias Puhle (Mainz: Philipp von Zabern, 2009), 494–513.
2. See, for example, Frances Gies and Joseph Gies, *Cathedral, Forge, and Waterwheel: Technology and Invention in the Middle Ages* (New York: HarperCollins, 1994); see also, for example, John Cherry, *Medieval Goldsmiths* (London: British Museum, 2011); and Ittai Weinryb, *The Bronze Object in the Middle Ages* (Cambridge: Cambridge University Press, 2016). See also Pamela H. Smith, Christy Anderson, and Anne Dunlop, eds., *The Matter of Art: Materials, Practices, Cultural Logics, c. 1250–1750* (Manchester: Manchester University Press, 2015).
3. Leadsmith Colin Torode, who produces historical pewter replicas, including medieval badges, using molds he makes himself, speculates that the simplest of these medieval workshops were mobile and could easily have followed trade from, for example, fair to fair or from one site's veneration days to the next. See Lionheart Replicas at https://www.lionheartreplicas.co.uk/about-lionheart-replicas.aspx.
4. Figures 5.15 and 5.16, both simple, flat badges from Aachen, show traces of the casting processes; the tattered edges created by lead oozing out from an imperfectly closed mold have not been broken off or sanded away. The crudeness of the casting process is especially visible in figure 5.16, which may well be a discard.
5. H. J. E. van Beuningen, "Technische aspecten," in *HP1*, 16–25, especially the table showing the chemical composition of tested badges on p. 23; D. Berger, "Herstellungstechnik hoch- und spätmittelaltlicher Kleinobjekte aus Zinn," in *HP3*, 39–55.
6. The historical paradox here is that these were artisans who were in effect mass-producing objects. See, for example, Geoff Egan and Hazel Forsyth, *Toys, Trifles, and Trinkets: Base Metal Miniatures from London, 1200–1800* (London: Unicorn, 2005). In fact, many small, lead-tin alloy objects were manufactured in the same way and in the same workshops as badges, such as embellishments or functional items of various kinds: clasps; large, garment-closing brooches; belt stretchers; belt buckles; bridle and harness gear; mirror frames; and so on.
7. See Carina Brumme, "Pilgerzeichen: Erhaltungsbedingungen und Verbreitungsräume," in *Das Zeichen am Hut*, 127–42.
8. See John Clark, "Medieval Finds from the River Thames: Accidental Loss, Rubbish

or Ritual?" Seminar, Centre for Medieval and Renaissance Culture, University of Southampton, England, November 11, 2013, 1–7; and Jennifer M. Lee, "Medieval Pilgrim Badges in Rivers: The Curious History of a Non-Theory," *Journal of Art Historiography* 11 (2014): 3–11. Clark and Lee both argue that badges might be found in waterways because they had been discarded. Lee also dismantles the explanation often found in scholarly literature that medieval badges are found in waterways because people threw them into rivers as votive offerings. Lee shows that the "river offering" explanation was a tentative hypothesis put forth by badge research pioneer Brian Spencer and then picked up and carried forward as fact by other scholars.

9. Kurt Köster, "Pilgerzeichen-Studien: Neue Beiträge zur Kenntnis eines mittelalterlichen Massenartikels und seiner Überlieferungsformen," in *Bibliotheca docet: Festgabe für Carl Wehmer*, ed. Joost Siegfried (Amsterdam: Verlag der Erasmus-Buchhandlung, 1963), 77–100, here p. 82, translation by Ann Marie Rasmussen.
10. See Jennifer Lee, "Material and Meaning in Lead Pilgrim Signs," *Peregrinations: Journal of Medieval Art and Architecture* 2.3 (2009): 152–69.
11. From Diane Webb, ed., *Pilgrims and Pilgrimage in the Medieval West*, International Library of Historical Studies, vol. 12 (London: Tauris, 1999), 129; original Latin in James Craigie Robertson, *Materials for the History of Thomas Becket, Archbishop of Canterbury*, 7 vols., vol. 1 (London: Longman, 1875–1885), 474.
12. A. M. Koldeweij, "Pelgrimsinsignes van Elisabeth uit Marburg," in *HP1*, 69–75.
13. The idea of a vertical pin has generated a certain amount of discussion among specialists, because it seems on the face of it an unsatisfactory way of attaching an object, which surely would simply fall off. Could these pins have been worn in a different way? Or perhaps medieval woolen cloth, which was of a high quality and durability nearly unknown today, had qualities of (for lack of better word) stickiness that made slippage less of a problem. In any case, as leadsmith Colin Torode explained to me, a vertical pin makes the most sense from the perspective of casting a badge; pewter hardens so quickly that the molten ore must be directed to flow from the widest to the narrowest points in the design.
14. The badges are datable because they were found under a strata of burnt material that can be linked to the burning of Harburg in 1397 by the rival cities of Lübeck and Hamburg. I thank archaeologist Kay-Peter Suchowa (Hamburg) for this information and for his generosity in sharing his findings and photographs.
15. In medieval England, bending a coin was part of making a vow to a saint. See Ralph Merrifield, *The Archaeology of Religion and Magic* (New York: New Amsterdam, 1987), 91. The practice of bending coins for magical purposes continued well into the early modern period, and thus such folded coins are found in archaeological excavations of sixteenth- and seventeenth-century European settlements in North America. See Sara Rivers Cofield, "Keeping a Crooked Sixpence: Coin Magic and Religion in the Colonial Chesapeake," *Historical Archaeology* 48.3 (2014): 84–105.
16. The archaeologists may not have recognized the badge fragment in figure 3.15 as being part of the Saint Servatius badge, which might explain why the measuring stick (not shown) is on the top of the image, not on the bottom where it normally belongs.
17. On the Wilsnack pilgrimage site see Caroline Walker Bynum, *Wonderful Blood: Theology and Practice in Late Medieval Northern Germany and Beyond* (Philadelphia: University of Pennsylvania Press, 2007); Felix Escher and Hartmut Kühne, eds., *Die*

Wilsnackfahrt: Ein Wallfahrts- und Kommunikationszentrum Nord- und Mitteleuropas im Spätmittelalter (Frankfurt: Peter Lang, 2006); Ann Marie Rasmussen, "Materiality and Meaning: What a Medieval Badge Can Tell Us About Translation," in *Un/Translatables: New Maps for German Literatures*, ed. Catriona McLoed and Bethany Wiggin (Chicago: Northwestern University Press, 2016), 215–28. On other holy or precious blood pilgrimage sites near Wilsnack see Hartmut Kühne, "Zur Konjunktur von Heilig-Blut-Wallfahrten im spätmittelalterlichen Mecklenburg," *Jahrbuch für Mecklenburgische Kirchengeschichte / Mecklenburgia Sacra* 12 (2009): 76–115. Some Holy Blood pilgrim sites were associated with anti-Jewish, anti-Semitic host desecration accusations that gave rise to the persecution and murder of Jews, for example at Sternberg (Mecklenburg-Vorpommern). See Kristin Skottki, "Sternberg," in *Pilgerspuren—Orte, Wege, Zeichen*, Exhibition catalogue (Petersberg, Germany: Michael Imhof, 2020), 326–34.

18. See Aden Kumler, "The Multiplication of the Species: Eucharistic Morphology in the Middle Ages," *Res: Anthropology and Aesthetics* 59/60 (Spring/Autumn 2011): 179–91.
19. See, for example, Folker Reichert, "Ein cleins ringlein, an allen heiligen Stätten angerührt," *Deutsches Archiv für Erforschung des Mittelalters* 67 (2010): 609–23, here p. 614: "Doch Pilger und Sammler nahmen es mit den Begriffen nicht so genau und brachten das eine mit dem anderen in Reliquien zusammen. Man kann von 'Ortsreliquien' sprechen, denen segensreiche Kraft zugesprochen wurde." (Pilgrims and collectors, however, paid less heed to such definitions and put both together in what might be termed site-focused reliquaries, to which beneficial power was attributed.)
20. Kumler, "Multiplication," 181. The designs on the badges could of course have influenced the designs engraved on the holy wafers, and vice versa.
21. See Barbara Baert, "The Blaffer Foundation's Saint John's Head: The *Johannesschüssel* Phenomenon," in *A Golden Age of European Art: Celebrating Fifty Years of the Sarah Campbell Blaffer Foundation*, ed. James Clifton and Melina Kervandjian (New Haven, CT: Sarah Campbell Blaffer Foundation, distributed by Yale University Press, 2016), 115–31.
22. I have not been able to find a technical term for this kind of phrase truncation. I hesitate to call them initialisms because in modern parlance this term refers to an acronym that is pronounced (CBC; DNA), which is not what is happening here.
23. On indecipherable badge inscriptions as examples of pseudoliteracy, see Thomas A. Bredehoft, "Literacy Without Letters: Pilgrim Badges and Late Medieval Literate Ideology," *Viator* 37 (2006): 433–45; on letters on badges, see Jennifer M. Lee, "Beyond the Locus Sanctus: The Independent Iconography of Pilgrims' Souvenirs," *Visual Resources* 21 (2009): 363–81; and Ann Marie Rasmussen, "Pilgerzeichen als sprechende Objekte," in *Stimme und Performanz in der mittelalterlichen Literatur*, ed. Monika Unzeitig and Florian Schmid (Berlin: de Gruyter, 2017), 469–91.
24. Barbara Newman, *Medieval Crossover: Reading the Secular Against the Sacred* (Notre Dame, IN: University of Notre Dame Press, 2013).

Chapter 4

1. The discussion will return shortly to the seeming contradiction of badges cast into the fabric of bells where they were presumably out of human sight.
2. Discussions of medieval tokens and seals are not included. While these objects share salient characteristics with badges because they, too, use images to create claims or

broadcast identities, tokens and seals functioned differently because they were not worn by people to be seen by others. Nevertheless, the areas of semiotic overlap between badges, tokens, and seals are worthy of further research. Tokens could be employed to make memorable the oral agreements and oaths that underwrote legal, political, economic, and social life. They belong to a category of concrete symbols, which Richard Firth Green calls "a very large category of similar objects whose handing over registered the actual *traditio* visible, clothing the abstract trothplight with a thing-like physicality." *A Crisis of Truth: Literature and Law in Ricardian England* (Philadelphia: University of Pennsylvania Press, 1999), 50. Tokens were also used as countercurrency, whether within large trading firms or dispensed by charitable associations to be exchanged for goods, or perhaps even as mock currency in carnival times. See William J. Courtenay, "Token Coinage and the Administration of Poor Relief During the Late Middle Ages," *Journal of Interdisciplinary History* 3.2 (1975): 275–95. On seals see Toni Diederich, "Frische Brise für die Siegelforschung: Überlegungen zu einer neuartigen Siegelpublikation," *Herold-Jahrbuch* 13 (2008): 9–23; the work by Brigitte Miriam Bedos-Rezak, *When Ego Was Imago: Signs of Identity in the Middle Ages*, Visualizing the Middle Ages, vol. 3 (Leiden: Brill, 2010); Bedos-Rezak, "Medieval Identity: A Sign and a Concept," *American Historical Review* 105.5 (2000): 1489–533; Bedos-Rezak, "Seals and Sigillography," in *Women and Gender in Medieval Europe: An Encyclopedia*, ed. Margaret Schaus (New York: Routledge, 2006), 732–33; Bedos-Rezak, "Mobile Technologies and the Mobilization of Medieval Urban Identity," *Mediaeval Journal* 8.1 (2018): 137–78; and Markus Späth, ed., *Die Bildlichkeit korporativer Spiegel im Mittelalter: Kunstgeschichte und Geschichte im Gespräch*, Sensus: Studien zur mittelalterlichen Kunst, vol. 1 (Cologne: Böhlau Verlag, 2009). For a study of medieval Jewish seals and sealing practices, see Andreas Lehnertz, *Judensiegel im spätmittelalterlichen Reichsgebiet. Begläubigungstätigkeit und Selbstrepräsentation von Jüdinnen und Juden*, 2 vols. (Wiesbaden: Harrassowitz, 2020).

3. On the agentive force of bells in the Middle Ages, see Michelle E. Garceau, "'I Call the People': Church Bells in Fourteenth-Century Catalunya," *Journal of Medieval History* 37 (2011): 197–214.
4. See Jennifer M. Lee, "Louis XI, A French Monarch in Pilgrim's Garb: Badges," *Fifteenth-Century Studies* 34 (2009): 113–32; and Lee, "Beyond the Locus Sanctus: The Independent Iconography of Pilgrims' Souvenirs," *Visual Resources* 21.4 (2009): 363–81.
5. See Chris Fern, Tania Dickinson, and Leslie Webster, eds., *The Staffordshire Hoard: An Anglo-Saxon Treasure* (London: Society of Antiquaries of London, 2020).
6. See, for example, Richard Kieckhefer, *Magic in the Middle Ages* (Cambridge: Cambridge University Press, 1989); and R. W. Scribner, "Cosmic Order and Daily Life: Sacred and Secular in Pre-Industrial German Society," in *Popular Culture and Popular Movements in Reformation Germany* (London: Hambleton, 1987), 1–16.
7. On medieval religion, see Patrick J. Geary, "Peasant Religion in Medieval Europe," *Cahiers d'Extrême-Asie* 12 (2001): 185–209. See also Caroline Walker Bynum, *Christian Materiality: An Essay on Religion in Late Medieval Europe* (New York: Zone, 2011).
8. Ruth Mellinkoff, *Averting Demons: The Protective Power of Medieval Themes and Motifs*, vol. 1 (Los Angeles: Ruth Mellinkoff Publications, 2004), 44.
9. As quoted by Mellinkoff, *Averting Demons*, 45.

10. Valerie J. Flint, "A Magic Universe," in *A Social History of England 1200–1500*, ed. Rosemary Horrox and W. Mark Ormrod (Cambridge: Cambridge University Press, 2006), 340–55.
11. Mellinkoff, *Averting Demons*, 45.
12. Mellinkoff, *Averting Demons*.
13. Mellinkoff, *Averting Demons*, 47–48. See also Michael David Bailey, *Battling Demons: Witchcraft, Heresy, and Reform in the Late Middle Ages* (College Park: Pennsylvania State University Press, 2003), 148.
14. Mellinkoff, *Averting Demons*, 48.
15. Mellinkoff, *Averting Demons*, 49. See also Clarence Maloney, ed., *The Evil Eye* (New York: Columbia University Press, 1976).
16. Simona Slanicka, "Male Markings: Uniforms in the Parisian Civil War as a Blurring of the Gender Roles (AD 1410–1420)," *Medieval History Journal* 2.2 (1999): 209–44, here p. 210.
17. See, for example, Diane Owen Hughes, "Distinguishing Signs: Ear-Rings, Jews and Franciscan Rhetoric in the Italian Renaissance City," *Past & Present* 112 (1986): 3–59; Alan Hunt, *Governance of the Consuming Passions: A History of Sumptuary Law* (New York: St. Martin's, 1996); and the marvelous work by Michel Pastoureau, for example, *The Devil's Cloth: A History of Stripes and Striped Fabric* (New York: Columbia University Press, 2001).
18. The scholarship on sumptuary laws is equally vast. A good place to start is Valentin Groebner, *Der Schein der Person: Steckbrief, Ausweis und Kontrolle im Europa des Mittelalters* (Munich: C. H. Beck, 2004). Translated by Mark Kyburz and John Peck as *Who Are You? Identification, Deception, and Surveillance in Early Modern Europe* (New York: Zone, 2007).
19. See Michel Pastoureau, *Heraldry: An Introduction to a Noble Tradition* (New York: Harry N. Abrams, 1997).
20. A certain amount of confusion can arise when working on this topic in different languages. The word *emblem* is sometimes used as a synonym for *device*, although I do not do so in this book because *emblem* is, to my ear, a more abstract and less precise term in this context. In German, moreover, the word *Devise*, which is the same word as the English *device*, means *motto*; that is to say, in German it refers not to an image but to a linguistic slogan or phrase of some kind.
21. When discussing medieval and early modern Europe, scholars do not ordinarily employ the term *corporate identity* in the modern sense of referring to a company that acts as a single entity, although the modern meaning of the term derives from the medieval understanding of the word *corporate* as historians employ it.
22. Slanicka, "Male Markings," 210.
23. See, for example, a recent study of the use of King Wenceslas IV's personal device, the torque or love knot, in book illuminations. Maria Theisen, "The Emblem of the Torque and Its Use in the Willehalm Manuscript of King Wenceslas IV of Bohemia," *Journal of the British Archaeological Association* 17.1 (2018): 131–53.
24. Slanicka, "Male Markings," 212.
25. Eloquent on this topic is Jennifer Lee, "'Reckless Effrontery': Conflict and the Abuse of Badges in Late Medieval England," *Mediaeval Journal* 8.1 (2018): 109–36, here pp. 110–11.

26. Lee, "Louis XI."
27. The account books of Landgrave Ludwig I of Hesse record a visit to Wilsnack and the purchase of pilgrim badges (see Pilgerzeichendatenbank, Testimonium #1972): "Ausgabe-Register des Kammerschreibers Siegfried Schrunter 1430 Aug. 4–1431 Juli 31: Desselbin mitwochin [20. Juni 1431] quam myn herre zur Wilsenach. Daselbs vor zceichen drii beh.[Groschen] Item der pharrer sandte myme herren bier, synem knechten vier beh. Opperte mym herre dem heiligen blude 24 gulden zu zcweien malen, zu iglichem male 12 gulden. Item den pristeren drii gulden gegebin. Opperte myn herre 1 gulden zur messe. Ist vertzert daselbs nun [neun] gulden. Der wertynnen 2 gulden, dem gesinde seß beh. Item umbe gots willen eyntzeln gegebin daselbs 1 gulden. Item vor phandlosunge dryer pilgeryme uß Mießen [Meißen] achte beh." (Chamber scribe Siegfried Schrunter's Register of Outlays, 4. August 1430–31. July 1431: On that same Wednesday [20. June 1431] my lord arrived at Wilsnack. From there for badges three pennies [Groschen]. Item the priest sent beer to my lord, to his servant, four pennies. Offered by my lord to the Holy Blood 24 guilders [Gulden] twice, each time twelve guilders. Item gave the priests three guilders. My lord offered for a mass one gulden and has now used for that nine guilders. To the female innkeeper two guilders, to the servants six pennies. Item for the sake of Our Lord to individuals each one guilder. Item for the hostage redemption of three pilgrims from Meissen eight pennies.) Friedrich Küch, "Eine Quelle zur Geschichte des Landgrafen Ludwig I," *Zeitschrift des Vereins für hessische Geschichte und Landeskunde* 42 (1908): 144–277, here p. 250.
28. An excellent analysis of Fuetrer's modes of constructing narratives can be found in Gerhard Wolf, "Im Mantel der Geschichte? Interferenzen zwischen chronikalischem und fiktionalem Wiedererzählen bei Ulrich Fuetrer." *Beiträge zur mediävistischen Erzählforschung* 2 (2019): 202–54.
29. For an analysis of this political conflict, see Christof Paulus, *Machtfelder: Die Politik Herzog Albrechts IV. von Bayern (1447/1465–1508) zwischen Territorium, Dynastie und Reich*, Forschungen zur Kaiser- und Papstgeschichte des Mittelalters: Beihefte und J. F. Böhmer, Regesta Imperii, vol. 39 (Cologne: Böhlau Verlag, 2015), 138–47. An excellent online summary of the Böcklerbund or Böckler League is provided by Hans-Josef Krey, "Böcklerbund," Historisches Lexikon Bayerns, accessed January 11, 2020, https://www.historisches-lexikon-bayerns.de/Lexikon/Böcklerbund.
30. "Under dem und den zeitten erhueb sich under dem adel in Nyder Bayrn und vor dem Behaimer wald ain püntnüss und machten ain gesellschaft und truegen ir yeder ainen pock, die ritter guldein, die andern sylbren, und welcher in dem pundt was, der muest den pock an im tragen. ... [und] hies man sy die Böckler." Ulrich Fuetrer, "Bayerische Chronik," reprinted in *Quellen und Erörterungen zur Bayerischen und Deutschen Geschichte*, ed. Reinhold Spiller, Neue Folge, Band 2, Abteilung 2 (Aalen, Germany: Scientia Verlag, 1969), 224.
31. Internecine political conflicts among the brothers who were heirs to the Bavarian Duchy also played a role in the Bock league; at least two of Albert's brothers were or had been members of the league. See Krey, "Böcklerbund."
32. "Also ward zbischen der selben fürsten und der Böckler gen Rengspurg ain güetlicher tag und da ain vertrag gemacht, das die Böckler Iren pundt und pöck muessten abthain. Und da die Böckler gen Rengspurg zu dem tag kumen, da verparg etlicher

seinen pock, etlicher under die zotten der kappen, etlicher under den übergebarssen rogk oder mantel, das sy sich des schambten vor herzog Albrechten, vor aus, zu den er sein nit traunüss het; so trueg in etlicher zu trotz offenlich." Fuetrer, "Bayerische Chronik," 226.

33. See, for example, Valentin Groebner, "Trügerische Zeichen: Praktik und das politische Unsichtbare am Beginn der Neuzeit" in *Geschichtszeichen*, ed. Heinz Dieter Kittsteiner, (Cologne: Böhlau, 1999), 63–80; A. M. Koldeweij, "Het zijn niet allen slagers die lange messen dragen: Valse pelgrims en hun herkenningstekens," in *HP1*, 33–38; and Lee, "Reckless Effrontery."
34. As quoted in Slanicka, "Male Markings," 227. See also Emily J. Hutchison, "Partisan Identity in the French Civil War, 1405–1418: Reconsidering the Evidence on Livery Badges," *Journal of Medieval History* 33.3 (2007): 250–74.
35. Slanicka, "Male Markings," 232.
36. See Valentin Groebner, "Mobile Werte, informelle Ökonomie: Zur 'Kultur' der Armut in der spätmittelalterlichen Stadt," in *Armut im Mittelalter*, ed. Otto Gerhard Oexle (Ostfidern, Germany: Jan Thorbecke, 2005), 165–87.
37. Shannon McSheffrey, "Sanctuary and the Legal Topography of Pre-Reformation London," *Law and History Review* 27.3 (2009): 483–514.
38. Shannon McSheffrey, *Seeking Sanctuary: Crime, Mercy, and Politics in English Courts, 1400–1550* (Oxford: Oxford University Press, 2017), 153–56.
39. Leigh Ann Craig, *Wandering Women and Holy Matrons: Women as Pilgrims in the Later Middle Ages*, Studies in Medieval and Reformation Traditions, vol. 138 (Leiden: Brill, 2009).
40. Bernardus Guidonis, *Le livre des sentences de l'inquisiteur Bernard Gui*, vol. 1 (2002): 628, as quoted in Craig, *Wandering Women*, 194. According to Craig, Gui also at times assigned pilgrimage that could be undertaken "uncrossed." These uncrossed, compulsory pilgrimages were usually assigned to women, often young, dutiful women from heretical homes where exposure to heresy was difficult if not impossible to avoid. The yellow color of the cross is also significant. Crusaders were also understood to be pilgrims. They took the cross, and to designate their status as *cruci signati* wore on their clothing a red cross.
41. Craig, *Wandering Women*, 194.
42. See Flora Cassen, "From Iconic O to Yellow Hat: Anti-Jewish Distinctive Signs in Renaissance Italy," in *Fashioning Jews: Clothing, Culture and Commerce*, ed. Leonard J. Greenspoon (West Lafayette, IN: Purdue University Press, 2013), 29–48; and *Marking the Jews in Renaissance Italy: Politics, Religion, and the Power of Symbols* (Cambridge: Cambridge University Press, 2017). On medieval anti-Jewish iconography and the visual stereotyping of Jewishness in medieval Christian art, see Sara Lipton, *Dark Mirror: The Visual Origins of Anti-Jewish Iconography* (New York: Henry Holt, 2014). On Jews in medieval cities, see Miri Rubin, "Jews: Familiar Strangers," chapter 4 of *Cities of Strangers: Making Lives in Medieval Europe* (Cambridge: Cambridge University Press, 2020), 50–70.
43. The entire document "Fourth Lateran Council: 1215" can be found in a reliable translation at *Papal Encyclicals Online*, https://www.papalencyclicals.net/councils/ecum12-2.htm.
44. Cassen, "From Iconic O," 31.
45. See Lipton, *Dark Mirror*, esp. Chap. 5.

46. See, for example, Elisheva Baumgarten and Judah D. Galinsky, eds., *Jews and Christians in Thirteenth-Century France* (New York: Palgrave Macmillan, 2015).
47. See Sebastian Ostkamp, "The World Upside Down: Secular Badges and the Iconography of the Late Medieval Period—Ordinary Pins with Multiple Meanings," *Journal of Archaeology in the Low Countries* 1–2 (2009): 107–25.
48. For an introduction to Urs Graf's drawings, see Christiane Andersson, *Dirnen, Krieger, Narren: Ausgewählte Zeichnungen von Urs Graf* (Basel: G-S Verlag, 1978), 34; for a lucid discussion of this drawing, see her article, "Harlots and Camp Followers: Swiss Renaissance Drawings of Young Women ca. 1520," in *The Youth of Early Modern Women*, ed. Elizabeth S. Cohen and Margaret Reeves (Amsterdam: Amsterdam University Press, 2018), 117–34, here pp. 121–23.

Chapter 5

1. See also R.M. van Heeringen, A. M. Koldeweij, and A.A. Gaalman, eds., *Heiligen uit de modder: In Zeeland gevonden pelgrimstekens* (Zutphen, Netherlands: Walburg Pers, 1987) and Andreas Haasis-Berner, *Pilgerzeichen des Hochmittelalters* (Würzburg, Germany: Veröffentlichungen zur Volkskunde und Kulturgeschichte, 2003).
2. For an excellent, short general introduction to medieval pilgrimage, see Simon Yarrow, "Pilgrimage," in *Routledge History of Medieval Christianity: 1050–1500*, ed. R. N. Swanson (Abington, UK: Routledge, 2015), 159–71. For studies focused on the art historical aspects of pilgrimage, see Sarah Blick and Rita Tekippe, eds., *Art and Architecture of Late Medieval Pilgrimage in Northern Europe and the British Isles* (Leiden: Brill, 2005); and J. Stopford, "Some Approaches to the Archaeology of Christian Pilgrimage," *World Archaeology* 26.1 (1994): 57–72, which has useful maps of pilgrim routes through France and northern Spain (p. 58), the Mediterranean to the Holy Land (p. 62), and Denmark to Rome overland (p. 64).
3. Sarah Blick, "Bringing Pilgrimage Home: The Production, Iconography, and Domestic Use of Late-Medieval Devotional Objects by Ordinary People," *Religions* 10.6 (2019): 392.
4. Lars Andersson gives two examples of parchment and paper badges found in non-manuscript contexts: a small (45 × 30 mm) piece of parchment onto which has been pressed an oval medallion featuring a female saint and written S URSULA, which was found under the floor of Hopperstad church in Norway (p. 80) and an arc of parchment badges painted with the Vera icon found in the convent of Wienhausen (Germany). *Pilgrimsmärken och vallfart: medeltida pilgrimskultur i Skandinavien* (Lund, Sweden: Almqvist & Wiksell International, 1989), 79–80.
5. Blick, "Bringing Pilgrimage Home."
6. On the increasing involvement of the laity in the late medieval church see Hartmut Kühne, Enno Bünz, and Thomas T. Müller, eds., *Alltag und Frömmigkeit am Vorabend der Reformation in Mitteldeutschland: Katalog zur Ausstellung, "Umsonst ist der Tod"* (Petersberg, Germany: Michael Imhof, 2014).
7. See Dee Dyas, "To Be a Pilgrim: Tactile Pilgrimage, Virtual Piety and the Experience of Place in Christian Pilgrimage," in *Matter of Faith*, 1–7.
8. Translation from A. T. Hatto has been lightly amended; for the original, *zeichen*, which Hatto translated as "token," I have substituted "badge." Gottfried von Strassburg, *Tristan*, ed. Rüdiger Krohn, (Stuttgart: Reclam, 1984), p. 164, lines 2620–37; Gottfried von Strassburg, *Tristan and the 'Tristan' of Thomas*, trans. A.T. Hatto (London: Penguin, 1960), 74.

9. See Hanneke van Asperen, "Jacobus als pelgrim naar Santiago en andere anachronismen," in *HP3*, 23–27.
10. See the photo in the Kunera database (Kunera 05000), which shows a medieval grave in situ during an archaeological excavation in Esslingen, Germany. Two Saint James shell badges are placed on what would have been the chest of the deceased.
11. Roberta Gilchrist notes that other items have been found in medieval Christian graves, for example, red coral in the graves of infants and children and wooden staffs on top of coffins. See *Medieval Life: Archaeology and the Life Course* (Woodbridge, UK: Boydell, 2012).
12. See, for example, the Saint James badge made of jet and found in Turku, Finland (Kunera 08073).
13. See Miri Rubin's work on the Blessed Virgin Mary, *Mother of God: The History of the Virgin Mary* (London: Allen Lane, 2009), and Rubin, *Emotion and Devotion: The Meaning of Mary in Medieval Religious Culture* (Budapest: Central European University Press, 2009).
14. Brigitte Miriam Bedos-Rezak, "Medieval Identity: A Sign and a Concept," *American Historical Review* 105.5 (2000): 1489–533; and Bedos-Rezak, *When Ego Was Imago: Signs of Identity in the Middle Ages*, Visualizing the Middle Ages, vol. 3 (Leiden: Brill, 2010).
15. Ian Short, ed. and trans., *A Life of Thomas Becket in Verse (La Vie de saint Thomas Becket), by Guernes de Pont-Sainte-Maxence* (Toronto: Pontifical Institute of Medieval Studies, 2013), 169.
16. See Jennifer M. Lee, "Searching for Signs: Pilgrims' Identity and Experiences Made Visible in the Miracula Sancti Thomae Cantuariensis," in *Art and Architecture of Late Medieval Pilgrimage in Northern Europe and the British Isles*, ed. Sarah Blick and Rita Tekippe (Leiden: Brill, 2005), 473–90.
17. Sarah Blick, "Reconstructing the Shrine of St. Thomas Becket, Canterbury Cathedral," in *Art and Architecture of Late Medieval Pilgrimage in Northern Europe and the British Isles*, ed. Sarah Blick and Rita Tekippe (Leiden: Brill, 2005), 407–41. See also Lloyd de Beer and Naomi Speakman, *Thomas Becket: Murder and the Making of a Saint* (London: British Museum, 2021).
18. See, for example, Brian Spencer, "Canterbury Pilgrim Souvenirs Found in the Low Countries," in *HP2*, 105–11; and A. M. Koldeweij, "'Tsente Thomaes te Cantelberghe': Pelgrimstochten vanuit de Nederlanden naar Canterbury—teruggevonden insignes en berichten uit andere bron," in *HP2*, 88–104.
19. Short, *A Life of Thomas Becket*, 169.
20. On reliquaries, see Cynthia Hahn, *Strange Beauty: Issues in the Making and Meaning of Reliquaries, 400–ca. 1204* (University Park: Pennsylvania State University Press, 2012); and Hahn, "The Voices of the Saints: Speaking Reliquaries," *Gesta* 36.1 (1997): 20–31. See also Hartmut Kühne, "Pilgerzeichen: Signum des Pilgers und Devotionalie," in *Liturgisches Jahrbuch* 61 (2011): 45–63.
21. Holy ground relics were also collected from other sites. On this phenomenon see Lucy Donkin, "Stones of St. Michael: Venerating Fragments of Holy Ground in Medieval France and Italy," in *Matter of Faith*, 23–31.
22. Hartmut Kühne, "Kreuzwege, Heilig-Kreuz-Kapellen und Jerusalempilger im Raum der mittleren Elbe um 1500," in *Heilige Grab: Heilige Gräber—Aktualität und Nach-*

leben von Pilgerorten, ed. Ursula Röper and Martin Treml (Berlin: Lukas, 2014), 44–54.

23. See Julia Weitbrecht, "The Vera Icon (Veronica) in the Verse Legend *Veronicia II*: Medializing Salvation in the Late Middle Ages," *Seminar* 52.2 (2016): 173–93. See also Alexa Sand, "Saving Face: The Veronica and Visio Dei," in *Vision, Devotion and Self-Representation in Late Medieval Art* (Cambridge: Cambridge University Press, 2014), 27–82.
24. The procession for the veil of Veronica became an annual event that continued into the early sixteenth century when the relic disappeared.
25. The late medieval pilgrimage landscape of northern Germany, for example, was full of locally and regionally important pilgrimage sites. See Hartmut Kühne and Jörg Ansorge, "'Holiness' from the Mud: Badges and Pilgrimage in German-Speaking Lands—A Case Study from the North German City of Stade (Lower Saxony) in the Former Diocese of Bremen," *Medieaval Journal* 8.1 (2018): 11–56. See also Hartmut Kühne and Nadine Mai, "Zur Einführung: Pilgerfahrten und Wallfahrtskirchen in Norddeutschland," in *Pilgerspuren—Orte, Wege, Zeichen*, Exhibition catalogue (Petersberg, Germany: Michael Imhof, 2020), 14–27.
26. Sarah Blick, "Common Ground: Reliquaries and the Lower Classes in Late Medieval Europe," in *Matter of Faith*, 110–15. See also Hartmut Kühne, "Das Rheinland als Pilgerlandschaft im Spiegel von Pilgerzeichen auf Glocken des 14.–16. Jahrhunderts," in *Wallfahrt und Kulturbegegnung: Das Rheinland als Ausgangspunkt und Ziel spätmittelalterlicher Pilgerreisen*, ed. Helmut Brach-Tuchel, Schriften des Heimatvereines der Erkelenzer Lande, vol. 26 (Erkelenz, Germany: Heimatverein der Erkelenzer Lande, 2012), 49–87; and Denis Bruna, "Enseignes de pèlerinage d'origine française découvertes aux Pays-Bas," in *HP2*, 31–36.
27. All examples and citations in the following pages are drawn from chap. 6 of Diana Webb, *Pilgrims and Pilgrimage in the Medieval West* (London: Tauris, 1999), 133–47. Numerous late medieval wills survive from the cities of Lübeck, Stralsund, and Rostock, as well as from other northern German cities. On the wills from northern Germany, see, for example, Heinrich Dormeier, "Pilgerfahrten Lübecker Bürger im späten Mittelalter: Forschungsbilanz und Ausblick," *Zeitschrift des Vereins für Lübeckische Geschichte und Altertumskunde* 92 (2012): 9–64; and Jörg Ansorge, "*Pelgrimmatze in de ere des almechteghen godes*: Pilgerzeichen und Schriftquellen zum mittelalterlichen Wallfahrtswesen in Rostock," in *Verknüpfungen des neuen Glaubens: Die Rostocker Reformationsgeschichte in ihren translokalen Bezügen*, ed. Heinrich Holze and Kristin Skottki, Academic Studies, vol. 56 (Göttingen: Vandenhoeck-Ruprecht, 2020), 29–83.
28. Webb, *Pilgrims*, 133.
29. See, for example, Gabriela Signori, *Das Wunderbuch Unserer Lieben Frau im thüringischen Elende (1419–1517)* (Cologne: Böhlau Verlag, 2006); and Hartmut Kühne, "Das Mirakelbuch der Fronleichnamkapelle von Heiligenleichnam bei Altenburg," in *Vor- und Frühreformation in thüringischen Städten (1470–1525/30)*, ed. Joachim Emig, Volker Leppin, and Uwe Schirmer (Cologne: Böhlau Verlag, 2013), 19–39.
30. See, for example, Hartmut Kühne and Carina Brumme, "Ablässe und Wallfahrten in Braunschweig und Königslutter: Zu einem Detail des Briefes Heinrich Hanners an

Thomas Müntzer," in *Thomas Müntzer—Zeitgenossen—Nachwelt: Siegfried Brauner zum 80. Geburtstag*, ed. Hartmut Kühne, Hans Jürgen Goertz, Thomas T. Müller, and Günter Vogler (Mühlhausen, Germany: Thomas-Müntzer-Gesellschaft, 2010), 39–72.

31. Webb, *Pilgrims*, 141.
32. Webb, *Pilgrims*, 138.
33. Webb, *Pilgrims*, 140.
34. Webb, *Pilgrims*, 139.
35. Webb, *Pilgrims*, 138.
36. On other iconographical traditions to be found on pilgrim badges from Rome, see Holger Grönwald, "Am Einzelfund ins Detail: Das mittelalterliche Bild des Pantheon und seiner Ikone im Spiegel von Pilgerzeichen," in *Wallfahrer aus dem Osten: Mittelalterliche Pilgerzeichen zwischen Ostsee, Donau und Seine—Beiträge der Tagung Perspektiven der europäischen Pilgerzeichenforschung 21. bis 24. April 2010 in Prag*, ed. Hartmut Kühne, Lothar Lambacher. and Jan Hrdina (Frankfurt: Peter Lang, 2013), 275–320.
37. David Morgan, *Visual Piety: A History and Theory of Popular Religious Images* (Berkeley: University of California Press, 1998).
38. Numerous medieval Aachen badges have been found in Gdańsk, for example. See Henryk Paner, *Średniowteczne świadectwa Kultu Maryjnego: Pamiątki pielgrzymie w zbiorach Muzeum Archeologicznego w Gdańsku* (Gdańsk, Poland: Muzeum Archeologizne w Gdańsku, 2013), 164–205.
39. The Virgin Mary's garment is sometimes referred to as a cloak or as a tunic in the secondary literature, but the item shown on the badges appears to be the medieval linen undergarment worn closest to the body by both men and women, which is usually called a shift or chemise in English. A similar garment was revered at Chartres Cathedral; see E. Jane Burns, "Saracen Silk and the Virgin's Chemise: Cultural Crossings in Cloth," *Speculum* 81.2 (2006): 365–97.
40. On the badge in figure 5.15, see Renate Samariter, "Pilgerzeichen und religiöse Zeichen aus der Stralsunder Frankenvorstadt," *Bodendenkmalpflege in Mecklenburg-Vorpommern Jahrbuch* 56 (Jahrbuch 2008; Schwerin 2009): 191–212, here p. 205.
41. For example, the small aureole pendant (Kunera 00433) or single-letter M badges.
42. See Jörg Ansorge, "Pilgerzeichen und Pilgerzeichenforschung in Mecklenburg-Vorpommern," in *Wallfahrer aus dem Osten*, 81–143, here p. 134; and "Pilgerzeichen sowie religiöse und profane Zeichen aus Stralsund," in *Das Zeichen am Hut*, 83–114, here p. 95, fig. 4.
43. See Sarah Blick, "Votives, Images, Interaction and Pilgrimage to the Tomb and Shrine of St. Thomas Becket, Canterbury Cathedral," in *Push Me, Pull You: Art and Devotional Interaction in Late Medieval and Renaissance Art*, ed. Sarah Blick and Laura Gelfand (Leiden: Brill, 2011), 21–58.
44. See, for example, Suzannah Biernoff, "Seeing and Feeling in the Middle Ages," in *Visual Sense: A Cultural Reader*, ed. Elizabeth Edwards and Kaushik Bhaumik (Oxford: Berg, 2008), 51–59.
45. Katherine Park, *Secrets of Women: Gender, Generation, and the Origins of Human Dissection* (New York: Zone, 2006), 73.
46. See H. J. E. van Beuningen, "Een middeleeuws diptiek uit Aken, gevonden in Dordrecht," in *HP2*, 54–58; and A. M. Koldeweij, "Een tweede diptiek uit Aachen," in *HP3*, 39–55.

47. See Ann Marie Rasmussen, "Pilgerzeichen als sprechende Objekte," in *Stimme und Performanz in der mittelalterlichen Literatur*, ed. Monika Unzeitig and Florian Schmid (Berlin: deGruyter, 2017), 469–91.
48. Fragments of these badges survive; for example, see Kunera 16331.
49. Historian Esther Cohen's work on the long-running legal disputes between badge-making families in southern France is relevant here: "*In haec signa*: Pilgrim-Badge Trade in Southern France," *Journal of Medieval History* 2.3 (1976): 193–214.

Chapter 6

1. Gösta Ditmar-Trauth, Arnold Muhl, and Heinrich Wunderlich, "Magdeburger Ritter in Miniaturformat: Mitteleuropas erster Zinnsoldat," in *Fund des Monats: Landesmuseum für Vorgeschichte* (Halle, Germany: Landesamt für Denkmalpflege und Archäologie Sachsen-Anhalt: November 2005), http://www.lda-lsa.de/de/landesmuseum_fuer_vorgeschichte/fund_des_monats/2005/november/. On the type of pewter object imagined as a crown in the opening sketch, see Daniel Berger, "Composition and Decoration of the so-called *Zinnfigurenstreifen* found in Magdeburg, Saxony-Anhalt, Germany," *Restaurierung und Archäologie* 7 (2014): 65–80.
2. Medieval children's toys that are miniaturized versions of ordinary objects can be found on display at the Musée de Cluny–Musée national du Moyen Âge in Paris, the Museum of London, and the Metropolitan Museum of Art in New York City. On children's toys from the Middle Ages, see Annemarieke Willemsen, *Kinder delijt: Middeleeuws speelgoed in de Nederlanden* (Nijmegen: Nijmegen University Press, 1998); Geoff Egan and Hazel Forsyth, *Toys, Trifles, and Trinkets: Base Metal Miniatures from London, 1200–1800* (London: Unicorn, 2006); and Geoff Egan and J. Bayley, *The Medieval Household: Daily Living, c. 1150–1450* (Woodbridge, UK: Boydell, 2010). On childhood in the Middle Ages, see Nicholas Orme, *Medieval Children* (New Haven, CT: Yale University Press, 2001); and Orme, *From Childhood to Chivalry: The Education of English Kings and Aristocracy, 1066–1530* (London: Methuen, 1984).
3. The hypothesis that knight badges and knight toys select images reflecting the prestige of knightly warfare might explain the manufacture of war elephant badges, which have been found in Ypres and in London. The war elephant might also be a heraldic device or livery for a fourteenth-century English lord (recall the area in London named Elephant and Castle). In any case, images of war elephants are not uncommon in the Middle Ages.
4. On chivalry, see David Crouch, *The Chivalric Turn: Conduct and Hegemony in Europe Before 1300* (Oxford: Oxford University Press, 2019); Maurice Keen, *Chivalry* (New Haven, CT: Yale University Press, 2005); and Richard Barber, *The Reign of Chivalry* (Woodbridge, UK: Boydell & Brewer, 2005). On the realities of medieval warfare within the world of chivalric virtue, see Richard A. Kaeuper, *Chivalry and Violence in Medieval Europe* (Oxford: Oxford University Press, 1999).
5. The *Codex Manesse* contains some 150 author portraits and was produced in the 1320s in Zurich, Switzerland, for a wealthy patrician family. For an excellent, brief overview in English on the *Codex Manesse*, see Marion E. Gibbs and Sidney Johnson, *Medieval German Literature: A Companion* (New York: Garland, 1997).

6. On the powerful gaze of women watching men fight, see Sandra Lindemann Summers, *Ogling Ladies: Scopophilia in Medieval German Literature* (Gainesville: University of Florida Press, 2013).
7. An excellent introduction to the medieval discourses of chivalry is provided by the articles in Robert W. Jones and Peter Coss, eds., *A Companion to Chivalry* (Rochester, NY: Boydell, 2019).
8. On tournaments see David Crouch, *Tournament* (London: Hambleton and London, 2005); and, for example, Andrew Brown, "Urban Jousts in the Later Middle Ages: The White Bear of Bruges," *Revue belge de philologie et d'historie* 78.2 (2000): 315–30. Some of the most famous jousts in medieval German literature take place in Wolfram von Eschenbach's *Parzival*, written around 1220. In book 2, Parzival's father, Gahmuret, inadvertently wins the hand of Parzival's mother, Herzeloyde, in marriage by winning a series of tournament jousts. I write "inadvertently" because Herzeloyde, both the lady in charge of the two-day tournament and its prize, falls in love with Gahmuret at first sight and uses a legal technicality to halt competition at the end of the first day. Wolfram von Eschenbach, *Parzival*, ed. Rüdiger Krohn. 2 vols. (Stuttgart: Reclam, 1981), 104–32; and *Parzival and Titurel*, trans. Cyril Edwards (Oxford: Oxford University Press, 2006), 26–36.
9. Maurice Delbouille, ed., *Le Tournoi de Chauvency* (Liège: Vaillant-Charmanne; Paris: Droz, 1932), 11. English translation by F. Regina Psaki, Michelle Loew, Caitlin Bradley, Keith Evans, Sabina Carp, and Natalie Brenner. See also Mireille Chazan and Nancy Freeman Regalado, eds., *Lettres, musique et société en Lorraine médiévale: Autour du Tournoi de Chauvency—Ms. Oxford Bodleian Douce 308* (Geneva: Librairie Droz, 2012).
10. See Karma Lochrie, "Medieval Masculinities Without Men," in *Rivalrous Masculinities: New Directions in Medieval Gender Studies*, ed. Ann Marie Rasmussen (Notre Dame, IN: University of Notre Dame, 2019), 209–33.
11. For scholarly discussions of other ladies' tournaments in medieval literature, see Sarah Westphal-Wihl, "*The Ladies' Tournament*: Marriage, Sex, and Honor in Thirteenth-Century Germany," *Signs* 14.2 (1989): 371–98; Helen Solterer, "Figures of Female Militancy in Medieval France," *Signs* 16.3 (1991): 522–49; Ute von Bloh, "Heimlich Kämpfe: Frauenturniere in Mittelalterlichen Mären," *Beiträge zur Geschichte der deutschen Sprache und Literatur* 121 (1999): 214–38; Ann Marie Rasmussen, *Wandering Genitalia: Sexuality and the Body in German Culture Between the Late Middle Ages and Early Modernity*, King's College London Medieval Studies, Occasional Series 2 (London: Centre for Late Antique & Medieval Studies, King's College London, 2009); and Jutta Eming, "Der Kampf um den Phallus: Körperfragmentierung, Textbegehren und groteske Ästhetik im *Nonnenturnier*," *German Quarterly* 85.4 (2012): 380–400.
12. For an outstanding, wide-ranging discussion of women and gender in medieval chivalry, including noblewomen's use of heraldry, see Louise J. Wilkinson, "Gendered Chivalry," in *A Companion to Chivalry*, ed. Robert W. Jones and Peter Coss (Rochester, NY: Boydell, 2019), 219–39.
13. Ann Marie Rasmussen and Sarah Westphal-Wihl, "Die Beichte einer Frau" [A woman's confession], in *Ladies, Whores, and Holy Women: A Sourcebook in Courtly, Reli-*

gious and Urban Cultures of Late Medieval Germany, ed. Ann Marie Rasmussen and Sarah Westphal-Wihl (Kalamazoo, MI: Medieval Institute, 2010), 9–45, here p. 31.

14. See, for example, the arguments made by James A. Schultz, *Courtly Love, the Love of Courtliness, and the History of Sexuality* (Chicago: University of Chicago Press, 2006). See arguments in chap. 12 in particular.
15. See Hartmut Kühne, Carina Brumme, and Helena Koenigsmarkova, eds., *Jungfrauen, Engel, Phallustiere: Die Sammlung mittelalterlicher französischer Pilgerzeichen des Kunstgewerbemuseums in Prag und des Nationalmuseums Prag* (Berlin: Lukas Verlag, 2012), 151–57.
16. See Michel Pastoureau, *Heraldry: An Introduction to a Noble Tradition*, trans. Francisca Garvie (New York: Harry N. Abrams, 1997), 13. This small, handsomely illustrated introductory volume by one of the world's leading medievalists is full of accessible knowledge on this arcane topic. See also Brigitte Bedos-Rezak, "Heraldry," in *Women and Gender in Medieval Europe: An Encyclopedia*, ed. Margaret Schaus (New York: Routledge, 2006), 360–61. On heraldry in badges see Wim van Anrooij, "Heraldische aspecten van insignes," in *HP2*, 225–33. See also the articles in "Wappen als Zeichen: Mittelalterliche Heraldik aus kommunikations- und zeichentheorischer Perspektive," special issue, *Das Mittelalter: Perspektiven mediävistischer Forschung* 11.2 (2006), ed. Wolfgang Achnitz.
17. Pastoureau, *Heraldry*, 43.
18. For an outstanding and brief introduction to blazon, see Megan L. Cook, "Blazon," *New Literary History* 50 (2019): 363–68; and Torsten Hiltmann, "Heraldry as a Systematic and International Language? About the Limitations of Blazonry in Describing Coats of Arms," Heraldica Nova: Medieval and Early Modern Heraldry from the Perspective of Cultural History, last modified May 30, 2016, https://heraldica.hypotheses.org/4623.
19. See Laurent Hablot, "Revêtir l'armoirie: Les vêtements héraldiques au moyen âge, mythes et réalités," *Espacio, tiempo y forma* 1.6 (2018): 55–87; Torsten Hiltmann and Laurent Hablot, eds. *Heraldic Artists and Painters in the Middle Ages* (Ostfildern, Germany: Thorbecke, 2018); Torsten Hiltmann and Miguel Metelo de Seixas, eds., *Heraldry in Medieval and Early Modern State-Rooms* (Ostfildern, Germany: Thorbecke, 2019).
20. I am generalizing here; the rules for using heraldry differed somewhat between England and the continent. For more information on heraldry see Torsten Hiltmann, "L'héraldique dans l'espace domestique: Perspectives historiques sur les armoiries et le décor héraldique dans l'espace profane (espace germanique, XIIIe–XVIe siècle)," *Le Moyen Âge* 123.3 (2017): 527–70; Hiltmann, "Potentialities and Limitations of Medieval Armorials as Historical Source: The Representation of Hierarchy and Princely Rank in Late Medieval Collections of Arms in France and Germany," in *Princely Rank in Late Medieval Europe: Trodden Paths and Promising Avenues*, eds. T. Huthwelker, J. Peltzer, and M. Wemhöner (Ostfildern, Germany: Thorbecke, 2011), 157–98.
21. For an outstanding discussion of such an object, see Benjamin L. Wild, "Emblems and Enigmas: Revisiting the 'Sword' Belt of Fernando de la Cerda," *Journal of Medieval History* 37 (2011): 378–96. The object in question is a sumptuous belt decorated with small, three-sided shields that have been painted with heraldic devices.
22. See Katie Stevenson, ed., *The Herald in Late Medieval Europe* (Woodbridge, UK: Boydell, 2009); Michael Powell Siddons, *Heraldic Badges in England and Wales* (Wood-

bridge, UK: Boydell, 2009); Torsten Hiltmann, *Spätmittelalterliche Heroldskompendien: Referenzen adeliger Wissenskultur in Zeiten gesellschaftlichen Wandels (Frankreich und Burgund, 15. Jahrhundert)*, Pariser Historische Studien, vol. 92 (Munich: Oldenbourg Verlag, 2011).

23. See Stephen Selzer, "Devisen an reichsfürstlichen Höfen des Spätmittelalters: Umrisse eines Forschungsfeldes," in *Reiche Bilder: Aspekte zur Produktion und Funktion von Stickereien im Spätmittelalter*, ed. Uta-Christine Bergemann and Annemarie Stauffer (Regensburg, Germany: Schnell & Steiner, 2010), 115–28.

24. Other examples that can be accessed on the Kunera website include a knight wearing a fine robe and a garland on his head, who is holding a shield featuring a rampant lion (found in Ypres, Belgium, now housed at Yper Museum, Kunera 16954); a now headless fragment of a standing knight holding a banner in his right hand and shield in his left, wearing a robe covered in the cross potent, also known as the crutch cross or Crusader's cross, which has tiny bars at the four ends and which was the heraldic device of the Knights of the Order of the Holy Sepulcher, a chivalric order founded in Jerusalem around the time of the First Crusade (1099). The device came to be used generally as the Crusader's Cross (found in Schwerin, Germany, now housed at Archäologisches Landesmuseum Mecklenburg-Vorpommern; Kunera 13657).

25. On animals in heraldry see Heiko Hartmann, "Tiere in der historischen und literarischen Heraldik des Mittelalters: Ein Aufriss," in *Tiere und Fabelwesen im Mittelalter*, ed. Sabine Obermaier (Berlin: de Gruyter, 2009), 147–79.

26. In Old French, he is known as the Chevalier au Cygne, and the oldest version of the story dates from around 1200. The Swan Knight appears in medieval German in Wolfram von Eschenbach, *Parzival*, lines 824,1–826,30 (around 1220); in Konrad von Würzburg, *Der Schwanritter* (around 1250); and in the anonymous *Lohengrin*, which consists of 768 stanzas and was written in the 1280s. The well-known modern version is of course Richard Wagner's opera *Lohengrin*, which premiered in 1850. Konrad von Würzburg, *Der Schwanritter* Konrads von Würzburg, ed. Jan Habermehl (Frankfurt: n.p., 2015) https://d-nb.info/1144611792/34; *Lohengrin*, ed. Heinrich Rückert. Bibliothek des gesammten deutschen National-Literatur, vol. 36 (Quedlinburg/Leipzig: Druck und Verlag von Gottfr. Basse, 1858); Wolfram von Eschenbach, *Parzival*, ed. Rüdiger Krohn, 2 vols. (Stuttgart: Reclam, 1981); and *Parzival and Titurel*, trans. Cyril Edwards (Oxford: Oxford University Press, 2006). See also Alastair Mathews, *The Medieval German Lohengrin: Narrative Poetics in the Story of the Swan Knight* (Rochester, NY: Camden House, 2016).

27. Laurent Hablot, "Emblématique et mythologie médiévale, le cygne, une devise princière," *Histoire de l'art: Bulletin d'information de l'Institut national d'histoire de l'art publié en collaboration avec l'Association des Professeurs d'Archéologie et d'Histoire de l'Art des Universités* (2001): 51–64.

28. See D. A. J. D. Boulton, *The Knights of the Crown. The Monarchical Orders of Knighthood in Later Medieval Europe, 1325–1520* (Woodbridge, UK: Boydell, 1987). For a lively cultural history of a chivalric order from its medieval foundations to the present see Stephanie Trigg, *Shame and Honor: A Vulgar History of the Order of the Garter* (Philadelphia: University of Pennsylvania Press, 2012).

29. According to H. F. K. Nierop, van Wassenaer accompanied Emperor Maximilian on his Italian campaign, where in 1509 at the storming of the Padua city walls van Wasse-

naer was wounded by a bullet in the jaw, causing him to lose seven teeth, presumably the cause of the facial scar on the portrait. See *The Nobility of Holland: From Knights to Regents 1500–1650*, trans. Maarten Ultee (Cambridge: Cambridge University Press, 1993), 4–5.

30. Hanneke van Asperen, "Secular Power, Divine Presence: The Badges of Our Lady of Aarschot," *Mediæval Journal* 8.1 (2018): 79–108.
31. Van Asperen, "Secular Power," 79.
32. On Oswald see Ulrich Müller and Margarete Springeth, eds., *Oswald von Wolkenstein: Leben—Werk—Rezeption* (Berlin: de Gruyter, 2011).
33. The three manuscripts are (1) Vienna, Österreichische Nationalbibliothek, cod. 2777, 108 poems, written in 1425 with additions from 1436, known as *Liederhandschrift* A (it opens with a now damaged author portrait); (2) Innsbruck, Universitätsbibliothek (UB), no signature, 107 poems, dated 1432 with additions from 1438, known as *Liederhandschrift* B (it opens with the author portrait shown in plate 11); and (3) Innsbruck, Tirol Landesmuseum Ferdinandeum, F.B. 1950, 117 poems, manuscript from ca. 1450, known as *Liederhandschrift* C (it is a copy of B, the Innsbruck manuscript).
34. See Leo Andergassen, "Oswald von Wolkenstein und die Kunst," in *Oswald von Wolkenstein: Leben—Werk—Rezeption*, ed. Ulrich Müller and Margarete Springeth (Berlin: de Gruyter, 2011), 77–88. The lily and jar are also common symbols associated with the Virgin Mary.

Chapter 7

1. Cle Lesger, *The Rise of the Amsterdam Market and Information Exchange* (Burlington, VT: Ashgate, 2006). Jan de Vries, *The First Modern Economy* (New York: Cambridge University Press, 1997) is a solid overview of why the Netherlands was the first expression of the modern economy.
2. Further examples of such badges can be found in the Kunera database, for example, 09989 or 06818.
3. See Hanneke van Asperen, "Annunciation and Dedication on Aachen Pilgrim Badges: Notes on the Early Badge Production in Aachen and Some New Attributions," *Peregrinations* 4.2 (2013): 215–35.
4. The Shrine of Charlemagne was consecrated in 1215 and the Shrine of the Virgin Mary, in 1239.
5. See Tom Scott, *The City-State in Europe, 1000–1600: Hinterland, Territory, Region* (Oxford: Oxford University Press, 2012); and Scott, *Society and Economy in Germany, 1300–1600* (New York: Palgrave, 2002).
6. Miri Rubin, *Cities of Strangers: Making Lives in Medieval Europe* (Cambridge: Cambridge University Press, 2020).
7. Rubin, *Cities*, 95.
8. See Konrad Eisenbichler, ed., *Companion to Medieval and Early Modern Confraternities* (Leiden: Brill, 2019); and Gervase Rosser, "Finding Oneself in a Medieval Fraternity: Individual and Collective Identities in the English Guilds" in *Mittelalterliche Bruderschaften in europäischen Städten*, ed. Monika Escher-Apsner (Frankfurt: Peter Lang, 2009), 29–46, and Rosser, *The Art of Solidarity in the Middle Ages: Guilds in England 1250–1550* (Oxford: Oxford University Press, 2015).

9. Franz-Josef Arlinghaus, "The Myth of Urban Unity: Religion and Social Performance in Late Medieval Braunschweig," in *Cities, Texts and Social Networks, 400–1500: Experiences and Perceptions of Medieval Urban Space*, ed. Caroline Goodson, Anne E. Lester, and Carol Symes (Farnham, UK: Ashgate, 2010), 215–32, here p. 223.
10. Arlinghaus, "Myth of Urban Unity," 215–16.
11. For example, in an uprising in Braunschweig in 1455, the rebellious faction apparently used a hare as their device. See Cordelia Hess, "The Writing on the Barn: Content and Materiality in Contested Documents of Northern German Towns," *Seminar* 52.2 (2016): 155–73, here p. 165: "Depictions of a hare, which was apparently used as a political device or sign by the rebels, played a central role in later accounts of these tense months. Recognized by both sides as the symbol of suppressed rebellion, the hare functioned as a visible and tangible sign of rebellious behaviors and actions, such as rumours and gossip spreading among the guilds or secret gatherings. For example, the young sword smiths were reprimanded by the council for their plans to paint a hare on their banner for the *swertdans*. In a detailed narration, Bote recounts that a gunman shot and skinned a hare, dressed up a cat in the hare's fur and flesh, and then sent the creature into an assembly of fur mongers (who were, the reader will recall, supporters of the uprising)." On the related use of shouted slogans ("cries"), see Jan Dumolyn, "'Criers and Shouters': The Discourse on Radical Urban Rebels in Late Medieval Flanders," *Journal of Social History* 42.1 (2009): 111–36.
12. See Jennifer Lee, "'Reckless Effrontery': Conflict and the Abuse of Badges in Late Medieval England," *Mediaeval Journal* 8.1 (2018): 109–36. On medieval beggars' marks, see Monika Escher-Apsner, "'Confraternitas pauperum'/'Confraternitas exulum': Inklusions- und Exklusionsmodi bruderschaftlicher Organisationen—die sog. Elendenbruderschaften als Sonderform?" in *Inklusion/Ekslusion: Studien zur Fremdheit und Armut in von der Antike bis zur Gegenwart*, ed. Lutz Raphael and Herbert Uerlings (Frankfurt: Peter Lang, 2008), 181–212. See Chapter 4 for a discussion of compelled badges.
13. Laura Crombie, *Archery and Crossbow Guilds in Medieval Flanders, 1300–1500* (Woodbridge, UK: Boydell, 2016), 3.
14. See the articles in Gerhard Krieger, ed., *Verwandtschaft, Bruderschaft, Freundschaft: Soziale Lebens- und Kommunikationsformen im Mittelalter* (Berlin: Akademie Verlag, 2009); and Rosser, *Art of Solidarity*, esp. chap. 3, "Friendship."
15. John M. Jeep, *Among Friends? Early German Evidence of Friendship Among Women* (Lincoln: University of Nebraska Press, 1999). Among the many publications on friendship, see, for example, Laura Gowing, Michael Hunter, and Miri Rubin, eds., *Love, Friendship, and Faith in Europe, 1300–1800* (New York: Palgrave, 2005).
16. On the Old Testament roots of the notion of friendship as companionship and the cultural changes it undergoes in the Middle Ages, see Ruth Mazo Karras, "David and Jonathan: A Late Medieval Bromance," in *Rivalrous Masculinities: New Directions in Medieval Gender Studies*, ed. Ann Marie Rasmussen (Notre Dame, IN: University of Notre Dame Press, 2019), 151–73.
17. See Heinrich Seuse, "Das Buch von dem Diener" [The life of the servant], chap. 45 in *Heinrich Seuse: Deutsche Schriften*, ed. K. Bihlmeyer (1907), 153–55. Translated by Frank Tobin as *The Exemplar, with Two German Sermons* (New York: Paulist, 1989).

18. These initials stand for the Latin *in hoc signo* (by this sign), an abbreviation that is itself a ritual instrument of power. See Jeffrey Hamburger, *Script as Image* (Walpole, MA: Peeters, 2014). The Christian IHS monogram was widely used in many modalities, including badges and precious jewelry; Bernhard Strigel's portrait of Bianca Maria Sforza from ca. 1505–1510 shows Sforza, the second wife of Emperor Maximilian, wearing a costly IHS pendant made of gold and pearls (Tiroler Landesmuseum, Ferdinandeum, Innsbruck, Ältere Kunstgeschichtliche Sammlungen). See also the embroidered IHS sewn onto a manuscript page in plate 5.
19. Enoch, "Clasp of Astonishment: Amateur Treasure Hunter Finds Tiny 14th Century Heart-Shaped Gold Brooch Worth £25,000 in Farmer's Field," *Daily Mail*, May 2, 2012, https://www.dailymail.co.uk/news/article-2138354/Amateur-treasure-hunter-finds-tiny-14th-century-gold-brooch-worth-25-000-farmers-field.html.
20. In medieval German the clasping of hands was a performative legal gesture called a *hanttruwe* (modern German, *Handtreue*) used to indicate the acceptance of an obligation or oath, for example, in marriage; the corresponding term in English would be *hand troth*, *hand plighting*, or *handfasting*.
21. Enoch, "Clasp of Astonishment."
22. From Anne L. Klinck, *Anthology of Ancient and Medieval Woman's Song* (New York: Palgrave Macmillan, 2004), 136. The poem's title, "Rybbe ne rele ne spynne yc ne may" (I cannot scrape, wind, nor spin), refers to the steps involved in producing linen thread from flax and hemp, a laborious process of beating and scraping plant fibers, winding them and spinning thread, and then weaving the cloth. This work was traditionally done by women. This poem is a fifteenth-century English carol, a song to accompany dancing, with separate sections for the leader and the dancers, who would have chorally sung the refrain (Middle English, *burden*), which opens every song and follows all stanzas, which are sung solo by the leader.
23. Judith M. Bennett, "Ventriloquisms: When Maidens Speak in English Songs, c. 1300–1550," in *Medieval Woman's Song: Cross-Cultural Approaches*, ed. Anne Klinck and Ann Marie Rasmussen (Philadelphia: University of Pennsylvania Press, 2002), 187–204.
24. H. Moser and H. Tervooren, eds., "Namenlose Lieder VII," in *Des Minnesangs Frühling*, 37th ed., vol. 1 (Stuttgart: Hirzel, 1982), 21.
25. Chrétien de Troyes, *Yvain: The Knight of the Lion*, trans. Burton Raffel (New Haven, CT: Yale University Press, 1987), 43.
26. See Frank Tobin, Kim Vivian, and Richard H. Lawson, trans., *Arthurian Romances, Tales, and Lyric Poetry: The Complete Works of Hartmann von Aue* (State College: Pennsylvania State Press, 2001).
27. Tobin et al., *Works of Hartmann von Aue*, 296.
28. For similar objects see also Bernard Prokisch and Thomas Kühtreiber, eds., *Der Schatzfund von Fuchsenhof: The Fuchsenhof Hoard—Poklad Fuchsenhof* (Linz, Austria: Oberösterreichisches Landesmuseum, 2004). An especially handsome example of a fourteenth-century silver brooch using the iconography of clasped hands (the so-called *Handtrouwebratzen*) can be seen in the so-called Pritzwalker Silberschatz (the silver treasure from Pritzwalk, Brandenburg, Germany); see Stefan Krabath and Lothar Lambacher, *Der Pritzwalker Silberfund: Schmuck des späten Mittelalters* (Pritzwalk, Germany: Stadt- und Brauerei Museum, 2006).
29. Arlinghaus, "Myth of Urban Unity," 228.

30. Arlinghaus, "Myth of Urban Unity," 230.
31. Arlinghaus, "Myth of Urban Unity," 232.
32. See Carol Symes, "Out in the Open, in Arras: Sightlines, Soundscapes and the Shaping of a Medieval Public Sphere," in *Cities, Texts and Social Networks, 400–1500: Experiences and Perceptions of Medieval Urban Space*, ed. Caroline Goodson, Anne E. Lester, and Carol Symes (Farnham, UK: Ashgate, 2010), 279–302. This article distills the arguments made by the author in her award-winning book regarding the political complexity of medieval cities.

Chapter 8

1. See, for example, the essays in Catherine Emerson, Adrian P. Tudor, and Mario Longtin, eds., *Performance, Drama and Spectacle in the Medieval City: Essays in Honour of Alan Hindley* (Leuven, Belgium: Peeters, 2010).
2. As an example, for discussions on Palm Sunday processions using a so-called *Palmesel* (wooden statue of Christ on donkey) that was pulled through the street, see R. W. Scribner, *Popular Culture and Popular Movements in Reformation Germany* (London: Hambledon, 1987), 25; and the museum catalog *Der Palmesel: Geschichte, Kult und Kunst—Eine Ausstellung im Museum für Natur und Kultur Schwäbisch Gmünd, 24. März–18 Juni 2000*, Museumskatalog 6, Reihe Museum für Natur und Kultur (Schwäbisch Gmünd, Germany: Museum und Galerie Schwäbisch Gmünd, 2000).
3. On all this see Carol Symes, *A Common Stage: Theater and Public Life in Medieval Arras* (Ithaca, NY: Cornell University Press, 2007).
4. Eckehard Simon, "Organizing and Staging Carnival Plays in Late Medieval Lübeck: A New Look at the Archival Record," *Journal of English and German Philology* 92.1 (1993): 57–72, here p. 59.
5. For a general overview of Christianity, see Gary Macy and Bernard Cooke, *Christian Symbol and Ritual: An Introduction* (New York: Oxford University Press, 2005).
6. On carnival in German-speaking lands, see, for example, Glenn Ehrstine, "Aufführungsort als Kommunikationsraum: Ein Vergleich der fastnächtlichen Spieltradition Nürnbergs, Lübecks und der Schweiz," in *Fastnachtspiele: Weltliches Schauspiel in literarischen und kulturellen Kontexten*, ed. Klaus Ridder (Tübingen, Germany: Max Niemeyer Verlag, 2009), 83–97; and Ehrstine, "Of Peasants, Women, and Bears: Political Agency and the Demise of Carnival Transgression in Bernese Reformation Drama," *Sixteenth-Century Journal* 31.3 (2000): 675–97. A collection and English translation of Dutch carnival plays can be found in Ben Parsons and Bas Jongenelen, *Comic Drama in the Low Countries, c. 1450–1560: A Critical Anthology* (Cambridge: D. S. Brewer, 2012).
7. See Eckehard Simon, ed., *The Theatre of Medieval Europe: New Research in Early Drama* (Cambridge: Cambridge University Press, 1991).
8. See Eckehard Simon's wonderful article on carnival activities in medieval German towns, "Carnival Obscenities in German Towns," in *Obscenity: Social Control and Artistic Creation in the European Middle Ages*, ed. Jan Ziolkowski (Leiden: Brill, 1998), 193–213. For German-speaking lands, see Bernd Neumann, *Geistliches Schauspiel im Zeugnis der Zeit: Zur Aufführung mittelalterlicher religiöser Dramen im deutschen Sprachgebiet*, 2 vols. (Munich: Artemis, 1987); and Eckehard Simon, *Die Anfänge des weltlichen deutschen Schauspiels 1370–1530: Untersuchung und Dokumentation* (Munich: Artemis, 2003).

9. "1480—Tercia post Dorothee (Februar 8) . . . Item Jorgen Gumler auß verschonung seins alters und swacheit, damit er sich meldet beladen sein, ist des tantzens mit seinem handwerck vertragen worden, doch daz er danach neben dem tantz gee." Simon, *Die Anfänge*, 425–26.
10. "1420: Als man dis hochzit [= *Weihnachten*] und davor bischofe machet, bede, herren und schu[o]ler, und denen zu dienst tüfel louffent, heissent üch unser herren sagen, daz sy nit wellent, dz yemant in tüfels wise louffen sole in den kilchen noch in der stadt, wand dadurch gotz dienst gehindert und gewirret wird"; "1432: [*Die Behörde*] verbietent menglichem, dz niemand in tüfels hüten louffen solle"; this injunction was repeated in a ruling reissued in 1436, 1441, and 1447. See Neumann, *Geistliches Schauspiel*, vol. 1, here p. 124.
11. "1488: Item der jhenenhalb, die uber ettlich, so in der vanacht gelaufen sind, weere gezuckt haben, auch deshalb, der ein schampar unzuchtig manns gemacht gelid getragen hat und anderer unzuchtigen Rotthalb zu erkunden und dem pfenter ze Rugen bevelhen." See Simon, *Die Anfänge*, 430.
12. For a bibliography on the Nuremberg carnival plays, see Ann Marie Rasmussen, "Reading in Nuremberg's Fifteenth-Century Carnival Plays," in *Literary Studies and the Question of Reading*, ed. Richard Benson, Eric Downing, and Jonathan Hess (Columbia, NY: Camden House, 2012), 106–29.
13. On the Aristotle and Phyllis tales in German-speaking lands, see Ann Marie Rasmussen, "Problematizing Medieval Misogyny: Aristotle and Phyllis in the German Tradition," in *Verstellung und Betrug im Mittelalter und in der mittelalterlichen Literatur*, ed. Mathias Meyer and Alexander Sager (Göttingen: V & R Unipress, 2015), 195–220. See also Christoph Huber, "Der zwiespaltige Gelehrte. Zur Ambiquität der Aristoteles-Figur in mittelalterlichen Darstellungen (Artes-Repräsentant, Fürstenerzieher, Liebhaber)," in *Diz vliegende bîspel: Ambiquity in Medieval and Early Modern Literature*, ed. Marian E. Polhill and Alexander Sager (Göttingen: V & R Unipress, 2020, 115–37. On the sexual badges in general see Ben Reiss, "Pious Phalluses and Holy Vulvas: The Religious Importance of Some Sexual Body-Part Badges in Late-Medieval Europe (1200–1550)," *Peregrinations* 6 (2017): 151–76; and Christopher Retsch, "'Geflügelte Genitalien, Phallusbäume und kopulierende Paare: Zur Motivik auf obszön-sexuellen Tragenzeichen / Winged Genitalia, Phallus Trees, and Copulating Couples: On the Motifs of Obscene-Sexual Badges," in *Mittelalterliche Tragezeichen*, 210–69.
14. "Darnach volget die Maria, Johannes und andere jüngern. Darnach kam ein grosser hauf, alle in gestalt der bösen geist. Darnach viel armbrustschützen." Neumann, *Geistliches Schauspiel*, vol. 2, 925–26, here p. 926.
15. Simon, "Carnival Obscenities in German Towns," 211.
16. Neumann, *Geistliches Schauspiel*, vol. 1, p. 251: "Brugg, around 1505: Der schuelmeister und sin frou mögen ouch wol mit inen essen und trincken die selben zit, und was den schuolern an gelt wirt, darzue sölln allwegs zwœnschueler zue seckelmeisteren gesetzt und denselben das ingezelt werden, dasselb dann zimlich und ordenlich ze nießen gebruchen, ouch damit des tüfels kleidung jaerlich erbesseren." (The schoolmaster and his wife should also eat and drink at the same time with them [the pupils], and when the pupils receive money, for this two pupils should always be appointed as masters of the purse and the received money paid over to them so that it can be used and enjoyed in a proper and orderly manner, and also so that the

devil clothing can be repaired annually with it.) See also Simon's discussion of devil clothes and leather in "Carnival Obscenities in German Towns," 204–6.

17. "Darnach kam einer in der gestalt Sanct Georgen auf einem grossen waidlichen hengst geritten." Neumann, *Geistliches Schauspiel*, vol. 2, 925–26, here p. 926.
18. Timothy Husband, *The Wild Man: Medieval Myth and Symbolism* (New York: Metropolitan Museum of Art, 1980).
19. See Konrad Eisenbichler and Wim Hüsken, eds., *Carnival and the Carnivalesque: The Fool, the Reformer, the Wildman, and Others in Early Modern Theatre* (Amsterdam: Rodopi, 1999). On wild men masquerades at court, see Susan Crane, "Wild Doubles in Charivari and Interlude," chapter 5 of *The Performance of Self: Ritual, Clothing, and Identity During the Hundred Years War* (Philadelphia: University of Pennsylvania Press, 2002), 140–74.
20. "Carnival Obscenities in German Towns," 199.
21. For example, the giant-like wild men on the greater (royal) coat of arms of Denmark; https://en.wikipedia.org/wiki/Coat_of_arms_of_Denmark
22. See, for example, Martha Bayless, *Parody in the Middle Ages: The Latin Tradition* (Ann Arbor: University of Michigan Press, 1996); and Sylvie Bethmont-Gallerand, "Un croquemitane dans les stalles," in *The Playful Middle Ages: Meanings of Play and Plays of Meaning—Essays in Memory of Elaine C. Block*, ed. Paul Hartwick, Medieval Texts and Cultures of Northern Europe, vol. 3 (Turnhout, Belgium: Brepols, 2010), 143–60; and Ruth von Bernuth, *Wunder, Spott und Prophetie: Natürliche Narrheit in den "Historien von Claus Narren,"* Frühe Neuzeit, vol. 113 (Tübingen, Germany: Max Niemeyer Verlag, 2009.)
23. A. M. Koldeweij, "A Barefaced *Roman de la Rose* (Paris, B.N., ms. fr. 25526) and Some Late Medieval Mass-Produced Badges of a Sexual Nature," in *Flanders in a European Perspective*, ed. M. Smeyers and B. Cardon (Leuven, Belgium: Peeters, 1993), 499–516. On wandering penis creatures, see George Ferzoco, *Il Murale Di Massa Marittima / The Massa Marittima Mural* (Florence: Consiglio Regionale della Toscana; Leicester: University of Leicester, 2004); Johann H. Winkelmann and Gerhard Wolf, *Erotik, aus dem Dreck gezogen*, special issue, *Amsterdamer Beiträge zur älteren Germanistik*, 59:1 (2004), with its thirteen pathbreaking articles advancing a variety of theories about sexual badges; Malcolm Jones, "Wicked Willies with Wings: Sexuality in Late Medieval Art and Thought," in *The Secret Middle Ages* (Westport, CT: Praeger, 2003), 248–68, 356–58; and Willy Piron, "Schreitende Vulven und fliegende Phalli: Spätmittelalterliche sexuelle Abzeichen und ihre Funktion / Walking Vulvas and Flying Phalluses: Late Medieval Sexual Badges and Their Function," in *Mittelalterliche Tragezeichen*, 270–89.
24. Ann Marie Rasmussen, *Wandering Genitalia: Sexuality and the Body in German Culture Between the Late Middle Ages and Early Modernity*, King's College London Medieval Studies, Occasional Series 2 (London: Centre for Late Antique & Medieval Studies, King's College London, 2009); Rasmussen, "Wanderlust: Gift Exchange, Sex, and the Meanings of Mobility," in *Liebesgaben: Kommunikative, performative und poetologische Dimensionen in der Literatur des Mittelalters und der Frühen Neuzeit*, ed. Margreth Egidi, Ludger Lieb, and Marielle Schnyder (Berlin: Erich Schmidt, 2012), 219–29.
25. "Nu schweigt ain weil und redt nit vil / und hört, was ich euch sagen will! / Hie ist ain mayster in medicinis / Und kan die kunst des mayster Plinis / und des hohen

Masters Kunst Origenis / und kumpt auss der höchsten schul Athenis." "Meister Aristoteles" [Master Aristotle], in *Fastnachtspiele aus dem 15. Jahrhundert*, ed. Adelbert von Keller, Bibliothek des Litterarischen Vereins Stuttgart, vols. 28–30 and 46 (Stuttgart: Litterarischer Verein, 1853–58), here vol. 46, pp. 216–30, lines 1–6.

26. Another literary parallel to the imagery in these badges can be found in the fourteenth-century medieval Netherlandish farce *De truwanten* [Vagabonds]. See Robert E. Lerner, "Vagabonds and Little Women: The Medieval Netherlandish Dramatic Fragment *De truwante*," *Modern Philology* 65.4 (1968): 301–6.
27. This badge and the worldview it suggests are discussed in more detail in Ann Marie Rasmussen, "Moving Beyond Sexuality in Medieval Sexual Badges," in *From Beasts to Souls: Gender and Embodiment in Medieval Europe*, ed. E. Jane Burns and Peggy McCracken (Notre Dame, IN: University of Notre Dame Press, 2013), 296–335. Reprinted in *Nahrung, Notdurft, Obszönität*, ed. Andrea Grafetstätter (Bamberg, Germany: Bamberg University Press, 2013), 125–54.
28. Appearing in the same week as I was sending this manuscript to the press, Sarah Hinds's article argues that sexual badges found in London belonged to urban youth culture, an interpretation with which I agree and that supports the fictional sketch in Chapter 1. See Hinds, "Late Medieval Sexual Badges as Sexual Signifiers: A Material Culture Reappraisal," *Medieval Feminist Forum: A Journal of Gender and Sexuality* 55.2 (2020): 170–91, https://ir.uiowa.edu/mff/vol55/iss2/8.

Concluding Remarks

1. Kristen B. Neuschel, *Living by the Sword: Weapons and Material Culture in France and Britain, 600–1600* (Ithaca, NY: Cornell University Press, 2020), 162.
2. Ann Marie Rasmussen and Hanneke van Asperen, "Introduction: Medieval Badges," *Medieval Journal* 8.1 (2018): 2.
3. Rasmussen and van Asperen, "Introduction," 3.

Bibliography

Achnitz, Wolfgang, ed. "Wappen als Zeichen: Mittelalterliche Heraldik aus kommunikationsmittel- und zeichentheorischer Perspektive." Special issue, *Das Mittelalter: Perspektiven mediävistischer Forschung* 11.2 (2006).

Andergassen, Leo. "Oswald von Wolkenstein und die Kunst." In *Oswald von Wolkenstein: Leben—Werk—Rezeption*, edited by Ulrich Müller and Margarete Springeth, 77–88. Berlin: de Gruyter, 2011.

Andersson, Christiane. *Dirnen, Krieger, Narren: Ausgewählte Zeichnungen von Urs Graf.* Basel: G-S Verlag, 1978.

———. "Harlots and Camp Followers: Swiss Renaissance Drawings of Young Women ca. 1520." In *The Youth of Early Modern Women*, edited by Elizabeth S. Cohen and Margaret Reeves, 117–34. Amsterdam: Amsterdam University Press, 2018.

Andersson, Lars. *Pilgrimsmärken och vallfart: Medeltida pilgrimskultur i Skandinavien.* Lund, Sweden: Almqvist & Wiksell International, 1989.

van Anrooij, Wim. "Heraldische aspecten van insignes." In *HP2*, 225–33. (See van Beuningen et al.)

Ansorge, Jörg. "*Pelgrimmatze in de ere des almechteghen godes*: Pilgerzeichen und Schriftquellen zum mittelalterlichen Wallfahrtswesen in Rostock." In *Verknüpfungen des neuen Glaubens: Die Rostocker Reformationsgeschichte in ihren translokalen Bezügen*, edited by Heinrich Holze and Kristin Skottki, 29–83. Göttingen: Vandenhoeck-Ruprecht, 2019.

———. "Pilgerzeichen und Pilgerzeichenforschung in Mecklenburg-Vorpommern." In *Wallfahrer aus dem Osten: Mittelalterliche Pilgerzeichen zwischen Ostsee, Donau und Seine: Beiträge der Tagung Perspektiven der europäischen Pilgerzeichenforschung 21. bis 24. April 2010 in Prag*, edited by Hartmut Kühne, Lothar Lambacher, and Jan Hrdina, 81–143. Frankfurt: Peter Lang, 2013.

———. "Pilgerzeichen sowie religiöse und profane Zeichen aus Stralsund." In *Das Zeichen am Hut im Mittelalter: Europäische Reisemarkierungen—Symposium in memoriam Kurt Köster (1912–1986) und Kataloge der Pilgerzeichen im Kunstgewerbemuseum und im Museum für Byzantinische Kunst der Staatlichen Museen zu Berlin*, edited by Hartmut Kühne, Lothar Lambacher, und Konrad Vanja, 83–114. Frankfurt: Peter Lang, 2008.

Arlinghaus, Franz-Josef. "The Myth of Urban Unity: Religion and Social Performance in Late Medieval Braunschweig." In *Cities, Texts and Social Networks, 400–1500: Experiences and Perceptions of Medieval Urban Space*, edited by Caroline Goodson, Anne E. Lester, and Carol Symes, 215–32. Farnham, UK: Ashgate, 2010.

van Asperen, Hanneke. "Annunciation and Dedication on Aachen Pilgrim Badges: Notes on the Early Badge Production in Aachen and Some New Attributions." *Peregrinations* 4.2 (2013): 215–35.

———. "The Book as Shrine, the Badge as Bookmark: Religious Badges and Pilgrims' Souvenirs in Devotional Manuscripts." In *Domestic Devotions in the Early Modern World*, edited by Marco Faini and Alessia Meneghin, 288–312. Leiden: Brill, 2018. https://doi.org/10.1163/9789004375888_016.

———. "Jacobus als pelgrim naar Santiago en andere anachronismen." In *HP* 3, 23–27. (See van Beuningen et al.)

———. "Kunera: A Dutch Saint and a Database of Badges and Ampullae." *Peregrinations: International Society for the Study of Pilgrimage Art* 1.4 (2004). http://peregrinations.kenyon.edu/.

———. "'Ou il y a une Véronique atachiée dedens': Images of the Veronica in Religious Manuscripts, with Special Attention for the Dukes of Burgundy and Their Family." In *The European Fortune of the Roman Veronica in the Middle Ages*, edited by Amanda Murphy, Herbert L. Kessler, Marco Petoletti, Eamon Duffy, and Guido Milanese, with the collaboration of Veronika Tvrzníková, Convivium Supplementum 2, 232–48. Turnhout, Belgium: Brepols, 2018.

———. *Pelgrimstekens op perkament: Originele en nageschilderde bedevaartssouvenirs in religieuze boeken (ca. 1450–ca. 1530)*. Nijmegen, Netherlands: Stichting Nijmeegse Kunsthistorische Studies, 2009. Translated into English as *Silver Saints: Prayers and Badges in Late Medieval Books*. Turnhout, Belgium: Brepols, 2021.

———. "A Pilgrim's Additions: Traces of Pilgrimage in the Belles Heures of Jean de Berry." *Quaerendo* 38.2–3 (2008): 175–94. Reprinted in *The Limbourg Brothers: Reflections on the Origins and the Legacy of Three Illuminators from Nijmegen*, edited by R. Dückers and P. Roelofs, 85–104. Leiden: Brill, 2009.

———. "Die Reliquienbüste der Anna: Abzeichen aus Düren in spätmittelalterlichen Handschriften / The Reliquary Bust of Saint Anne: Badges from Düren in Late Medieval Manuscripts." In *Mittelalterliche Tragezeichen: Social Media des Mittelalters / Medieval Badges: Social Media of the Middle Ages*, edited by André Dubisch, 290–321. Exhibition Catalog. Lübeck: European Hansamuseum, 2020.

———. "Secular Power, Divine Presence: The Badges of Our Lady of Aarschot." *Mediæval Journal* 8.1 (2018): 79–108.

van Asperen, Hanneke, and Willy Piron. "Het is geen insigne: Een korte verkenning van middeleeuwse objecten in lood-tin." In *HP4*, 23–34. (See van Beuningen et al.)

Awais-Dean, Natasha. *Bejewelled: Men and Jewellery in Tudor and Jacobean England*. London: British Museum, 2017.

Baert, Barbara. "The Blaffer Foundation's Saint John's Head: The *Johannesschüssel* Phenomenon." In *A Golden Age of European Art: Celebrating Fifty Years of the Sarah Campbell Blaffer Foundation*, edited by James Clifton and Melina Kervandjian, 115–31. New Haven, CT: Sarah Campbell Blaffer Foundation, distributed by Yale University Press, 2016.

Bailey, Michael David. *Battling Demons: Witchcraft, Heresy, and Reform in the Late Middle Ages*. College Park: Pennsylvania State University Press, 2003.

Barber, Richard. *The Reign of Chivalry*. Woodbridge, UK: Boydell & Brewer, 2005.

Baudat, Michel. "La dévotion à saint Antoine abbé à travers des enseignes de pèlerinages récemment découvertes." *Bulletin des Amis du vieil Arles* 111 (2001): 39–46.

Baumgarten, Elisheva, and Judah D. Galinsky, eds. *Jews and Christians in Thirteenth-Century France*. New York: Palgrave Macmillan, 2015.

Bayless, Martha. *Parody in the Middle Ages: The Latin Tradition.* Ann Arbor: University of Michigan Press, 1996.

de Beer, Lloyd, Anna Harnden, and James Robinson, eds. *Matter of Faith: An Interdisciplinary Study of Relics and Relic Veneration in the Medieval Period.* London: British Museum, 2014.

de Beer, Lloyd, and Naomi Speakman, *Thomas Becket: Murder and the Making of a Saint.* London: British Museum, 2021.

Bedos-Rezak, Brigitte Miriam. "Heraldry." In *Women and Gender in Medieval Europe: An Encyclopedia,* edited by Margaret Schaus, 360–61. New York: Routledge, 2006.

———. "Medieval Identity: A Sign and a Concept." *American Historical Review* 105.5 (2000): 1489–533.

———. "Mobile Technologies and the Mobilization of Medieval Urban Identity." *Mediæval Journal* 8.1 (2018): 137–77.

———. "Seals and Sigillography." In *Women and Gender in Medieval Europe: An Encyclopedia,* edited by Margaret Schaus, 732–33. New York: Routledge, 2006.

. *When Ego Was Imago: Signs of Identity in the Middle Ages.* Visualizing the Middle Ages, 3. Leiden: Brill, 2010.

Bennett, Judith M. "Ventriloquisms: When Maidens Speak in English Songs, c. 1300–1550." In *Medieval Woman's Song: Cross-Cultural Approaches,* edited by Anne Klinck and Ann Marie Rasmussen, 187–204. Philadelphia: University of Pennsylvania Press, 2002.

Berger, Daniel. "Composition and Decoration of the so-called *Zinnfigurenstreifen* found in Magdeburg, Saxony-Anhalt, Germany." *Restaurierung und Archäologie* 7 (2014): 65–80.

———. "Frühe Belege mittelalterlicher Zinngiesser in Zerbst, Lkr. Anhalt-Bitterfeld." *Archäologie in Sachsen-Anhalt* 7 (2014): 88–134.

———. "Gussform für Zeichen mit Kreuzigungsszene und Dreiecksspange." In *Aufbruch in die Gotik. Der Magdeburger Dom und die späte Stauferzeit.* Landesaustellung Sachsen-Anhalt aus Anlass des 800. Domjubiläums, ed. Mathias Puhle, 2, 494–513. Mainz: Philipp von Zabern, 2009.

———. "Herstellungstechnik hoch- und spätmittelaltlicher Kleinobjekte aus Zinn." In *HP3,* 39–55. (See van Beuningen et al.)

Berger, Jean. "Les enseignes de pélerinage du Puy." In *Jubilé et culte marial,* edited by Bruno Maes, Daniel Moulinet, and Catherine Vincent, 87–114. Saint-Étienne, France: Publications de l'Université Saint-Étienne, 2009.

von Bernuth, Ruth. *Wunder, Spott und Prophetie: Natürliche Narrheit in den "Historien von Claus Narren."* Frühe Neuzeit, 113. Tübingen, Germany: Max Niemeyer Verlag, 2009.

Bethmont-Gallerand, Sylvie. "Un croquemitane dans les stalles." In *The Playful Middle Ages: Meanings of Play and Plays of Meaning— Essays in Memory of Elaine C. Block,* edited by Paul Hartwick. Medieval Texts and Cultures of Northern Europe, 3, 143–60. Turnhout, Belgium: Brepols, 2010.

van Beuningen, H. J. E. "Een middeleeuws diptiek uit Aken, gevonden in Dordrecht." In *HP2,* 59–66. (See van Beuningen et al.)

———. "Technische aspecten: Gietvormen, metaalsamenstelling." In *HP1,* 16–25. (See van Beuningen et al.)

van Beuningen, H. J. E., and A. M. Koldeweij, eds. *Heilig en profaan: 1000 laat-middeleeuwse insignes uit de collectie H. J. E. van Beuningen*, Rotterdam Papers, 8. Cothen, Netherlands: Stichting Middeleeuwse Religieuze en Profane Insignes, 1993 (hereafter *HP1*).

van Beuningen, H. J. E., A. M. Koldeweij, and D. Kicken, eds. *Heilig en profaan: 1200 laat-middeleeuwse insignes uit openbare en particuliere collecties*, Rotterdam Papers, 12. Cothen, Netherlands: Stichting Middeleeuwse Religieuze en Profane Insignes, 2001 (hereafter *HP2*).

van Beuningen, H. J. E., A. M. Koldeweij, D. Kicken, and H. van Asperen, eds. *Heilig en profaan: 1300 laatmiddeleeuwse insignes uit openbare en particuliere collecties*, Rotterdam Papers, 13. Langbroek, Netherlands: Stichting Middeleeuwse Religieuze en Profane Insignes, 2012 (hereafter *HP3*).

van Beuningen, H. J. E., H. van Asperen, A. M. Koldeweij, and H. W. J. Piron, eds. *Heilig en profaan: 800 laatmiddeleeuwse insignes uit openbare en particuliere collecties*, Rotterdam Papers, 14. Langbroek, Netherlands: Stichting Middeleeuwse Religieuze en Profane Insignes, 2018 (hereafter *HP4*).

Biernoff, Suzannah. "Seeing and Feeling in the Middle Ages." In *Visual Sense: A Cultural Reader*, edited by Elizabeth Edwards and Kaushik Bhaumik, 51–59. Oxford: Berg, 2008.

Blick, Sarah. "Bringing Pilgrimage Home: The Production, Iconography, and Domestic Use of Late-Medieval Devotional Objects by Ordinary People." *Religions* 10.6 (2019): 392.

———. "Common Ground: Reliquaries and the Lower Classes in Late Medieval Europe." In *Matter of Faith: An Interdisciplinary Study of Relics and Relic Veneration in the Medieval Period*, edited by James Robinson, Lloyd de Beer, and Anna Harnden, 110–15. London: British Museum, 2014.

———. "Reconstructing the Shrine of St. Thomas Becket, Canterbury Cathedral." In *Art and Architecture of Late Medieval Pilgrimage in Northern Europe and the British Isles*, edited by Sarah Blick and Rita Tekippe, 407–41. Leiden: Brill, 2005.

———. "Votives, Images, Interaction and Pilgrimage to the Tomb and Shrine of St. Thomas Becket, Canterbury Cathedral." In *Push Me, Pull You: Art and Devotional Interaction in Late Medieval and Renaissance Art*, edited by Sarah Blick and Laura Gelfand, 21–58. Leiden: Brill, 2011.

Blick, Sarah, and Rita Tekippe, eds. *Art and Architecture of Late Medieval Pilgrimage in Northern Europe and the British Isles*. Leiden: Brill, 2005.

von Bloh, Ute. "Heimlich Kämpfe: Frauenturniere in mittelalterlichen Mären." *Beiträge zur Geschichte der deutschen Sprache und Literatur* 121 (1999): 214–38.

Boulton, D'Arcy Jonathan Dacre. *The Knights of the Crown: The Monarchical Orders of Knighthood in Later Medieval Europe, 1325–1520*. Woodbridge, UK: Boydell, 1987.

Bredehoft, Thomas A. "Literacy Without Letters: Pilgrim Badges and Late Medieval Literate Ideology." *Viator* 37 (2006): 433–45.

Brown, Andrew. "Urban Jousts in the Later Middle Ages: The White Bear of Bruges." *Revue belge de philologie et d'historie* 78.2 (2000): 315–30.

Brumme, Carina. "Der heilige Antonius und die Hanse: Pilgerzeichen als Indikator für den Einfluss mittelalterlicher Handelsbündnisse auf den Wallfahrtsverkehr / Saint Anthony and the Hanse: Pilgrim Badges as Indicators for the Influence of Medieval

Trading Alliances on Pilgrimage Traffic." In *Mittelalterliche Tragezeichen: Social Media des Mittelalters / Medieval Badges: Social Media of the Middle Ages*, edited by André Dubisch, 326–63. Exhibition catalog. Lübeck: European Hansemuseum, 2020.

———. "Pilgerzeichen: Erhaltungsbedingungen und Verbreitungsräume." In *Das Zeichen am Hut im Mittelalter: Europäische Reisemarkierungen—Symposion in Memoriam Kurt Köster (1912–1986) und Katalog der Pilgerzeichen im Kunstgewerbemuseum und im Museum für Byzantinische Kunst der Staatlichen Museen zu Berlin*, edited by H. Kühne, L. Lambacher, and K. Vanja, 127–42. Frankfurt: Peter Lang, 2008.

Brumme, Carina, and Hanneke van Asperen. "Kleine Objekte und große Kontexte: 170 Jahre Forschung zu mittelalterlichen Zeichen / Small Objects, Larger Contexts: 170 Years of Research into Medieval Badges." In *Mittelalterliche Tragezeichen: Social Media des Mittelalters / Medieval Badges: Social Media of the Middle Ages*, edited by André Dubisch, 150–77. Exhibition catalog. Lübeck: European Hansemuseum, 2020.

Bruna, Denis. "Enseignes de pèlerinage de la *Vita Tolosana* Provence et Languedoc: Nouvelles découvertes et état de la question." In *Saint Jacques et la France: Actes du colloque des 18 et 19 Janvier 2001*, edited by Adeline Rucquoi, 65–82. Paris: CERF, 2003.

———, ed. *Enseignes de pèlerinage et enseignes profanes: Catalogue d'exposition*. Paris: Éditions de la Réunion des Musées Nationaux, 1996.

———. "Enseignes de pèlerinage d'origine française découvertes aux Pays-Bas." In *HP2*, 31–36. (See van Beuningen et al.)

———. *Enseignes de plomb et autres menues chosettes du Moyen Âge*. Paris: Léopard d'Or, 2006.

———. *Saints et diables au chapeau: Bijoux oubliés du Moyen Âge*. Paris: Seuil, 2007.

———. "Témoins de dévotions dans les livres d'heures à la fin du Moyen Âge." *Revue Mabillon* (1998): 127–36.

Bund, Konrad, and Rüdiger Pfeiffer-Rupp, eds. *Varia Campenologiae: Studia Cyclica—25 Jahre Deutsches Glockenmuseum auf Burg Greifenstein, Festschrift für Jörg Poettgen*. Schriften aus dem Deutschen Glockenmuseum 6. Greifenstein, Germany: Deutschen Glockenmuseum, 2009.

Burns, E. Jane. "Saracen Silk and the Virgin's Chemise: Cultural Crossings in Cloth." *Speculum* 81.2 (2006): 365–97.

Bynum, Caroline Walker. "Are Things 'Indifferent'? How Objects Change Our Understanding of Religious History." *German History* 34.1 (2016): 88–112.

———. *Christian Materiality: An Essay on Religion in Late Medieval Europe*. New York: Zone, 2011.

———. *Wonderful Blood: Theology and Practice in Late Medieval Northern Germany and Beyond*. Philadelphia: University of Pennsylvania Press, 2007.

Carru, D., and S. Gagnière. "Notes sur quelques objets de dévotion populaire, ampoules et enseignes de pèlerinage au Moyen-Âge tardif provenant d'Avignon." *Mémoires de l'Académie de Vaucluse*, 8.1 (1992): 55–92.

Cassen, Flora. "From Iconic O to Yellow Hat: The Shifting Symbolic Meaning of Jewish Distinctive Signs in Renaissance Italy." In *Fashioning Jews, Clothing, Culture, Commerce*, edited by L. Greenspoon, 29–49. Indianapolis: Purdue University Press, 2013.

———. *Marking the Jews in Renaissance Italy: Politics, Religion, and the Power of Symbols*. Cambridge: Cambridge University Press, 2017.

Chazan, Mireille and Nancy Freeman Regalado, eds., *Lettres, musique et société en Lor-*

raine médiévale: Autour du "Tournoi de Chauvency" (Ms. Oxford Bodleian Douce 308). Publications Romanes et Françaises 255. Geneva: Librairie Droz, 2012.

Cherry, John. *Medieval Goldsmiths*. London: British Museum, 2011.

Clark, John. "Medieval Finds from the River Thames: Accidental Loss, Rubbish or Ritual?" Seminar, Centre for Medieval and Renaissance Culture, University of Southampton, England, November 11, 2013, 1–7.

Cohen, Esther. "*In haec signa*: Pilgrim Badge Trade in Southern France." *Journal of Medieval History* 2.3 (1976): 193–214.

Cohen, Jeffrey, ed. *Animal, Vegetable, Mineral: Ethics and Objects*. Washington, DC: Oliphaunt, 2012.

Cook, Megan L. "Blazon." *New Literary History* 50.3 (2019): 363–68.

Courtenay, W. J. "Token Coinage and the Administration of Poor Relief During the Late Middle Ages." *Journal of Interdisciplinary History* 3 (1972): 275–95.

Craig, Leigh Ann. *Wandering Women and Holy Matrons: Women as Pilgrims in the Later Middle Ages*. Studies in Medieval and Reformation Traditions 138. Leiden: Brill, 2009.

Crane, Susan. *The Performance of Self: Ritual, Clothing, and Identity During the Hundred Years War*. Philadelphia: University of Pennsylvania Press, 2002.

Crombie, Laura. *Archery and Crossbow Guilds in Medieval Flanders: 1300–1500*. Woodbridge, UK: Boydell, 2016.

Crouch, David. *The Chivalric Turn: Conduct and Hegemony in Europe Before 1300*. Oxford: Oxford University Press, 2019.

———. *Tournament*. London: Hambleton and London, 2005.

Delbouille, Maurice, ed. *Le Tournoi de Chauvency*. Liège et Paris: Vaillant-Charmann, 1932.

Dewilde, Marc, Anton Ervynck, and Alexis Wielemans, eds. *Ypres and the Medieval Cloth Industry in Flanders: Archaeological and Historical Contributions*. Archeologie in Vlaanderen, 2. Zellik, Belgium: Instituut voor het Archeologisch Patrimonium, 1998.

Diederich, Toni. "Frische Brise für die Siegelforschung: Überlegungen zu einer neuartigen Siegelpublikation." *Herold-Jahrbuch* 13 (2008): 9–23.

Ditmar-Trauth, Gösta, Arnold Muhl, and Heinrich Wunderlich. "Magdeburger Ritter in Miniaturformat: Mitteleuropas erster Zinnsoldat." In *Fund des Monats: Landesmuseum für Vorgeschichte*. Halle: Landesamt für Denkmalpflege und Archäologie Sachsen-Anhalt, November 2005.

Donkin. Lucy. "Stones of St. Michael: Venerating Fragments of Holy Ground in Medieval France and Italy." In *Matter of Faith: An Interdisciplinary Study of Relics and Relic Veneration in the Medieval Period*, edited by James Robinson, Lloyd de Beer, and Anna Harnden, 23–31. London: British Museum, 2014.

Dormeier, Heinrich. "Pilgerfahrten Lübecker Bürger im späten Mittelalter Forschungsbilanz und Ausblick." *Zeitschrift des Vereins für Lübeckische Geschichte und Altertumskunde* 92 (2012): 9–64.

Dubisch, André, ed. *Mittelalterliche Tragezeichen: Social Media des Mittelalters / Medieval Badges: Social Media of the Middle Ages*. Exhibition catalogue. Lübeck: European Hansemuseum, 2020.

Dumolyn, Jan. "'Criers and Shouters: The Discourse on Radical Urban Rebels in Late Medieval Flanders." *Journal of Social History* 42.1 (2009): 111–36.

Dyas, Dee. "To Be a Pilgrim: Tactile Pilgrimage, Virtual Piety and the Experience of Place in Christian Pilgrimage." In *Matter of Faith: An Interdisciplinary Study of Relics and Relic Veneration in the Medieval Period*, edited by James Robinson, Lloyd de Beer, and Anna Harnden, 1–7. London: British Museum, 2014.

Egan, Geoff, and Justine Bayley. *The Medieval Household: Daily Living, c. 1150–1450*. Woodbridge, UK: Boydell, 2010.

Egan, Geoff, and Hazel Forsyth. *Toys, Trifles, and Trinkets: Base Metal Miniatures from London, 1200–1800*. London: Unicorn, 2005.

Ehrstine, Glenn. "Aufführungsort als Kommunikationsraum: Ein Vergleich der fastnächtlichen Spieltradition Nürnbergs, Lübecks und der Schweiz." In *Fastnachtspiele: Weltliches Schauspiel in literarischen und kulturellen Kontexten*, edited by Klaus Ridder, 83–97. Tübingen, Germany: Max Niemeyer Verlag, 2009.

———. "Of Peasants, Women, and Bears: Political Agency and the Demise of Carnival Transgression in Bernese Reformation Drama." *Sixteenth-Century Journal* 31.3 (2000): 675–97.

Eisenbichler, Konrad, ed. *Companion to Medieval and Early Modern Confraternities*. Leiden: Brill, 2019.

Eisenbichler, Konrad, and Wim Hüsken, eds. *Carnival and the Carnivalesque: The Fool, the Reformer, the Wildman, and Others in Early Modern Theatre*. Amsterdam: Rodopi, 1999.

Emerson, Catherine, Adrian P. Tudor, and Mario Longtin, eds. *Performance, Drama and Spectacle in the Medieval City: Essays in Honour of Alan Hindley*. Leuvens, Belgium: Peeters, 2010.

Eming, Jutta. "Der Kampf um den Phallus: Körperfragmentierung, Textbegehren und groteske Ästhetik im *Nonnenturnier*." *German Quarterly* 85.4 (2012): 380–400.

Enoch, Nick. "Clasp of Astonishment: Amateur Treasure Hunter Finds Tiny 14th Century Heart-Shaped Gold Brooch Worth £25,000 in Farmer's Field." *Daily Mail*, May 2, 2012. https://www.dailymail.co.uk/news/article-2138354/Amateur-treasure-hunter-finds-tiny-14th-century-gold-brooch-worth-25-000-farmers-field.html.

Escher, Felix, and Hartmut Kühne, eds. *Die Wilsnackfahrt: Ein Wallfahrts- und Kommunikationszentrum Nord- und Mitteleuropas im Spätmittelalter*. Frankfurt: Peter Lang, 2006.

Escher-Apsner, Monika. "'Confraternitas pauperum'/'Confraternitas exulum': Inklusions- und Exklusionsmodi bruderschaftlicher Organisationen—die sog. Elendenbruderschaften als Sonderform?" In *Inklusion/Exklusion: Studien zu Fremdheit und Armut von der Antike bis zur Gegenwart*, edited by A. Gestrich, L. Raphael, and H. Uerling, 181–212. Frankfurt: Peter Lang, 2008.

Feller, Laurent, and Ana Rodríguez, eds. *Objets sous contrainte: Circulation des richesses et valeur des choses au Moyen Âge*. Paris: Publications de la Sorbonne, 2013.

Fern, Chris, Tania Dickinson, and Leslie Webster, eds. *The Staffordshire Hoard: An Anglo-Saxon Treasure*. London: Society of Antiquaries of London, 2020.

Ferrando, Philippe. "Quatre enseignes de pèlerinage inédites pour Sainte-Croix de Montmajour." *Bulletin des Amis du Vieil Arles* 110 (March 2001): 5–13.

Ferrier, A. "A Collector and His Collections: Subject and Objects." In *Gevonden voorwerpen: Opstellen over middeleeuwse archeologie voor H. J. E. van Beuningen*, edited by D. Kicken, A. M. Koldeweij and J. R. ter Molen. Rotterdam Papers 11, 8–11. Rotterdam: BOOR, 2000.

Ferzoco, George. *Il Murale Di Massa Marittima / The Massa Marittima Mural*. Florence: Consiglio Regionale della Toscana; Leicester: University of Leicester, 2004.

Flint, Valerie J. "A Magic Universe." In *A Social History of England 1200–1500*, edited by Rosemary Horrox and W. Mark Ormrod, 340–55. Cambridge: Cambridge University Press, 2006.

Forgeais, Arthur. *Collection des plombs historiés trouvés dans la Seine*, 5 vols. Paris: Chez l'Auteur, Quai d'Orfèvres, 54, 1861–1865.

Foster Campbell, Megan H. "Pilgrimage Through the Pages: Pilgrim's Badges in Late Medieval Devotional Manuscripts." PhD diss., University of Illinois, Urbana-Champaign, 2011.

Füetrer, Ulrich. "Bayerische Chronik." Reprinted in *Quellen und Erörterungen zur Bayerischen und Deutschen Geschichte*, edited by Reinhold Spiller, 224. Neue Folge, Band 2, Abteilung 2. Aalen, Germany: Scientia Verlag, 1969.

Garceau, Michelle E. "'I Call the People': Church Bells in Fourteenth-Century Catalunya." *Journal of Medieval History* 37 (2011): 197–214.

Geary, Patrick J. "Peasant Religion in Medieval Europe." *Cahiers d'Extrême-Asie* 12 (2001): 185–209.

Gerson, Paula, Annie Shaver-Crandell, and Alison Stone, eds. *The Pilgrim's Guide to Santiago de Compostela: A Critical Edition*, 2. London: Harvey Miller, 1998.

Gibbs, Marion E., and Sidney Johnson. *Medieval German Literature: A Companion*. New York: Garland, 1997.

Gies, Frances, and Joseph Gies. *Cathedral, Forge, and Waterwheel: Technology and Invention in the Middle Ages*. New York: HarperCollins, 1994.

Gilchrist, Roberta. *Medieval Life: Archaeology and the Life Course*. Woodbridge, UK: Boydell, 2012.

Gottfried von Strassburg. *Tristan*. Edited by Rüdiger Krohn. Stuttgart: Reclam, 1984.

Gottfried von Strassburg. *Tristan and the 'Tristan' of Thomas*. Translated by A.T. Hatto. London: Penguin, 1960.

Gowing, Laura, Michael Hunter, and Miri Rubin, eds. *Love, Friendship, and Faith in Europe, 1300–1800*. New York: Palgrave, 2005.

Green, Richard Firth. *A Crisis of Truth: Literature and Law in Ricardian England*. Philadelphia: University of Pennsylvania Press, 1999.

Groebner, Valentin. "Mobile Werte, informelle Ökonomie: Zur "Kultur" der Armut in der spätmittelalterlichen Stadt." In *Armut im Mittelalter*, edited by Otto Gerhard Oexle, 165–87. Ostfidern, Germany: Jan Thorbecke, 2005.

———. *Der Schein der Person: Steckbrief, Ausweis und Kontrolle im Europa des Mittelalters*. Munich: C. H. Beck, 2004. Translated by Mark Kyburz and John Peck as *Who Are You? Identification, Deception, and Surveillance in Early Modern Europe*. New York: Zone, 2007.

———. "Trügerische Zeichen: Praktik und das politische Unsichtbare am Beginn der Neuzeit." In *Geschichtszeichen*, edited by Heinz Dieter Kittsteiner, 63–80. Cologne: Böhlau, 1999.

Grönwald, Holger. "Am Einzelfund ins Detail: Das mittelalterliche Bild des Pantheon und seiner Ikone im Spiegel von Pilgerzeichen." In *Wallfahrer aus dem Osten: Mittelalterliche Pilgerzeichen zwischen Ostsee, Donau und Seine—Beiträge der Tagung Perspektiven der europäischen Pilgerzeichenforschung 21. bis 24. April 2010 in Prag*, edited by Hartmut Kühne, Lothar Lambacher, and Jan Hrdina, 275–320. Frankfurt: Peter Lang, 2013.

Haasis-Berner, Andreas. *Pilgerzeichen des Hochmittelalters*. Würzburg, Germany: Veröffentlichungen zur Volkskunde und Kulturgeschichte, 2003.

Habermehl, Jan, ed. *Der Schwanritter Konrads von Würzburg. Aus der Frankfurter Handschrift neu ediert und mit einem Kommentar versehen*. Frankfurt am Main; n.p., 2015; https://d-nb.info/1144611792/34.

Hablot, Laurent. "Emblématique et mythologie médiévale, le cygne, une devise princière." *Histoire de l'art: Bulletin d'information de l'Institut national d'histoire de l'art publié en collaboration avec l'Association des Professeurs d'Archéologie et d'Histoire de l'Art des Universités* (2001): 51–64.

———. "Revêtir l'armoirie: Les vêtements héraldiques au moyen âge, mythes et réalités." *Espacio, tiempo y forma* 1.6 (2018): 55–87.

Hahn, Cynthia. *Strange Beauty: Issues in the Making and Meaning of Reliquaries, 400–ca. 1204*. University Park: Pennsylvania State University Press, 2012.

———. "The Voices of the Saints: Speaking Reliquaries," *Gesta* 36.1 (1997): 20–31.

Hamburger, Jeffrey. *Script as Image*. Walpole, MA: Peeters, 2014.

Hanawalt, Barbara. *Growing Up in Medieval London*. New York: Oxford University Press, 1993.

Harthan, John. *The Book of Hours*. London: Thames and Hudson, 1977.

Hartmann, Heiko. "Tiere in der historischen und literarischen Heraldik des Mittelalters: Ein Aufriss." In *Tiere und Fabelwesen im Mittelalter*, edited by Sabine Obermaier, 147–79. Berlin: de Gruyter, 2009.

van Heeringen, R. M., A. M. Koldeweij, and A. A. Gaalman, eds. *Heiligen uit de modder: In Zeeland gevonden pelgrimstekens*. Zutphen, Netherlands: Walburg Pers, 1987.

Herbers, Klaus, and Hartmut Kühne. "Einführung: Mittelalterliche Pilgerzeichen—zur Geschichte und den gegenwärtigen Perspektiven ihrer Erforschung." In *Pilgerzeichen—Pilgerstraßen*, edited by K. Herbers and H. Kühne, 7–27. Tübingen, Germany: Narr, 2013.

———, eds. *Pilgerzeichen—Pilgerstrasse*. Tübingen, Germany: Narr, 2013.

Hess, Cordelia. "The Writing on the Barn: Content and Materiality in Contested Documents of Northern German Towns." *Seminar* 52.2 (2016): 155–73.

Hiltmann, Torsten. "Heraldry as a Systematic and International Language? About the Limitations of Blazonry in Describing Coats of Arms." Heraldica Nova: Medieval Heraldry in Social and Cultural-Historical Perspectives, May 25, 2016. https://heraldica.hypotheses.org/4623.

———. "L'héraldique dans l'espace domestique: Perspectives historiques sur les armoiries et le décor héraldique dans l'espace profane (espace germanique, XIIIe–XVIe siècle)." *Le Moyen Âge* 123.3 (2017): 527–70.

———. "Potentialities and Limitations of Medieval Armorials as Historical Source: The Representation of Hierarchy and Princely Rank in Late Medieval Collections of Arms in France and Germany." In *Princely Rank in Late Medieval Europe: Trodden Paths and Promising Avenues*, edited by T. Huthwelker, J. Peltzer, and M. Wemhöner, 157–98. Ostfildern, Germany: Thorbecke, 2011.

———. *Spätmittelalterliche Heroldskompendien: Referenzen adeliger Wissenskultur in Zeiten gesellschaftlichen Wandels (Frankreich und Burgund, 15. Jahrhundert)*. Pariser Historische Studien, 92. Munich: Oldenbourg, 2011.

Hiltmann, Torsten, and Laurent Hablot, eds. *Heraldic Artists and Painters in the Middle Ages*. Ostfildern, Germany: Thorbecke, 2018.

Hiltmann, Torsten, and Miguel Metelo de Seixas, eds. *Heraldry in Medieval and Early Modern State-Rooms*. Ostfildern, Germany: Thorbecke, 2019.

Hinds, Sarah. "Late Medieval Sexual Badges as Sexual Signifiers: A Material Culture Reappraisal." *Medieval Feminist Forum: A Journal of Gender and Sexuality* 55.2 (2020): 170–91. https://ir.uiowa.edu/mff/vol55/iss2/8.

Howell, Martha. "Credit Networks and Political Actors in Thirteenth-Century Ypres." *Past and Present* 242 (February 2019): 3–26.

Huber, Christoph. "Der zwiespaltige Gelehrte. Zur Ambiquität der Aristoteles-Figur in mittelalterlichen Darstellungen (Artes-Repräsentant, Fürstenerzieher, Liebhaber)." In *Diz vliegende bîspel: Ambiquity in Medieval and Early Modern Literature*, edited by M. E. Polhill and A. Sager, 115–37. Göttingen: V & R Unipress, 2020.

Hughes, Diane Owen. "Distinguishing Signs: Ear-Rings, Jews and Franciscan Rhetoric in the Italian Renaissance City." *Past and Present* 112 (1986): 3–59.

Hunt, Alan. *Governance of the Consuming Passions: A History of Sumptuary Law*. New York: St. Martins, 1996.

Husband, Timothy. *The Wild Man: Medieval Myth and Symbolism*. New York: Metropolitan Museum of Art, 1980.

Hutchison, Emily J. "Partisan Identity in the French Civil War, 1405–1418: Reconsidering the Evidence on Livery Badges." *Journal of Medieval History* 33.3 (2007): 250–74.

Jeep, John M. *Among Friends? Early German Evidence of Friendship Among Women*. Lincoln: University of Nebraska Press, 1999.

Jones, Malcolm. "Sacred and Profane: Reinforcement and Amuletic Ambiguity in the Late Medieval Lead Badge Corpus." *Amsterdamer Beiträge zur älteren Germanistik* 59 (2004): 111–37.

———. "The Secular Badges." In *HP1*, 99–109. (See van Beuningen et al.)

———. "Wicked Willies with Wings: Sexuality in Late Medieval Art and Thought." In *The Secret Middle Ages*, 248–68, 356–58. Westport, CT: Praeger, 2003.

Jones, Robert W., and Peter Coss, eds. *A Companion to Chivalry*. Rochester, NY: Boydell, 2019.

Kaeuper, Richard A. *Chivalry and Violence in Medieval Europe*. Oxford: Oxford University Press, 1999.

Karras, Ruth Mazo. "David and Jonathan: A Late Medieval Bromance." In *Rivalrous Masculinities: New Directions in Medieval Gender Studies*, edited by Ann Marie Rasmussen, 151–73. Notre Dame, IN: University of Notre Dame Press, 2019.

Keen, Maurice. *Chivalry*. New Haven, CT: Yale University Press, 2005.

von Keller, Adelbert, ed. "Meister Aristoteles." In *Fastnachtspiele aus dem 15. Jahrhundert*, vols. 28–30 and 46. Bibliothek des Litterarischen Vereins Stuttgart, 46, 216–30. Stuttgart: Litterarischer Verein, 1853–58.

Kieckhefer, Richard. "Erotic Magic." In *Sex in the Middle Ages: A Book of Essays*, edited by Joyce E. Salisbury. Garland Medieval Casebooks, 3, 30–55. New York: Garland, 1991.

———. *Magic in the Middle Ages*. Cambridge: Cambridge University Press, 1989.

Klinck, Anne L. *Anthology of Ancient and Medieval Woman's Song*. New York: Palgrave Macmillan, 2004.

Koldeweij, A. M. "A Barefaced *Roman de la Rose* (Paris, B.N., ms. fr. 25526) and Some

Late Medieval Mass-Produced Badges of a Sexual Nature." In *Flanders in a European Perspective*, edited by M. Smeyers and B. Cardon, 499–516. Leuven, Belgium: Peeters, 1993.
———. "De insignie collectie van H. J. E. van Beuningen en zijn zestig 'mooisten.'" In *HP4*, 7–22. (See van Beuningen et al.)
———. "Een tweede diptiek uit Aachen." In *HP* 3, 39–55. (See van Beuningen et al.)
———. "Die Sammlung H. J. E. van Beuningen und ihre Vorgänger / The H. J. E. van Beuningen Collection and its Predecessors." In *Mittelalterliche Tragezeichen: Social Media des Mittelalters / Medieval Badges: Social Media of the Middle Ages*, edited by André Dubisch, 132–49. Exhibition catalog. Lübeck: European Hansemuseum, 2020.
———. "Het zijn niet allen slagers die lange messen dragen: Valse pelgrims en hun herkenningstekens." In *HP1*, 33–38. (See van Beuningen et al.)
———. "Pelgrimsinsignes van Elisabeth uit Marburg." In *HP1*, 69–75. (See van Beuningen et al.)
———. "Shameless and Naked Images: Obscene Badges as Parodies of Religious Devotion." In *Art and Architecture of Late Medieval Pilgrimage in Northern Europe and the British Isles*, edited by Sarah Blick and Rita Tekippe, 493–510. Leiden: Brill, 2005.
———. "'Tsente Thomaes te Cantelberghe': Pelgrimstochten vanuit de Nederlanden naar Canterbury—teruggevonden insignes en berichten uit andere bron." In *HP2*, 88–104. (See van Beuningen et al.)
———. "The Wearing of Significative Badges, Religious and Secular: The Social Meaning of a Behavioral Pattern." In *Showing Status: Representations of Social Positions in the Late Middle Ages*, edited by Wim Blockmans and Antheun Janse, 307–28. Turnhout, Belgium: Brepols, 1999.
Konrad von Würzburg. *Der Schwanritter Konrads von Würzburg*, edited by Jan Habermehl. Frankfurt am Main: n.p., 2015; https://d-nb.info/1144611792/34.
Köster, Kurt. "Gemalte Kollektionen von Pilgerzeichen und religiösen Medaillen in flämischen Gebets- und Stundenbüchern des 15. und 16. Jahrhunderts: Neue Funde in Handschriften der Gent-Brügger Schule." In *Liber Amicorum Herman Liebaers*, edited by Frans Vanwijngaerden, Jean-Marie Duvosquel, Josette Mélard, and Lieve Viaene-Awouters, 485–535. Brussels: Koninklijke Bibliotheek Albert I, 1984.
———. "Pilgerzeichen-Studien: Neue Beiträge zur Kenntnis eines mittelalterlichen Massenartikels und seiner Überlieferungsformen." In *Bibliotheca docet: Festgabe für Carl Wehmer*, edited by Joost Siegfried, 77–100. Amsterdam: Verlag der Erasmus-Buchhandlung, 1963.
———. "Religiöse Medaillen und Wallfahrts-Devotionalien in der flämischen Buchmalerei des 15. und frühen 16. Jahrhunderts: Zur Kenntnis gemalter und wirklicher Kollectionen in spät-mittelalterlichen Gebetbüchern." In *Buch und Welt: Gustav Hofmann zum 65. Geburtstag*, edited by Hans Striedl and Joachim Wieder, 459–504. Wiesbaden, Germany: Harrassowitz, 1965.
Krabath, Stefan, and Lothar Lambacher. *Der Pritzwalker Silberfund: Schmuck des späten Mittelalters*. Pritzwalk, Germany: Stadt- und Brauerei Museum, 2006.
Krey, Hans-Josef. "Böcklerbund." Historisches Lexikon Bayerns, accessed January 11, 2020, https://www.historisches-lexikon-bayerns.de/Lexikon/Böcklerbund.
Krieger, Gerhard, ed. *Verwandtschaft, Bruderschaft, Freundschaft: Soziale Lebens- und Kommunikationsformen im Mittelalter*. Berlin: Akademie Verlag, 2009.

Küch, Friedrich. "Eine Quelle zur Geschichte des Landgrafen Ludwig I." *Zeitschrift des Vereins für hessische Geschichte und Landeskunde* 42 (1908): 144–277.

Kühne, Hartmut. "Kreuzwege, Heilig-Kreuz-Kapellen und Jerusalempilger im Raum der mittleren Elbe um 1500." In *Heilige Grab: Heilige Gräber—Aktualität und Nachleben von Pilgerorten*, edited by Ursula Röper and Martin Treml, 44–54. Berlin: Lukas, 2014.

———. "Das Mirakelbuch der Fronleichnamkapelle von Heiligenleichnam bei Altenburg." In *Vor- und Frühreformation in thüringischen Städten (1470–1525/30)*, edited by Joachim Emig, Volker Leppin, and Uwe Schirmer, 19–39. Cologne: Böhlau Verlag, 2013.

———. "Pilgerzeichen: Signum des Pilgers und Devotionalie." *Liturgisches Jahrbuch* 61 (2011): 45–63.

———. "Das Rheinland als Pilgerlandschaft im Spiegel von Pilgerzeichen auf Glocken des 14.–16. Jahrhunderts." In *Wallfahrt und Kulturbegegnung: Das Rheinland als Ausgangspunkt und Ziel spätmittelalterlicher Pilgerreisen*, edited by Helmut Brach-Tuchel, 49–87. Schriften des Heimatvereines der Erkelenzer Lande, 26. Erkelenz, Germany: Heimatverein der Erkelenzer Lande e.V., 2012.

———. "Zur Konjunktur von Heilig-Blut-Wallfahrten im spätmittelalterlichen Mecklenburg." *Jahrbuch für Mecklenburgische Kirchengeschichte / Mecklenburgia Sacra* 12 (2009): 76–115.

Kühne, Hartmut, and Jörg Ansorge. "'Holiness' from the Mud: Badges and Pilgrimage in German-Speaking Lands—A Case Study from the North German City of Stade (Lower Saxony) in the Former Archdiocese of Bremen." *Mediæval Journal* 8.1 (2018): 11–56.

Kühne, Hartmut, and Carina Brumme. "Ablässe und Wallfahrten in Braunschweig und Königslutter: Zu einem Detail des Briefes Heinrich Hanners an Thomas Müntzer." In *Thomas Müntzer—Zeitgenossen—Nachwelt: Siegfried Brauner zum 80. Geburtstag*, edited by Hartmut Kühne, Hans Jürgen Goertz, Thomas T. Müller, and Günter Vogler, 39–72. Mühlhausen, Germany: Thomas-Müntzer-Gesellschaft, 2010.

Kühne, Hartmut, Carina Brumme, and Helena Koenigsmarková, eds. *Jungfrauen, Engel, Phallustiere: Die Sammlung mittelalterlicher französischer Pilgerzeichen des Kunstgewerbemuseums in Prag und des Nationalmuseums Prag.* Berlin: Lukas, 2012.

Kühne, Hartmut, Enno Bünz, and Thomas T. Müller. *Alltag und Frömmigkeit am Vorabend der Reformation in Mitteldeutschland: Katalog zur Ausstellung "Umsonst ist der Tod."* Petersberg, Germany: Michael Imhof, 2013.

Kühne, Hartmut, Hans Jürgen Goertz, Thomas T. Müller, and Günter Vogler, eds. *Thomas Müntzer—Zeitgenossen—Nachwelt: Siegfried Brauner zum 80. Geburtstag.* Mühlhausen, Germany: Thomas-Müntzer-Gesellschaft, 2010.

Kühne, Hartmut, Lothar Lambacher, and Jan Hrdina, eds. *Wallfahrer aus dem Osten: Mittelalterliche Pilgerzeichen zwischen Ostsee, Donau und Seine.* Frankfurt: Peter Lang, 2012.

Kühne, Hartmut, Lothar Lambacher, and Konrad Vanja, eds. *Das Zeichen am Hut im Mittelalter: Europäische Reisemarkierungen. Symposion in Memoriam Kurt Köster (1912–1986) und Katalog der Pilgerzeichen im Kunstgewerbemuseum und im Museum für Byzantinische Kunst der Staatlichen Museen zu Berlin.* Frankfurt: Peter Lang, 2008.

Kühne, Hartmut and Nadine Mai. "Zur Einführung: Pilgerfahrten und Wallfahrtskirchen in Norddeutschland." In *Pilgerspuren—Orte, Wege, Zeichen*, 14–27. Exhibition catalogue. Petersberg, Germany: Michael Imhof, 2020.

Kumler, Aden. "The Multiplication of the Species: Eucharistic Morphology in the Middle Ages." *Res* 59/60 (Spring/Autumn 2011): 179–91.

Labaune-Jean, Françoise. *Le plomb et la pierre: Petits objets de dévotion pour les pèlerins du Mont-Saint-Michel de la conception à la production (XIVe–XVe siècles)*. Caen, France: Publications du Craham, Série antique et médiévale, 2016.

Lassure, J.-M. "Enseignes de pèlerinage du XIVe siècle trouvées à Toulouse et au Pouget (Hérault)." *L'Auta* 35 (2002): 200–6.

Lee, Jennifer M. "Beyond the Locus Sanctus: The Independent Iconography of Pilgrims' Souvenirs." *Visual Resources* 21 (2009): 363–81.

———. "Louis XI, A French Monarch in Pilgrim's Garb: Badges." *Fifteenth-Century Studies* 34 (2009): 113–32.

———. "Material and Meaning in Lead Pilgrim Signs." *Peregrinations: Journal of Medieval Art and Architecture* 2.3 (2009): 152–69.

———. "Medieval Pilgrim Badges' in Rivers: The Curious History of a Non-Theory." *Journal of Art Historiography* 11 (2014): 3–11.

———. "'Reckless Effrontery': Conflict and the Abuse of Badges in Late Medieval England." *Mediæval Journal* 8.1 (2018): 109–36.

———. "Searching for Signs: Pilgrims' Identity and Experiences Made Visible in the *Miracula Sancti Thomae Cantuariensis*." In *Art and Architecture of Late Medieval Pilgrimage in Northern Europe and the British Isles*, edited by Sarah Blick and Rita Tekippe, 473–90. Leiden: Brill, 2005.

———. "Signs of Affinity: Canterbury Pilgrims' Sign Contextualized, 1171–1538." PhD diss., Emory University, Atlanta, Georgia, 2003.

Lehnertz, Andreas. *Judensiegel im spätmittelalterlichen Reichsgebiet. Begläubigungstätigkeit und Selbstrepräsentation von Jüdinnen und Juden*. 2 vols. Forschungen zur Geschichte der Juden, Abteilung A: Abhandlungen, 30. Wiesbaden: Harrassowitz, 2020.

Lerner, Robert E. "Vagabonds and Little Women: The Medieval Netherlandish Dramatic Fragment *De truwante*." *Modern Philology* 65.4 (1968): 301–6.

Lesger, Cle. *The Rise of the Amsterdam Market and Information Exchange*. Burlington, VT: Ashgate, 2006.

Lipton, Sara. *Dark Mirror: The Visual Origins of Anti-Jewish Iconography*. New York: Henry Holt, 2014.

Lochrie, Karma. "Medieval Masculinities Without Men." In *Rivalrous Masculinities: New Directions in Medieval Gender Studies*, edited by Ann Marie Rasmussen, 209–33. Notre Dame, IN: University of Notre Dame, 2019.

van der Lof, R. F. C. "Een plankje voor pelgrimsinsignes in Weesp en zijn verwanten." *Antiek* 25.6 (1990): 307–11.

Lohengrin, edited by Heinrich Rückert. Bibliothek des gesammten deutschen National-Literatur, 36. Quedlinburg/Leipzig: Druck und Verlag von Gottfr. Basse, 1858.

van Loon van de Moosdijk, Elly. "Pelgrimsinsignes op 'Nederlandse' klokken." In *HP2*, 112–27. (See van Beuningen et al.)

van Loon-van de Moosdijk, Elly. "Pilgrim Badges and Bells." In *Art and Symbolism in Medieval Europe: Papers of the "Medieval Europe Brugge 1997" Conference, Volume 5*, edited by Guy de Boe and Frans Verhaeghe, 149–54. Zellik, Belgium: Instituut voor het Archeologisch Patrimonium, 1997.

Macy, Gary, and Bernard Cooke. *Christian Symbol and Ritual: An Introduction*. New York: Oxford University Press, 2005.

Maloney, Clarence, ed. *The Evil Eye*. New York: Columbia University Press, 1976.

Mathews, Alastair. *The Medieval German Lohengrin: Narrative Poetics in the Story of the Swan Knight*. Rochester, NY: Camden House, 2016.

McSheffrey, Shannon. "Sanctuary and the Legal Topography of Pre-Reformation London." *Law and History Review* 27.3 (2009): 483–514.

———. *Seeking Sanctuary: Crime, Mercy, and Politics in English Courts, 1400–1550*. Oxford: Oxford University Press, 2017.

Mellinkoff, Ruth. *Averting Demons: The Protective Power of Medieval Themes and Motifs*, vol. 1. Los Angeles: Ruth Mellinkoff Publications, 2004.

Merrifield, Ralph. *The Archaeology of Religion and Magic*. New York: New Amsterdam, 1987.

ter Molen, J. R. "H. J. E. van Beuningen: Levensschets van een bevlogen verzamelaar." In *Gevonden voorwerpen: Opstellen over middeleeuwse archeologie voor H. J. E. van Beuningen* edited by D. Kicken, A. M. Koldeweij, and J. R. ter Molen. Rotterdam Papers, 11, 12–28. Rotterdam: BOOR, 2000.

Morgan, David. *Visual Piety: A History and Theory of Popular Religious Images*. Berkeley: University of California Press, 1998.

Moser, H., and H. Tervooren, eds. "Namenlose Lieder VII." In *Des Minnesangs Frühling*, vol. 1, 37th ed., 21. Stuttgart: Hirzel, 1982.

Müller, Ulrich, and Margarete Springeth, eds. *Oswald von Wolkenstein: Leben—Werk—Rezeption*. Berlin: de Gruyter, 2011.

Neumann, Bernd. *Geistliches Schauspiel im Zeugnis der Zeit: Zur Aufführung mittelalterlicher religiöser Dramen im deutschen Sprachgebiet*, 2 vols. Munich: Artemis, 1987.

Neuschel, Kristen B. *Living by the Sword: Weapons and Material Culture in France and Britain, 600–1600*. Ithaca, NY: Cornell University Press, 2020.

Newman, Barbara. *Medieval Crossover: Reading the Secular Against the Sacred*. Notre Dame, IN: University of Notre Dame Press, 2013.

Nierop, H. F. K. *The Nobility of Holland: From Knights to Regents 1500–1650*, translated by Maarten Ultee. Cambridge: Cambridge University Press, 1993.

Oefelein, Cornelia. "The Signs and Bells of Mass Pilgrimage." In *Mobs: An Interdisciplinary Inquiry*, edited by Nancy Van Deusen and Leonard Michael Koff, 231–68. Leiden: Brill, 2012.

Orme, Nicholas. *From Childhood to Chivalry: The Education of English Kings and Aristocracy, 1066–1530*. London: Methuen, 1984.

———. *Medieval Children*. New Haven, CT: Yale University Press, 2001.

Ostkamp, Sebastian. "The World Upside Down: Secular Badges and the Iconography of the Late Medieval Period—Ordinary Pins with Multiple Meanings." *Journal of Archaeology in the Low Countries* 1–2 (2009): 107–25.

Der Palmesel: Geschichte, Kult und Kunst—Eine Ausstellung im Museum für Natur und Kultur Schwäbisch Gmünd, 24. März–18 Juni 2000. Museumskatalog 6, Reihe Museum für Natur und Kultur. Schwäbisch Gmünd, Germany: Museum und Galerie Schwäbisch Gmünd, 2000.

Paner, Henryk. *Gdańsk na pielgrzymkowych szlakach średniowiecznej Europy*. Gdańsk, Poland: Muzeum Archeologizne w Gdánsku, 2016.

———. *Średniowteczne świadectwa Kultu Maryjnego: Pamiątiki pielgrzymie w zbiorach Muzeum Archeologicznego w Gdańsku*. Gdańsk, Poland: Muzeum Archeologizne w Gdańsku, 2013.

Park, Katherine. *Secrets of Women: Gender, Generation, and the Origins of Human Dissection*. New York: Zone, 2006.

Parsons, Ben, and Bas Jongenelen. *Comic Drama in the Low Countries, c. 1450–1560: A Critical Anthology*. Cambridge: D. S. Brewer, 2012.

Pastoureau, Michel. *The Devil's Cloth: A History of Stripes*. New York: Columbia University Press, 2001.

———. *Heraldry: An Introduction to a Noble Tradition*. New York: Harry N. Abrams, 1997.

Paulus, Christof. *Machtfelder: Die Politik Herzog Albrechts IV. von Bayern (1447/1465–1508) zwischen Territorium, Dynastie und Reich*. Forschungen zur Kaiser- und Papstgeschichte des Mittelalters: Beihefte und J. F. Böhmer, Regesta Imperii, 39. Cologne: Böhlau Verlag, 2015.

Piron, Willy. "Pilgrim Badges and GIS: A Northern Affair?" In *Wallfahrer aus dem Osten: Mittelalterliche Pilgerzeichen zwischen Ostsee, Donau und Seine*, edited by Hartmut Kühne, Lothar Lambacher, and Jan Hrdina, 475–86. Frankfurt: Peter Lang, 2012.

———. "Schreitende Vulven und fliegende Phalli: Spätmittelalterliche sexuelle Abzeichen und ihre Funktion / Walking Vulvas and Flying Phalluses: Late Medieval Sexual Badges and Their Function." In *Mittelalterliche Tragezeichen: Social Media des Mittelalters / Medieval Badges: Social Media of the Middle Ages*, edited by André Dubisch, 270–89. Exhibition catalog. Lübeck: European Hansemuseum, 2020.

Poettgen, Jörg. "Europäische Pilgerzeichenforschung: Die Zentrale Pilgerzeichenkartei (PZK) Kurt Kösters (1986)." In *Nürnberg und der Forschungsstand nach 1986*. Reprinted in *Jahrbuch für Glockenkunde* 7/8 (1995/96): 195–207. http://www.pilgerzeichen.de/html/poettgen-koester.html.

———. "Pilgerzeichen auf Glocken: Studien zur Geschichte, Verbreitung und Motivation ihrer Verwendung." In *HP2*, 128–36. (See van Beuningen et al.)

Prokisch, Bernard, and Thomas Kühtreiber, eds. *Der Schatzfund von Fuchsenhof: The Fuchsenhof Hoard—Poklad Fuchsenhof*. Linz, Austria: Oberösterreichisches Landesmuseum, 2004.

Rasmussen, Ann Marie. "Materiality and Meaning: What a Medieval Badge Can Tell Us About Translation." In *Un/Translatables: New Maps for German Literature*, edited by Catriona McLoed and Bethany Wiggin, 215–28. Chicago: Northwestern University Press, 2016.

———. "Moving Beyond Sexuality in Medieval Sexual Badges." In *From Beasts to Souls: Gender and Embodiment in Medieval Europe*, edited by E. Jane Burns and Peggy McCracken, 296–335. Notre Dame, IN: University of Notre Dame Press, 2013. Reprinted in *Nahrung, Notdurft, Obszönität*, ed. Andrea Grafetstätter, 125–54. Bamberg, Germany: Bamberg University Press, 2013.

———. "Pilgerzeichen als sprechende Objekte." In *Stimme und Performanz in der mittelalterlichen Literatur*, edited by Monika Unzeitig und Florian Schmid, 469–91. Berlin: de Gruyter, 2017.

———. "Das Porträt von Herzog Heinrich V. von Mecklenburg in North Carolina (USA)." *Mecklenburgisches Jahrbuch* 135 (2020): 349–352.

———. "Problematizing Medieval Misogyny: Aristotle and Phyllis in the German Tradition." In *Verstellung und Betrug im Mittelalter und in der mittelalterlichen Literatur*, edited by Mathias Meyer and Alexander Sager, 195–220. Göttingen: V & R Unipress.

———. "Reading in Nuremberg's Fifteenth-Century Carnival Plays." In *Literary Studies and the Question of Reading*, edited by Richard Benson, Eric Downing, and Jonathan Hess, 106–29. Columbia, NY: Camden House, 2012.

———. *Wandering Genitalia: Sexuality and the Body in German Culture Between the Late Middle Ages and Early Modernity*. King's College London Medieval Studies, Occasional Series 2. London: Centre for Late Antique & Medieval Studies, King's College London, 2009.

———. "Wanderlust: Gift Exchange, Sex, and the Meanings of Mobility." In *Liebesgaben: Kommunikative, performative und poetologische Dimensionen in der Literatur des Mittelalters und der Frühen Neuzeit*, edited by Margreth Egidi, Ludger Lieb, and Marielle Schnyder, 219–29. Berlin: Erich Schmidt, 2012.

Rasmussen, Ann Marie, and Hanneke van Asperen. "Introduction: Medieval Badges." *Mediæval Journal* 8.1 (2018): 1–10.

Rasmussen, Ann Marie, and Sarah Westphal-Wihl, eds. and trans. "Die Beichte einer Frau." In *Ladies, Whores, and Holy Women: A Sourcebook in Courtly, Religious, and Urban Cultures of Late Medieval Germany, with Introductory Essays*, 9–15. Kalamazoo, MI: Medieval Institute Publications, 2010.

Reichert, Folker. "Ein cleins ringlein, an allen heiligen Stätten angerührt." *Deutsches Archiv für Erforschung des Mittelalters* 67 (2010): 609–24.

Reiss, Ben. "Pious Phalluses and Holy Vulvas: The Religious Importance of Some Sexual Body-Part Badges in Late-Medieval Europe (1200–1550)." *Peregrinations* 6 (2017): 151–76.

Retsch, Christopher. "Geflügelte Genitalien, Phallusbäume und kopulierende Paare: Zur Motivik auf obszön-sexuellen Tragezeichen / Winged Genitalia, Phallus Trees, and Copulating Couples: On the Motifs of Obscene-Sexual Badges." In *Mittelalterliche Tragezeichen: Social Media des Mittelalters / Medieval Badges: Social Media of the Middle Ages*, edited by André Dubisch, 210–69. Exhibition catalog. Lübeck: European Hansemuseum, 2020.

Rivers Cofield, Sara. "Keeping a Crooked Sixpence: Coin Magic and Religion in the Colonial Chesapeake." *Historical Archaeology* 48.3 (2014): 84–105.

Robertson, James Craigie. *Materials for the History of Thomas Becket, Archbishop of Canterbury*. 7 vols. London: Longman, 1875–85.

Rosser, Gervase. "Finding Oneself in a Medieval Fraternity: Individual and Collective Identities in the English Guilds." In *Mittelalterliche Bruderschaften in europäischen Städten*, edited by Monika Escher-Apsner, 29–46. Frankfurt: Peter Lang, 2009.

———. *The Art of Solidarity in the Middle Ages: Guilds in England 1250–1550*. Oxford: Oxford University Press, 2015.

Rubin, Miri. *Cities of Strangers: Making Lives in Medieval Europe*. Cambridge: Cambridge University Press, 2020.

———. *Emotion and Devotion: The Meaning of Mary in Medieval Religious Culture*. Budapest: Central European University Press, 2009.

———. *Mother of God: The History of the Virgin Mary*. London: Allen Lane, 2009.

Samariter, Renate. "Pilgerzeichen und religiöse Zeichen aus der Stralsunder Frankenvorstadt." *Bodendenkmalpflege in Mecklenburg-Vorpommern Jahrbuch* 56 (Jahrbuch 2008; Schwerin 2009): 191–212.

Rudy, Kathryn M. "Kissing Images, Unfurling Rolls, Measuring Wounds, Sewing Badges and Carrying Talismans: Considering Some Harley Manuscripts through the Physical Rituals they Reveal," *Electronic British Library Journal* (2011), Article 5. http://www.bl.uk/eblj/2011articles/article5.html.

———. "Sewing the Body of Christ: Eucharist Wafer Souvenirs Stitched into Fifteenth-Century Manuscripts, Primarily in the Netherlands," *Journal of Historians of Netherlandish Art* 8.1 (Winter 2016): DOI: 10.5092/jhna.2016.8.1.1.

Sand, Alexa. "Saving Face: The Veronica and Visio Dei." In *Vision, Devotion and Self-Representation in Late Medieval Art*, 27–82. Cambridge: Cambridge University Press, 2014.

Schmidt, Peter. *Gedruckte Bilder in handgeschriebenen Büchern: Zum Gebrauch von Druckgraphik im 15. Jahrhundert*. Pictura et Poesis, 16. Cologne: Böhlau, 2003.

Schultz, James A. *Courtly Love, the Love of Courtliness, and the History of Sexuality*. Chicago: University of Chicago Press, 2006.

Scott, Tom. *The City-State in Europe, 1000–1600: Hinterland, Territory, Region*. Oxford: Oxford University Press, 2012.

———. *Society and Economy in Germany, 1300–1600*. New York: Palgrave, 2002.

Scribner, R. W. *Popular Culture and Popular Movements in Reformation Germany*. London: Hambledon, 1987.

Selzer, Stephen. "Devisen an reichsfürstlichen Höfen des Spätmittelalters: Umrisse eines Forschungsfeldes." In *Reiche Bilder: Aspekte zur Produktion und Funktion von Stickereien im Spätmittelalter*, edited by Uta-Christine Bergemann and Annemarie Stauffer, 115–28. Regensburg, Germany: Schnell & Steiner, 2010.

Seuse, Heinrich. "Das Buch von dem Diener." In *Heinrich Seuse: Deutsche Schriften*, edited by Karl Bihlmeyer. Stuttgart: Kohlhammer, 1907.

———. *The Exemplar, with Two German Sermons*, translated by Frank Tobin. New York: Paulist, 1989.

Short, Ian, ed., trans., and intro. *A Life of Thomas Becket in Verse: La vie de saint Thomas Becket by Guernes de Pont-Sainte-Maxence*. Toronto: Pontifical Institute of Medieval Studies, 2013.

Siddons, Michael Powell. *Heraldic Badges in England and Wales*. Woodbridge, UK: Boydell, 2009.

Signori, Gabriela. *Das Wunderbuch Unserer Lieben Frau im thüringischen Elende (1419–1517)*. Cologne: Böhlau Verlag, 2006.

Simon, Eckehard. *Die Anfänge des weltlichen deutschen Schauspiels 1370–1530: Untersuchung und Dokumentation*. Munich: Artemis, 2003.

———. "Carnival Obscenities in German Towns." In *Obscenity: Social Control and Artistic Creation in the European Middle Ages*, edited by Jan Ziolkowski, 193–213. Leiden: Brill, 1998.

. "Organizing and Staging Carnival Plays in Late Medieval Lübeck: A New Look at the Archival Record." *Journal of English and German Philology* 92.1 (1993): 57–72.

———, ed. *The Theatre of Medieval Europe: New Research in Early Drama*. Cambridge: Cambridge University Press, 1991.

Skottki, Kristin. "Sternberg." In *Pilgerspuren—Orte, Wege, Zeichen*, Exhibition catalogue, 326–34. Petersberg, Germany: Michael Imhof, 2020.

Slanicka, Simone. "Male Markings: Uniforms in the Parisian Civil War as a Blurring of the Gender Roles (A.D. 1410–1420)." *Medieval History Journal* 2 (1999): 209–44.

Smith, Mathew Ryan. "Reconsidering the 'Obscene': The Massa Marittima Mural." *SHIFT: Queen's Journal of Visual and Material Culture* 2 (2009): 1–27.

Smith, Pamela H., Christy Anderson, and Anne Dunlop, eds. *The Matter of Art: Materials, Practices, Cultural Logics, c. 1250–1750*. Manchester: Manchester University Press, 2015.

Solterer, Helen. "Figures of Female Militancy in Medieval France." *Signs* 16.3 (1991): 522–49.

Späth, Markus, ed. *Die Bildlichkeit korporativer Spiegel im Mittelalter: Kunstgeschichte und Geschichte im Gespräch*. Sensus: Studien zur mittelalterlichen Kunst, 1. Cologne: Böhlau Verlag, 2009.

Spencer, Brian. "Canterbury Pilgrim Souvenirs Found in the Low Countries." In *HP2*, 105–11. (See van Beuningen et al.)

———. "Pilgrim Badge." Grove Art Online, Oxford University Press, 2003. https://doi.org/10.1093/gao/9781884446054.article.T067659.

———. *Medieval Pilgrim Badges from Norfolk*. Kings Lynn, UK: Norfolk Museums Service, 1980.

———. "Pilgrim Souvenirs." In *Age of Chivalry: Art in Plantagenet England, 1200–1400*, edited by Jonathan Alexander and Paul Binski, 205–24. London: Royal Academy, 1987.

———. *Pilgrim Souvenirs and Secular Badges: Medieval Finds from Excavations in London*, 2nd ed. Woodbridge, UK: Boydell, 2010.

———. *Salisbury Museum Medieval Catalogue*. Salisbury, UK: Salisbury and Wiltshire Museum, 1990.

Stahuljak, Zrinka. *Pornographic Archaeology: Medicine, Medievalism, and the Invention of the French Nation*. Philadelphia: University of Pennsylvania Press, 2012.

Stefanowitsch, Anatol. "Emojis als Tragezeichen / Emojis as Badges." In *Mittelalterliche Tragezeichen: Social Media des Mittelalters / Medieval Badges: Social Media of the Middle Ages*, edited by André Dubisch, 514–39. Exhibition catalog. Lübeck: European Hansemuseum, 2020.

Stevenson, Katie, ed. *The Herald in Late Medieval Europe*. Woodbridge, UK: Boydell, 2009.

Stopford, J. "Some Approaches to the Archaeology of Christian Pilgrimage." *World Archaeology* 26.1 (1994): 57–72.

Summers, Sandra Lindemann. *Ogling Ladies: Scopophilia in Medieval German Literature*. Gainesville: University of Florida Press, 2013.

Symes, Carol. *A Common Stage: Theater and Public Life in Medieval Arras*. Ithaca, NY: Cornell University Press, 2007.

———. "Out in the Open, in Arras: Sightlines, Soundscapes and the Shaping of a Medieval Public Sphere." In *Cities, Texts and Social Networks, 400–1500*, edited by Caroline Goodson, Anne Lester, and Carol Symes, 279–302. New York: Taylor & Francis, 2010.

Theisen, Maria. "The Emblem of the Torque and Its Use in the Willehalm Manuscript of King Wenceslas IV of Bohemia." *Journal of the British Archaeological Association* 17.1 (2018): 131–53.

Tixador, Arnaud. *Enseignes sacrées et profanes médiévales découvertes à Valenciennes: Un peu plus d'un kilogramme d'histoire*. Valenciennes, France: Valenciennes Service Archéologique, 2004.

Tobin, Frank, Kim Vivian, and Richard H. Lawson, trans. *Arthurian Romances, Tales, and Lyric Poetry: The Complete Works of Hartmann von Aue*. State College: Pennsylvania State Press, 2001.

Trigg, Stephanie. *Shame and Honor: A Vulgar History of the Order of the Garter*. Philadelphia: University of Pennsylvania Press, 2012.

de Troyes, Chrétien. *Yvain: The Knight of the Lion*. Translated by Burton Raffel. New Haven, CT: Yale University Press, 1987.

Vandi, Loretta. "The Holy Land in Paris: Embroidering, Depicting, and Stamping the Passion in a Fifteenth-Century Book of Hours (Paris, Bibliothèque de l'Arsenal, MS 1176 A rés.)." *Peregrinations: Journal of Medieval Art and Architecture* 7.1 (2019): 43–86. https://digital.kenyon.edu/perejournal/vol7/iss1/2.

de Vries, Jan. *The First Modern Economy*. New York: Cambridge University Press, 1997.

Webb, Diana, ed. *Pilgrims and Pilgrimage in the Medieval West*. International Library of Historical Studies, 12. London: Tauris, 1999.

Weinberg, Sam. *Historical Thinking and Other Unnatural Acts*. Philadelphia: Temple University Press, 2001.

Weinryb, Ittai, ed. *Agents of Faith: Votive Objects in Time and Place*. New Haven, CT: Yale University Press, 2018.

———. *The Bronze Object in the Middle Ages*. Cambridge: Cambridge University Press, 2016.

Weitbrecht, Julia. "The Vera Icon (Veronica) in the Verse Legend *Veronicia II*: Medializing Salvation in the Late Middle Ages." *Seminar* 52.2 (2016): 173–93.

Wenzel, Edith. "*zers* und *fud* als literarische Helden: Zum 'Eigenleben' von Geschlechtsteilen in mittelalterlicher Literatur." In *Körperteile. Eine kulturelle Anatomie*, edited by Claudia Benthien and Christoph Wulf, 274–93. Reinbek: Rowohlt, 2001.

Westphal-Wihl, Sarah. "*The Ladies' Tournament*: Marriage, Sex, and Honor in Thirteenth-Century Germany," *Signs* 14.2 (1989): 371–98.

Wild, Benjamin L. "Emblems and Enigmas: Revisiting the 'Sword' Belt of Fernando de la Cerda." *Journal of Medieval History* 37 (2011): 378–96.

Wilkinson, Louise J. "Gendered Chivalry." In *A Companion to Chivalry*, edited by Robert W. Jones and Peter Coss, 219–39. Rochester, NY: Boydell, 2019.

Willemsen, Annemarieke. *Kinder delijt: Middeleeuws speelgoed in de Nederlanden*. Nijmegen: Nijmegen University Press, 1998.

Winkelmann, Johan H., and Gerhard Wolf, eds. *Erotik aus dem Dreck gezogen*. Special issue. *Amsterdamer Beiträge zur älteren Germanistik* 59.1 (2004).

Wolf, Gerhard. "Im Mantel der Geschichte? Interferenzen zwischen chronikalischem und fiktionalem Wiedererzählen bei Ulrich Fuetrer." *Beiträge zur mediävistischen Erzählforschung* 2 (2019): 202–54.

Wolfram von Eschenbach. *Parzival*, edited by Rüdiger Krohn. 2 vols. Stuttgart: Reclam, 1981.

———. *Parzival and Titurel*, translated by Cyril Edwards. Oxford: Oxford University Press, 2006.

Yarrow, Simon. "Pilgrimage." In *Routledge History of Medieval Christianity: 1050–1500*, edited by R. N. Swanson, 159–71. New York: Routledge, 2015.

Index

Page references in italics refer to illustrations